THE SOUTH CHINA SEA

THE
SOUTH CHINA SEA
THE STRUGGLE FOR POWER IN ASIA

BILL HAYTON

YALE UNIVERSITY PRESS
NEW HAVEN AND LONDON

For information about this and other Yale University Press publications, please contact:
U.S. Office: sales.press@yale.edu   www.yalebooks.com
Europe Office: sales@yaleup.co.uk   www.yalebooks.co.uk

Typeset in Adobe Garamond Pro by IDSUK (DataConnection) Ltd
Printed in Great Britain by TJ International Ltd, Padstow, Cornwall

Library of Congress Control Number: 2014944966

ISBN 978-0-300-18683-3

A catalogue record for this book is available from the British Library.

10 9 8 7 6 5 4 3 2 1

MIX
Paper from
responsible sources
FSC   FSC® C013056
www.fsc.org

This book was begun while I was working in the BBC in London and finished while I was seconded to the reform of Myanmar Radio and Television. It is dedicated to my friends and colleagues in two very different newsrooms.

"News is what somebody does not want you to print. All the rest is advertising."
Anon (though attributed to many people)

Contents

Contents

The South China Sea – known as the East Sea in Vietnam and the West Philippine Sea in the Philippines.

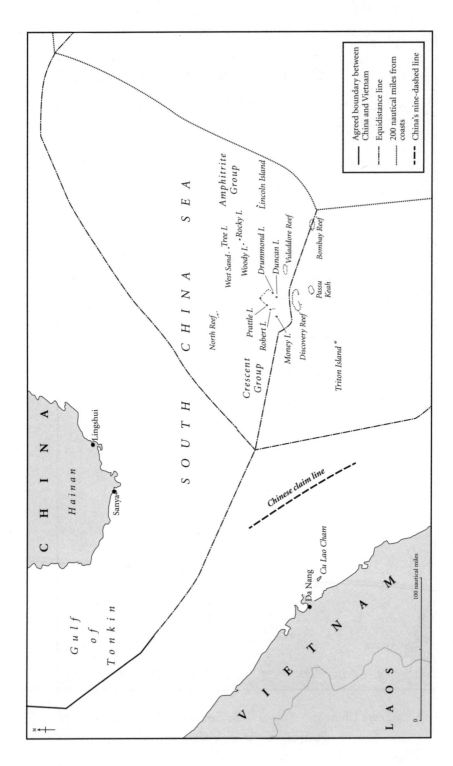

The Paracel Islands: occupied by China, which calls them the Xisha, but claimed by Vietnam, which calls them the 'Hoang Sa.

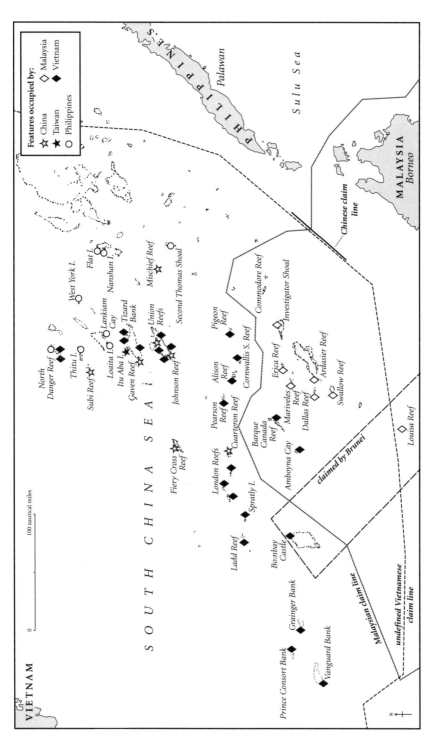

The Spratly Islands, known as the Nansha in China, the Truong Sa in Vietnam and the Kalayaan Island Group in the Philippines.

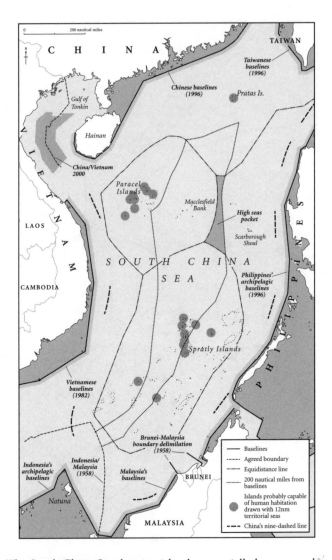

The South China Sea showing islands potentially large enough to be considered 'capable of sustaining human habitation or economic life'. The cartographer has drawn these islands with 12 nautical mile territorial seas and hypothetical Exclusive Economic Zones. The EEZs are shown with their maximum effect – half way between the island and the nearest coastline. Recent ICJ judgements suggest the line would be drawn closer to the islands. The map also shows how China's 'U-shaped line' claim cuts into every littoral country's EEZ drawn from their coastline. (Based on a map drawn by I Made Andi Arsana, Lecturer at the Department of Geodetic and Geomatic Engineering, Faculty of Engineering, Universitas Gadjah Mada, Indonesia.)

Introduction

ONE DAY IN the future, a pair of fishing boats might set out from the Philippine island of Luzon, heading west into the open sea. They will set a course for a coral atoll once named after the harbour they have just left, the Bajo de Masingloc. Over the past 300 years the atoll has had many names. The Spanish also called it Maroona Shoal, the British called it Scarborough Shoal, nationalist Chinese named it Min'zhu – Democracy – Reef, Communist Chinese renamed it Huangyan – Yellow Rock – and, most recently and least appropriately, nationalist Filipinos baptised it Panatag – Tranquil – Shoal. When they arrive, the crews will see very little: just the summit of a mountain that surges from the sea floor 4,000 metres below. A single tower of rock standing alone in the South China Sea.

If it were only 3 metres shorter, the mountain would be unremarkable, aside from the danger it would pose to passing ships. But even at high tide a few rocks break the surface, each just about large enough to stand on. And since the official definition of an island is 'a naturally formed area of land, surrounded by water, which is above water at high tide', those few metres make all the difference.[1] Recognised possession of an island gives the owner rights to the sea, to the fish swimming around it and to the minerals that may lie on or below the seabed. More recently, possession has come to mean much more. For some, it has become the difference between pride and humiliation, between the status of great power and also ran. Which is why on this day in the future the fishing boats are trying to reach it.

On this hypothetical day, the boats are carrying flag-waving Filipinos: members of Congress, former military officers and veteran street protestors. Under cover of darkness they try to slip past a ship of the China Coast Guard: there to prevent just such an incursion. They almost make it. While the Chinese ship is patrolling the far end of the atoll they dash for the entrance to the lagoon. It's a risky move. The entrance is 350 metres wide but currents and waves push the craft almost onto the reef. Just as they're getting close they hear a shot and the night is turned bright by a flare overhead. A small boat is barrelling towards them at high speed and a loud-hailer barks a warning in English: 'This is Chinese territory since ancient times. You must leave this area immediately. Leave or we will be forced to take action against you.' But the Filipinos press on: they're almost inside the lagoon. Another warning: 'If you do not leave immediately, we will take armed action against you. Turn your boats around.' With the first boat just 10 metres from the lagoon mouth, another shot. This time it's not a flare. Bullets splash in the water.

On the fishing boats the military men are urging the captains to press on. They've been under fire before. They're not intimidated. They've come too far to give up now. They will plant their flags on this piece of Philippine territory. Another burst of fire rakes the deck. A crewman is killed; a congressman is hit in the shoulder and two other activists seriously wounded. But the boats are inside the lagoon now – and the military men produce their own weapons and fire back. The Chinese speedboat backs off, but the mother ship is now blocking the only exit from the lagoon. On board the bullet-riddled boat there is panic. First aid is given and congressional assistants use satellite phones to call in help and favours. Live interviews are given to breathless TV news anchors. In Manila, crowds form around the Ministry of Defence and the Chinese consulate, demanding action. In Beijing, another crowd hurls rocks at the Philippine embassy, online wars break out, websites are hacked and defaced. Everyone is calling for action. The Chinese government refuses to allow the fishing boats to leave the lagoon, saying they have entered its territory illegally and must be dealt with by the law. The Philippine government demands the release of the boats and all on board and despatches its largest warship, the BRP *Gregorio del Pilar,* to the scene.

The Chinese don't back down, so the *Gregorio* fires a warning shot. No response. Philippine naval special forces are sent to board the Chinese ship, fist-fights break out on the bridge, tear gas is used and someone starts shooting. Then two Chinese jets try to strafe the *Gregorio*. They miss, but it's the last straw: having pulled out the special forces, the *Gregorio* shells the Chinese, hitting the ship near the stern. It limps away and the Filipino activists exit the lagoon and are hauled aboard the *Gregorio* for medical treatment. The provocation is too much for Beijing to bear. While the world urges calm and restraint an expeditionary force sets sail from Sanya, the headquarters of the South China Sea fleet on Hainan Island.

Maritime insurance premiums go through the roof, container ship sailings are cancelled, flights are re-routed, semiconductor supply lines are disrupted and just-in-time logistical networks begin to break down. Fishermen stop fishing, markets go empty, urban workers go hungry, activists get angrier, oil prices sky-rocket, politicians shout louder, warnings get direr: all to no avail. The Chinese make their first landing on Parola, the northernmost of the Spratly Islands, hundreds of kilometres west of Scarborough Shoal. The tiny Filipino garrison can put up only token resistance. But 3 kilometres away, the Vietnamese forces occupying Dao Song Tu Tay are better armed and regard this move as a mortal threat. With artillery and shore-based missiles they target the Chinese fleet. Both sides call in air support.

The fighting spreads to all the other islands in the Spratlys – landings are made on reefs and sandbars across a wide area of ocean. Washington repeats its threats about its vital national interest in the freedom of the seas. It moves carrier groups into the region; token vessels from other countries join them in a show of international resolve. Confrontations between Chinese and American vessels become increasingly tense: there are collisions at sea and submarines play cat and mouse beneath the waves. Japanese warships are ordered to escort oil tankers. In the post-Fukushima era the country's electricity industry needs a tanker to arrive every six hours to keep the power flowing. The Indian government offers help to its strategic partner Vietnam, upping the ante even higher. And then someone in Delhi decides that this would be the perfect moment to regain some lost territory in the Himalayas . . .

It's only a scenario and even as I write this good people are working on ways to prevent it ever unfolding. But there are also forces pushing

Asia in the opposite direction. Economic competition, superpower logic and populist nationalism are increasing the chances of conflict. The South China Sea is the first place where Chinese ambition has come face to face with American strategic resolve. Dozens of other players, from medium-sized countries to pint-sized politicians, are seeking to gain some advantage from the unfolding confrontation. Interests are being assessed and alliances formed and reformed: strategic partnerships, mutual defence treaties – a web of commitments binding the world to the future of this region. What happens if someone shoots an archduke?

* * * * * *

To understand the importance of the South China Sea to the wider world, fly from Singapore's Changi Airport on a clear day and, as you rise up, look down at the water below. Hundreds of vessels, from the smallest of fishing smacks to the very largest of crude carriers, fill the waterway: tugs, trawlers, container ships, car transporters and bulk freighters shifting the stuff of modern life. Oil heading east fuels the giant economies at the other end of the South China Sea: Taiwan, South Korea, China and Japan. To the west flows the combined output of the workshops of the world: hardware and software, headwear and footwear. The best guesses suggest that more than half the world's maritime trade goes through the Straits of Malacca, along with half the world's liquefied natural gas and one-third of its crude oil. If the ships stopped moving, it wouldn't be long before the lights in some parts of the world started going out.

The South China Sea is both the fulcrum of world trade and a crucible of conflict. There were battles in 1974 and 1988 and there have been dozens of less violent confrontations since. The United States has been involved since the beginning and India has begun to take an interest. The region deserves our attention and yet, outside a small circle of academics, paid experts and other obsessives, it is very poorly understood. Many of the accepted truths about the disputes, repeated in most media coverage, are either untrue or unproven. The Sea is not particularly rich in oil and gas resources, the military bases on the disputed islands are not particularly 'strategic' since almost all could be destroyed with a single missile strike, the territorial disputes involve six countries, not five, since Indonesia is affected although it pretends it isn't and the 'historic claims' of the disputants are actually very modern.

Many of the key writings on the South China Sea – at least in English – can trace their original references back to two Western academic works: a 1976 paper by the German historian Dieter Heinzig, entitled 'Disputed Islands in the South China Sea', and a 1982 book by the American geographer Marwyn Samuels, *Contest for the South China Sea*. They were pioneering and impressive pieces of work, bringing much needed insight to the subject. But the histories that both books recounted relied in large part on articles published in Chinese Communist Party journals following the Chinese invasion of the Paracel Islands in January 1974. One was published in the March 1974 edition of *The 70s Monthly* (*Ch'i-shi nien-tai yüeh-k'an*) and two in the May 1974 edition of *Ming Pao Monthly*. These were clearly not neutral pieces of scholarship: they were intended to justify the invasion. Heinzig and Samuels are not to be blamed for this. There was little other material available at the time.

However, by relying on these early works (and the works that rely on these works), too many academics and commentators are still, in effect, allowing these three Chinese articles to frame the entire debate about the South China Sea, 40 years after they were published. Knowledge about the history and current situation of the Sea has proliferated since then, allowing researchers to re-examine the old certainties. Too much of this new material is lying unread in academic journals. I hope that by bringing some of that work to wider attention, this book will make a contribution to changing the terms of the debate.

There is much more to the South China Sea than apparently Lilliputian squabbles over barren lumps of rock. Mysterious cultures have risen and fallen around its shores, invaders have come and gone, winds of trade and war have directly connected the Sea to the fates of faraway empires for centuries. Its history is also a global history. Its future should be a global concern. In our era, what happens in the South China Sea will define the future. Will China's rise lead to conflict between the superpowers? Does the Chinese leadership intend to play by the rules of the international game or challenge them? Does the United States have the will to stand its ground? Will the countries of Southeast Asia win or lose from superpower competition? How has the hunt for hydrocarbons affected the conflict? Above all, what can be done to prevent war ever breaking out? How could the resources of the Sea be equitably shared among the hundreds of millions of mostly poor people living around its shores? Read on.

Yangon, Myanmar
December 2013

CHAPTER 1

Wrecks and Wrongs
Prehistory to 1500

VICTOR PAZ DREW breath. In front of him lay three slabs, about the length of a person in all. This was going to take some effort. He took a moment to control his excitement: hope and caution battling for supremacy. As he paused, larks – *hinay hinay* in Tagalog – flitted among the *bili* trees, their songs echoing around the cave mouth, heralds for an archaeological revelation. Above the cave, the huge Illé limestone tower soared out of the paddy fields, dominating the wide, green valley floor. By now, the others had put down their tools to watch, forming an audience around him. The middle stone looked the easiest to lift. Victor reached down and grabbed it with both hands. Gingerly, he prised it away.

Beneath the slab was a ribcage: smashed but still recognisably human. Victor grinned. This was good, a fine reward after a season of digging. The small crowd pressed in around the edge of the pit, a metre above where Victor was kneeling. As the stone was placed aside they could see that the skeleton had been buried with ceremony. In the centre of the chest was a hammerstone: a vital tool for a Neolithic craftsman. Above it lay a small clutch of shells, still pressed together, although the pouch that once confined them had long rotted away. Two large bailer shells were placed to one side, but what would later prove to be the most significant find lay at the top of the chest: a necklace of discs interspersed with conus beads – jewelry made from tiny cone-shaped shells.

Victor removed the two remaining slabs, revealing the entire skeleton. Now he could see just how elaborate the burial had been. Around the body were more stones, enclosing it within a deliberate shape. Above the head, the stones formed a point with a polished pebble at the apex. As head of the Archaeological Studies Programme at the University of the Philippines, Victor was obliged to be a professional sceptic. But he knew this find could have an emotional importance as much as a scientific one. His predecessor in the role – and his mentor – had been Wilhelm Solheim and for decades Solheim had scoured this end of Palawan Island, piecing together evidence for a theory that would explain how and why peoples, languages and cultures spread across Southeast Asia. But after a lifetime of research around the South China Sea, Solheim was running out of time. At the age of 81 his faculties were slowly leaving him. The discoveries in the Illé Cave in April 2005 would be his reward.

Victor stood back and looked again at the stones surrounding the body. They were in the shape of a boat, heading into the shadows of the cave and the afterlife beyond. The polished stone marked the prow of the boat and bailer shells, as their name implies, are vital accessories for anyone taking a leaky canoe onto the ocean. But even Victor wasn't prepared for the next revelation. The conus beads were taken to the laboratory in Manila for testing. Because animals make shells from the nutrients and minerals they eat, they carry molecular markers of the time and place where they live and die. And these conus shells, which had been collected, crafted, turned into jewelry and placed in this burial, had lived and died at least 4,200 years ago. And that, to Victor Paz and Wilhelm Solheim, was the evidence they had been seeking for years. It gave them a chance to clinch a debate that has divided archaeologists: how and why did modern humans populate Southeast Asia? Their discovery appeared proof that the people who buried their dead at Illé Cave were already maritime people more than four millennia ago. That would knock out a key plank of the dominant explanation that Southeast Asian culture had simply diffused from southern China. 'We still have to know more,' admits Paz, 'but it is more and more becoming an argument that cannot be ignored.'

Paz, Solheim and their colleagues had journeyed to a remote valley in the wild northern tip of Palawan to try to win an argument. Their motivations were both personal and scientific. They were deliberately looking for evidence that might support a theory they had already formed but their methods were honest, their team was open and their reasoning was logical. Unfortunately, the independent pursuit of knowledge is only one of several motives for archaeological exploration in the South China Sea. Others are less interested in the big questions because they have chosen their answers already: their purpose is to find treasure or justify territorial claims. And those with less noble intentions have access to vastly greater resources.

Mixed motives among archaeologists and historians – and their masters – in Southeast Asia are nothing new. For centuries, the writing of the region's history has revealed as much about contemporary obsessions as about the past. Has Southeast Asia been anything more than a stage upon which outsiders have played imperial games? Are the people who live around the South China Sea descended from China or from somewhere else? Were the great civilisations of Champa, Angkor and Srivijaya home-grown or implanted? Did culture and civilisation flow from one source or from many? Who controlled territory and what did that actually mean? Colonialist, nationalist and internationalist historians have all answered these questions differently. Recent evidence from linguistics, ceramics, genetics, botany and sedimentology is shining new light. The more it reveals, the more complex the story becomes.

* * * * * *

The earliest evidence of humans in Southeast Asia dates from about 1.5 million years ago. Remains of 'Java Man', more formally known as *homo erectus*, have been found both in Java and in China. But he, and his wives and children, appear to have died out around 50,000 years ago, possibly chased into oblivion by his smarter relative, *homo sapiens*. Modern humans probably reached Australia around 50,000 years ago, suggesting they had already settled Southeast Asia en route. Skulls found in Borneo and the Philippines indicate that modern humans had arrived in those places by 40,000 and 22,000 years ago respectively. The problem is that there's very little other evidence – mainly because the world then looked very different. Sea level 17,000 years ago was around 120 metres lower than it is today. The modern islands of Java, Sumatra and Borneo were joined to the mainland and Australia was joined to New Guinea. If, as seems likely, *homo sapiens* lived along the sea shore, then the villages he built and the tools he manufactured now lie well beyond the reach of archaeology, 120 metres under water. There are huge gaps in our under-standing and very little evidence with which to close them.

But as we come closer to the present – a few thousand years ago – the evidence multiplies and so do the arguments. How did scattered subsist-ence settlements evolve into urban centres? How did people who knew only stone tools come to master bronze and iron smelting? And how were these innovations spread? The first explanations sprang from a remark-able insight by a German scholar, Otto Dempwolff. Around the start of the twentieth century he began to demonstrate similarities between the different languages of Southeast Asia. By the time the American linguist Robert Blust came to develop this work at the end of the twentieth century, links had been discovered between more than 1,000 languages spoken as far apart as Taiwan, Hawaii, Easter Island, New Zealand, Malaysia and Madagascar. The implications were extraordinary. They demonstrated that people separated by thousands of miles of ocean – covering half the world's circumference – shared cultural roots. Blust argued that these roots could all be traced back to a single language spoken in Taiwan around 5,500 years ago, a language he called 'proto-Austronesian'. And by showing how this language had divided and multiplied, he devised a theory linking the diffusion of Austronesian languages across the islands of Southeast Asia to the migration of peoples, the settlement of new territories and the spread of agricultural and other technologies. It became known as the 'Out of Taiwan' model.

But where had these proto-Austronesian speakers come from? The Australia-based archaeologist Peter Bellwood believes that they were descendants of the farmers who had first mastered the art of rice-growing in the Yangtze Valley around 8,500 years ago. In this period 'China' was home to many different language groups apart from proto-Austronesian including Sino-Tibetan (from which evolved Chinese, Tibetan and Burmese), Austroasiatic (from which Vietnamese and Khmer developed) and Tai (Thai). In addition to growing rice, these peoples also kept pigs and poultry, made pottery and used stone tools. Over the following millennia, pressures at home and opportunities abroad caused these groups to move across East and Southeast Asia. In Bellwood's account, the proto-Austronesian speakers gradually spread east and south, eventually reaching the Chinese coasts by around 5,500 years ago.

So far, these migrations had travelled over land. But the next phase of the Austronesian odyssey was radically different. Sea levels 5,000 years ago were pretty much the same as they are now, making the Taiwan Strait about 130 kilometres wide at its narrowest point. Yet this hurdle appears to have been overcome, because archaeologists have recovered evidence of rice-growing dating from around this time on Taiwan. Over the next thousand years or so, enough Austronesian speakers had arrived or reproduced on the island to overwhelm any remnants of previous migrations and their language had already begun to split into dialects. In Bellwood's model, the next step was 'out of Taiwan'.

The first step was the journey southwards across the Luzon Strait. By hopping to the Batanes Islands, the longest single stretch was about 80 kilometres. Further hops would have brought the voyagers to Luzon, the main island of the Philippines, where, again, they would have encountered humans from much earlier migrations. The new arrivals, with their more advanced technology and culture, established settlements, prospered, grew in number and moved on again. Bellwood argues that from about 4,000 years ago (2000 BCE) the people who came 'out of Taiwan' spread throughout the rest of the Philippines and then west into present-day Indonesia. Others went east. By 1500 BCE, some had reached the Mariana Islands, 2,500 kilometres from Luzon and then carried on to Fiji. By 800 BCE Tonga had been settled, by 300 CE Hawaii, and by 1200 New Zealand.

It's a dramatic story and there is plenty of evidence to support it: the languages themselves, archaeological finds and genetic research. But there are also several problems with it. Some finds in the Batanes Islands are newer than those in Luzon, suggesting people moved there from the south, not the north. Burial techniques found in southern Vietnam are older than similar ones found in Taiwan and Luzon. Evidence for early rice-growing in Taiwan is rare, suggesting it was not widespread there before about 4,000 years ago; genetic analysis of rice suggests that different strains – from India and Java – may have travelled through the region from south to north before 'Chinese' varieties travelled in the opposite direction. Genetics also shows that the Pacific pig and the Pacific rat came from Indochina, not Taiwan. The objections have mounted up.

As a result, a rival explanation for the spread of language and culture around the South China Sea has emerged. Rather than stressing a flow of people 'out of Taiwan', it proposes a constantly communicating network transporting information and technology in many directions. It also makes coastal China both a recipient and a transmitter of this culture, but not its sole source. And that is why Bill Solheim found himself celebrating the discovery of a grave in northern Palawan.

Solheim had begun his search for the origins of Southeast Asian civilisations more than half a century before, studying at Berkeley and Arizona and digging in the Philippines in the 1950s. It was his work on pottery that drew him to develop a very different model to Peter Bellwood's. He argued that similarities between 2,500-year-old pots he found in Kalanay on the Philippine island of Masbate and others recovered in the 1920s from Sa Huynh on the coast of southern Vietnam were not coincidental. Many of them were marked with very precise geometric patterns – triangles, zigzags, parallel lines and hatchings – cut or pressed into the clay. Some of the pots had sophisticated shapes and many were coloured with a distinctive red slip. From this beginning, Solheim's perspective widened to include pottery from other sites spread around Southeast Asia, other kinds of objects – in particular tools and jewelry – and then other time periods, both later and earlier. Many of his colleagues disagreed, arguing the definition of 'similarity' had now become too vague to be useful. Nonetheless, Solheim pressed on. His next task was to try to explain how these similarities had come about.

One crucial insight was that although similar objects could be found in many places, they appeared there at different times. So while the 'stepped adze' (an early cutting tool) was developed in southeastern China about 5,000 years ago and spread to Taiwan and Vietnam over the following millennium, burial jars found in Vietnam and Palawan date from 4,000 years ago but only 1,000 years ago in Luzon and Taiwan. Similarly, the curious jade ear pendant known as the 'lingling o' (shaped like a circle, broken near the top and with points facing down and to the sides) has been dated to 4,000 years ago in Vietnam but to more recent periods in Taiwan and the Philippines. To Solheim, this meant that objects, knowledge and culture had developed in different places and then spread backwards and forwards over huge distances around mainland Southeast Asia and the islands, evolving as they travelled.

So he began to develop the idea of a maritime network: semi-nomadic communities travelling by sea and river and living by hunting, gathering and trading. The problem for Solheim was that these people, if they existed, left little trace: no permanent settlements, no monuments and no written records. It required a leap of imagination to believe in their existence. But then he realised that the evidence was actually still around. As late as the 1950s the American anthropologist Alexander Spoehr encountered women from the Samal people on the Philippine island of Mindanao who had never been on land and were convinced they would be attacked by evil spirits if they ever did so. Even today, many of the Badjao 'sea gypsies' of the Philippines, the Bajau of Malaysia, the Orang Laut of Indonesia, the Tanka of southern China and the Dan of Vietnam continue to live in and around the sea, surviving by fishing and trading. Indeed, all around the region, from China to Vietnam and Thailand, there are still communities of maritime peoples carrying on a form of life that, in essence, began many thousands of years ago. Solheim coined a word for these people derived from the Austronesian words for 'south island' and 'people'. He called them the Nusantao.

To really understand them we have to invert our ideas about land as a place of safety and the sea as a place of danger. Land can be hostile, home to dangerous creatures, thieves and tax collectors. The sea is full of food and, for the most part, easy to travel on. Supplies of fruit and vegetables can be harvested from river banks or traded and, as the New Zealand anthropologist Atholl Anderson has explained, even the problem of fresh water can be overcome.[1] Large quantities can be carried inside stoppered lengths of bamboo. It's robust, easily packed and, when emptied, the bamboo can be used to repair the boat. Add in some rainwater and fluid from raw fish and sea journeys of up to three or four weeks become unproblematic.

The beauty of Solheim's model, which he called the Nusantao Maritime Trading and Communication Network, is that it doesn't require any major rupture with the past, or any single great act of migration. It doesn't rely on, or exclude, any particular ethnic group. Technologies and cultures evolved gradually. Some Nusantao speak Austronesian languages, others don't; some are semi-settled, some are entirely nomadic; some live on the sea, some in river mouths, others far inland. They interacted with settled people and the populations must have mixed. They never consciously acted as a team and their technology was simple, yet by small acts of travelling and trading the Nusantao created a vast network of sail and paddle power which could transport sea slugs from northern Australia to the dining tables of southern China and banana trees from the forests of New Guinea to the gardens of Madagascar. And on each journey goods, knowledge and culture passed back and forth.

It's a wonderfully haphazard model and joyously *human*. It means that the people who really discovered the islands of the South China Sea had no ethnic identity that we would recognise today and certainly no attachment to anything like a state. As political units developed on land, the Nusantao would try to live beyond their clutches. The distinction between trading and smuggling, piracy and sedition was blurred. It's ironic that when modern-day states make territorial claims in the sea, they often base them upon the activities of people whom, in previous eras, those states tried to restrict or even eradicate.

The Nusantao aren't an ethnic group, so it makes little sense to ask where they came from. However, Solheim argues that a key hub of the Nusantao network was the area of coast between central Vietnam and Hong Kong. From here it reached all the way to Madagascar in the west and Easter Island in the east, Australia in the south and Japan in the north. We know that Indian glass beads were brought to China by people described, in Chinese texts, as 'Malays' around 400 BCE and that distinctive bronze 'Dong Son' drums, made in northern Vietnam around 2,000 years ago, have been found in burials all around Southeast Asia and southern China. This was a time of rapid development, when complex societies and empires began to emerge in many parts of the world – and linking them all was a maritime network.

For if there were maritime communities trading up and down coasts and communicating over long distances then it's ridiculous to think that these links would have stopped at boundaries between what we now call 'East Asia', 'Southeast Asia', 'India', 'Arabia' or 'Europe'. Coastal traders would have had contacts with their fellows to the north, south, east and west. Both information and goods would have flowed across these networks, people in one place would have been aware of ideas and materials from elsewhere; folk memories about visitors from afar would have endured and exotic heirlooms would have been passed down between generations. The maritime route wasn't the only way to travel, of course. Others went by land but sea could be quicker and safer.

In 1939 an Indian ivory figurine was found under the ash in Pompeii and archaeologists began to accept that long-distance trade between Rome and South Asia had been well developed by the time Vesuvius erupted in 79 CE. It wasn't just statues that arrived from the east. A Roman document, the 'Periplus of the Erythraean Sea' dated to about 63 CE, mentions a place called 'Thina' well known as a source of silk. It seems that 2,000 years ago some Europeans were aware of a maritime route to China. There's debate about whether the Roman historian Pliny really described cloves in the first century CE but they are listed as imports to Egypt about 180 CE. There was only one place in the world where cloves were then grown: the northern Moluccan Islands, in present-day Indonesia. And by 284 CE, the eastern Roman Empire had sent its first envoys to China, via the coast of Linyi in what is now Vietnam.

* * * * * *

Dotted across Southeast Asia, from Champa in Vietnam and Angkor in Cambodia to Borobudur and Prambanan in Indonesia, are dozens of immense towers and temples that appear utterly alien to their surroundings. Their obvious Indian styling, ripe with voluptuous maidens and blessed with altars to bejewelled gods, seems like flotsam now, left by a receding Hindu tide. Smothered in jungle for centuries, they were discovered by Europeans once colonialism had matured to the extent that it could pay for archaeologists to go poking around the imperial recesses.

And these archaeologists quickly jumped to conclusions about who had built these great structures, and why. Eager to justify their own societies' presence in these foreign lands, they imagined that the temples were the work of an earlier generation of outsiders. Just as Europeans had brought civilisation and progress to the natives, so too had the builders of these monuments, centuries before. The builders must have come from India, imposed their language and way of life on the benighted inhabitants and lifted them up several rungs on the ladder of civilisation in the process. It meant European colonialism was merely the continuation of a long-established pattern of behaviour in Southeast Asia.

These ideas endured a long time. As late as 1964, the French historian George Coedès could write that 'the peoples of Further India shared a late Neolithic civilization when the Brahmano-Buddhist culture of India was first brought into contact with them'. In other words, the region had been stuck in the Stone Age until around 400 CE when it was colonised by Hindus and Buddhists from the west. The peoples of Southeast Asia had been written out of the story; history was just something that happened to them, rather than something they shaped. It's taken a half-century of digging, translating and thinking to overturn that view.

As a result, we can now see a direct link between the builders of the great temples and the Nusantao nomads who had plied the waters to the east and west for centuries. Indeed, it now seems that Southeast Asians were trading with India centuries before Indian culture took root in Southeast Asia. Products and knowledge moved backwards and forwards across the trading networks. Austronesian speakers had passed their names for boats into southern Indian languages by the first century CE. Indian techniques for manufacturing glass beads had been transferred around Southeast Asia even earlier.

Between the first and fifth centuries CE the coasts of Southeast Asia grew rich on the proceeds of trade with the various Indian civilisations: sandalwood, cardamoms, camphor, cloves, jewels and precious metals. Indian writings refer to the 'Islands of Gold' – Swarnadvipa – and the 'Land of Gold' – Swarnabhumi. With the trade travelled elements of the different cultures: from pottery designs to religion and then philosophy and politics. It seems that rather than being colonised by South Asians, Southeast Asian rulers chose to adopt South Asian ideas about kings, priests and power to reinforce their hold over their populations and hold onto territory against rivals.

From the little we know, the dominant power in Southeast Asia in the first centuries CE seems to have been a place that Chinese records call 'Funan'. Funan was based in the Mekong Delta, straddling what is now southern Vietnam and Cambodia. Through a combination of fortuitous geography and political cunning it built an empire from its crucial position on the trading routes between Europe and India to the west and China in the east. It grew rich as Rome developed tastes for Chinese silk and South-eastern Asian spices, as the Chinese sought frankincense and myrrh from

Arabia and as glass, pottery, metalwork, ivory, horn and precious minerals flowed between all of them.

The pioneers were the Nusantao, moving from place to place, exchanging goods and profiting from the proceeds. Chinese texts describe Malay ships (known as *kunlun bo*) arriving as early as the third century BCE. Gradually others from the Indian and Middle Eastern coasts joined them. There's no archaeological evidence that any Chinese ships made trading voyages across the South China Sea until the tenth century CE. This would seem to undermine many Chinese claims to the contrary, such as the assertion of the Foreign Ministry's website that 'Yang Fu of the East Han Dynasty (23–220 A.D.) made reference to the Nansha Islands in his book entitled Yiwu Zhi (Records of Rarities)'.[2] The available evidence suggests Yang Fu's research is more likely to have involved questioning foreign traders arriving at ports than independent voyaging. Although some Chinese did travel abroad on other people's ships, the inhabitants of what is now southern China seem to have been content to let others take the risk of going to sea and then manage the trade at the point of arrival.

Funan's position was literally pivotal because trade in this period was a relay. Few, if any, ships made the entire journey. Instead, traders probably carried goods over the part of the journey they knew best: from Europe to India, from India to the Malay Peninsula, then by land over the Isthmus of Kra at the narrowest point of the Malay Peninsula (where a 40-kilometre portage avoids a 1,600-kilometre sea voyage), by sea again to Funan and finally from Funan to southern China. To be successful, a trader needed to master the rhythm laid down by the annual pattern of winds that we now know by the Arabic word for season – *mawsim* or monsoon.

During the northern hemisphere's summer, continental Asia heats up. The air over it rises, drawing in more air from the seas to the south, creating strong and sustained winds towards the continent: the southwest monsoon. As Asia cools during the autumn and winter, the air over it sinks and is pushed out from the continent: the northeast monsoon. Sailing from the Malay Peninsula to Funan was easiest between December and January because of winds blowing away from South Asia but there was then a long wait, until June, before the journey from Funan to southern China could begin. Ships needed to be in port before the start of the typhoon season in mid-July. Travelling in the opposite direction, the easiest time to sail from China to Southeast Asia is in January and February, when winds and currents flow from the northeast. There's then another pause before the South Asian monsoon pattern makes its safe and convenient to sail on to the west.

This period of unfavourable winds and currents, from February to June each year, provided prosperity for the coast of what is now Vietnam for centuries. Back then, it obliged traders to pause in Funan and resupply from local sources. A Chinese account from the third century describes what these 'Malay' ships might have looked like: over 50 metres long with as many as four sails and able to carry 700 people and 600 tons of cargo.[3] The large numbers of ships, and their passengers and crew, provided a healthy market for local farmers and commodities dealers and a steady flow of duties and taxes for rulers and their courts to live from. It also made Funan a great place to do business and by the second century CE it was an entrepôt for Persians, Indians, Chinese and traders from all round Southeast Asia. Although China's influence was substantial, it was India that provided Funan's cultural and political inspiration. Its rulers adopted Hinduism, took Indian names and borrowed political ideas from their Indian counterparts. Even its town planning appears to have followed Indian lines.

Funan was only one of many empires, chiefdoms and fiefs around the South China Sea that emerged, thrived and faded into obscurity during the first millennium CE. Their histories are still being unearthed: both literally from archaeological digs and metaphorically from the pages of Chinese and other texts. Often we see them only in reflection, as they were recorded by others. And too often we view them through our present-day preoccupations: trying to trace the pedigrees of modern states through the shifting borders and migrating peoples of earlier centuries. But our present borders and identities would have made no sense to people actually alive in this early period. The historian Michael Churchman has shown that texts written in the Han–Tang period (from 111 BCE to 938 CE) made no linguistic distinction between 'Chinese' and 'Vietnamese', for example. It was nineteenth- and twentieth-century historians who forced modern national identities upon these ancient peoples.[4] During the period when the French imperial administrators were trying to define a clear border between their realm and 'China', French historians were simultaneously dividing ancient people into different categories by transcribing their names in either 'Chinese' or 'Vietnamese' styles.

What is now China looked very different two millennia ago. Peoples referred to as Yue or Viet in Chinese texts lived all along the southern coast, including the Red River Delta in present-day Vietnam. They were briefly conquered by the Qin Dynasty in 221 BCE but within 15 years the Qin had collapsed and the south coast regained independence for about a century. It wasn't until 111 BCE that the south fell to the Han Dynasty – and even then the region remained largely autonomous for another century. In the early years of the Common Era the Han imposed more direct rule, prompting occasional revolts and punitive military campaigns, and this state of ambiguous control persisted until the collapse of the Han in 220 CE. When the Han finally fell, their empire fractured into three, with the Wu Dynasty taking over much of the area south of the Yangtze River. But the Wu state only lasted until around 265 when it was defeated by its northern rivals, the Jin. Then, just 80 years later in 316, the Jin were forced out of the north and became a southern-based state until they too collapsed in 420 and were superseded by a series of other southern-based states.

Where then is 'China' in this era? Historians of China have tended to describe 'a civilization pretending to be a state', to use Lucian Pye's formulation, a continuous culture that has controlled the landmass of East Asia for millennia.[5] This is not how it appears from the perspective of the South China Sea. For many centuries, the dynasties and peoples who controlled the Sea's northern shore were different from those controlling the inland areas of 'China'. While the northern-based kingdoms looked inwards, those of the south looked outwards. They were directly connected to the maritime trading networks and through them to Funan and the rest of the region.

Throughout most of this period, Funan possessed two things that have proved to be crucial for every successful Southeast Asian trading centre since: beneficial relationships with whoever was ruling India and southern China. In times of crisis, and particularly after political changes, Funan would send 'embassies' to China seeking to preserve its position as preferred trading partner. Its representatives would make 'tribute' offerings to facilitate the discussions. Much has been made of these tributary relations.

Some nationalist Chinese historians argue that they prove Southeast Asian societies were vassals to Chinese emperors. This is how old Chinese texts tend to record them. However, contemporary Southeast Asian accounts suggest that 'tribute' wasn't viewed as some kind of feudal relationship between master and servant but simply as a trading partnership. Chinese rulers welcomed this 'tribute' as foreign recognition of their right to rule. Tribute ensured good relations abroad and symbolically reinforced the domestic power of rulers against potential rivals. For the 'tributaries', it was just the formality required to gain access to the ports. It was this status as a 'tributary relation' that made Funan a gatekeeper both to the riches within its sphere of influence and to those over the far horizon.

For almost three centuries Funan seems to have dominated the South China Sea trade, despite competition and attacks from its rivals. It used both diplomacy and force to maintain its position, coping with the ups and downs of the long-distance sea trade until the middle of the fourth century CE. Around that time high tolls and corruption in Chinese ports depressed business, out-of-work merchants turned to piracy and competing traders learnt to navigate their way around the Malay Peninsula, ending Funan's grip on the Isthmus of Kra. Merchants from other parts of Southeast Asia started to bypass Funan and deal directly with other ports further up the coast. Gradually Funan was eclipsed by its rivals. By the time sea trade revived again, after the fall of the Jin in China in 420 CE, it was other ports that would reap the benefits, in particular those further up the coast, in Champa.

In contrast to Funan, where little remains, Champa has left massive monuments: great red brick towers dotted across what is now central Vietnam. Their Indian imagery is obvious; indeed even the name 'Champa' seems to have been borrowed from an Indian kingdom. Champa's roots lie in the Stone Age Sa Huynh culture that Wilhelm Solheim identified as part of the Nusantao network and its prosperity was built, like that of Funan before it, on a marriage between sea trade and the export of inland commodities: elephant ivory and rhino horn were two of the more exotic products which its forests could provide. Champa was not a centralised state, more a collection of settlements based in river valleys along the coast that recognised a main ruler. Throughout its thousand-year history, power frequently moved between the different valleys.

Champa was rarely peaceful. It emerged out of the piracy that followed the decline in legitimate trade with China at the end of the fourth century. After the fall of the Jin, overland routes from China to the west were closed to southern China's new rulers, the Liu Song. As a result, they became dependent on maritime trade – which was being damaged by Champa's piracy. The threat was so bad that Liu Song forces invaded Champa in 446 and destroyed its capital. But they also declared themselves open to trade and Champa became an entrepôt – while continuing to tolerate, and sometimes encourage, piracy. At about the same time, Guangzhou on the Pearl River Delta became the main port of southern China and trade between the two – linked by the annual monsoon cycle – became highly profitable.

But although Champa dominated maritime trade with China, it did not have a monopoly. Other trading ports began to develop relations too. The kingdom of Taruma in western Java and other rulers in Sumatra had sent embassies by 460. One thing all these places had in common was their adoption of elements of Indian religious and political culture: Hinduism at first and later Buddhism. Kingdoms referred to themselves by the Sanskrit term *mandala* – wheel – and the rulers as *cakravartin* – wheel-turner. They saw themselves as centres of networks, rather than states with defined borders. Their legitimacy came less from physical control over territory and more from recognition by other rulers. Relations between them were fluid and less powerful centres might have allegiances to more than one *mandala*. But this legitimacy needed to be backed up by military power. To maintain their centrality *mandalas* needed to be able to force subordinate polities into line when necessary.

The use of 'Indian' ways of governing and the continuing spread of Indian religion in the region is evidence of the strong trading links between Southeast Asia and places to the west throughout the rest of the first millennium. Aromatic woods, resins, gold, spices and sometimes slaves were all in high demand. The evidence is not clear-cut but it seems that commerce with Indian kingdoms was more significant than with China for most of Southeast Asia in this period. There was a particular slump in trade with China at the end of the sixth century. However, once the Tang Dynasty had taken power in China in 618 and unified the lowlands for the first time in 200 years, the South China Sea trade seems to have taken

off again. Conditions were ripe for the emergence of other *mandalas* to
take advantage of it. This was the era of the great 'Indianised' civilisations:
Champa, Srivijaya and Angkor: the builders of the monuments which so
excited European colonists and continue to fascinate us today.

While Champa was still engaging in occasional acts of piracy, a more
reliable trading partner emerged much further to the south, on the southeastern coast of Sumatra. For a long time, almost all that was known about
Srivijaya came from Chinese descriptions. Even its location was a mystery.
It wasn't until 1993 that the French archaeologist Pierre-Yves Manguin
was able to confirm earlier suspicions that Srivijaya was located along the
banks of the Musi River in what is now the Indonesian city of Palembang.
Sadly, it seems that most of the remains of one of the most important
Southeast Asian civilisations now lie beneath the PIHC fertiliser factory.
The company used to be called PT Pupuk Sriwijaya but even that vestigial
trace of the ancient city has gone, just like the ruins the company unknowingly obliterated in the 1960s.

Srivijaya was a classic *mandala* – the dominant power among a group
of trading settlements along the main east–west trade route. From its base
it controlled access through both the Straits of Malacca to the north and
the Sunda Strait to the south. By 683 it could command a military force
around 20,000 strong – many of whom were probably nomadic Nusantao
who could both trade and fight on behalf of the ruler.[6] East–west maritime
trade was practically impossible without Srivijaya's consent. It was such a
significant power that in 683 the Chinese Tang court sent its first embassy
to what it called the Nanyang – island Southeast Asia – in order to seal
the relationship between the two.[7] Srivijaya became, in effect, the Tang
Dynasty's gatekeeper in the region.

* * * * * *

Sea cucumbers, *trepang* in Indonesian, have been exported from Southeast
Asia to China as both a delicacy and a medicine for at least 2,000 years.
So it was fitting that a *trepang* diver should literally stumble on a find that
radically changed our understanding of the history of trade in the South
China Sea. In August 1998, while pursuing the slithering creatures across
the seabed nearly 2 kilometres off the northern coast of the Indonesian

island of Belitung, the diver found a strange mound. It turned out to be an Arab dhow laden with more than 55,000 pieces of Chinese pottery – a cargo that would eventually sell for $32 million, though neither he nor his country would see much of that. Markings on the pottery would reveal that the ship had sunk in 826 CE in the middle of the Tang Dynasty, making this the earliest concrete evidence of direct sea trade between the Arab world and China.

Evidence is what all historians seek and, in contrast to China with its centuries of written records, Southeast Asia lacks it. Few documents survive, waterside settlements have been swept away and a combination of tropical climate and voracious insects has disposed of most of the rest. The great lost cities bear useful inscriptions but there are still gaping holes in the historical record. The best chances of filling them lie in the discovery of physical artifacts. The smallest details, from the molecular composition of shells to the techniques used in building boats, can unlock revelations about where and how people moved, what they ate, what kind of societies they lived in and how they related to others. As a result, modern archaeologists are fastidious about recording everything about their excavations: the layout of a ship's living space might hint at the culture and the hierarchy of the people on board and the arrangement of the cargo might reveal the order of its ports of call. Every scrap of evidence could be useful. Moreover, colleagues will only regard the interpretations as valid if the findings are accurately logged and made open to review and reinterpretation. These things did not happen at the Belitung wreck; at least not at first. There were other, more pressing priorities.

After the *trepang* divers had extracted a few bowls and sold them in the market, word spread and a local company, Sulung Segara Jaya, obtained a licence to excavate the wreck from the Indonesian national committee for shipwreck salvage. It was quickly joined by Seabed Explorations, owned by a German construction engineer turned underwater explorer, Tilman Walterfang. The two companies worked fast. They knew from bitter experience the site would be swiftly looted by others if they did not. In August 1998 Indonesia was in meltdown. General Suharto had been deposed, over a thousand people had been killed in rioting, separatism was flaring up and expatriates and their wealth were fleeing the country. Walterfang stayed put: his future wealth still lay on the bottom of the sea. The teams kept working, removing as much of the cargo as they could during September and October before the monsoon stopped their work. As they feared, local treasure hunters moved in almost immediately. Walterfang contracted a separate company, Maritime Explorations, owned by another former engineer, Michael Flecker, to excavate the remainder of the site in the new year and do a more scientific analysis of what remained. Flecker had excavated dozens of wrecks in the area and also had a PhD in marine archaeology.

We now know that the pottery on board the Belitung wreck was mass-produced in at least five separate places across China, that it was transhipped around the Chinese coast to Guangzhou where it was loaded aboard a ship reminiscent of those still used in Oman, made from timber originally grown in Central Africa and India. The crew was probably a polyglot assemblage of Arabs, Persians and Malays and the end customers for the cargo were the upper and middle classes of the Abbasid Caliphate, centred on Baghdad. The ship sailed on the monsoon winds southwest from Guangzhou, probably stopping en route to refresh stocks of food and water before being wrecked on a reef within Srivijaya's sphere of influence. So to whom did the cargo rightfully belong? In Walterfang's view the answer was simple: him – and whoever was prepared to buy it from him. As the pottery was taken away for conservation and cleaning and the remains of the ship examined for clues about its origin, the haggling started.

In the end only Singapore wanted the treasure enough to pay the sum that Walterfang sought. The driving force behind the acquisition of the cargo was Pamelia Lee, then head of the Singapore Tourist Board and a sister-in-law of Singapore's long-serving prime minister, Lee Kuan Yew. 'I thought it was time for Singapore to look for the finer things in life,' she recalls. 'Like every other nation that becomes wealthy you have to look at building your roots.'[8] Lee hoped that the cargo would repay the purchase price by attracting visitors to the huge resort then being planned for Sentosa Island in Singapore. In April 2005 the state-owned Sentosa Corporation, part of the Singapore Ministry of Trade and Industry, announced an agreement to buy the hoard from Walterfang's company for $32 million. Half the cost was contributed by the estate of one of Southeast Asia's richest men: the banking and hotel magnate Tan Sri Khoo. The deal was described as a key part of Sentosa's plans to create a new maritime museum filled with artifacts salvaged from shipwrecks.

In early 2011, while the maritime museum was being built, some of the 'Tang Treasure' went on display at the ArtScience Museum on the Singapore waterfront. The plan was to transfer the exhibition to the Smithsonian Institution in Washington DC the following year. But then a coalition of American archaeologists intervened. They were furious that a private company had been allowed to excavate such a rare and precious site. Some accused the Institution of promoting looting. It became an argument between idealists and cynics – between those who believed that best archaeological practice should be observed in every case and those who felt that the real-world problems of looting and of financing exploration demanded real-world solutions. In April 2011, the Smithsonian gave in and cancelled the exhibition. Walterfang accused his critics of being 'social climbers' playing 'yet another political game'.[9] Relations haven't improved much since.

Even worse, the Maritime Experiential Museum on Sentosa has also snubbed the Tang Treasure. There are pieces there from other wrecks but not a single piece from Belitung. At the time of writing, only a tiny fraction of the cargo is on public display, in a few cases inside the Goodwood Park Hotel in Singapore, formerly owned by Mr Khoo. It seems Singaporeans have little interest in one of the world's most remarkable archaeological discoveries. Pamelia Lee is disappointed that the people of the island state, in many ways the modern equivalent of Funan or Srivijaya, have not understood the significance of the treasure. 'My vision is that in years to come, when they have the best of all gadgets, they will look for something tangibly different,' she sighs[10]. But perhaps there's a more profound message here. It appears that not only do Singaporeans have no sense of 'ownership' of the cargo, they have no sense of ownership towards the sea either, despite the fact that their entire country owes its existence to seaborne trade. Singapore is an entrepôt, capitalising on the east–west currents passing its harbours, but that doesn't translate into a sense of entitlement to its riches.

Its modern meaning aside, what the Belitung wreck proves to archaeologists is that by the middle of the Tang era (the three centuries between 618 and 907) the South China Sea trade had become a highly integrated export industry. Enterprises in many parts of China were designing products for specific markets (decorated with Buddhist symbols or Koranic inscriptions as required) and mass-producing them. Local agents were then transporting the goods over land, down rivers and around the coast to the entrepôts where foreign merchants would handle the long-distance shipping. There was a clear division of labour between domestic manufacture and foreign trade.

The Tang court took special measures to encourage the relationship. Early on it ordered that provisions be made available to foreigners arriving in Guangzhou and created an official position to supervise the trade. Malay traders (perhaps those Nusantao again) moved to Guangzhou in significant numbers along with Arabs, Persians, Armenians and Indians. They brought with them the finest products from their home countries: pearls, rugs and minerals from Persia (including the cobalt blue used in pottery glazes), frankincense, myrrh, and dates from Arabia, jewels and glassware from India and spices and perfumes from Southeast Asia. They exchanged them for the ceramics, silks and metalwork of China. The maritime silk route, the Abbasid–Tang superhighway from Guangzhou to Baghdad, by way of Srivijaya and Sri Lanka, created vast wealth for those who could control it.

Under the Tang, trade was the preserve of the court and only appointed officials could handle imports: eunuchs who had every incentive to demand bribes and exploit traders at their most vulnerable. The corruption became worse and worse until, in October 758, there was a riot. Persian and Arab traders sacked the city and took their trade elsewhere. The rulers of the Red River Delta in what is now Vietnam (nominally under Tang rule but largely autonomous) jumped at the opportunity. Their port, at Long Bien, became the trade terminus for a few decades. However, Guangzhou must have regained its position by the time the Belitung ship departed there around 826. But 40 years after that, in 878, anti-Tang rebels occupied Guangzhou. One Arab account says they singled out and slaughtered thousands of Arabs, Persians, Jews and Christians who were resident there. Nonetheless, the surviving foreign traders seem to have clung on to their toeholds on the coast.

The revolt was a taste of things to come. In 906 the Tang Dynasty collapsed, their former realm fractured and the coast became independent again. The ramifications changed the whole region. On the southwest coast, the area around Guangzhou broke away to form the Nan Han kingdom and then the rulers of the Red River Delta broke away from that to form Dai Viet. Dai Viet would grow to rival and ultimately conquer the lands of Champa (and over the next thousand years evolve into Viet Nam).

On the southeast coast, in the modern province of Fujian, the kingdom of Minnan emerged. Cut off from the north, Minnan embraced the sea. Over the course of the tenth century, it became a fully maritime trading state. The port of Quanzhou emerged from obscurity to become a hive of entrepreneurial energy and the destination of choice for merchants from the Middle East. After more than a thousand years of trading with foreigners, the people whom we would now call 'Chinese' set sail across the oceans on their own vessels for the first time.[11] It was the start of a seafaring tradition that would carry Fujianese – and members of the Min or Hokkien ethnic group in particular – across the South China Sea and beyond.

By 970, after 60 years of independence, the south came under the control of the Song Dynasty, with its capital in the northern city of Kaifeng. Initially the Song regarded the sea in the way inland rulers traditionally had: as a source of threat. It was a place where 'bad elements' could hide – whether smugglers or political rivals – and where foreign ideas could propagate. In 985 all Chinese merchants were banned from travelling abroad. The Song followed their predecessors and imposed a state monopoly on trade. Private dealings were banned, forcing foreign merchants to import their cargoes through official channels, so that the court could then impose taxes on ships, customs duties on imports and also confiscate a proportion of the cargo and profit from its resale to domestic consumers.

But within a few years the Song initiated a remarkable policy U-turn. In 987 the court sent four missions abroad to encourage foreign states to trade. But that wasn't enough. Pressure on the court to relax its controls grew further: from coastal merchants, who wanted the profits; from consumers, who wanted the foreign goods; and from the treasury, which needed revenue to support the bureaucracy. In 989 private Chinese shipping was allowed to sail abroad for trade. Finally, after centuries of being on the receiving end of trade, in the late tenth century Chinese mariners were officially permitted to make their own trading voyages. There were tax incentives too. The proportion of inbound cargo that was automatically commandeered by the state was cut to just half and later reduced further. Boat-builders learnt to construct ocean-going vessels. They adopted inventions from the Chinese inland water trade, such as watertight compartments and sternpost rudders, but they also copied elements of the Malay ships that had been visiting their shores for centuries. Even the name they gave these vessels – *po* – was of Malay origin.

In the years after 1069, a Song court official, Wang Anshi, pioneered reforms intended to increase government income by stimulating trade. In a very early experiment with liberal economics, import taxes were reduced and the management of trade devolved to each port. It was a success: within 20 years, the value of trade had doubled. One other reform had far-reaching consequences. The court lifted its ban on the export of copper money. The currency spread rapidly around the South China Sea trading network and Song coinage became a medium of exchange as far away as Sumatra and Java.

By 1090 Chinese ships were being allowed to sail abroad from any port, spreading the income from trade much more widely. The move also allowed Fujianese traders to break into a business previously monopolised by foreigners. And just like the foreigners, they too were obliged to follow the monsoons and wait in foreign ports for winds to change. While sojourning they began to put down roots: dedicating temples to their seafaring goddess Mazu and creating embryonic Chinatowns. Nonetheless restrictions remained. Chinese ships were only allowed to be away from port for nine months, one monsoon cycle. They could only reach as far as Sumatra before having to return home. Westward trade into the Indian Ocean remained the preserve of Arab, Indian and Srivijayan ships. However, the more adventurous Chinese merchants began to push onwards to India and the Persian Gulf regardless.

But at home, the Song court was under increasing pressure. In 1126 it lost control of its northern lands to Jurchen invaders from Manchuria and moved its capital to Hangzhou on the eastern coast. In the resulting crisis it banned Chinese ships from sailing abroad and stopped almost all luxury imports (with the notable exception of the ivory required to make officials' belt buckles). But even this crisis only lasted, at most, six years before the Song started to liberalise trade once again. Within 14 years trade policies had pretty much reverted to their pre-crisis positions. The imperative to trade was overwhelming. By the 1160s the expat community in Quanzhou had become so large that it required a special cemetery. Many of these traders were Muslim, Islam having taken root in Champa by this time, and they had good connections with both Muslims from the Middle East and China's growing Muslim population.

The Song Dynasty would last another century. Taken as a whole, the period from the fall of the Tang Dynasty in 906 until the fall of the Song in 1279 seems to have been an early 'golden age' of commerce around the South China Sea. Changes in China and India and the growth of Islamic commerce unleashed large increases in trade and wealth creation.[12] The most powerful of the Champa states, Vijaya, prospered at this time. Srivijaya, on the other hand, declined following an invasion from the southern Indian Chola kingdom in 1025. That allowed other ports to emerge along the coasts of Sumatra, Java, Bali, Borneo and mainland Southeast Asia. Islands in the Philippines (known as Butuan and Ma-yi in Chinese texts) start to be recorded as trading entities too. The discovery, in 1981, of a spectacular hoard of golden treasure in the Philippine city of Surigao, on the tip of Mindanao Island, suggests a wealthy Hindu-ised elite was already in place there by this time.

New commodities were being exchanged, bringing more and more people and territories into the regional, and ultimately global, trading system. But by the end of the thirteenth century, boom seems to have turned to bust. In 1275, Srivijaya's main port, Jambi, was destroyed by raiders from Java. At the same time Mongols were advancing from the north into the Song's territory. The Mongols' eventual conquest of Fujian and Guangzhou by 1279 seems to have triggered a general decline in regional trade that lasted until they lost power almost a century later. Instead, the Sea became an arena of conflict as the Mongol 'Yuan Dynasty' sought influence. Kublai Khan, the ruler of the Yuan Dynasty, sent 14 maritime missions abroad and launched destructive attacks against Champa and Java in particular. Without the wealth from maritime trade, however, the Yuan Dynasty couldn't generate the surpluses needed to maintain their own power. By 1368 they were in the dustbin of history.

They were replaced by the Ming Dynasty who almost immediately tried to abolish private overseas trade and bring it, once again, entirely under state control. Trading relations officially reverted to 'tribute' arrangements rather than the open market and Guangzhou was designated the 'legiti-mate' port for ships from Southeast Asia. But after nearly four centuries of private trading by Chinese merchants and with an infrastructure of agents and family networks in place around the region, unofficial trade was never eliminated, particularly among the entrepreneurs of Fujian province. In the end the smuggling became dominant, particularly when Chinese communities abroad started to use the 'tribute' trade as cover. In time the Ming would turn their backs on the sea and focus on inland problems, but not before the most spectacular assertion of Chinese state power in the sea: the 30 years of the 'eunuch voyages'.

* * * * * *

Geoff Wade is an Australian historian, a level-headed expert on the Ming Dynasty and its written annals, the *Ming Shi-lu*. But if you want to upset him, just ask about the writer Gavin Menzies and his book *1421: the Year China Discovered the World*, describing the alleged exploits of the Chinese eunuch admiral Zheng He. Wade is derisive. Menzies' book, he says, 'is quite remarkable in that not one of the claims made in the volume has any veracity whatsoever. The eunuch admirals that he claims circumnavigated the world did not travel past Africa, there are no Chinese or other texts which support the voyages suggested, there has been no Chinese shipwreck found beyond Asia, and there are no Ming settlement sites or structures beyond Asia. That a fiction of this scale could be published and marketed as non-fiction is a damning indictment of Mr Menzies, but even more so of his publisher.'[13] Wade might get angrier than most but this is the generally held view among professional historians about Menzies' claims.

Menzies may have invented large parts of his account but there's no doubt that Zheng He was a fascinating historical figure: a Muslim from Yunnan who was captured during the Ming invasions and castrated, and who later helped the third Ming emperor win a succession battle for the throne. Zheng is now so widely known that it's hard to believe there was a time when he was an obscure figure. That changed in October 1984 when the Chinese leader Deng Xiaoping used the admiral to justify his 'open door' policy of engagement with the West in a speech to the Communist Party's Central Advisory Commission. In the years since, Zheng has become the poster boy for Beijing's policy of 'peaceful rise', an exemplar of China's engagement with the world. In 2004 the man responsible for organising the huge commemorations marking the 600th anniversary of the admiral's first voyage, Vice-Minister of Communications Xu Zu-yuan, summarised the official view of his achievements. 'These were thus friendly diplomatic activities,' he declared. 'During the overall course of the seven voyages to the Western Ocean, Zheng did not occupy a single piece of land, establish any fortress or seize any wealth from other countries. In the commercial and trade activities, he adopted the practice of giving more than he received, and thus he was welcomed and lauded by the people of the various countries along his routes.'[14]

However, Geoff Wade argues that this account of Zheng is almost as misleading as Gavin Menzies' version. Wade's study of the *Ming Shi-lu* has revealed there were 25 voyages led by several different eunuch commanders in the years between 1403 and the early 1430s, of which Zheng led only five. The vast majority of the voyages were to Southeast Asia but Zheng became famous because his ships went much further – around the Indian Ocean. Wade argues that the voyages were not peace missions but clear shows of force. Each expedition – of between 50 and 250 ships – carried over 20,000 troops armed with the most advanced weapons of their time. The purpose was clearly to shock and awe. On the first voyage, ordered in 1405, Zheng stopped in Palembang on Sumatra where he chased down a fugitive from the Ming court, Chen Zu-yi. Five thousand people were reported killed in the fighting. On the same voyage Zheng's armada fought an army in Java, which Wade believes probably belonged to Majapahit, China's rival for supremacy in the South China Sea at the time. On another voyage, in 1411, Zheng invaded a Sri Lankan city, destroyed its military, appointed a puppet ruler and took the king back to China. In 1415 he intervened in a civil war in Sumatra and there are also suggestions that his forces committed atrocities on the Arabian Peninsula.[15]

Wade argues that the fact that so many rulers and ambassadors were transported to China on board Zheng's ships suggests they must have been coerced into travelling and that this coercion gave the Ming Dynasty access to ports and shipping lanes. In 1405 the admiral established a garrison in Malacca (Melaka in Malay), a city established just three years before, which enabled Ming forces to control the Straits in which it sits. He awarded the ruler a kingship in return. The overall purpose of the voyages appears to have been two-fold: to control trade routes and to give the usurping emperor legitimacy at home through the enforced paying of homage to him by foreign rulers. This is a long way from the official picture of the 'outstanding envoy of peace and friendship' promoted by Beijing. In the end, this 'gunboat diplomacy' lasted just 30 years. Jealous court officials curbed the eunuch's powers. Policy priorities turned inwards: Zheng's maps were burned and his boats left to rot away. China didn't possess another naval ship capable of reaching the islands of the South China Sea until it was given one by the United States 500 years later.

But the Chinese Communist Party knows that myth is stronger than history and Zheng the kindly diplomat still sets sail whenever 'maritime cooperation' needs to be discussed in Southeast Asia or an investment deal celebrated in East Africa. 'Official history' plays a vital role in Communist China generally, as even a brief visit to the National Museum of China in Tiananmen Square will attest. It buttresses the Party's right to rule and denigrates rivals. Once a particular historical narrative becomes Party dogma, challenging it becomes a career-limiting act of dissent. Supporting it with evidence brings rewards.

In 1986, China's State Administration of Cultural Heritage created an Underwater Archaeological Heritage Centre (UWARC) to be managed by the National Museum. The decision was prompted, in part, by a fear that China was losing its 'ownership' of faraway shipwrecks to well-financed foreign excavators. But it also had another purpose. UWARC's first open-water expedition was to the Chinese-occupied but Vietnamese-claimed Paracel Islands. In March 1999 the centre's director, Zhang Wei, announced that his divers had recovered 1,500 relics dating from 907, 'proving that the Chinese were the earliest inhabitants' of the Paracels. Less partisan archaeologists guffawed. In 907 the Tang Dynasty had just fallen so it is conceivable that the wreck could have been from one of the very first ships ever to sail from the newly independent state of Minnan. However, it's much more likely that the vessel was Malay or Arab. Chinese pottery was traded all around the region, and beyond. The presence of pottery on any shoal is no more proof of Chinese historical possession than the presence of thousands of cowry shells in a Bronze Age tomb in the Chinese city of Anyang is proof that Henan Province should rightfully belong to the Philippines.

Zhang, the Centre's original director, was not appointed to be an independent analyst of historical evidence. When presenting UWARC to the International Council on Monuments and Sites in 2005, Zhang explained that the organisation was preparing 'one or two excavations of shipwrecks in the Nansha Islands' and that: 'The results from the excavation can demonstrate that China has the unarguable sovereignty of the South China Sea Islands.'[16] There is a symbiotic relationship between the Centre and Chinese foreign policy. UWARC has a budget that other archaeologists in the region can only dream about.[17] Its 'research base' in the city of Qingdao alone cost $24 million and UWARC has other centres in Hubei, Hainan and Fujian plus a new research vessel.[18] The excavation of the 'Nanhai One' shipwreck in the mouth of the Pearl River was funded to the tune of $150 million. And UWARC repays the favour with loyal service to the state: finding 'evidence' that reinforces the official history and thus the narrative of China's indisputable sovereignty in the South China Sea.

Across that sea, other underwater archaeologists have found it more difficult to research an alternative narrative. In April 2012, a joint Franco-Filipino expedition organised by the National Museum in Manila was investigating a wreck on the Scarborough Shoal, 220 kilometres west of the main island of the Philippines, Luzon. Based on board a support ship, the MV *Sarangani*, they were following best practice: investigating the site in situ, non-commercially and with the intention of publishing their findings for others to review. But then a Chinese Marine Surveillance ship arrived and ordered them to leave – on the grounds that the wreck belonged to China. Only Chinese archaeologists would be allowed to investigate the site so that they could again find 'evidence' of indisputable Chinese sovereignty.

Despite these difficulties, archaeologists such as Victor Paz, Peter Bellwood, Wilhelm Solheim, Pierre-Yves Manguin and all their colleagues have accumulated enough evidence to tell a very different story about the South China Sea: that it was a polyglot place of exchange and trade where questions of sovereignty were utterly different from the way they are posed today. Until the early sixteenth century, a series of Indianised *mandalas* dominated maritime Southeast Asia. There was no neat succession from one power centre to the next. Their ascents were gradual, as were their falls, and for long periods they coexisted – sometimes peacefully, often not. Funan, in the Mekong Delta, held sway from the first to the fourth century; Champa, in what is now central Vietnam, from the sixth until the fifteenth; Srivijaya, on Sumatra, from the seventh until the twelfth; Angkor, in the lower Mekong, from the early ninth century to the 1430s;

Majapahit, on Java, from the twelfth to the sixteenth; and Malacca, on the Malay Peninsula, from the early fifteenth until the Portuguese arrived in the early sixteenth. At times the governing power on the north shore of the South China Sea, the area that today we call China, intervened in the affairs of the other polities – but rarely and only for limited periods. In no sense did any state or people 'own' the Sea. In September 1975 Deng Xiaoping is said to have told his Vietnamese counterpart Le Duan that the islands of the South China Sea 'have belonged to China since ancient times'.[19] The phrase appeared in public for the first time in three Chinese publications in November 1975.[20] The words have been repeated innumerable times since but, as we shall see, a review of the evidence tells us that this sense of ownership is not ancient, but very recent.

CHAPTER 2

Maps and Lines
1500 to 1948

IN JANUARY 2008, in the light- and humidity-controlled basement of the Bodleian Library in Oxford, about 5,500 nautical miles from the Spratly Islands, Robert Batchelor unrolled a document that has radically changed our understanding of the history of the South China Sea. It was a map, a metre and a half long by a metre wide, covering what we now call East and Southeast Asia: from Japan in the northeast to Sumatra and Timor in the south. It was also a work of art. During the 350 years it had been in the library, many people had admired its delicately painted 'mountain water' scenes: the pale green sea fringed with bamboo, pine and sandalwood trees; hills, rivers and plants drawn as they might be seen in life. But what Batchelor spotted – which no-one else had noticed for centuries – was a network of pale lines radiating from the southern Chinese port of Quanzhou. The lines linked Quanzhou with almost every port in the region: from Nagasaki to Manila, Malacca and beyond. More surprisingly, each route was marked with navigational instructions: Chinese compass bearings and indications of distance.

What Batchelor, an American historian, had rediscovered was a guide to the trading highways of Asia. It demolished the traditional image of seventeenth-century China as an inward-facing, isolationist power. Instead it showed a China that was engaged with the sea and, through the sea, to the wider world. It was also a picture of a region untroubled by formal borders, where kingdoms and fiefs were all connected. The map was the product of an era when the boundaries between rulers had entirely different characters to those that divide the region today. But it was drawn at a time when the nature of those boundaries was starting to change because of battles between empires, and debates between thinkers, on the other side of the world. Those battles and debates both laid the foundations for modern international law and also imposed new ideas about boundaries that continue to disturb the waters of the South China Sea today.

The map's own biography makes that plain. It shows just how strongly connected Europe and Asia had become, even by the 1600s. It was presented to the Bodleian in 1659 after the death of its owner, John Selden, one of the most important legal figures in seventeenth-century England. In his will, Selden said the map had been 'taken by an English commander' though he didn't say which one. After years of diligent research, Robert Batchelor believes he knows. In the summer of 1620, a ship of the English East India Company, the *Elizabeth*, stopped at Taiwan and spotted a vessel – Chinese or Japanese – carrying among its passengers a Portuguese pilot and two Spanish priests. The captain of the *Elizabeth*, Edmund Lenmyes, used this as justification to seize the ship, its cargo and, Batchelor believes, the map.[1] Selden says in his will that the English commander (whoever he was) was 'pressed exceedingly to restore it at great ransome' but refused to give it back to its owners. The commander must have immediately recognised the map's value.

We don't know how Selden obtained the map but he had been a Member of Parliament and knew the key investors in the English East India Company.[2] Robert Batchelor believes the map arrived in England in 1624 after a long and difficult journey. Perhaps it was sold as booty or presented as a gift to an influential patron. John Selden would have been an ideal recipient. He was right at the heart of England's political and trading elite and a pioneer of legal thinking. He's now best known for providing some of the earliest legal arguments for countries to claim territorial waters around their shores. What is less well known is that Selden's contribution, a key foundation of international law, started with an argument about a small oily fish. The fate of the European herring would be caught up in a fight over access to Asia. It was a battle about freedom of the seas, free trade and the economic domination of the world, a battle that had its roots in discoveries a century before.

* * * * * *

Vasco da Gama's arrival in India in May 1498 had started well but, in a taste of things to come, relations quickly deteriorated. Being the first person to sail all the way from Europe provided initial celebrity status but his Portuguese gifts didn't impress the Zamorin of Calicut. Compared to the silks, ivories and gold the Zamorin was used to, da Gama's offering of scarlet cloaks, hats, oil and honey looked more like an insult. Worse, the Arab and Persian merchants who already handled Calicut's trade with Europe recognised the threat da Gama posed and conspired to run him out of town. The Zamorin sent him away and, lacking understanding of the monsoons, da Gama endured a terrible voyage back to Portugal, losing two-thirds of his crew. Nonetheless, he brought back enough spice to more than pay for the cost of the expedition and his sponsor, King Manuel, was delighted. By sailing around Africa, Portuguese merchants could now outflank the infidel Arabs and also break the trade monopoly formerly enjoyed by the merchants of Venice through their stranglehold over the eastern Mediterranean.

Transporting spices and other luxuries from Asia to Europe in a single sea journey was much cheaper and safer than the traditional Arab–Venetian route combining short voyages with overland caravans. The Portuguese in their modern *carracks* – able to carry both cargo and cannon – quickly came to dominate the trade. In only a few years they had a base in Goa and found their way past Calicut, across the Bay of Bengal and to the Straits of Malacca: the gateway to the Spice Islands. Unfortunately, the Sultan of Malacca had no intention of letting them through. His rule depended on taxing the trade that passed between what we now call Indonesia and Malaysia. Malacca was the new regional entrepôt, the heir to Funan and Srivijaya and rival to Majapahit. The city teemed with foreign merchants brokering trade between their ancestral homes and the rest of the known world. It held at least 100,000 residents and transients, among them Malays, Tamils, Gujaratis, Javanese, Chinese and Luçoes – traders from Luzon.

A Portuguese ambassador met the Sultan in 1509, presenting a more impressive consignment of gifts than Vasco da Gama had carried a decade before and his countrymen were granted a 'factory' from which to trade. However, other merchants – in particular the Gujaratis – objected and persuaded the Sultan to arrest the Christians on charges of treason. In June 1511, Portuguese gunboats arrived under the command of Admiral Afonso de Albuquerque. As negotiations dragged on, his spies gathered intelligence about the city's defences and cultivated sympathisers among the Chinese merchants. The Sultan refused to release his captives so, on the feast of Saint James, de Albuquerque attacked. After two weeks, the Sultan fled and on 10 August 1511 Malacca fell to the Portuguese. It would remain in their control for the next 130 years.

Among de Albuquerque's fleet was a 31-year-old officer, Ferdinand Magellan. Perhaps after the battle he wandered the streets of the city and encountered the Luçoes and their tales. Ten years later, having transferred his loyalties to Spain, Magellan set off to try to reach Luzon and its gold mines from the east and, in 1521, he became the first European to reach Asia via the Pacific. As in the previous voyages, the welcome was initially warm: the ruler of the island of Cebu and most of his subjects apparently converted to Christianity. According to the scholar accompanying Magellan, Antonio Pigafetta, the islanders pulled out their finest porcelain, proof they were already trading with China. Magellan arrived with faith and steel but he underestimated the reluctance of the other islanders to submit to either Jesus or Spain. Only a month later, on 27 April 1521, Magellan was hacked to death on the island of Mactan.

The Portuguese weren't much friendlier. They despatched a fleet to intercept Magellan, eventually discovering some of the expedition's survivors aboard the ship *Trinidad* off the spice island of Tidore and promptly imprisoning them. Having fought so hard to reach the Spice Islands (the Moluccan or Maluku Islands as we know them today) from the west, the Portuguese weren't about to hand their advantage to interlopers arriving from the other direction. This was only one of many disagreements between the two Christian empires. To resolve them, the king of Spain, Charles V, married off his sister to his Portuguese counterpart and three years later wed his new brother-in-law's sister, Isabella. A later fruit of these arranged unions was the 1529 Treaty of Zaragoza. For the first time, outsiders drew a line through Southeast Asia, dividing it between European empires. Although the map-making was inexact, it resulted in the Portuguese retaining the Spice Islands of what became Indonesia and the Spanish retaining what would become the Philippines. Five centuries later that division still exists. The Muslim rebellion in the southern Philippines and the Philippines' continuing claim over the Malaysian province of Sabah, which prevents the two countries reaching a border agreement in the South China Sea, ultimately stem from the Treaty of Zaragoza.

The Portuguese had come to Malacca seeking mace, nutmeg and cloves but found themselves, serendipitously, at the gateway to the mysterious land that Europeans then called 'Cathay'. With Malacca in their grasp there was no military force able to stop them pushing east, certainly not from Ming Dynasty China. After the eunuch admirals' 30-year spell of gunboat diplomacy a century before, the navy had rotted away. The court became more concerned about threats to its northern borders and an internal financial crisis. The Ming had been the first economy in history to issue paper money – and the first to suffer hyperinflation. Worthless money couldn't keep the navy afloat.

In the decades afterwards, as the official fleets declined, an unofficial private sector had emerged to meet Chinese demand for imported goods and to supply the market for silk and porcelain in places like Cebu. At this time trade in China was supposed to be a state-owned enterprise imbued with the rituals of 'tribute'. The southeastern province of Fujian, however, became notorious for smuggling. Its ships carried goods around the region and also took away many thousands of Fujianese to set up trading operations in distant ports. They created the first, small, Chinatowns around the shores of the South China Sea.[3] It was some of these people who assisted the Portuguese in Malacca – both in the battle and afterwards.

Encouraged by the Fujianese, the Portuguese pressed on in search of the sources of silk and porcelain. It was the Portuguese who first gave the waters east of Malacca the name by which we know them today: Mare da China or the Sea of China. Later, as they pushed towards Japan, they realised they had to distinguish the 'South Sea of China' from the other stretch of water off China's east coast. To the Chinese it was just 'the sea' or to the literate, the southern sea – the Nanhai.

The local pilots had no maps as Europeans understood the term – just their accumulated knowledge written in the form of rutters: instructions for navigating from place to place. Those rutters also included a dose of mythology – notably a belief in the Wan-li Shi-tang. According to a Chinese account of 1178 – Chou Ch'u-fei's 'Information on what lies beyond the passes' – this was a long embankment in the ocean near where the waters descend into the underworld. Advised by their pilots, the Portuguese explorers also came to believe in the Wan-li Shi-tang, a vast archipelago of dangerous reefs and islands stretching all along the coast of what is now Vietnam. The Portuguese deployed the best tools Renaissance science could offer but even they were fooled. A sail-shaped Wan-li Shi-tang was copied and recopied on every map of the region for the following 300 years – until surveys in the late 1700s and early 1800s revealed that, apart from the Paracel Islands at its northerly end, it didn't actually exist. For 300 years the mistaken belief in the existence of the archipelago deterred most sailors from venturing into the centre of the South China Sea.

The 'China' that the Portuguese reached in the early 1500s was not a single unified state[4] and large parts of the southern coast were outside the control of the Ming rulers in Beijing. The Portuguese found it much easier to deal with individual merchants from Fujian than with the hostile state authorities based in the official entry port of Guangzhou. China at this time was in desperate need of one particular commodity that the Portuguese were perfectly placed to provide. The earlier hyperinflation had caused merchants to turn away from paper money and demand payments in silver. The nearest source of silver was only a short sail away in Japan but relations between the two countries were so bad that in 1549 the Ming court had banned direct sailing between them. The Portuguese showed up at exactly the right moment to become middlemen – shuttling between Nagasaki and Macao, trading Japanese silver for Chinese silk.[5]

In 1567 the Ming emperor finally conceded the impossibility of control-ling smuggling and ended – in Fujian province – the official ban on private trade. The result was an explosion of commerce – around 200 junks sailed south each monsoon.[6] For the first time, large private Chinese trading fleets began to outnumber those of the Southeast Asian traders who had dominated the 'China trade' for the previous millennium. The German scholar Angela Schottenhammer has shown how this change came to be reflected in language: the term *hai shang* – maritime merchant – began to appear in Chinese texts for the first time and even the meaning of the

Chinese word for sea itself – *hai* – shifted. In earlier times it had implied a meeting place between civilisation and the unknown. From the mid-sixteenth century onwards it lost its mystical connotations and evolved into a simple description of geography.[7]

A further Ming reform would change not just China but the entire world. In 1570 the government gave in to the inevitable and decreed that taxes also had to be paid in silver. But there simply wasn't enough silver in China, or Japan, to meet demand. The price soared to unaffordable levels. What saved the Ming administration was the discovery of the world's largest silver mine in Potosi, 20,000 kilometres away, high up in the Spanish-controlled Andean mountains.

The Treaty of Zaragoza had allowed the Spanish to retain their toehold in the Philippines and in 1571 the heirs to Magellan established a trading base in Manila. They learnt of the rocketing price of silver across the water and so began the 'Acapulco Trade'. For more than a century, galleons shipped around 150 tons of silver a year across the Pacific from Mexico to Manila where it was traded for gold, silks and ceramics from China. Similarly large amounts of silver travelled eastwards from Potosi, via Europe. The price of silver in China – as measured against gold – was double that in Europe. Simply by shipping Andean silver to China, exchanging it for gold and selling that gold in Europe, the Spanish Empire was able to make vast profits – and pay for its wars in Europe.[8] At the same time the European elite rapidly developed a taste for the luxuries of Chinese silk and porcelain.

Faced with such a 'silver opportunity', the Chinese population of Manila swelled, reaching 10,000 within 30 years. Most of them came from just four townships in the Jinjiang region of Fujian.[9] Manila became a key stop on the eastern trading route around the South China Sea. As well as silver, Fujianese shipped home the seeds of southern China's future growth – literally. The Spanish brought maize, sweet potato and peanuts from South America and farmers discovered they all grew well in the soils of southern China – leading to an agricultural revolution and a rapid increase in population.

For better and for worse the Chinese coast was now firmly integrated into the global economy. Networks of Chinese, Malays, Arabs and Europeans transmitted the impacts of cannons and currency around the world. By the end of the sixteenth century, the united Spanish–Portuguese Empire dominated European trade with Asia. But the empire was rotting from within. In 1581, after two decades of unrest and repression, the rulers of seven Dutch provinces declared independence from their Spanish Habsburg rulers. In response, the Portuguese tried to cut the supply of Asian spices. The Dutch response would shake the world. All they needed was a good map.

The answer to their Calvinistic prayers was Jan Huyghen van Linschoten, a Dutchman who had travelled to Spain as a teenager and sailed with the Portuguese between their outposts in Goa, Malacca and Macao (the nearest anchorage to Guangzhou the Portuguese could rent from the Chinese authorities). He assiduously copied their maps and sailing directions until his ship's trunk held, in effect, the keys to Asia. In 1594, after a perilous journey back to the Netherlands, he gave them to a compatriot, Cornelis de Houtman, who organised, the following year, the first Dutch expedition to reach Southeast Asia. It was a disaster. Two-thirds of the crew died, de Houtman offended the Sultan of Banten, ordered murders and rapes and only just made it back alive. Nonetheless he had proved that the Dutch could trade independently with the Spice Islands.

In 1596 Jan Huyghen shared his knowledge with the rest of Europe. His *Itinerario* – the story of his voyages – and his maps (quickly translated into English and German) smashed the Portuguese monopoly of knowledge about how to sail the spice routes.[10] For northern European entrepreneurs this was a double opportunity – a chance both to hit the Habsburgs and to make a personal fortune. On 31 December 1600, Queen Elizabeth of England granted 216 aristocrats and merchants a Royal Charter to form the East India Company. Two years later, in Amsterdam, six small companies were merged to form its Dutch equivalent, the Vereenigde Oostindische Compagnie (VOC). The VOC was both a trading company and an arm of the state – specifically licensed to fight the Portuguese. But the Portuguese wouldn't give up easily. The contest between the two would ultimately lead to the first 'world war', reshape Southeast Asia and give us the system of international maritime law which underlies the conflict in the South China Sea to this day.

* * * * * *

By late 1602 the VOC had established a trading and military bridgehead on the southern tip of the Malay Peninsula. The Sultan of Johor's dislike of the Portuguese was just as strong as that of the Duch since he was a descendant of the defeated ruler of Malacca. In September 1601 the Portuguese had captured and executed 17 members of a Dutch crew that was attempting to reach Guangzhou (known to Europeans as Canton) and break into the China trade. Now, after learning of the Dutch–Johor alliance, they blockaded and shelled Johor's coast.

On 25 February 1603, the Dutch and Johorese hit back. Admiral Jakob van Heemskerk and his new ally were alerted to a heavily laden Portuguese ship nearby – sailing from Macao to Malacca. By the standards of the time, the *Santa Catarina* was vast. Its cargo included 1,200 bales of raw silk, chests of damask and taffeta, 70 tons of gold, 60 tons of porcelain and large amounts of cotton, linen, sugar, spices and wooden furniture. There were probably around 1,000 people on board: 700 troops, 100 women and children plus a large number of merchants and the crew. Amazingly this vast prize was pitifully defended. The Portuguese had a practice of selling the officers' positions to the highest bidders, not to the most skilled. The Dutch, on the other hand, trained well.[11]

Shortly after sunrise, Van Heemskerk's flotilla (two Dutch ships and several from Johor) found the *Santa Catarina* at anchor in the mouth of the Johor River (close to Changi Airport in modern Singapore). With their first fusillades, they shredded the *Catarina*'s sails so it couldn't move and they spent the rest of the day firing occasional shots into its hull (but not so many as to seriously damage the cargo). With his ship leaking and casualties mounting, the captain, Sebastião Serrão, surrendered. In exchange for their lives, the passengers and crew forfeited the ship and its contents.

When, eventually, the *Santa Catarina*'s cargo reached the Netherlands the quantities of precious metals, luxury textiles and fine porcelain caused a sensation. Merchants were tantalised by the obvious opportunities that lay in the Orient. At auction the cargo sold for 3.5 million guilders – equal to half the total capital of the VOC. But there was a problem. Some of the VOC's shareholders felt the company should be concentrating on maximising its profits rather than fighting a costly war. The Dutch political elite, however, believed their new country needed both profits and war. They needed a good persuader. They sent for the 21-year-old Hugo Grotius.

Hugo Grotius (the Latinised version of Huig de Groot) was, in effect, a celebrity lawyer. Born into a powerful family, he was regarded as a prodigy, graduating from college at 11 and being sent to meet the king of France at the age of 15. He became a barrister and then official historian of Holland (a position more like a modern spin doctor than an earnest academic). In late 1604 he was hired by the directors of the VOC to justify the seizure of the *Santa Catarina*. The apologia he produced would protect the VOC's dual role as trader and fighter but would also evolve into one of the founding documents of international law. It would lay the intellectual foundations for Dutch colonisation and bring about a 'clash of civilisations' between European and Southeast Asian concepts of political power and territory.

Most of the conventional wisdom about Hugo Grotius has been overturned in recent years by a pair of historians: Martine Julia van Ittersum and Peter Borschberg. Their careful re-reading of his personal and public writings has allowed us to see that – far from being a disinterested political thinker – Grotius was a lobbyist for the VOC and a determined advocate of Dutch commercial and political rights. He chose his arguments to suit the occasion, misconstrued the positions of others and relied on shaky references. Nonetheless, his writings have had a lasting impact.

The Portuguese argued that they had exclusive rights to trade in Asia because they had discovered the sailing routes to it. In the Iberian Catholic worldview, discovery by non-Christians simply didn't count. Grotius, however, argued a radical new line: Asian rulers were a part of humanity and could therefore make their own decisions about whom to trade with. Whereas Portugal's rulers argued that they had the right to decide who could sail the seas in their domain, Grotius argued that the sea, like air, couldn't be occupied by any one power and was therefore free for all to use. While these ideas might sound modern and progressive, they were also self-interested. They were intended to defend the right of the VOC to sign contracts with Asian rulers. Grotius would later argue that these contracts could legitimately exclude everyone else and also justify the use of force against anyone who tried to impede shipping or renege on contracts.

Grotius lobbied successfully behind the scenes but his arguments remained private until 1609 when they were published anonymously in a seminal pamphlet, *Mare Liberum – The Free Sea*. Once again he was writing for a political purpose – to try to influence peace negotiations between the Dutch and the Spanish. The VOC was terrified that, as a condition of peace, the Dutch government would concede the right of Spain and Portugal to exclude its ships from Asia. Grotius the spin doctor set to work. Again he was successful: the Treaty of Antwerp, signed on 10 April 1609, granted Dutch merchants the right to trade wherever Spain and Portugal didn't already have settlements.

But Grotius also had another target in mind: herring. Even worse than interfering with navigation, in his view, was interfering with fishing. At one point in *Mare Liberum* he calls it 'insane cupidity'. King James I of England (who was also King James VI of Scotland) was infuriated by the Dutch fleet that sailed along the Scottish and English coasts to intercept the annual migration of herring – upon which hundreds of communities depended for their livelihood. James wanted to keep the Dutch out of what he saw as 'his' waters but didn't want to start a fight with one of his few allies in Europe. On 16 May 1609, shortly after *Mare Liberum* had been published, he banned foreigners from fishing along the British coasts without an official licence. But James felt the need to bolster his edict with legal justification. A law professor, William Welwood, wrote a treatise in 1613 using biblical, Roman and (what we would now call) environmental arguments in favour of the king's right to limit foreign fishing. James can't have thought it good enough because, in 1619, he sent for another lawyer – John Selden.

Selden's pamphlet was finished that summer and sent for the king's approval. But at the last minute, James became concerned that his brother-in-law, King Christian of Denmark, might object to English attempts to claim the seas and then stir up a wider dispute about the whole North Atlantic. The pamphlet was quietly shelved and the legal argument temporarily suspended. Over the following decades both Grotius and Selden played active roles in national politics, fell out of favour in their respective countries and were even imprisoned for a while. By the mid-1630s Selden needed to ingratiate himself with England's new king, Charles I, who took a harder line on maritime disputes than his predecessor. In 1635 he offered a set of legal arguments to rebut the claims of Hugo Grotius. Even the title was a direct challenge to the Dutch: *Mare Clausum – The Closed Sea*.

Although Selden agreed with Grotius that ships had the right of 'innocent passage' through another country's waters, he insisted that states also had a right to restrict access to those waters in some circumstances. He argued that sovereigns ought to be able to claim specific areas – even of the high seas – based on long-standing usage.[12] The open sea could, he claimed, be 'occupied' and therefore not necessarily open to all: particularly if it contained plenty of herring.[13] It must have been around this time – with Selden a leading player in court politics – that he came into possession of the Chinese map.

The argument between Grotius and Selden – between open sea and closed sea – continues to this day. Selden was clearly in favour of drawing imaginary lines through waves but ultimately even Grotius conceded that bays, gulfs and straits could be possessed. However, although they both concluded that it was possible and right to draw lines through the sea, they disagreed about exactly where these lines should be drawn. By the end of the seventeenth century, European states had reached a compromise, sometimes called the 'cannon shot' rule, allowing a country to control the waters up to three or four nautical miles from its coast. For several centuries it appeared that Selden had lost the argument – mainly because England (Britain after 1707) became a maritime power. From then on, London's interests were better served by Grotius' arguments than Selden's. The British Empire was based on the presumed right of countries – and one country in particular – to trade freely around the world. Rather than arguing for wider territorial waters to save the herring, Britannia now argued for narrower ones so that it could rule more of the waves. That required minimising other rulers' rights to limit navigation. The Royal Navy could usually be relied upon to resolve any major disagreements over this point of legal principle with the application of its own version of the 'cannon shot' rule.

In each era, the global hegemon – the Netherlands, then Britain and today the United States – has argued in favour of freedom of navigation and used military force to prevent others challenging that freedom. But Selden's point of view continues to have its adherents, mainly among those on the receiving end of naval gunfire. The question of whether and how coastal states can assert their sovereignty offshore remains with us now and there are few places where this question is more vexed than in the South China Sea.

* * * * * *

The taking of the *Santa Catarina* was the opening shot of what became the first 'world war'. For most of the first half of the seventeenth century the Dutch and Portuguese were fighting in parts of Europe, Latin America, Africa and Asia. For a short period the English East India Company (EIC) and the Dutch VOC formed an alliance – which is why, in 1620, Captain Lenmyes of the *Elizabeth* felt entitled to capture a Chinese ship off Taiwan on the grounds that it was carrying Portuguese and Spanish passengers, and to steal its cargo and perhaps its beautifully illustrated map. The Dutch became the dominant force in the South China Sea for most of the seventeenth century – both as long-distance traders and as middlemen in voyages between Asian destinations. With superior fire-power they had squeezed the Portuguese out of the Japanese silver trade and most of the spice ports and even squashed their English allies in the 'Amboyna Massacre' of traders on the (today Indonesian) island of Ambon in 1623.

By 1625, and for the following 50 years, the Dutch Republic dominated global trade. At its peak the Dutch merchant fleet was larger than the Spanish, Portuguese, French, English, Scottish and German fleets combined, with 6,000 ships and 50,000 sailors. Amsterdam was the commercial capital of the world and Batavia (modern Jakarta) was its eastern outpost – in charge of the trade to Taiwan and Japan. In 1641 the VOC finally achieved a crucial breakthrough in Southeast Asia – conquering Malacca to become the dominant force in the Straits.

It was never total dominance though. The VOC always depended on local allies, such as the Sultan of Johor, for support. The company became more enmeshed in regional politics and gradually it acquired territory. Using Grotius' arguments about the inviolability of contracts, it enforced harsh deals with cold steel: brutalising and sometimes massacring those who resisted. The Chinese authorities were strong enough to keep the VOC out, however, so the Dutch had to deal through the merchants of Fujian. Batavia became the new regional entrepôt, the meeting point of Europe and the Chinese junk trade.

Throughout this period, the Chinese demand for silver appeared to be insatiable; coins of Latin American silver became the regional currency. But after 70 years of the Acapulco trade, the Spanish had shipped so much silver bullion to China that its value started to fall – it just didn't buy as much gold or grain as it once had. In China, the economic imbalances led, ultimately, to the fall of the Ming Dynasty in 1644 and its later replacement by the invading Qing. But the consequences rippled wider. Without the surplus from the Acapulco galleons, Spain could no longer afford to fight the Thirty Years War. The result, in 1648, was the Peace of Westphalia that created the basic political structure of modern Europe and the beginnings of the international state system as we know it today.

The change of regime in China was bloody and drawn-out. In the face of resistance by an independent Fujianese leader known as Koxinga, the new Qing authorities had, in 1656, banned trade once again and instituted one of history's most devastating 'scorched earth' campaigns along the southern coast. Huge numbers of people were forced to move inland and for the first time in Chinese texts the phrase 'maritime frontier' – *hai jiang* – began to be used. However, the policies were counter-productive: both trade and emigration increased as people sought any means to survive.

The drastic campaign eventually consolidated the Qing's hold over the coast and, in 1684, the new authorities felt secure enough to end their ban on private overseas trade. All along the southern Chinese coast, merchants set sail for new markets. By the end of the seventeenth century, with home advantage and low margins (no need for costly war-fighting), they had turned the Europeans into 'also rans' in the South China Sea. The Portuguese had Macao and Timor but little else. The Spanish were running a thriving trade between Latin America and Manila but not beyond. The Dutch – who had dominated for decades – had been expelled from Taiwan, pulled out of Tonkin (northern Vietnam) and Cambodia and lost their special relationship with Japan. The English 'empire' in the region consisted of a trading factory in Canton. In short, the Europeans were just another group of foreign merchants: tolerated so long as they respected local customs. It was the beginning of a 'Chinese Century' in the South China Sea region.

Now the barriers to migration had been lifted, great numbers of Chinese set off to seek their fortunes. Some travelled back and forth but others stayed away, most as traders but a few as administrators for local rulers. Then labourers started to travel abroad too. As demand for pepper, gold and tin grew back home, many thousands of Chinese migrated to

Southeast Asia to set up plantations or work in mines. In some places they created self-governing communities – *gongsi* – and in others they became an integral part of the settlements created by the European trading companies. The colonial cities of Portuguese Macao, Spanish Manila or Dutch Batavia couldn't have run without Chinese labour.

The Europeans feared their dependency on the Chinese and adopted racist policies to keep them marginalised. This – combined with grossly unfair business practices – frequently caused unrest and sometimes massacres. Nonetheless, overseas Chinese communities endured, generating wealth and contributing the skills and labour to enable their host communities to develop. The result was what's been described as an 'informal empire' around the rim of the South China Sea: 'informal' in the sense that it wasn't systematically exploited by the Qing authorities. For them it was a source of revenue, not territory. They paid little attention to the world beyond the coast.

The Chinese merchants who used the sea generally regarded it as a dangerous inconvenience and stuck to its edges, still convinced that the Wan-li Shi-tang – the mythical 10,000-mile archipelago along the coast of Indochina – blocked the direct route.[14] Chinese rutters such as the *Tung Hsi Yang Kao* – published in 1617 – make this clear.[15] It was Europeans who were foolish enough to try to find a direct route through its centre. Their successes and failures are now memorialised on sea charts: the Macclesfield Bank, in the middle of the South China Sea, was first described by John Harle, the captain of the English ship *Macclesfield*, in 1701.[16] One notable failure gave its name to the Scarborough Shoal, after the British ship wrecked upon it on 12 September 1748.[17] These maritime disasters were tragedies for the Europeans but provided useful business for others with the skills to plunder the wrecks. The business was so good that the Nguyen rulers of what would later become central Vietnam licensed a band of seamen to salvage the cargoes – a practice now used in support of Vietnam's claim to the Paracel Islands.[18]

In 1795 the English East India Company hired the man who would revolutionise travel in the South China Sea: the hydrographer James Horsburgh. Between 1807 and 1810, EIC ships mapped most of the coasts of the South China Sea and finally disproved the existence of the Wan-li Shi-tang. In 1809 and 1811 Horsburgh published his two-volume

India Directory of navigational instructions and then, in 1821, a chart of the South China Sea containing the first reasonably accurate mapping of what are today called the Paracel Islands and Spratly Islands.[19] This European knowledge did not transfer quickly to Chinese geographers. As late as 1843, the writer Wang Wen Tai could still contrast the route taken by European navigators with that taken by Chinese mariners. In his publication, *Hong mao fan ying ji li kao lue* (*To Study the Foreigners*), the name he used for the Macclesfield Bank – Hong Mao Qian – translates as 'the bank of the barbarians with red hair', the Chinese translation of Banc des Anglais or English Bank, the name used on French maps before it was renamed Macclesfield Bank.[20]

Two decades after the publication of Horsburgh's chart, Wang still believed the Paracels were 1,000 *lis* (500 kilometres) long and in what's thought to be a reference to the Spratly Islands, he wrote 'in the Qi Zhou Da Yang there are big rocks, but we do not know anything about it'.[21]

But Horsburgh did discover some local seafarers who did know how to navigate among the reefs and rocks. In his description of the Paracel Islands in the 1852 edition of the *India Directory* he noted that:

> There are numerous fishing boats belonging to [Hainan] Island, built of a heavy and hard wood instead of the fir which the Chinese boats are built with, and they sail fast; many of them go every year on fishing voyages for two months and navigate to seven or eight hundred miles from home, to collect the bicho de mer [sea cucumber], and procure dry turtle and sharks' fins, which they find amongst the numerous shoals and sand-banks in the south-east part of the China Sea. Their voyages commence in March, when they visit the Northern Banks, and leaving one or two of their crew and a few jars of fresh water, the boats proceed to some of the large shoals in the vicinity of Borneo, and continue to fish until the early part of June, when they return and pick up their small parties and their collections. We met with many of these fishing boats when we were about the shoals in the China Sea.[22]

Why did Horsburgh make a distinction between the hardwood vessels and 'Chinese' boats? Perhaps it was because their crews weren't Chinese in the sense that he understood the term. Their semi-nomadic lifestyle suggests that they might have been 'sea gypsies' – part of the Tanka people or the U-tsat, or the Dan-Jia – relics of the Nusantao network (see Chapter 1) who lived along the coasts of Vietnam and southern China. (The Dan-Jia can still be found in Hainan, living in floating villages.) Others may have come from further away: Badjao from the Philippines, Orang Laut from Malaysia and other nomadic groups are all known to have fished among the islands. Wherever they were from, the sea nomads lived lives that were largely separate from land-based authorities. They were treated with suspicion, often regarded as brigands or pirates and not seen as full citizens. It is ironic that these people are now regarded as the pioneers of the modern state sovereignty claims currently being put forward in the Sea.

The English EIC was prepared to spend money on surveys because its China trade was so lucrative. From small beginnings it came to subsidise the entire British Empire. In the first half of the eighteenth century, 90 per cent of the EIC's exports to Canton were in the form of silver. But, just as it had done a century before, the price of silver would fall drastically. After 1775 it comprised only 65 per cent of the company's exports to Canton.[23] In 1780 the EIC suddenly needed a new business model. The British government had dropped its tax on Chinese tea and demand for the brew exploded. The EIC needed something else to sell in exchange and found the answer growing on its lands in Bengal: opium. The exchange of an Indian narcotic for a Chinese stimulant grew to immense proportions: imports of tea in London fetched £23 million by 1800. Customs duties on the tea subsidised the British government, which funded the Royal Navy, which ultimately protected the traders and the empire. It was all built on opium.

The EIC, like its predecessors, now desperately needed a base in the Malacca Straits, a port where it could do as the Portuguese, Spanish and Dutch had done before and connect to the Chinese junk trade. In 1786 it leased the island of Penang at the northern end of the Straits but with only modest success. It was the acquisition of Singapore in 1819 that gave the British the edge. Perfectly sited to receive trade from all directions and free from traditional rulers, overbearing religion and cumbersome bureaucracy, Singapore rapidly developed from a malarial swamp into an Anglo-Chinese (or perhaps more accurately a Sino-British) regional hub.

With its victory over France in the Napoleonic War, Britain became the new global hegemon and, like its predecessors, sought to control access to the China trade through the Straits of Malacca. The Dutch could protest but they were in no position to resist.

Up until the nineteenth century, the interventions of European powers in East and Southeast Asia had been significant but generally local and temporary. With the power of the industrial revolution behind them, however, that would change. Trading empires would evolve into territorial ones and these new empires would create boundaries and new conflicts. The stories of two territorial disputes illustrate this well. In the middle of the seventeenth century, the Vietnamese Lê emperor and the Lao king were fighting over a section of the upper Mekong Valley. The conflict was eventually resolved when the two rulers agreed that people whose houses were built on stilts (the 'Lao') owed allegiance to the king, whereas those who lived on the ground (the 'Vietnamese') owed allegiance to the emperor. A defined boundary was much less important than the personal allegiances of the people.[24] In total contrast, the British and the Dutch resolved their nineteenth-century dispute in the Straits of Malacca with a very different kind of agreement. The 1824 Anglo-Dutch treaty drew a line through the sea – British activities were confined to the north side and Dutch to the south. It meant the British had to abandon their settlement at Bencoolen on Sumatra and the Dutch had to evacuate Malacca. Personal ties meant nothing; nationality and place were everything. It resolved a European problem but created many more for the indigenous Malay communities who had long roamed across both sides of the imaginary line. Those who tried to live in the traditional way were called 'smugglers', those who tried to resist were called 'pirates'.[25]

By the beginning of the nineteenth century, Europeans and Southeast Asians had radically different ideas about what constituted a 'country'. The traditional Southeast Asian political unit was defined by its centre: by the personal prestige of its ruler. In this *mandala* system, the ruler's authority diminished with distance from the centre of the kingdom. In Europe, at least since the Peace of Westphalia, a political unit had become defined by its edges: laws, rights and duties applied equally across the territory but stopped completely at its boundary. In the Asian system there could be gradual transitions in authority and even gaps where no ruler was acknowledged. Smaller units might recognise more than one sovereign or possibly none at all. Traditionally, boundaries in Southeast Asia had been fluid – and maritime borders vague in the extreme. The ambiguity allowed relations between rulers to evolve and frontiers to shift: sometimes peacefully, though more often violently. In the European system there were no gaps – everywhere was supposed to belong to a sovereign – and to only one. Hard choices were inbuilt.

As a result of the arguments between Grotius and Selden (and their successors) there was now a consensus among Western rulers about how these definite boundaries could be extended into the sea. As their empires expanded, that consensus travelled east and was imposed upon a region that had a completely different understanding of maritime boundaries. The transition from fluid frontier to fixed frontline laid the foundations for the current conflict in the South China Sea.

* * * * * *

European trading companies had ventured to East Asia as both merchants and mercenaries, ready to fight for their right to profit. They were licensed by their governments but acted in their own interests. By the nineteenth century the two most successful – the British and the Dutch – had become governments in their own right. The necessities of making alliances, squashing rivals, charging customs duties and preventing smuggling had obliged them to grab territory and rule populations – often in the most vicious and capricious manner. As the governments back home tried to control these abuses and fix the companies' financial problems, the interests of business and state became utterly intertwined. The VOC bankrupted itself in 1800 and its territory was taken over by the Dutch state. The EIC was repeatedly in trouble but survived on the profits of the opium–tea trade. The Qing authorities were demanding payment in silver but the silver price was rocketing because of independence wars being fought in Latin America. Without opium, British cash would flow out of the country to pay for tea and other imports from China. When the Qing tried to stop the EIC's trade they implicitly threatened the British economy with a balance of payments crisis. The combined response of the EIC and the British government was to try to force open China's markets – not just for opium but for all products – and restore the balance of trade. The 'Opium Wars' of 1840 and 1860 did just that. Gunboats of the EIC and the Royal Navy, subsidised by opium, overwhelmed their Qing opponents. While these ships blockaded the coast, British-commanded troops forced the emperor to cede Hong Kong and open five other ports for international trade. The Treaty of Nanjing was the first of 26 similarly 'unequal treaties' that the Qing would be forced to sign with a total of ten countries over the following 60 years.

The Opium Wars were the final flourish of the EIC. By 1874 bankruptcy and rising disgust at its behaviour had led to its forcible nationalisation. But that didn't end the confusion of British commercial and colonial motives in Southeast Asia. In 1842, the adventurer James Brooke had become Rajah of Sarawak and in 1882 the North Borneo Chartered Company took over what is now Sabah. They were identified as 'British' territories but only gradually were they formally included in the British Empire.

The French and German imperial projects, on the other hand, were state-led operations from the start. With a pretext provided by the mistreatment of Catholic missionaries, the French Navy shelled the city of Danang in central Vietnam in 1858. The following year French forces seized Saigon and within a decade 'Cochinchina' was a colony. Cambodia and Annam became French protectorates soon after but what the French were really after was an independent route – by river or rail – to the potentially huge markets of the Chinese interior. Success required control of the northern province of Tonkin – a prospect that deeply alarmed the court in Beijing. The Chinese government sponsored the Black Flags (who were, depending on one's point of view, either a band of brigands or a semi-autonomous political unit) to stop them. But after the resulting war (from 1884 to 1885) China was obliged to recognise French control of Tonkin and agree to a defined border between it and the Qing realm.

Around the same time, the German Reich was also seeking territory in Asia. In preparation it sought to establish a string of naval bases connecting the homeland with a hoped-for colony in China. Its navy conducted a series of surveys around the Paracel Islands between 1881 and 1884. Germany neither sought nor received permission from China or France for the surveys and neither government seems to have noticed, let alone issued a protest. (Some Chinese writers claim that a Chinese protest was issued but there appears to be a lack of proof.) The German authorities actually published their survey in 1885 and it became the reference for later English and French maps of the islands, but not, strangely, for the Chinese.[26] In 1897, the mistreatment of European missionaries again provided a pretext for imperial intervention. Within months Germany had seized what became Tsingtao (Qingdao) in northeastern China.

The American imperial project in Asia began with Commodore Perry's exemplary display of gunboat diplomacy in Tokyo harbour in 1853: plenty of gunpowder but no casualties. Rather than resist, as the Qing court had done, the Japanese elite embraced modernisation and, within half a century, were to join in the dismemberment of China. American success in Japan led to greater ambitions. In 1890 the president of the US Naval War College, Alfred Mahan, published *The Influence of Sea Power upon History, 1660–1783* – analysing Britain's success in creating a global empire. Mahan argued that for the United States to prosper, it needed to secure new markets abroad and protect trade routes to them through a network of naval bases. His argument resonated with a new generation of politicians. The opportunity came eight years later. By the end of the Spanish–American War, the US had truly become a Pacific power, annexing the Philippines, Hawaii and Guam.

All this territory-taking by the colonial powers provided the foundations for the current boundaries in the South China Sea. They created the states and they created the borders between them, from which the maritime frontiers were measured. The Philippines and Indonesia were split by an agreement between Portugal and Spain in 1529, the line between Malaysia and Indonesia was largely fixed by the British and the Dutch in 1842; the Chinese–Vietnamese border was dictated to the Chinese by the French in 1887, the general frontiers of the Philippines were set by the US and Spain in 1898 and the border between the Philippines and Malaysia by the US and Britain in 1930.

This was part of a much wider process of defining and marking the borders between the different colonial states, a process that generated great resentment and resistance. It took the Dutch almost a century to enforce them in Borneo and the other islands. As late as the early twentieth century, they were still dealing with 900 different indigenous political units.[27] But these are the borders the post-colonial states emerged with and they have become sacred national symbols – despite the grief they continue to cause. Even more deeply rooted now is the way of thinking about these borders. The Westphalian system has become so dominant that its notions of fixed borders and territorial sovereignty are often assumed to have existed for millennia. But in Southeast Asia it goes back little more than a century and extrapolating modern political borders from those that may have existed under the *mandala* system can be both meaningless and dangerous.

The main reason for the sensitivity about borders and sovereignty in the region is, of course, the experience of China during the period its ideologues call 'the century of national humiliation'. The memory of the Qing regime's impotence in the face of industrialised European invasion still motivates China's leadership today. But in contrast to its physical occupations in other parts of the world, nineteenth-century Western imperialism in China wasn't really territorial: the areas of land seized up until 1900 (Hong Kong and the other international concessions) were a tiny fraction of China's territory. Nor was it particularly about lives lost. Around 20,000 people were killed during the 'Opium Wars' of 1840 and 1860 for sure, but vastly more – 20 to 30 million – died in the mid-century 'Taiping Rebellion'. The humiliation was ideological. It combined the sense of violation by 'others' with a knowledge that it was internal corruption and decay which had allowed it to happen. By contrast, Japan had adapted to the new world system quite successfully and was ready to challenge the established East Asian order.

* * * * * *

In 1894 and 1895, in a sign of developments to come, Japan seized control of Korea and Taiwan from Qing China. The defeat by Japan was closely followed, in 1901, by the multinational invasion to suppress the 'Boxer Rebellion'. The Qing Dynasty was in crisis and acutely sensitive to accusations that it could not defend the country's territory. Groups such as the Society to Recover the Nation's Rights, the Society to Commemorate the National Humiliation and the Self-Government Society instigated boycotts of British, American, Japanese and other foreign goods.[28] Which is why, in 1909, a Chinese government decided to turn the sovereignty of islands in the South China Sea into a question of national pride for the first time. Then, as now, the issue was the fate of almost uninhabitable dots in the sea, far from land. The posturing would result in the drawing of the line that has since become the basis for China's claims in the Sea.

As early as October 1907 rumours had been circulating about a band of Japanese explorers landing upon Pratas Island, a guano-covered coral reef 400 kilometres southwest of (Japanese-occupied) Taiwan and about 260 kilometres from the Chinese mainland.[29] The rumours weren't confirmed until a Chinese ship paid a visit to Pratas in March 1909 and discovered Nishizawa Yoshiji and around hundred colleagues digging up bird droppings. When challenged, Nishizawa declared that he had discovered the island, that it was previously uninhabited and that it now belonged to him. His motive was simple. The droppings were a rich and valuable fertiliser for the paddy fields back home and Nishizawa hoped to make a fortune.

When news reached Canton (Guangzhou), the Self-Government Society launched another boycott of Japanese goods and demanded the government do something. Its outraged middle-class members also collected evidence to try to prove that Pratas belonged to China. The armchair nationalists leafed through old books and interviewed ancient mariners for proof of the island's ties to the mainland. With popular pressure rising, the Chinese decided to make the problem disappear with cold hard cash. The Japanese government was willing to assist. The Chinese boycott was seriously hurting many Japanese companies and Japan could see little value in occupying Pratas.[30] The authorities in Tokyo offered to recognise Chinese sovereignty if its claim could be proved.[31]

On 12 October 1909 the Viceroy of Canton and the Japanese consul in the city agreed the deal. Japan would recognise Chinese sovereignty and Mr Nishizawa would vacate the island in exchange for 130,000 silver dollars in compensation.[32] The Cantonese authorities hoped to recoup the money by adopting Mr Nishizawa's business plan. They even hired a couple of his guano-mining experts to advise them. Sadly it all came to nothing. Without a wharf to load large ships, the whole project was uneconomic. By Christmas 1910 it had been abandoned and Pratas was reported to be deserted again.[33]

But the anxieties about China's maritime border persisted and the Governor of Guangdong, Zhang Yen Jun, felt that wielding a sword would be more effective than just a pen and turned his attention to the Paracel Islands, several hundred kilometres to the southwest. At this time, official Chinese maps (whether national, regional or local) showed Hainan Island as the southernmost point of Chinese territory. This had been the case on maps published in 1760, 1784, 1866 and 1897.[34] While the negotiations over Pratas unfolded, Governor Zhang despatched a boat to the Paracels in May 1909 – and then two more the following month. Chinese accounts talk of a flotilla spending three weeks cruising around, making surveys and firing off the occasional salvo of cannon to claim the islands for China. However, the French owner of a shipping company plying routes across the sea, P.A. Lapicque, gave a different version in a book published 20 years later.[35] He says the expedition (which was guided by two Germans from the massive trading firm Carlowitz and Company) spent two weeks at anchor off Hainan waiting for good weather and then sped to the Paracels on 6 June before returning to Canton the following day. This visit is now the basis for China's claim to sovereignty over the islands. In the aftermath of the expedition a new map of Guangdong was published showing, for the first time on any Chinese map, the Paracel Islands as part of the province.[36]

That was one of the final acts under the dying Qing dynasty: it was finally overthrown in 1911. The first map the new republican government produced, in its 1912 *Almanac*, showed no borders at all. The new national leadership was avowedly 'modern' – it aspired to become part of the international system – but as the geographer William Callahan has pointed out, it couldn't resolve the contradiction between China's new identity as a nation-state and its old one as the centre of a *mandala*-based series of hierarchical relationships. The first constitution of the Republic of China illustrated this perfectly when it asserted that 'The *sovereign territory* of the Republic of China continues to be the same as the *domain* of the former Empire.' This simple equation of the old 'domain' with the new 'sovereign territory' is fundamental to the current disagreement over 'borders' in the South China Sea.[37]

This was the situation when a private cartographer, Hu Jinjie, set to work drafting a new guide to China's historic territory. When it was eventually published in December 1914 the *New Geographical Atlas of the Republic of China* contained the first Chinese map to include a line drawn across the South China Sea demonstrating which islands rightfully belonged to the mainland. Hu entitled the map the 'Chinese territorial map before the Qianglong–Jiaqing period'.[38] In other words, the line represented the extent of Chinese state 'control' before 1736 and, significantly, the only islands within the line were Pratas and the Paracels.[39] It went no further south than 15° N. Throughout the turbulent 'warlord era' of the 1920s and into the early 1930s this was the line published on Chinese maps. It took 20 years and another international crisis out at sea for the line to assume the location that China asserts today.

The sense of national violation grew even stronger on 9 May 1915 when the republican government was forced to accept new Japanese demands to cede territory and other rights.[40] The National Teachers' Association declared 9 May to be 'National Humiliation Commemoration Day'. In 1916 the Central Cartographic Society in Shanghai published a 'Map of National Humiliation' showing the territories lost to foreigners. Interestingly, Hong Kong, Taiwan and Tonkin were prominently marked but no mention was made of anywhere else in the South China Sea. For much of the following decade China was consumed by civil war between competing factions and warlords but after the Kuomintang took power in 1927, they used 'national humiliation' as a unifying idea to bring the country together. It even made 'National Humiliation Commemoration Day' an official holiday.

On 13 April 1930, the French warship *Malicieuse* dropped anchor off Spratly Island, hundreds of kilometres to the south of Pratas and the Paracels, and fired a 21-gun salute. The only witnesses to this display of imperial pomp were four marooned and starving fishermen unaware that they were witnessing the opening salvo in a still-unfinished battle for control of their fishing grounds. The *Malicieuse* had been sent by the French governor of Cochinchina following reports that the Japanese government was about to grab the island, 500 kilometres from his coast.[41] The French government publicised its occupation but, strangely, failed to formally annex it until the British government asked for a copy of the annexation document three years later. The Chinese government had failed to notice the 1930 occupation but when the annexation was announced on 26 July 1933, claiming Spratly Island and five others – Amboyna Cay, Itu Aba, North Danger

Reef (Les Deux Iles), Loaita and Thitu – its reaction was explosive, but also somewhat confused.

On the day of the announcement, the Chinese consul in Manila, Mr Kwong, asked the American colonial authorities in the Philippines for a map of the islands. It's clear from contemporary reports carried by the influential Shanghai newspaper *Shen Bao* (formerly transliterated as *Shun Pao*) that the Chinese government was unable to work out which islands had been annexed or where they were located. On 28 July, the newspaper reported that the Chinese Ministry of Foreign Affairs had asked the government to send a ship to investigate what was going on. Two days later, the paper's Paris reporter informed readers that the islands were uninhabited coral reefs and different from the Paracels. Nonetheless arguments about the islands' location raged in the paper for several weeks. It seems the Chinese government believed the French had changed the names of the islands just to confuse the situation. It had to turn to foreign governments for advice. On 1 August the Americans in Manila gave Mr Kwong a map. He was reportedly surprised to learn that the Paracels and Spratlys were in fact different places.[42] It wasn't until 15 August that the map reached the government in Nanjing. The Chinese government continued to dither even as protests continued on the streets.

Instead, Japan became the first country to protest against the French move, on 21 August, arguing that a Japanese company, Rasa Industries, had been mining yet more guano in the islands until very recently. However, it turned out that they too were confused: Rasa had been active on Pattle Island in the Paracels. *Shen Bao* continued to report disarray among the authorities for many weeks. Despite all the bluster and outrage, the Chinese government never actually formally protested against the French move.[43] The reason seems to be that, at this stage, the Chinese government regarded the Paracels as its southernmost territory and not the Spratlys. A once-secret report for its Military Council, from 1 September 1933, seems to confirm this:

All our professional geographers say that Triton Island [in the Paracels] is the southernmost island of our territory. But we could, maybe, find some evidence that the nine islands [in the Spratlys] were part of our territory in the past . . . We need to cool down the game with the French, but let our fishermen continue their activities to protect our fishing rights. Our

Navy is weak and these nine islands are not useful for us now . . . We must focus only on the Xisha Islands [Paracel Islands] because the points of evidence of our sovereignty on them are so numerous that the whole world accepts it, with the exception of Japan.[44]

Unable to exert any physical leverage, the Chinese government turned instead to its map-makers. On 7 June 1933, just as rumours of the French occupation of the Spratlys began to circulate, it established the Review Committee for Land and Water Maps. While the committee deliberated, another cartographer, Chen Duo, published his *Newly-Made Chinese Atlas* in which the Chinese sea border stretched down to 7° N – firmly including those Spratly Islands which France had just claimed.[45] This may have influenced the committee because, after a year and a half of study, it finally responded to Paris' provocations. Instead of a 21-gun salute, the committee deployed a list. The first volume of its journal, published in January 1935, included Chinese names for the 132 islands and islets in the South China Sea that the committee believed rightfully belonged to China. Of these, 28 were in the Paracels and 96 in the Spratlys. The list was not a collection of traditional Chinese names for the features but transliterations and translations of the Western names printed on navigation charts. In the Spratly Islands, for example, North Danger became Běi xiǎn (the Chinese for 'north danger'), and Spratly Island became Si-ba-la-tuo (the Chinese transliteration of the English name) and in the Paracels, Antelope Reef became Líng yang (the Chinese word for antelope). Another island in the Paracels (the westernmost outcrop of the Amphitrite group), was called 'West Sand' in English and it seems likely that this name was given to the entire Paracels which became Xisha ('west sand' in Chinese). The Macclesfield Bank, in the centre of the sea, was named Nansha ('southern sand') and the Spratlys named Tuansha ('chaotic sand').[46] It's significant, of course, that at this juncture the Macclesfield Bank was regarded as 'southern'.

It's clear that in many cases the committee simply translated the names of the features on the British maps into Chinese, including many of the existing errors and adding some of their own. James Shoal seems to be a case in point. The committee gave it the Chinese name of Zengmu (the transliteration of James) Tan. But *tan* is the Chinese word for a beach or sandbank – something that sticks out of the water. In English nautical terminology, however, a shoal is an underwater feature – a raised area of seabed (the word is derived from an Old English word for 'shallow'). James Shoal is in fact 22 metres below the surface. But because of the committee's unfamiliarity with the area they declared it to be a land feature. Thus it would seem that China's claim in the South China Sea is, to some extent, based on a translation error. What's now described as the 'southernmost point of Chinese territory' doesn't exist – any more than the Wan-li Shi-tang did eight centuries before.

The committee continued with its territorial mission. Three months later, in April 1935, it published *The Map of Chinese Islands in the South China Sea*, taking the country's sea border right down to 4° N – the location of James Shoal, only 107 kilometres from the coast of Borneo and over 1,500 kilometres from the Chinese mainland.[47] Then one of China's most eminent geographers, Bai Meichu, added his own innovation. Bai had been one of the founders of the China Geographical Society. He was also an ardent nationalist and in 1930 had drawn his own version of the 'Chinese National Humiliation Map' to educate his countrymen about just how much territory they had lost.[48] In the year Bai became director of the society's editorial board, he declared: 'Loving the nation is the top priority in learning geography, while building the nation is what learning geography is for.'[49] In 1936, at the age of 60, he created his most enduring legacy: a map in his *New China Construction Atlas* including a U-shaped line snaking around the South China Sea as far south as James Shoal. This was then copied by others. Between 1936 and 1945 versions of the line were published on 26 other maps. Some stretched down to the James Shoal, though most only included the Spratlys.[50] A decade later, it was Bai's line that would be taken up by the Chinese government, copied and asserted to define China's historic island territories.

All this list-making and map-drawing came to an abrupt end with the Japanese invasion of China in 1937. The job of protecting the country's sovereignty was passed to the military and the previous objects of Chinese nationalistic anger – Britain, Russia and the United States in particular – became allies against the greater enemy. But the Second World War would reset the territorial battle in the South China Sea. Japan had occupied Taiwan in 1895, so when American forces in the Philippines surrendered in May 1942 almost the entire coast of the Sea, from Taiwan to Singapore and back again, fell under the control of a single power for the first time in its millennia-long history. The South China Sea became a 'Japanese lake' and would remain so until January 1945. The Japanese occupied Woody Island in the Paracels and Itu Aba in the Spratlys. The base on Itu Aba was virtually destroyed when American planes napalmed and strafed it on 1 May 1945 and the island was abandoned sometime before the arrival of a US reconnaissance mission on 18 November 1945.[51] Two Australian commandos were landed on Woody Island in the Paracels by the American submarine, USS *Pargo*, on 3 February 1945 and observed two Japanese and a European living there under a French tricolour. After the commandos withdrew, the *Pargo* shelled all the buildings.[52] On 8 March American aircraft bombed radio stations on both Woody Island and Pattle Island[53] and when another submarine, the USS *Cabrilla*, visited Woody Island on 2 July, the tricolour was still flying, but this time with a white flag above it.[54]

As the course of the war turned, the allies began to debate where lines would be drawn on maps once it had ended. As early as May 1943, a few weeks after the battle of Guadalcanal, the US State Department drew up document T–324 to help decide what should be done about the islands of the South China Sea. Allowing Japan to hold on to them was a non-starter, but since they were 'of no vital interest to any single country or territory', the American position remained vague.[55] Later documents continued the theme, arguing that no single country had a clear-cut claim on the islands. Document CAC–301, 'Spratly and other islands (Shinnan Gunto)', prepared on 19 December 1944 ahead of the Yalta Conference, recommended that the Spratlys be placed under 'the projected international organization' – the future United Nations – although noting that this would require the approval of France. Another document, CAC–308, recommended three options for the Paracels: international trusteeship, a deal between China and France, or thirdly – 'unless France should provide evidence of the alleged transfer of the Paracels to Annam by China in 1816' – support for China's claim.[56] After the war, however, the State Department recognised the improbability that any of the islands would be placed under UN control because it would require an unlikely degree of flexibility from France. As a result, the US left its position vague.

On 4 July 1946, the Philippines became independent of the United States and less than three weeks later Vice-President Elpidio Quirino declared the Spratly Islands part of its sphere of influence. The French authorities, trying to reassert their control over Indochina, sent a mine-sweeper, the FR *Chevreuil*, out to the Spratlys. It found them uninhabited and, on 5 October 1946, placed a stone marker on Itu Aba asserting French sovereignty. On 9 December 1946 the Chinese Navy – having just received several ships, trained crews and charts of the waters from the United States – despatched two vessels to the Paracels and two to the Spratlys.[57] The *Taiping* (formerly the USS *Decker*) and the *Zhongye* (probably the former USS LST–1056) arrived at Itu Aba on 12 December where their crews erected a rival stone marker, claiming the island for China. Then, in January 1947, Chinese and French forces landed on different islands in the Paracels – again making rival claims (for more on this see Chapter 3).

In May 1947 the Chinese parliament approved a motion calling on the government to recover all the Paracels from France, by force if necessary, and to clearly 'delimit our territory'. Force was out of the question but delimiting territory was easier. The Geography Department of the Ministry of Internal Affairs drafted a list of new names for all the islands in the South China Sea. Itu Aba was renamed Taiping Island and Thitu Island was renamed Zhongye (after the ships on the 1946 expedition) and other features were awarded similarly patriotic titles: Spratly Island became Nanwei – 'noble south' – for example. Perhaps realising their mistake, the committee changed James Shoal from a sandbank (*tan*) into a reef (*ansha*). The names of the four sets of features were also adjusted: the Paracels remained Xisha – West Sand – but Pratas became East Sand – Dongsha. The name Nansha – South Sand – which had previously referred to the Macclesfield Bank was moved south to describe the Spratlys and the Macclesfield Bank (previously the Nansha) was re-designated the Zhongsha – Central Sand.

By the end of 1947, the department had finalised a cross-reference table for all the old and new names of the islands and islets – whose number had crept up to 159.[58] The list was officially announced on 1 December, the same day the islands were all formally placed under the administration of the Hainan Special District.[59] Around the same time, the department printed a new 'Location Map of the South China Sea Islands', which was formally published by the Ministry in February 1948 as an adjunct to its new 'Administrative Division Map of the Republic of China'. All the

new names were included – along with the line originally drawn on Bai
Meichu's map a decade earlier. Eleven dashes raced down the eastern side
of the South China Sea from Taiwan to the coast of Borneo and then
northward to the Gulf of Tonkin in a great U-shape. No official explanation of the meaning of the line was provided although one of its cartographers, Wang Xiguang, is reported to have said that the dashes simply
indicated the median line between China's territory – in other words, each
claimed island – and that of its neighbours.[60]

On 12 June 1947 a meeting between officials of the Republic of China's
Navy, Defence and Interior ministries agreed that the government claimed
everything within the line but would negotiate precise maritime boundaries with other countries at a later date and according to the international
laws in operation. No border had been delimited – it was the beginning of
what would later be called 'strategic ambiguity' in the South China Sea.[61]
But by then the days of the Republic of China were numbered. Within
months its leadership had fled to Taiwan and the Communist Party had
proclaimed the People's Republic. The Communists adopted the maps
and lines of its predecessors although, in 1953, in what is assumed to
have been a special favour to brother Communists struggling for independence, their cartographers reduced the number of dashes to nine by
removing two from the Tonkin Gulf between China and Vietnam.[62] The
border in that piece of sea was only finally defined by the two countries in
1999. In June 2013, the Chinese State Bureau of Surveying and Mapping
issued a new official map of the country and added a tenth dash, to the
east of Taiwan, making clear that it too was firmly part of the national
territory.[63]

In May 2009, the Chinese authorities attached a map of the 'U-shaped
line' to its submission to the United Nations Commission on the Limits
of the Continental Shelf, the first time it had ever used the line in an
official international context. The response around the region was angry
and vociferous. It showed how far ideas about boundaries and borders had
shifted since an unknown Chinese cartographer drew the 'Selden Map'
nearly 400 years before. The idea of drawing fixed lines on maps to demar-
cate political allegiance would have been nonsensical then and the idea
that the sea could be 'owned' just ridiculous. These are all concepts that
emerged in seventeenth-century Europe and were brought to Southeast

Asia by trading companies and empires. The Europeans drew new maps and then new lines and in the process spread new ways of thinking about both. It was the transition from one set of ideas to the other, from the *mandala* system to the Westphalian system, that left a legacy of historical confusion and, in the years since the 'U-shaped line' was published, spawned a rush for territory in the South China Sea.

CHAPTER 3

Danger and Mischief
1946 to 1995

IMMEDIATELY AFTER THE end of the Second World War, for just over a year, none of the Paracel or Spratly islands was occupied or controlled by anyone. But 50 years later, almost all of them were. There was not one single battle for control nor was the transition slow and steady; there were intense episodes in 1946–7, 1956, the early 1970s, 1988 and 1995 when actions by one side usually triggered reactions from others. Each time the original occupation was driven by a particular vision – of nationalistic legitimacy, strategic advantage or economic reward – but none delivered the expected results.

Chiang Kai-shek's vision was to use the islands to bolster his leadership in the face of the advances by Communist forces. He saw an opportunity to demonstrate his fitness to rule China by standing up to the Westerners who had once ravaged the country. In the closing months of 1946 his government despatched its newly acquired decommissioned US warships to stake a Chinese claim. His adversary would be a former monk turned naval admiral, Georges Thierry d'Argenlieu. Admiral d'Argenlieu had served France with distinction during the First World War but then adopted the cassock and sandals of a Catholic monastic order. He served the order with distinction too, becoming its head in France. However in September 1939, with the country facing the threat of German invasion, Father d'Argenlieu hung up his cassock, re-rendered his services to Caesar and rejoined the navy.

D'Argenlieu rose through the upper ranks of the Free French forces, serving as General de Gaulle's envoy and commander on missions to France's remaining colonies in Africa and Asia. Honours and promotion followed and in mid-August 1945 de Gaulle put him in charge of restoring French control in Indochina. The colony was in turmoil: Japan surrendered, a Communist-led revolution followed and Ho Chi Minh became president of the new 'Democratic Republic of Vietnam' which he proclaimed on 2 September. Meanwhile Chinese units began to move in from the north while British forces landed in the south. The Brits used Japanese troops to quell the local revolution and handed the colony over to d'Argenlieu. The admiral was no liberation theologist. In uniform his guiding belief was an all-encompassing devotion to the French empire.[1] Clever but ultra-conservative, one critic joked that he possessed 'the most brilliant mind of the twelfth century'.[2]

Throughout 1945 and 1946 d'Argenlieu worked hard to undermine both the Vietnamese nationalists and the politicians back in Paris who favoured compromise with them. Tricky negotiations ensued between d'Argenlieu, the French government, Ho Chi Minh's nationalists and the Chinese nationalist government. The French and Vietnamese both wanted the Chinese to leave but couldn't agree on much else. D'Argenlieu wouldn't even use the word 'Vietnam', preferring the colonial name 'Annam'.[3] The political situation became worse as d'Argenlieu pursued his own agenda. In June 1946 he proclaimed the creation of a rival 'Republic of Cochin-China', destroying Paris' hopes of a peaceful compromise with Ho Chi Minh's 'Vietnam'. Amid the infighting, the fate of the Paracel Islands, a couple of hundred kilometres off the coast, slipped down the agenda.

Unlike the better-known Spratlys, most of the Paracels are proper islands: dry enough to sustain human habitation. They lie about 350 kilometres south of Hainan Island and about the same distance east of Danang and have been used by fisher-folk and pirates from the Chinese and Vietnamese coasts and beyond for centuries. The Paracels are divided into two clusters. The northwestern Amphitrite group (named after the French ship that 'discovered' them in 1698)[4] has six islands (including the imaginatively named Woody, Rocky and Tree islands along with South, Middle and North islands). The largest, Woody, is nearly 2 kilometres long and just over 1 kilometre wide. A seventh island, Lincoln, is sometimes included in the group. The Crescent group lies 64 kilometres southwest of the Amphitrites and contains a further seven islands: Pattle and Robert are the most significant. The others are: Triton, Duncan, Money, Drummond and Passu Keah. During the war French, 'Annamite' and then Japanese forces had occupied the islands – sometimes at the same times. But by late 1945 they were empty.

A year later, rumours of a Chinese plan to annex the islands reached Paris and on 22 October 1946 the Minister of Overseas France ordered d'Argenlieu to send a garrison to occupy the Paracels. D'Argenlieu ignored him and decided instead to teach the Vietnamese nationalists 'a lesson' for daring to resist French rule. On 23 November 1946, following clashes between French and Vietnamese forces in the port of Haiphong, d'Argenlieu ordered the cruiser *Suffren* and four other ships to shell the city. The bombardment levelled several districts and killed around 6,000 Vietnamese. Retaliation was not long coming. On 19 December, street fighting between the French and the Vietnamese rebels erupted in Hanoi. The first phase of the Vietnam War had begun. If d'Argenlieu had sent the *Suffren* to the Paracels instead, as Paris had ordered him to do, history might have been different.

D'Argenlieu was now so preoccupied with the war he had just started that he refused a further request from Paris to occupy the Paracels 'without delay', citing bad weather. The historian Stein Tønnesson has tracked down what happened next. The weather didn't dent Chiang Kai-shek's ambitions. His Chinese government despatched its new warships to the South China Sea. On 4 January 1947, the minesweeper *Yongxing* (formerly the USS *Embattle*) and the *Zhongjian* (formerly USS LST–716) landed around 60 Chinese troops on Woody Island. By this time d'Argenlieu had finally despatched a rival expedition aboard the ship *Tonkinois*. When the French arrived, two weeks after the Chinese, their captain attempted to bribe – and then force – the Chinese to leave, even firing shots in the air.[5] The Chinese held out and a furious diplomatic row erupted between the two governments. France backed down and ordered its ship to sail away and deploy troops on Pattle Island in the Crescent group instead. Nationalist China had its victory and France could only watch.

While the historical and legal arguments about the Paracels' sovereignty date back much further than 1947, it's possible that if d'Argenlieu had followed his instructions and occupied Woody Island before China did, the islands would still be in Vietnamese hands today. Within six weeks, then, Admiral d'Argenlieu's bellicose choice of priorities had condemned Vietnam to three decades of war and also to an enduring antagonism with China about the fate of the Paracels. The French government was livid and shortly afterwards sacked d'Argenlieu. While the war he'd started raged on, he returned to God and the Carmelites. He lived out the remaining years of his life with the order, finally passing away in 1967 at a monastery in Brittany.

After January 1947, rival claimants occupied the two halves of the Paracels: nationalist Chinese on Woody Island and Franco-Vietnamese on Pattle Island. But Chiang Kai-shek's island victory was pyrrhic. His position continued to weaken and his government was forced to flee to Taiwan. In 1950 the Communists captured Hainan Island and the nationalists chose to withdraw their forces from Woody Island and also from Itu Aba in the Spratlys. The colonial French meteorology service in Indochina noted that weather reports from the two islands ceased on 4 and 5 May 1950 respectively.[6] France knew the islands had been abandoned but never occupied them, partly for fear of provoking unnecessary diplomatic rows with Taipei and Beijing but mainly because they had a more pressing war to fight on the mainland.

For five years after May 1950, Pattle Island was the only South China Sea feature to be occupied by any country. The US, Britain and France controlled the waters, particularly during the Korean War that began in June 1950. Beijing simply didn't have the means to contest their supremacy. That didn't mean it had abandoned its claims, however, and by 1955 Communist Chinese units were established on Woody Island. Mao Zedong's forces had quietly trumped Chiang Kai-shek's proud gesture. But rather than a flag-waving expedition, their interest was more down to earth: to mine guano as fertiliser for the paddy fields back home. Chiang Kai-shek's vision for the islands had turned to excrement.

* * * * * *

Tomas Cloma's vision for the islands also featured guano – in conjunction with canned fish – but his dream was more personal: to make a fortune.

Just 165 centimetres tall, what he lacked in height he made up in ambition. He left his native island of Bohol to work as a tailor's assistant in Manila, put himself through high school, got a job as a telegraph operator, then as a freight broker and then, in 1933, as assistant shipping editor for the *Manila Bulletin* newspaper. He wrote about shipping movements by day and studied law by night, eventually passing his bar exams in 1941. Within months, though, his putative legal career had been destroyed by Japan's invasion of the Philippines. To feed and clothe his family, Cloma went to sea for three years, using his Boholano fishing skills to sail passengers and cargo between the islands. The family survived the war and life was just starting to get better when Cloma's six-year-old son Basilio was killed in a traffic accident in the city of Calamba. Tomas' heart-broken wife, Luz, stopped going to church. Tomas buried his grief in his work.

In March 1947 Tomas and Luz Cloma, along with his brother Filemon and three friends, formed the Visayan Fish Corporation. With the compensation money they received after Basilio's death they converted some decommissioned US military tugs into fishing boats. They hired experienced crews and set them to work. Business was good but Tomas was always quick to see other opportunities. When, in September 1948, the government-run Philippine Nautical School (PNS) was closed by a strike, Cloma set up the rival Philippine Maritime Institute (PMI). It offered three-month courses, only half the length of those at the PNS, from a cut-price base: a barge near the mouth of the Pasig River in Manila. After a while the institute moved to a fishing boat that gave on-the-job training (while also providing the Visayan Fish Corporation with cheap labour). Within 18 months the institute had been formally recognised by the government and had classrooms on dry land. Another idea came from a near disaster. In 1947 Filemon had been fishing off Palawan when Typhoon Jennie, one of the strongest storms on record, forced him to seek shelter among a mysterious group of offshore islands. Over the following years, the brothers made plans to open a fish-canning factory there and also mine the guano.

In later accounts of their adventures Tomas Cloma would say that he checked various maps but could find nothing that mentioned the islands. Even today, Cloma is often described in the Philippines as the man who 'discovered' the islands. But Cloma must have known this wasn't true. It seems unlikely that a man who had worked as an assistant shipping editor on a national newspaper for eight years, and as an international freight broker before that, would have not known about the reefs and islands lying off the country's coast.

Cloma may have claimed to be ignorant of the Spratly Islands but his government had been well aware of their existence for some time. Remembering that they had been used as a jumping-off point for the Japanese invasion, local newspapers had been pressing for government action to secure them. In July 1946, immediately after the Philippines became independent of the United States, the then Vice-President and Foreign Secretary, Elpido Quirino, told a press conference that the Philippines would claim the islands as essential to its security.[7] On 17 May 1950, by which time he was president, Quirino declared that the islands belonged to the Philippines but added that the country would not press its claim so long as nationalist (Taiwanese) Chinese forces remained in control. He can't have been aware that they'd actually left 12 days earlier. Things would be different – he warned – if the Communists moved in. Strangely, however, the Philippines did not press its claim at the San Francisco peace conference in 1951.[8] It's hard to believe that Cloma was unaware of all these developments.

Cloma had a key ally, Carlos P. Garcia, another Boholano, with whom he had been at high school. Garcia was elected to the Senate in 1946 and became Vice-President and Foreign Minister in 1953. Cloma and his brother organised fund-raising for Garcia's election campaigns and – says Filemon's son – Garcia provided government contracts and other favours in return.[9] This connection would become crucial as Cloma manoeuvred himself ever deeper into the murky waters of international politics.

There's evidence to suggest the Clomas were engaged in smuggling and, in 1955, Filemon was jailed for six months for stockpiling small arms and explosives. He was freed in that year's Christmas amnesty, however, and the plotting to claim the islands continued.[10] On 1 March 1956 Vice-President Garcia was the guest of honour at a send-off dinner for Filemon's occupation party.[11] Garcia failed to persuade the rest of President Magsaysay's government to support the Clomas but the mission set off anyway. On 15 March, Filemon and his merry band landed on the islands.[12] Two months later, on 15 May, Tomas sent letters to Garcia and several embassies in Manila claiming for himself a hexagonal area of sea off the coast of Palawan totalling 64,976 square miles and all the islands, reefs and cays within it (Spratly Island itself was deliberately left out of the claim). He based the claim 'on the rights of discovery and/or occupation'. Then, six days later, he issued a second notice declaring he had named the territory, tautologically, as 'The Free Territory of Freedomland'.

Garcia made a public statement of support on 17 May but, according to press reports at the time, President Magsaysay ordered him to 'cut short Cloma's comic opera before it got really serious'. Magsaysay wasn't the only one with this opinion. The French chargé d'affaires in Manila, Jacques Boizet, initially referred to the incident as a 'ridiculous quarrel' among 'pygmies' but warned that it had the potential to cause deep problems if Communist China decided to intervene. Exactly what was happening behind the scenes is still unclear. Many of the Philippine government records were subsequently destroyed in fires. The French geographer François-Xavier Bonnet, who has studied the period extensively, believes Garcia and Magsaysay – despite their public differences – were acting in consort: Garcia backing Cloma and Magsaysay holding high-level talks with the Taiwanese government to try to keep the situation under control.[13] The presidency issued an official communiqué stating that Cloma was acting as an individual and that the Philippines had not officially claimed the islands. But while Cloma's actions appeared ridiculous to some, they were indeed deeply provocative to others and set in chain a series of events that still mark the region today.

On 31 May 1956, the Beijing government declared it would not tolerate any infringements of its claims in the islands. By now the French had left Vietnam and the country had been 'temporarily' divided between Communist north and capitalist south. On 1 June the Republic of Vietnam (RVN or 'South Vietnam') condemned Cloma's actions and the following day even France joined in, reiterating its own unabandoned claim dating back to 1933. But Tomas Cloma was not deterred. On 6 July he issued the 'Freedomland Charter' describing his new country as an independent entity seeking official recognition from the Philippines 'under protectorate status'. He had in mind something like the position Brunei then had as a British colony. Tomas declared himself head of state with sole executive powers. His sons and friends were named as cabinet ministers. He also unveiled the flag of 'Freedomland', which, rather ominously given what was to happen next, bore a large white albatross.

The following day, 7 July, just to make sure the message had been received, Cloma, his son Jaime and several of his PMI cadets marched to the (Taiwanese) Chinese embassy in Manila and presented its diplomats with a flag that Jaime said he'd removed from Itu Aba (or as he renamed it, MacArthur Island). This provoked both a protest from Taipei and criticism from the Philippine government. It was all becoming too much. The RVN Navy sent a ship to one of the Spratlys where the crew erected a monument and hoisted the national flag on 22 August.[14] The nationalist government on Taiwan resolved to sort out the Clomas once and for all and despatched part of its navy under a Commodore Yao.[15] They would meet at a place called Danger.

In the early morning of 1 October 1956, Vessel IV of the PMI fleet was anchored off North Danger Reef (which Cloma had renamed 'Ciriaco Island' in the northernmost tip of 'Freedomland') when it was challenged by two ships of the Taiwanese Navy. Captain Filemon Cloma was 'invited' aboard one of them to discuss his claim. A four-hour argument about the niceties of international law ensued – during which the Taiwanese boarded the PMI IV and confiscated all the weapons, maps and relevant documents they could find.[16] The next day Filemon was invited on board again and presented with a statement in which he acknowledged he'd been trespassing in Chinese territory and pledged not to do so again. According to Filemon's son, he signed it under duress. The navy ships then departed and Filemon's crew checked the nearby islands – all the structures they'd previously built there had been destroyed.[17]

Tomas Cloma wasn't a man to take this lying down. So, later that month, he took himself to New York with the intention of making a formal complaint to the United Nations. But by now the Philippine government was also fed up with him. After a press conference in the coffee shop of the Waldorf Astoria Hotel, Cloma was taken aside by the Philippine ambassador to the UN, Felixberto Serrano, who explained that only recognised governments could present matters to the UN and the Philippines was not going to waste any more time on the matter. Garcia and his allies in the Foreign Affairs Association back in Manila made a last-ditch lobbying effort to persuade President Magsaysay to change his mind but failed.

On 8 February 1957 Garcia wrote a carefully worded letter to Cloma in which he made a somewhat arbitrary distinction between the seven islands known as the 'Spratlys' and the rest of the land features, which he called 'Freedomland'. Speaking on behalf of the Foreign Ministry (not the government), he said Cloma was welcome to claim any unoccupied islands in Freedomland, just as long as no other country's sovereignty over them had been recognised. It meant nothing.[18]

That should have been the end of Tomas Cloma's involvement with international politics, but there was a curious coda to the whole Freedomland project. After 1956, Cloma directed his energies into his business activities but he never abandoned his dream. He enjoyed being referred to as 'Admiral' Cloma and wore a gleaming white uniform on special occasions at the PMI. Gradually, though, his expedition faded from public memory. In the early 1970s, however, it earned unwelcome attention from President Ferdinand Marcos. Oil exploration had begun off the coast of Palawan in 1970 and, by July 1971, Philippine forces had landed on three of the Spratly Islands: Thitu, Nanshan and Flat (respectively Pagasa, Lawak and Patag in Filipino). They also seem to have tried to land on Itu Aba but were repelled by Taiwanese forces.[19] Later that month, Marcos ordered the military to create a Western Command to protect its interests in the area.

It was during this period that the Philippine government made its first attempts to formalise a coherent territorial claim over the islands, but it was one that relied on rather shaky geographical and legal foundations. Firstly, following Garcia, it tried to argue that the area included in Freedomland was different from the island group known internationally as the Spratlys and secondly it claimed that the Philippines had title over Freedomland because of the activities of Tomas and Filemon Cloma 25 years before. Cloma saw an opportunity and wrote to the *Daily Express* newspaper in January 1974 calling on the government to sponsor his original claim at the International Court of Justice. It caught Marcos' attention and the following month Cloma was invited to a meeting at the presidential palace during which he pledged to cede the islands. All that needed to be worked out was the small matter of a contract and a purchase price. Cloma appointed three politicians to act as his legal team and the negotiations dragged on.

On 3 October 1974, Cloma, by then aged 70, was invited to the national police headquarters at Camp Crame. After a long conversation with a police colonel he was shown to his new home in Stockade No. 3. At around the same time, the government confiscated one of his vessels, the MS *Philippine Admiral*, crippling Cloma's shipping company. After a few days Cloma was told he would be charged with 'illegally wearing uniform and insignia'. Marcos' martial law regime had taken the 'admiral' joke a little too seriously. Cloma understood what was really going on. He held out for 57 days but in the end the old man was broken. He signed over Freedomland to the Philippine government for a single peso.

Marcos renamed Freedomland the Kalayaan Islands – *kalayaan* being the Tagalog word for freedom – and in June 1978 issued Decree 1596 incorporating Kalayaan as a municipality of Palawan province. The municipality still exists, although for most of the year it's based in an office in the suburbs of Puerto Princesa on Palawan. At the time of writing, the Philippine military occupies nine islands and reefs and tries to keep watch on the rest. The largest Philippine-occupied island – formerly called Thitu but renamed Pagasa (from the word for hope in Filipino) – is now home to a small statue of Tomas Cloma. It stands next to the runway, looking mournfully out to sea: at what for a few years was Cloma's domain. In July 1987, after the overthrow of the Marcos regime, Cloma and his associates requested compensation from the democratically elected government of President Corazon Aquino. They asked for 50 million pesos. Tomas Cloma died on 18 September 1996 without receiving a reply. His dream of a guano and canned fish conglomerate remained unfulfilled.

* * * * * *

Comic as they were to some, Cloma's activities reignited regional anxiety over the Spratlys. Taiwan returned to Itu Aba in 1956, after six years away, motivated by the same nationalism that had inspired its first expedition in 1946. By the time of the next island-grabbing episode, when Ferdinand Marcos ordered Philippine forces to seize three islands in 1971, the motivation was oil. A couple of years later, oil was also the reason for the Republic of Vietnam to join the race. President Nguyen Van Thieu was trying to win a war against Communism while simultaneously rescuing a smashed economy over-stretched by military spending and rapidly declining American aid. On 20 July 1973, a month after the US Congress had voted to ban all US combat activities in Indochina, the RVN awarded its first oil concessions. Eight blocks off its southern and eastern coasts were awarded to Mobil, Exxon, a Canadian consortium and a subsidiary of Shell called Pecten. In September 1973, to protect the exploration, South Vietnam formally annexed ten of the Spratly Islands. It deployed hundreds of troops to Spratly Island itself and to Namyit Island – just across the lagoon from Itu Aba. The protests from Taipei and Manila were loud. Beijing took time to consider its options.[20]

The Communist Party leadership in Beijing had to weigh up the effects of some momentous global and regional changes. Although they were all nominally Communist, relations between the governments in Beijing, Moscow and Hanoi were far from fraternal. An ideological split between China and the Soviet Union had become progressively worse during the 1960s and the two had fought a border war in 1969. By that time, the Chinese leader Mao Zedong had begun to see the USSR as a greater threat than the US. Simultaneously, the US Secretary of State, Henry Kissinger, realised that China could be a useful ally in the global struggle against the Soviet Union and started to cultivate a relationship. His secret visit to Beijing in July 1971 paved the way for President Nixon's fanfare-filled foray in February 1972.

Vietnam found itself stuck in the middle of this triangle. The Communist north had long tried to balance its relations with Moscow and Beijing, the better to fight its war against the Washington-backed south. Weapons, aid and advice came from both but Hanoi didn't want to be beholden to either. Vietnam's modern national identity is more or less built around the story of its millennia-long struggle against China. The Communist Party leadership in Hanoi was determined not to become a vassal state all over again. There were political differences too. Hanoi was determined to liberate (as it saw it) the entire territory of Vietnam while Beijing wanted Hanoi to fight a long and protracted war to keep the US bogged down.[21] As a result, Hanoi started to lean in the direction of Moscow.

Two concerns sharpened Chinese apprehensions. If Hanoi won the war, the Soviet Fleet might have access to bases in the South China Sea, with the potential to throttle China's supply lines. Secondly, if there was oil there, others were getting their hands on it first. From Beijing's perspective whoever controlled the Paracels could hunt for oil in the waters around them and control access to southern China. At the time the islands were still divided: the Amphitrite group was occupied by Communist Chinese forces and the Crescent group by the South Vietnamese. The RVN government, however, was more concerned about events on the mainland than on these specks in the sea. The garrison on Pattle Island was little more than a weather station, a small squad of guards and a herd of goats. Over in the Amphitrite group though, things were quite different. Starting in 1970, the Chinese had surveyed all the islands and constructed a new harbour on Woody Island. It was the jumping-off point for an operation that would propel a quiet American into the news.

Gerald Kosh had believed in the United States' mission in Vietnam. He volunteered for the army straight out of high school, the words of JFK's 'ask not what your country can do for you' speech ringing in his ears. His father, a wounded Second World War veteran, had opposed the idea but Kosh was a determined man. In May 1967 he graduated from Airborne Ranger School as the Outstanding Leader of his class and was sent to Vietnam. He transferred to Special Forces and became a captain in the Green Berets. A veteran of long-range reconnaissance patrols, he was the epitome of the American jungle warrior. After his tour ended he remained in the army, based with the 10th Special Forces Group, periodically returning to Southeast Asia to train anti-Communist forces.

He left the military but – his family says – didn't enjoy civilian life. Bored, he headed back to Vietnam with $300 in his pocket and the promise of a job via the US Embassy. On 10 December 1973 the Naval Attaché in Saigon appointed him one of 12 Regional Liaison Officers assigned to monitor the use of American military equipment transferred to the Vietnamese government. His reports must have made grim reading, particularly as the official ceasefire, in place since the previous January, crumbled. On 4 January 1974, President Thieu announced that war had restarted in Vietnam.

Just a week later a Chinese spokesman renewed Beijing's sovereignty claim over the Paracels but hardly anyone in Saigon noticed. And if Washington had any inkling of what was coming, it didn't let on. Mao Zedong's vision was to secure a strategic fastness off China's southern coast and enable the hunt for oil around the Paracels and beyond. Beijing's relations with North Vietnam were deteriorating fast and South Vietnam had lost American military support. January 1974 was a moment when the Beijing leadership could act without fearing the consequences. For Kissinger and Nixon, the fate of South Vietnam's island possessions was much less important than the US's improving relations with China. A tacit US–China alliance would be much more significant to the outcome of the Cold War than whatever would happen in Saigon.

We now know that the operation had been planned for some time. An official history of the Chinese Navy published in Beijing in 1987 tells us that the order came from the very top: it was issued by Mao Zedong and Zhou Enlai in 1973. The man they put in charge was Deng Xiaoping, later to be the country's de facto leader but who, at that time, had only just been recalled to the capital after six years in political disgrace. Preparations were kept highly secret but we know from a declassified US military document later written by Gerald Kosh that the Chinese military began training for some kind of operation around September 1973. American intelligence had a source in the Chinese port of Beihai who reported a tightening of security around this time – although the connection to what subsequently happened would only be made later. From mid-December onwards, hundreds of Chinese commandos were observed leaving the port each day on six fishing trawlers and returning each evening. This continued for around ten days. They were ready for action by early January.[22]

As Vietnamese made preparations for the Tet festival, news reached Saigon of strange boats appearing around the Paracels. A Vietnamese Navy ship was despatched to find out what was happening. On Monday, 14 January the high command's fears were confirmed. Two Chinese trawlers lay at anchor 300 metres off Robert Island. Suddenly the navy had to switch gear. More used to supporting army manoeuvres on land or patrolling the waterways of the Mekong Delta, it now faced the possibility of a battle at sea. At the same time the admirals couldn't rule out the chance that the Chinese operation was merely a distraction to allow Communist forces to make a breakthrough on land.

It was clear that alarm was spreading. On Tuesday, 15 January, President Thieu himself made a special visit to the Navy HQ in Danang.[23] And sometime that day Jerry Scott of the American Consulate in Danang contacted the regional naval commander, his good friend Commodore Ho Van Ky Thoai, with a special request. Could one of his staff, a Regional Liaison Officer called Gerald Kosh, board one of the ships about to depart for the Paracels? It was quickly agreed and Kosh joined the crew of HQ–16.[24] The ship was one of seven former US Coastguard cutters that had been given to Vietnam in the early 1970s. Although built in the Second World War, their 5-inch guns made them the most heavily armed vessels in the Vietnamese Navy.

The next day, HQ–16 delivered 14 members of the Vietnamese SEAL naval commando unit to guard Robert Island. But when they reached Drummond and Duncan islands they discovered they were too late. Chinese troops were already onshore with support vessels nearby. All this was urgently reported back to Danang. That evening Vietnam's foreign minister publicly condemned the Chinese occupation of the islands and reserved the right to take all appropriate means to deal with the situation.[25]

Behind the scenes there was panic. The navy's third highest-ranking officer, Deputy Chief of Staff for Operations Kiem Do, was urging a swift and determined response. 'If we act now, we can retake the islands,' he recalls urging his overall commander, Admiral Tran Van Chon.[26] Instead, in Kiem's account, Chon dithered, demanding proof of Vietnam's historical claims to the islands. While the hours slipped away Kiem was reduced to searching the navy's library and filing cabinets to find the appropriate documents. At the same time, through his official American liaison officer, Kiem formally requested the US 7th Fleet to form an interdiction line to block the Chinese Navy from reaching the islands. Nothing was done. The Vietnamese were on their own.

On Thursday, 17 January, 15 SEALS were landed on Money Island. Of the seven islands in the Crescent group, three were now occupied by Vietnamese forces and two by Chinese. Three more ships were hurriedly despatched to the Paracels: HQ–5 (another ex-US Coastguard cutter), HQ–4 (the former USS *Forster*, a destroyer armed with 3-inch guns) and HQ–10 (the former minesweeper USS *Serene*, now a patrol craft). By the morning of Friday, 18 January, all four were on station in the islands and the flotilla's commander, Captain Ha Van Ngac, decided to stage a show of strength and attempt to land SEALS on Duncan Island. While four other Chinese ships stood by, two Chinese corvettes (Russian-built submarine chasers constructed in the 1950s) manoeuvred in front. Using signal lamps, they started a historical argument in English. 'These islands belong to China since the Ming Dynasty. Nobody can deny,' they flashed. The Vietnamese replied with the less erudite 'please leave our territorial waters immediately'. This went on for several minutes until the Chinese corvettes stopped the history lesson and began a game of 'chicken', steaming into the path of the Vietnamese vessels. Ngac decided not to play and aborted the landing. First round to the Chinese.

At 8 p.m. that Friday, Kosh was called across to the HQ–5 to meet Ngac, along with a group of Vietnamese Army combat engineers who'd also been sent out with the flotilla. Ngac told him that since combat was imminent all the non-sailors should go ashore. Kosh and the engineers were delivered to Pattle Island, along with some provisions and ten boxes of Capstan cigarettes, to wait out the battle with the meteorologists and their guards. While they were bedding down for the night in the weather station, a coded message was being transmitted to Ngac from Danang. The order was contradictory: repossess Duncan Island peacefully. Quite how the four-ship flotilla and its small complement of SEALS were going to persuade the larger fleet of Chinese vessels, and their entrenched ground forces, to depart was not specified. Ngac decided to make a landing the following morning, Saturday, 19 January. At 8 a.m., 20 SEALS climbed down into two inflatables and sped towards the shore with a mission to talk to the Chinese and ask them to leave. At 8.29 a.m. they beached. As they waded through the surf, the Chinese opened fire, killing one of the SEALS. A second man was killed while trying to retrieve the body. The SEALS retreated.

Ngac radioed for orders. In Navy HQ in Saigon, Kiem Do looked for Admiral Chon. He'd disappeared. An assistant told him Chon had boarded a flight to Danang. Kiem called up Chon's deputy in Danang. He'd disappeared too: gone to the airport to pick up Chon. At the very moment when the fate of the islands hung in the balance, the South Vietnamese Navy's two most senior officers had both made themselves unavailable. In the end, it was Kiem himself who had to give the order to shoot. He also put in a second request for assistance from the US 7th Fleet. Again, nothing came of it.

So, at 10.29 a.m., two hours after the SEALS had been killed, the four Vietnamese ships opened fire on the six Chinese vessels. They were just a mile away from each other. Unfortunately for the Vietnamese, the forward gun on HQ–4 wasn't working and the ship was quickly hit by one of the Chinese corvettes. HQ–5 seriously damaged the other corvette but was then hit itself. Then, 15 minutes later, HQ–5 managed to accidentally hit HQ–16. The shell smashed into the engine room below the waterline. HQ–16 quickly lost electrical power and started listing 20 degrees. Then HQ–5 was hit again, losing its gun turret and radio. Finally, HQ–10, the smallest vessel of the four, was hit by a Chinese rocket-propelled grenade, which destroyed its bridge and killed the captain. Within half an hour, although they'd seriously damaged two of the Chinese ships, the Vietnamese flotilla was totally out of action. HQ–10 sank and the other three limped back to Danang. By any independent assessment the encounter was disastrous but the sailors returned to a heroes' welcome. Vietnamese media had been told that they'd sunk two Chinese ships and seen off a much larger Chinese fleet. It was spun as a good news story, just in time for the Tet celebrations.

Meanwhile Gerald Kosh, and the others on the three remaining Vietnamese-controlled islands, could only await their fate. The two groups of SEALS on Money and Robert were battle-hardened veterans. On Pattle, the meteorologists and their guards were not. Only Kosh knew what combat felt like. They didn't have long to wait. Kosh watched the professionalism of the Chinese invasion with admiration, particularly in comparison with the incompetence of the Vietnamese defence. He watched as they prepared to land on Robert Island, two miles away. At 9 a.m., three Chinese gunboats took up positions offshore and an hour later started to systematically shell the island. Half an hour after that, two fishing trawlers arrived. Their numbers revealed them to be the same boats that had been observed training out of Beihai a month before.

At least 100 soldiers then appeared on the deck of each trawler and offloaded dark grey rubber rafts. As Kosh sat in his vantage point, viewing the activity through his binoculars, six to eight soldiers climbed down rope ladders into each raft. By the time they were done, 30 rafts had assumed an attack formation and paddled off. As they passed over the coral reef, one of the rafts fired a red flare and the ships stopped their shelling and moved off towards Pattle Island. The landing force carried on towards the beach, remaining in close formation. The SEALS opened fire but didn't cause any casualties. Outnumbered more than ten to one, it wasn't long before they surrendered. Unknown to Kosh, the 15 SEALS on Money Island had worked out what was coming. They took to the water before they could be captured. After nine days drifting for 200 miles on a rubber raft, fishermen eventually rescued them 35 miles off the Vietnamese coast.

Kosh's respect for the Chinese assault became even stronger when they turned their attention to Pattle. Again, the island was swept with artillery. Kosh and the Vietnamese had to take shelter around the weather station for nearly an hour as the shells came down. Fortunately, none of them was hit. Then two more trawlers arrived and another set of rafts landed another 200 or so Chinese troops. Kosh remained hidden while observing how they systematically swept across the island with each unit focused on particular objectives. Within an hour the operation was complete. Communist China's first foreign seaborne invasion had been successful.

For Kosh, though, the situation looked dark. He was going to have a hard time explaining why he was in the Paracels. The Chinese were bound to assume he was a spy and treat him accordingly. Two CIA officers, John T. Downey and Richard G. Fecteau, shot down while trying to re-supply anti-Communist rebels in China in 1952, had only just been released after spending 20 years in jail. He told the Chinese he was a civilian, an observer, and he'd only come to the islands to assess what the engineers were planning to do. They transferred him to Hainan and then to the Chinese mainland.

Meanwhile, in both Vietnam and the US, officials scrambled to find out what had happened to him. Aware of the urgency of the situation, Henry Kissinger invited the acting Chinese 'deputy ambassador' in Washington for a chat on 23 January. According to the declassified minutes of the meeting, Kosh was the first item on the agenda. Kissinger made plain that the US took no position at all on the rights and wrongs of the Paracels dispute but urged that Kosh be released very soon, 'and that would certainly defuse the situation as far as the United States is concerned', he told the quasi-ambassador.[27]

Kosh spent almost a week in jail before Kissinger's urging had the desired effect. On 29 January he walked across the border into Hong Kong (then a British colony) with four of the Vietnamese prisoners. US officials went to great lengths to keep questions at bay. Journalists were told he had hepatitis and needed to be quarantined. He was helicoptered to the airport, flown immediately to Clark airbase in the Philippines and then back to Philadelphia Naval Hospital in the US. He gave no interviews. Instead he seems to have put his energies into drafting an assessment of the Chinese assault for the army's Special Research Detachment, a report that was declassified 20 years later.

Kosh was far from beaten. Just a month after arriving at the Naval Hospital, he was back at his post in Vietnam. Then, after his assignment ended there, he worked as a civilian contractor with the UN peacekeeping force in the Sinai and then in other overseas jobs where, presumably, he maintained his reporting activities. But tragically for him and his family, Gerald Kosh was not to enjoy a long and happy retirement full of the world's best war stories. The man who had dedicated his life to the service of his country and who had, in a way, fought the war in Vietnam almost to its very end would eventually become a casualty of it. During those long-range patrols as a Green Beret he had been soaked in Agent Orange – the herbicide sprayed by American planes in order to destroy the jungle vegetation and expose the enemy hiding within it. Contaminated with dioxin, Agent Orange was highly toxic. In 2002, at the age of 56, Gerald Kosh was killed by chemicals sprayed from an American plane 30 years before.

* * * * * *

Mao Zedong's vision for the islands came to nothing. No oil has yet been found around the Paracels and their strategic value remains unproven. The occupation of the Crescent group certainly didn't prevent the Soviet Navy using the harbour at Cam Ranh Bay on the Vietnamese coast after Hanoi had won the war, just as Beijing had feared. Tiny bases such as those on Woody and Pattle islands are almost impossible to defend anyway. That was the Royal Navy's view as far back as the 1940s and it's been the US Navy's view since. But such doubts haven't stopped further occupations. In the wake of the Paracels invasion, the RVN government rushed to reinforce its garrisons in the Spratlys. At least 120 troops were despatched and five islands occupied. But China made no moves in that direction. In fact it did the opposite and de-escalated the conflict, releasing all the prisoners from the Paracels within a few weeks and silencing the nationalist rhetoric. But the Communist North Vietnamese leadership (which had been publicly silent about the battle) was convinced that Beijing intended to take over more islands. In April 1975, three weeks before the fall of Saigon, Hanoi seized six of the Spratly Islands from the RVN to ensure they didn't fall into Chinese hands. The lieutenant in charge of the South Vietnamese garrison on Southwest Cay (known to Vietnamese as Dao Song Tu Tay) chose to swim the 3 kilometres to the Philippine-occupied Northeast Cay (known to Filipinos as Parola Island) rather than be captured.

In November 1975, for the first time, the dispute between Beijing and Hanoi over the islands appeared in public when the Chinese paper *Guangming Ribao* criticised the Vietnamese territorial claims. At the time China simply didn't have the capacity to conduct a sustained military operation as far south as the Spratlys. Nonetheless, it was quietly making preparations. During the rest of the decade it consolidated its positions in the Paracels, enlarging the harbour and opening a runway on Woody Island in 1978. A decade later it would be able to make its presence felt in a decisive way.

For the first 30 years of its existence, the People's Liberation Army (PLA) Navy had been a junior service, dedicated to coastal defence. The Beijing leadership assumed that any war would be won on the land and the navy's role would be like guerrilla warfare at sea: hundreds of small boats harrying attackers from all angles and cutting off their supply lines. (The 1974 Paracels operation had been highly unusual and required months of special training.) But by 1982, the combination of Deng Xiaoping at the apex of the Communist Party and Admiral Liu Huaqing in charge of the navy would bring about major change. Liu had been a loyal Communist since childhood and made a name for himself in the most sensitive political and counter-infiltration sections of the military and in battles against nationalist forces during China's civil war.[28] The war also brought him into contact with Deng and their partnership became mutually beneficial. The story of the next decade was, to quote Professor John Garver, the 'interaction of bureaucratic and national interests'[29] or perhaps, to paraphrase the

Catch–22 character Milo Minderbinder, 'what's good for Liu is good for the Navy and what's good for the Navy is good for China'. Deng wanted China to regain its economic strength – for which it needed resources and reliable trade routes. He was also worried about the risk of the country being encircled by the Soviet Union and its allies, including Vietnam. Liu was ambitious and, along with the rest of the naval leadership, seeking prestige. Expanding China's position in the South China Sea was an objective that pleased them all.

In contrast to Mao, who had favoured self-reliance and built up industries in China's heartland, far from external threats, Deng's economic reforms favoured trade and, therefore, the coast. The first special economic zone was created in Shenzhen, close to Hong Kong, in 1980 and was followed by 14 more in other coastal cities in 1984. The first industry opened to foreign investment was offshore oil and the first two rounds of bidding, in 1982 and 1984, focused on blocks off the coast of Hong Kong and Hainan. Deng's policy depended upon access to international trade routes and as early as 4 March 1979, possibly after lobbying from Liu, he had issued the first instructions for the navy to organise long-distance missions.

As soon as Liu took charge of the navy, he began to formulate the strategy he called 'active green-water defence'. This meant controlling the sea between the inshore 'brown water' and the 'blue water' far offshore in order to allow for defence in depth and shield the rapidly growing coastal cities from attack.[30] Liu defined 'green water' as the area between the Chinese coast and what he called the 'first island chain' – stretching from Japan to Taiwan and on to the Philippines, Borneo and Singapore. New ships were commissioned, bases along the southern coast and in the Paracels were expanded and intelligence was gathered. According to the Chinese Navy's own published history, in April 1983 the Oceanographic Bureau was ordered to begin surveys of conditions just north of the Spratly Islands. Then, in May, two ships were sent as far south as James Shoal, the submerged coral reef over 1,500 kilometres from Hainan Island and just 100 kilometres from the Malaysian coast but declared the 'southernmost point of Chinese territory'. On board were dozens of navigators and naval college instructors.[31] In 1984, research vessels surveyed most of the area of the Spratlys, almost up to the coast of the Philippines. In February 1985 a flotilla made a long-distance cruise to Antarctica. By 1987, the navy was ready for expeditionary warfare.

The Chinese leadership was concerned that, even as it was becoming more dependent upon the South China Sea, it was losing ground in the Spratlys. In June 1983, Malaysia had joined Taiwan, Vietnam and the Philippines by occupying reefs. The list of options for a navy seeking forward bases in the South China Sea was getting shorter. It was time for action and the moment was opportune. The economy was growing and providing extra resources for the navy. Mikhail Gorbachev's reforms had ended the threat from the Soviet Union and relations with the United States were better than they'd ever been. China had nothing to lose in provoking a conflict with Vietnam. Ever since Vietnam's invasion of Cambodia in December 1978 and China's punitive invasion of northern Vietnam two months later, relations between the two had been little better than hostile.[32] Vietnam was internationally isolated because of its ongoing occupation of Cambodia and was unlikely to get more than verbal support from its main ally, Moscow. According to the China watcher Taylor Fravel, in early 1987 a decision was taken in Beijing to occupy territory.[33] Now all the leadership needed was a pretext.

In March 1987, a meeting of UNESCO mandated countries to establish monitoring stations as part of a survey of the world's oceans. No-one, not even the Vietnamese, seems to have noticed that one of the sites proposed by China was in the Spratlys. On 4 April the Chinese Academy of Sciences sent off another mission to survey the islands. In May the navy sent a flotilla to join them, practising resupply and war-fighting along the way and depositing a concrete block on Fiery Cross Reef (Yongshu in Chinese), declaring it Chinese territory. More surveys took place over the following months until, on 6 November 1987, the Beijing leadership gave the green light for an observation post to be built on Fiery Cross Reef. Unusually for a civilian research centre, the construction plans included a two-storey barracks, a wharf, a helicopter hangar and a landing pad.

Fiery Cross Reef would not have been anyone's first choice for a research station. At high water it was almost entirely submerged, except for a single metre-high rock at its southwestern end. The rest was composed of a ring of sharp coral, 25 kilometres long and 7 kilometres wide. The main reason it wasn't already occupied was that there was almost nothing there to occupy. But this did not deter Liu's navy. On 21 January 1988 four Chinese ships arrived with engineers and construction materials and set about creating something that could resemble dry land. The following day a Vietnamese ship arrived to see what was going on but left without incident.[34]

Up until that day the Vietnamese had probably felt quite secure in that part of the Spratlys: they occupied everything worth occupying. On London Reefs, 72 kilometres south of Fiery Cross, and on Union Bank, about 93 kilometres to its east, they controlled almost everything sticking out of the water. Fiery Cross was little more than a shipping hazard on the route back home. But they'd underestimated Chinese naval engineering. For nine days the new arrivals proved their commitment to the marine environment by blasting channels through the coral reef and then dredging up enough coral debris to form 8,000 square metres of dry land.[35]

The Vietnamese woke up to what was happening and on 31 January sent two ships to deposit a landing party on Fiery Cross Reef. But the mission failed in the face of severe weather and superior Chinese numbers. On 18 February the Chinese went one step further, landing sailors on the only feature on London Reefs that the Vietnamese didn't occupy: Cuarteron Reef (Huayang in Chinese), a bean-shaped rocky outcrop about a metre and a half above sea level. The Vietnamese were incensed and Hanoi made a public protest: Cuarteron was just 19 kilometres from their nearest outpost. The Vietnamese media warned that China would face 'all the consequences' if it didn't leave the two reefs. The sea was rough and the politics was about to get rougher.

Almost a month later, the Vietnamese, fearing a repeat of the Cuarteron incident, moved to secure the features on Union Bank that they didn't occupy. Union Bank is a large underwater mound, around 470 square kilometres in area, covered in coral reefs that stick out of the water in 31 places. The only feature on Union Bank that comes close to most people's definition of an 'island' is Sin Cowe Island which, in 1988, hosted a Vietnamese garrison. Seventeen kilometres southeast of Sin Cowe Island lies Johnson Reef (Chigua in Chinese, Da Gac Ma in Vietnamese) which is mostly underwater although a few rocks break the surface, the highest being just over a metre above the waves. Less than 2 kilometres to the north of Johnson Reef is Collins Reef (sometimes called Johnson Reef North) and 15 kilometres to its northeast is Lansdowne Reef, both equally inhospitable and mostly submerged at high tide.[36]

On the night of 13 March, the Vietnamese Navy despatched three ships: one each to Johnson, Collins and Lansdowne reefs. Unfortunately for those on board, the ancient rust-buckets[37] were detected by the Chinese side, which moved to intercept them with a larger and more heavily armed force. At first light on 14 March 1988, the Vietnamese successfully grabbed Collins and Lansdowne (and remain in control there to this day). The Johnson Reef operation turned into a disaster. The exact sequence of events is still disputed but it seems the Vietnamese landed first, in a small boat full of construction equipment, and planted their flags on the coral. Chinese troops then arrived and tried to remove the flags. The two sides shouted at each other and then scuffled. The Chinese accounts say a Vietnamese soldier shot and wounded one of the Chinese force that then retreated as the Vietnamese ships opened fire with machine guns. The Vietnamese say it was the other way around: the Chinese killed the deputy commander of the Vietnamese landing force and withdrew before their ships opened fire. Strangely, a propaganda film released by the Chinese Navy in 2009 to celebrate the navy's 60th anniversary gives more credence to the Vietnamese version. The video, now available on YouTube, was shot from one of the Chinese ships and shows the Vietnamese force standing knee deep in water as the tide rises over the reef. Huge spouts of water then erupt around the Vietnamese troops as the Chinese ships open fire. Within seconds the thin line of men has completely disappeared and 64 lie dead in the water: the machine guns are Chinese and the victims Vietnamese. The Chinese won the battle of Johnson Reef with a turkey shoot.

With the three ships that supported the Vietnamese operation also destroyed, the Chinese had a freer hand over the next few weeks. They already occupied three reefs: Fiery Cross, Cuarteron and Johnson. By 8 April 1988 they had occupied three more: Kennan or McKennan Reef – a part of Union Bank 19 kilometres east of Vietnamese-occupied Sin Cowe Island; Subi Reef – 15 kilometres from the Philippine-occupied Thitu Island; and Gaven Reef – part of Tizard Bank on which sit both Itu Aba Island, the largest of the Spratlys and the only one occupied by Taiwan, and Namyit Island, occupied by Vietnam.

The list demonstrates the degree of planning and resources that the Chinese state had devoted to the operation. In the face of armed resistance and bad weather it had occupied six mostly submerged coral reefs and constructed living platforms, resupply facilities and defensive emplacements in just over two months. Moreover, each of the six was strategically located within a few kilometres of the main islands held by China's rivals and yet each had been entirely unoccupied before 1988. The survey missions had done their jobs excellently. China now had much more than a toehold in the Spratlys.

Liu was triumphant. His 'green water' strategy was now a reality. Deng rewarded him with the rank of full admiral, a place on both the Party and state Central Military Commissions and a seat in the National People's Congress. Four years later, after Deng's retirement, he became a member of the innermost circle of the Chinese Communist Party: the Standing Committee of the Politburo. In all these roles he continued to push for more and more resources to be devoted to the navy. He demanded, and got, bigger ships, better technology and support for his dream of a fully capable 'blue water' navy. But what had China as a whole gained? It now had new bases in the South China Sea, but what else? The best that can be said is that the occupations have prevented other countries advancing their positions. No-one else has been able to drill for oil or monopolise fishing activity in the region but despite all the effort that has gone into seizing and building bases, neither has China.

* * * * * *

From the day he was elected, the Philippine president, Fidel ('Eddie') Ramos, had to contend with a powerful wave of anti-American feeling. Resentment at Washington's earlier support for the Marcos dictatorship had combined with a deeper current of nationalism, resulting in the Philippine Senate voting, in September 1991, to evict the United States from its two vast military sites. Clark Air Force Base had actually already closed on 15 June 1991 when Mount Pinutabo erupted, showering it with thousands of tons of volcanic debris. The vote meant it would not be repaired. On 24 November 1992, the Stars and Stripes was pulled down at Subic Bay Naval Base for the last time. The next day the Philippines was, in effect, defenceless. Worse, the annual subsidy that the US had provided to the Armed Forces of the Philippines (AFP) disappeared too. Underfunded for years, the navy and air force were in no position to fill the gap left by the Americans' departure. The navy of a country of innumerable islands comprised around 50 vintage Second World War American surplus patrol and transport ships and the air force possessed five functional F-5 jets, built in 1966.

After years of economic stagnation interspersed with political chaos, Ramos' vision was to try to use the country's untapped oil potential to lift its people out of grinding poverty. Ever since the first explorations of the early 1970s there had been hopes that further riches lay offshore. So, in May 1994, the Ramos government secretly approved an application from a Philippine company, Alcorn Petroleum (a subsidiary of an American company, Vaalco Energy), to conduct a paper assessment of the oil and gas potential in an area off the coast of Palawan. Although it didn't involve any survey or drilling work at sea, this was, arguably, a violation of the Manila Declaration, a 1992 agreement between the then six members of ASEAN (the Association of Southeast Asian Nations) to 'exercise restraint' in their actions in the South China Sea. In 1992 China had awarded drilling rights to an American company, Crestone, in an area further to the west and Vietnam had awarded another American company, Conoco, blocks that overlapped the Crestone concession (see Chapter 5 for more on this). Nonetheless, after news of the survey leaked out, China protested against what it saw as an infringement of its own sovereignty. The fuse was lit for a regional crisis.

Captain Joefel Alipustain was the first person to suffer the consequences. He and the rest of his crew aboard the fishing boat *Analita* were going about their usual business on 10 January 1995 when they made an unusual discovery. Sticking several metres out of the sea, raised above the waves on giant stilts, were four large platforms, each supporting three or four octagonal bunkers. During the typhoon season, in the crew's traditional fishing ground, a horseshoe-shaped rock formation submerged at high tide had been occupied. And the occupiers were far from pleased to have been discovered; the *Analita*'s crew quickly found themselves surrounded by hostile boats. To their astonishment, they discovered the interlopers were Chinese, 114 kilometres closer to the Philippines than they had been only a few months before. The crew were held for a week before being freed on condition they didn't tell anyone what they'd found. But that commitment lasted only as long as it took the *Analita* to reach home, and the world quickly learnt the apt name of the place where they'd been detained: Mischief Reef (Meiji Jiao in Chinese, Panganiban in Filipino).[38] And the location of Mischief Reef? Almost exactly in the middle of the area being surveyed by Alcorn Petroleum.[39]

The Philippine authorities went into denial. 'It couldn't be true', they maintained. The government had other things on its mind. Manila was hosting the largest Christian gathering in history: 4 million people watched Pope John Paul II celebrate Mass. (The region was also somewhat distracted by the Kobe earthquake in the same week.) It was only after the pontiff had left town that the Ramos administration could turn its attention to the sea. A navy plane was sent out but apparently failed to find any evidence of bunkers on stilts. The Chinese went into a different form of denial: there'd been no incident at all with a fishing boat, they said, and there was no base on Mischief Reef. But by 9 February the Ramos government had photographic proof to show the world's press and the Chinese story changed too. Yes, there were structures, they admitted, but they'd been built by the fisheries administration, not the navy. However, that didn't seem to explain the presence of satellite dishes on the huts or the eight armed navy transport vessels around the reef. Then they told the Philippine authorities that the base had been built by 'low-ranking' naval personnel without proper authorisation.[40] But the idea that hundreds of tons of wood and steel, prefabricated housing units, communications equipment and all the men and materials required to set up the four bases could be transported hundreds of kilometres without official permission was ludicrous.[41]

The reaction in Manila was furious, made worse by a sense of impotence. Following the fall of President Marcos and the end of the Cold War, the public and politicians had assumed the country did not face any external threats and voted accordingly. In 1989 Ramos, as Secretary of National Defence, had proposed a 15-year $12.6 billion military modernisation plan. He tried to prioritise it again after becoming president but it remained firmly on the shelf. It wasn't until a fortnight after Ramos demonstrated that Chinese naval forces had managed to build a base 209 kilometres offshore without anyone noticing that Congress finally found the time to debate the plan.[42] The Modernization Act was approved within days but the resolution to actually implement it wasn't passed for almost two further years.[43] (In 1997, as a result of the Asian financial crisis, most of the funding would disappear anyway.) In February 1995, because of the delays, Ramos had no military option. He was being lied to by Beijing. The United States, still upset about the termination of the bases agreement and more worried by events in Bosnia, wasn't rushing to help. He turned instead to his neighbours.

It was a turning point. Up until January 1995, Chinese expansion in the South China Sea had only really affected Vietnam – and at times when Hanoi was internationally isolated. The features China had seized were all either in the Paracels or along the western side of the Spratlys, far from the other claimants. But by taking Mischief Reef on the eastern side, China had, for the first time, encroached into waters claimed by a member of ASEAN. After the Chinese move, not just the Philippines but Malaysia, Brunei and Indonesia all felt directly threatened. Vietnam, due to join ASEAN that July, was also lobbying for a firm stand. Even Singapore, usually keen to keep on the right side of Beijing, was concerned. In a memorable interview with the BBC, its former prime minister, Lee Kuan Yew, later compared China's actions to 'a big dog going up to a tree and raising its leg and marking its presence, so that smaller dogs in the region will know that a big dog has been past and will come back'.[44]

But ASEAN didn't have a military option either: none of its members were prepared to risk hostilities with China. Sanctions were out too, so instead, on 18 March, it issued a strongly worded statement expressing its 'serious concern', calling upon all parties to 'refrain from taking actions that destabilize the region and threaten the peace and security of the South China Sea' and specifically calling for an 'early resolution of the problems caused by the recent developments in Mischief Reef'. This was pretty tough talk by ASEAN standards but it had no effect out at sea: the bunkers remained on their stilts. China kept stonewalling. In April, at the first ever ASEAN–China Forum, which might have been the obvious place to discuss the matter, Beijing simply refused to have it on the agenda. Instead it was raised, and by all accounts quite forcefully, at an informal meeting beforehand. The Philippine government said it was pleased with the support, but still the structures remained on the reef.

Beijing refused to discuss the issue at the official regional meetings that Ramos would have preferred. The refusal obliged Ramos to agree to China's preferred channel – bilateral discussions – instead, and in August the two sides agreed a 'code of conduct' to avoid future incidents: more statements, more paper, but still no practical change. From the outset, China offered the Philippines joint development of the oil prospects in the areas it claimed – asking the Philippines, in effect, to recognise its territorial rights in the Spratlys. This policy – which has been termed 'occupy and negotiate' or, more pithily, 'take and talk' – is something that none of the other claimants have been prepared to accept.

So why did China occupy Mischief Reef in late 1994? The initial trigger may well have been the Philippine announcement of plans for oil and gas development. But there were internal reasons too. The Singapore-based regional analyst Ian Storey argued that it was the result of jockeying for power within the upper echelons of the Chinese Communist Party as Deng Xiaoping's faculties diminished.[45] Deng's chosen successor, Jiang Zemin, was not a military man and needed support from the PLA leadership and more nationalist factions if he was to reach the top spot. In 1994, Deng's other protégé, Admiral Liu, was a key member of the Politburo Standing Committee and Vice-Chair of the Central Military Commission – the two key bodies in Chinese politics. It seems highly likely that he would have seen the occupation of Mischief Reef as a key part of his 'green water' strategy and that an astute politician like Jiang would have fully supported it. The move was clearly a success. Chinese forces occupy Mischief Reef to this day and the repercussions have been minimal.

The Philippines' neighbours learnt lessons from the crisis. In April 1995, the Indonesian government revealed that China had made a claim on waters near the Natuna Islands, within Indonesia's claimed Exclusive Economic Zone. Alarmed by the events at Mischief Reef, Jakarta decided its best option was deterrence. In August 1996, Indonesia, Malaysia and Brunei held joint military exercises in Borneo, on the southern fringe of the South China Sea. The following month, Indonesia held its largest-ever naval manoeuvres – around the Natunas: 27 ships, 54 aircraft and almost 20,000 personnel took part in war games, climaxing with an amphibious assault on the island where Exxon's multi-billion dollar natural gas project was due to be based. The Chinese Navy sent five ships to observe the exercises but just to make sure that the message was received in Beijing, the chief of China's General Staff, Fu Quanyou, was invited to Jakarta for meetings with President Suharto and his defence chiefs.[46] China still maintains a claim to the northern part of the gas field but, until very recently, took little action to assert it. (A few incidents since 2012 have given Indonesia renewed cause for concern, of which more later.)

After months of Indonesia talking softly but waving a big stick and the Philippines doing the opposite, the situation in the South China Sea stabilised in time for the annual meeting of the Asia-Pacific Economic Cooperation (APEC) group. By coincidence the November 1996 meeting, involving 21 heads of government, was being held in Manila. It gave Jiang Zemin the opportunity to make the first ever visit to the Philippines by a Chinese head of state. Once APEC was over, he spent three days meeting and greeting the country's business and political leaders. At the start of the second day, President Ramos treated Jiang and his delegation to an early morning boat trip around Manila Bay. As they breakfasted, a Philippine Navy band struck up a series of numbers from a specially produced songbook entitled *Sailing Together to the 21st Century*. The two leaders took to the floor and performed a duet of Elvis Presley's 'Love Me Tender'. As the 60 or so guests applauded, the enmity of Mischief Reef seemed far away. But out at sea, nothing changed. Almost exactly two years after the karaoke cruise, the Chinese Navy turned their stilt platforms on Mischief Reef into concrete blockhouses with wharfs and helipads. China had talked and taken.

The desire to grab islands in the South China Sea began with nationalist flag-waving and ended with a rush to claim potential oilfields and fishing rights. None of the occupations has yet delivered the hoped-for rewards. Instead they have created chronic insecurity, blocked development of the sea's resources and forced politicians into rhetorical battles and jingoistic gestures at times when they might have preferred to seek regional cooperation. China was a latecomer to the Spratlys party but each time it has occupied a feature, Beijing's negotiating position has become stronger. What practical benefits has it gained though? Only the negative effect of preventing others from making gains. Beijing clearly sees this as a long-term strategy that will eventually oblige other states to share sovereign rights. But will they? Is there an alternative to 'might is right'? Could the rule of international law provide an alternative?

CHAPTER 4

Rocks and Other Hard Places
The South China Sea and International Law

ON 29 MARCH 1843 the crew of the sailing barque *Cyrus* was hunting for oil in the South China Sea. Sadly for them, the oil was getting away. Five days before, the *Cyrus* had lowered its harpoon boats and come close, but the whales had escaped, heading off fast between the reefs. It was tough and perilous work. The ship was navigating an area known only as the 'dangerous ground' – from the warning printed on the first maritime charts. Despite the new charts the sea off the northern coast of Borneo remained a risky prospect for whalers – and whales – alike. But on this day the weather was fine and a steady breeze allowed the *Cyrus* to make good progress in pursuit of its prey.

Extracting oil from the blubber of a dead whale was a noxious process. As Ishmael complained, aboard the *Pequod* in *Moby Dick*, 'It has an unspeakable, wild Hindoo odor about it, such as may lurk in the vicinity of funeral pyres. It smells like the left wing of the day of judgment; it is an argument for the pit.' But once safely barrelled up, whale oil was prized cargo and the 281-ton *Cyrus* could carry tens of thousands of gallons of it. This was the prize its captain, Richard Spratly, was seeking. He'd left London 16 months before and wouldn't return for a further 17. It took nearly three years of hunting to fill the hold with enough oil to satisfy the ship's owners. Add in whalebone, whale ivory and ambergris and the trade was lucrative. In all, Spratly would make four long voyages as master of the *Cyrus*. Each one was marked by the birth of another child – though he never saw any of them before their second birthday. By the time each arrived, he had already departed on the next expedition.

The sea had been Richard Spratly's destiny from an early age. Born in the shadow of London's docks to a boat-builder father he was apprenticed to a whaling ship at 16. He transferred to the corrections industry, transporting British and Irish prisoners to Australia, and by the age of 30 had command of the convict ship *York*. Two years later, in 1834, he returned to his first vocation: chasing cetaceans through the South Seas.

As one of the most experienced captains in the fleet, Richard Spratly could weather the difficult conditions better than most. After years on deck he knew the treacherous waters well and would occasionally write to the authorities with discoveries of dangerous rocks and shoals he had encountered. He'd often learnt the hard way: in the spring of 1842 he told a fellow captain that in the many voyages he had made in the seas around what is now Indonesia, Malaysia and the Philippines he 'had been aground on nearly all these reefs and shoals' at some point. Even a decade later he would write to the *Nautical Magazine* complaining that he 'never yet could find one chart of this intricate Archipelago to be in the least depended upon'.

So it is somewhat ironic that this entire intricate archipelago now bears his name. At 9 a.m. that Wednesday, 29 March 1843, there came a shout from the masthead of the *Cyrus*. The lookout had spotted a low, sandy island: 12 miles to the southeast. Captain Spratly believed that it was uncharted. Others disagreed, saying the island had already been recorded by the East India Company's surveyor, James Horsburgh, but perhaps in deference to his long experience, the Royal Navy's Hydrographic Office chose to honour Spratly and since 1881 its charts have marked 'Spratly Island'. It was a fitting honour for an old sea dog, but perhaps in view of later developments, Horsburgh's original name of 'Storm Island' might have been more appropriate.

Spratly must have been only one of dozens of European ships' captains to have spotted his 'sandy isle' but he is the one credited with its discovery. It might have been an accident that it was he; but it was much less of an accident that he was British. Britain was the global hegemon, British cartographers were drawing the best maps and British committees were drawing up the rules for naming territory. Thousands of others probably saw Spratly Island during the preceding millennia, perhaps even landed on it, but they left no traces in any written records. The idea that this patch of land, just 750 metres long and 350 metres wide, could actually 'belong' to anyone didn't arise until 1877.

It was, unsurprisingly, Great Britain that first claimed it, initiating a process that led ultimately to the disputes of today. Over the century and a half since, claim has been laid upon claim with governments reaching far into the past and the furthest recesses of legal theory in search of evidence and arguments that might make their actions compatible with international law. Unfortunately, in the South China Sea the law is far from clear. There are two sets of laws to contend with: an older form governs 'historical claims' to territory and a newer form, defined by the United Nations Convention on the Law of the Sea (UNCLOS), governs the maritime claims that can be measured from territorial claims. The South China Sea is where the two forms intersect – and perhaps collide.

* * * * * *

The international rules about claiming territory were laid down by those most active in acquiring it. European rulers wanted their actions to be legitimate in the eyes of God and, more importantly, protected from the predations of rivals. In the fifteenth century, Portugal and Spain needed the authority of a man who purported to speak on behalf of God. The 1455 'Papal Bull' of Pope Nicholas V authorised King Alfonso of Portugal to conquer non-Christian lands and peoples and prohibited other Christians from 'meddling' with Portuguese possessions. Its sequels, the Treaty of Tordesillas in 1493 and the Treaty of Zaragoza in 1529, divided the world into Portuguese and Spanish realms. When the Dutch broke up this global duopoly in the seventeenth century they wrote new rules to legitimise their actions. The rules evolved further through the wars and conquests of the following two centuries until, by the time of the Conference of Berlin in 1884, European powers had developed a coherent set of principles justifying the grabbing of land around the world and arbitrating disputes between them.

In these bad old days, before the foundation of the League of Nations, they recognised five ways that territory could be acquired: conquest (the forcible acquisition of rights over territory), cession (another ruler giving up their rights through a formal treaty), occupation (establishing an administration over territory not belonging to any other ruler: what was called 'empty land' or *terra nullius* regardless of the presence of 'natives'), prescription (the gradual recognition of one ruler's rights by others) and accretion (where land is added to existing territory by, for example, reclaiming the sea). In the twentieth century, having acquired as much territory as they were likely to and, in the wake of two savagely destructive world wars, realising that the costs of conflict now firmly outweighed the benefits, the victorious states decided to strike conquest from the list. Further acquisitions of territory by force were outlawed by the United Nations Charter.

But the legacy of that imperial past is a system of international law that, when it comes to territorial disputes, prioritises discovery over proximity. The sound of that original Papal Bull still echoes, sometimes in the language of the playground: 'finders keepers, losers weepers'. Since there is no overarching global constitution, countries have agreed – to varying degrees – to be bound by a set of customs and practices that have grown up haphazardly in response to specific circumstances. Over the centuries, international law has fused the requirements of dominant states for a system that legitimises their territorial gains with the legalistic practices of a European civil court. It therefore demands demonstrable forms of evidence – papers, treaties and charts – rather than inchoate senses of national entitlement – such as 'the islands have been ours since ancient times'. The result in the South China Sea dispute is the apparently ridiculous situation whereby Britain or France might have as strong a legal claim to the islands as any of the states that border the Sea.

In September 1877, the authorities in the British colony of Labuan (an island off the coast of Borneo) licensed an American named Graham and two Britons named Simpson and James to claim Spratly Island and Amboyna Cay on behalf of the British Crown and then extract from it as many tons of guano as they could carry away on their ships. An announcement was duly posted in the *Government Gazette*.[1] Other countries may have been closer, other fishermen may have visited the island, other navies may even have sailed past it but Britain was the first to announce it in a newspaper – and that is the kind of evidence that tribunals value. From such humble beginnings, claims of empire grow. It was the first act of sovereignty by any state in what we now know as the Spratly Islands. Another British licence was issued to the Central Borneo Company in 1889. However, the imperial interest in guano never reached the levels of tea, opium or rubber and its interest in the islands remained mainly one of navigation. Nonetheless Britain has never formally renounced its claim to Spratly Island and Amboyna Cay.

Indeed, Britain discreetly revived its claim in the weeks after April 1930 when the French authorities announced that they'd despatched a warship, the *Malicieuse*, taken possession of Spratly Island and laid claim to all the other features within a large rectangular area of the South China Sea. The two governments exchanged diplomatic notes and legal arguments for the following two years. At the front of their minds was the apparent danger posed to their colonies by the expansion of the Japanese empire into the region. Faced with a common enemy, neither wished to relinquish its own claim but the British didn't want to undermine France's either. It wasn't until July 1933 that the French government formally annexed six named islands: Spratly or Storm, Amboyna Cay, Itu Aba, North Danger (known to the French as Les Deux Iles), Loaita and Thitu. Another newspaper announcement was placed – in the French government's *Journal Officiel*. The announcement prompted national hysteria in China but (as we saw in Chapter 2) once the Chinese government had realised that it related to the Spratlys and not to the Paracels, the fuss died down. Contrary to what Chinese officials claim today, newspapers remained bare of official protests or rival annexation notices. The French maintained their claim on paper but did little to enforce it on land until 1938 when they erected a weather station on Itu Aba,[2] which was occupied by Japanese forces during the Second World War. As we've seen, the Japanese abandoned it some time between a US bombing raid on 1 May 1945 and a US naval landing on 18 November 1945. The next sailors to arrive were French, aboard the minesweeper FR *Chevreuil*, on 5 October 1946. They erected a stele reclaiming the island for France and renewing the annexation of 1933. The Philippine government asserted a claim to the Spratlys in July 1946 but did nothing to enforce it for decades.

Until the end of the Second World War, the Chinese Navy had been incapable of even reaching the Spratly Islands. It was only with the supply of ships, maps and training by the United States that the Republic of China (ROC) government was able to mount an expedition and make the kind of claim that would be recognised by an international court. On 12 December 1946, two ROC Navy ships, the *Taiping* and *Zhongye* (the former USS *Decker* and USS *LST 1056* respectively), arrived at Itu Aba. According to Chinese accounts, the ships' crews removed a Japanese stele from the island and erected a Chinese one in its place. They appear not to have noticed the French one – or not thought it worth mentioning. This was the first act of sovereignty, in a form that an international tribunal would recognise, ever made by any Chinese government in the Spratlys. ROC forces then occupied the island, on and off, until they pulled out on 5 May 1950. By then the French had other priorities: Indochina was being prised from their grasp by Ho Chi Minh and his nationalist friends.

Threading a coherent case through the tapestry of what happened next will earn international lawyers some fine fees. To summarise two bloody decades: Vietnam was divided between Communist north and capitalist south in 1954, the French pulled out in 1956 and then the country was reunited under Communism in 1975–6. While it might seem logical that – since France was the colonial power in Vietnam – French territorial claims in the South China Sea would naturally fall to Vietnam after independence, that argument is unlikely to satisfy an international court. Just like Britain, France has never formally abandoned its claim to the Spratly Islands. It claimed them on its own account, not on behalf of Vietnam. (This situation contrasts strongly with its earlier claim on the Paracel Islands, which was ostensibly made on behalf of the protectorate of Annam, and later fell to Vietnam.) It was not until 1956 that the newly independent Republic of Vietnam ('South Vietnam') asserted a claim to the Spratly Islands, in response to the pretensions of the Filipino entrepreneur Tomas Cloma. That was also the cue for the Republic of China to reoccupy Itu Aba.

The situation becomes even more complex when one investigates the legal situation of the Republic of Vietnam (RVN) itself. One could take the view that the republic was an illegal puppet state created by the imperial powers (French and American). This was certainly the view of the leadership of the Communist Democratic Republic of Vietnam ('North Vietnam' or DRV) at the time. The DRV regarded itself as the legitimate government of the entire country, temporarily constrained to a part of the national territory by the 1954 partition. Alternatively one could see the DRV (North Vietnam) and the RVN (South Vietnam) as two legitimate states in separate areas of the national territory. To some extent the DRV leadership played along with this too – it sponsored a separate 'Provisional Revolutionary Government' that was officially in charge of the war in the south. When the Communists defeated the Republic in 1975 they officially created a southern Communist state with its own legal 'personality' for just over a year before uniting the two countries under a single 'Socialist Republic of Vietnam' in 1976.

Why does all this matter? Because the legalistic nature of international tribunals will require a claimant country to show it has established a formal claim to a territory, that it has maintained that claim and then asserted it in the face of actions by other claimants. Up until 1975 the DRV did very little to assert its claims in the South China Sea while the Republic of Vietnam did considerably more. If the DRV was the legitimate government of the whole country, then its earlier lack of action could harm its case. If the Republic's actions are taken into account – as a legitimate state within the national territory of Vietnam – then Vietnam's case would be much stronger.

There is one particular action taken by the leadership of DRV that has been used to undermine the Vietnamese claim to the islands. In 1958 the Prime Minister of the DRV, Pham Van Dong, sent a brief letter to his (Communist) Chinese counterpart in which he wrote that 'the Government of the Democratic Republic of Vietnam recognises and approves the declaration made on 4 September 1958 by the Government of the People's Republic of China regarding the decision taken with respect to China's territorial sea'. Again, this might seem a somewhat obscure reason to deny the Vietnamese claim to the islands but under the customs of international law it might amount to what's known as an 'estoppel'.

Estoppel is a key concept in European civil law. Its purpose is to stop claimants saying one thing and doing another. If, for example, one party agrees that a dispute is settled, they can't subsequently go back on their word. It's intended to promote transparency and honest behaviour and is supposed to do the same thing in international law too. If one state recognises the validity of another's territorial claim then, in theory, it should be 'estopped' from contesting the claim in future. In 1958, however, neither the Democratic Republic of Vietnam nor the People's Republic of China had acceded to the International Court of Justice and, as communist states, neither had much regard for the 'bourgeois, imperialist' rules of the international community. Rather, they were in the midst of an international anti-imperialist war against them.

On 23 August 1958 forces of the People's Republic of China began shelling their Nationalist rivals on the islands of Jinmen and Mazu, both within a few kilometres of the Chinese mainland. Eleven days later the Communist Chinese issued a 'Declaration on the Territorial Sea' claiming ownership of all waters up to 12 nautical miles offshore – encompassing both Jinmen and Mazu. The purpose was primarily to prevent American ships from resupplying or defending the islands. But the declaration also asserted a territorial claim to Taiwan and its surrounding islands, and to the Paracels, Macclesfield Bank and the Spratlys. In a gesture of solidarity against the American imperialists North Vietnam printed the declaration in the Communist Party newspaper *Nhan Dan* on 6 September and then, on the 14th, Pham Van Dong sent his letter. The letter didn't explicitly consent to Communist China's claim to the islands but neither did it explicitly reject it. That failure to protest might be sufficient grounds for a tribunal to regard the Vietnamese claim to the islands as estopped. However, the Vietnamese leadership would feel more than a little aggrieved if its gesture of brotherly solidarity with another Communist state during a period when neither was familiar with the minutiae of international law was used more than half a century later to undermine its country's territorial position.

In short, when subjected to the arcane rules and customs of international justice what might appear to be a 'natural' Vietnamese claim to the Spratly Islands off their country's coast is less strong than it might appear. Unless the French government formally cedes its claims to the Spratlys, Vietnam cannot rely on the actions of the French Empire in the 1930s and 1940s. There may also be legal argument over whether the current Socialist Republic of Vietnam is legitimately the successor to the Republic of Vietnam and its actions and whether Pham Van Dong's letter undermined the Democratic Republic of Vietnam's claim.

China's historic claim to the Spratlys relies on references to islands in ancient documents. However, a closer reading of those texts provides no information about exactly which islands are being referred to and nothing that amounts to proof of conquest, cession, occupation, prescription or accretion. An international court will have to grapple instead with China's complex modern history. The Republic of China was proclaimed in January 1912 and formally recognised by the 'great powers' in October 1913. But even before this had happened, seven southern provinces had rebelled against Beijing's control, beginning a revolt that would result in the establishment of a separate, rival government in Guangzhou in 1917 by Sun Yat-sen and his allies. It would be 11 years before this administration could fight its way to power over the whole country and become China's internationally recognised government. During this turbulent period, the authorities in southern China are said to have carried out a number of actions that form the basis of Chinese sovereignty claims over the Paracel Islands.

In particular, the southern administration placed the islands under the nominal administration of Hainan Island in 1921 and then granted permits for the extraction of guano. In 1923 and 1927 they sent patrols to inspect the activities of the guano collectors. (The historian Ulises Granados has found evidence in contemporary reports by British intelligence that these permits were actually agreed with a front company for Japanese interests which reportedly promised to provide weapons and funding in exchange for development rights over Hainan Island and the Paracels.[3]) The French authorities (on behalf of the protectorate of Annam) failed to protest against all this and this inaction is now used as evidence of French acquiescence to Chinese sovereignty. But how should a modern tribunal regard actions taken by a government that had no recognition from the 'great powers' before 1928?

The situation becomes more complex after the establishment of the (Communist) People's Republic of China on 1 October 1949 and the expulsion of the Republic of China to Taiwan. Beijing clearly doesn't recognise the legitimacy of the Republic of China in Taiwan but the Communist state's rights in the Spratly Islands rest entirely on the claim to Itu Aba, first made by forces of the Republic of China in 1946. The Communist authorities in Beijing now champion the voyage of the *Taiping* as a claim of sovereignty made on behalf of all China. They took a different view of the ship 60 years ago, during the first Taiwan Strait crisis, seeing it as a symbol of American imperialism. Communist forces sank the *Taiping* off the Tachen Islands on 14 November 1954. The incident highlights the problems the Beijing leadership might have constructing a legal case for its sovereignty over the Spratlys. If it is the successor state to the Republic of China, can it claim that actions taken by the Republic of China after the declaration of the Communist state on 1 October 1949 reinforce its own claim? For example, in 1956 it was the navy of the Republic of China that evicted the Cloma brothers' expedition from Itu Aba and North Danger Reef. That would appear to be a concrete assertion of sovereignty by the Republic of China – but is it one that can be appropriated by the People's Republic of China? If the Taiwan government ever chose to merge with the People's Republic of China on the mainland this is one point over which it would have considerable leverage.

None of these issues has been tested in an international court and, given the complexity and uncertainty of the intersecting legal difficulties, it seems unlikely that they ever will. All we can say is that, from historical perspective, none of the claims to the islands – whether by Britain, France, the Republic of China, the People's Republic of China, Vietnam or, as we shall see later, the Philippines – appears to be entirely convincing. If Britain had kept its flag flying on Spratly Island and France had done the same on Itu Aba or if either had formally ceded its rights to another claimant, the situation might be clearer. But they haven't, so the countries around the shores of the sea have, instead, created their own facts in the 'dangerous ground'.

* * * * * *

These days Richard Spratly's 'sandy isle' is known to its inhabitants as Truong Sa Lon – big Truong Sa. 'Big' is relative. It is the largest piece of dry land in the Spratlys under Vietnamese control – but that's not saying much. Its highest natural point is two and a half metres above sea level although there's very little that's natural about Spratly Island now. The beach has been enclosed behind a high concrete wall intended to keep out both waves and unwanted visitors. Over the wall protrude dozens of posts and pylons: solar-powered floodlights, electricity-generating windmills, radar towers and a huge mobile phone mast. Urban roofs mingle surreally with the trees: standard-issue Vietnamese state-sector buildings (red tiles, ochre walls, neo-classical balconies) transplanted from the mainland by the forces of socialist construction.

Viewed from above, the island forms a neatly isosceles triangle, like a way-marker pointing back towards the motherland, 470 kilometres away. Stretching right across its base, and occupying about a quarter of the entire area, lies a concrete runway – originally built by South Vietnamese forces and rebuilt in 2004. A mesh of pathways runs parallel and perpendicular among the imported trees, creating a garden suburb in the sea. Protruding from the base of the triangle into the sea, a cedilla of a jetty stretches 75 metres over the first bank of coral into water deep enough to welcome fishing boats and the occasional supply vessel. Less welcoming structures fill the water around the rest of the perimeter: hull-smashing spikes intended to wreck an invading force before it can reach the shore.

It's crucial for the Vietnamese cause that the island appears to be a settled, economically vibrant community, so great efforts are made to construct the appearance of 'normality'. Like almost every Vietnamese village, the island hosts a Buddhist pagoda, a temple devoted to a patron figure (in this case socialist Vietnam's 'founding uncle', Ho Chi Minh) and an overbearing grey monument to heroes who fell in the fight for national liberation ('the nation remembers your sacrifice'). There's also a large school building to cater for the tiny number of children living on the island. Visitors can enjoy the hospitality afforded by the 'Capital Guest House', paid for by donations from the people of Hanoi.

Such 'voluntary' collections and other state subsidies make the local government, or People's Committee, one of the best funded per capita in the country. In the past few years, its deputy chairman Nguyen Duc Thien told the official Vietnam News Agency in 2011, investments in solar and wind power mean the island has a regular supply of electricity, the construction of reservoirs allows it to store enough water to meet demand and communications links have given it access to the internet.[4] Chickens and ducks roam the island. Small vegetable plots have been established behind high screens that attempt to keep out wind, sand and salt. Bananas and other fruit trees line the pathways. A $170,000 project run by the Southern Vietnam Institute for Agricultural Science is trying to increase productivity but Truong Sa Lon is hardly self-sufficient.[5] The population has grown so large that food, water and even the soil in which the plants grow still have to be shipped in.

It's not just material needs that need to be catered for. The island population's moral welfare must also be protected. In April 2012 five monks from the official Vietnam Buddhist Sangha (motto: Dharma, Nation, Socialism) set sail for a six-month sojourn on Truong Sa Lon with a mission to improve the spiritual lives of the community. The Communist Party of Vietnam is also concerned about morale. Apart from the usual round of military inspections and national days, two anniversaries are carefully marked: the 1975 'liberation' of the islands from South Vietnamese control and the 1988 Battle of Johnson Reef. At these ceremonies young soldiers are urged to be eternally vigilant against the 'insidious schemes' of the unnamed 'enemy'.[6] Spratly Island is not a 'normal' island: it's an unsinkable bulwark. Hidden among the trees – between the school and the guesthouse and the pagoda – are bunkers, barracks, at least five battle tanks, 20 gun emplacements and a garrison to defend them.[7] But living there – or on one of the 21 other Vietnamese-controlled smaller islands and reefs – is tough. Keeping the troops and sailors motivated is crucial and the Party is ever keen to nurture emotional links between the units out at sea and the folks back home.

The Party excels at organising 'grassroots' solidarity activities and, as nationalist sentiments have swelled in recent years, participation in fund-raising campaigns for the soldiers and sailors out at sea has become ever greater. The sums involved are relatively small, easily within the gift of central government, but the mobilisational power of the campaigns cannot be measured in monetary value alone. They are powerful tools with which the leadership wins popular support. Newspapers have publicly committed themselves to 'propagandise' information about the islands and provinces organise gift-giving events at which coral branches and beach pebbles are exchanged for donations of karaoke DVDs, table tennis tables, electrical generators and cartons of cigarettes. TV programmes feature reporters in patriotic T-shirts extolling the courageous men and women who defend the faraway national territory. A decade ago these would have been dull rituals but now they are enthusiastically followed by an appreciative audience.

Vietnam did not enjoy 'first mover advantage' in its choice of positions in the Spratlys. The Republic of China reoccupied Itu Aba, the largest island, in 1956. The Philippines occupied Thitu (Pagasa in Filipino), Nanshan (Lawak) and Flat (Patag) Islands, and North Danger Reef, sometime before July 1971. (They considered landing on Itu Aba too but were deterred by Taiwanese ships.) By the time the South Vietnamese sent in the marines in September 1973, choices were becoming more limited. Spratly Island – Truong Sa Lon – was an obvious candidate as it was the closest proper island to the Vietnamese mainland and also outside the area claimed by the Philippines. They learnt from the Filipinos' mistake and didn't try to occupy Itu Aba: it had been heavily reinforced by this time. Instead they surreptitiously moved onto Namyit Island, another part of the same atoll – the Tizard Bank – about 20 kilometres across the lagoon.[8] Around the same time they also took over Sin Cowe Island (Dao Sinh Ton) on Union Bank (the seventh largest island) and, much further to the south, Amboyna Cay (Dao An Bang).

Another prize fell to the Vietnamese through a combination of alcohol and bad weather. The two northernmost islands of the Spratlys lie on what the British had named North Danger Reef. This was where, in October 1956, Filemon Cloma had been forced by the Taiwanese Navy to abandon his island-grabbing antics. As its French name – Les Deux Iles – suggests, the reef has two main features: the 2-kilometre-long Northeast Cay (Parola in Filipino) and the 650-metre-long Southwest Cay (Pugad in Filipino). In early 1975 Filipino garrisons occupied both and the two units would often socialise together. One night the officers and men from Pugad were invited to Parola for a party. According to General Juancho Sabban, former head of the Philippine Western Command, they were unable to return to Pugad because of severe weather. Unfortunately for the Filipinos, the weather wasn't severe enough to prevent South Vietnamese troops sneaking onto the island in their absence.[9] Pugad has been occupied by the Vietnamese ever since and is now known to its inhabitants as Dao Song Tu Tay.

That wasn't the end of the story, as we saw in Chapter 3. Only a few months later, in the closing weeks of the Vietnam War, Hanoi launched its 'East Sea Campaign' to grab all the islands that were under South Vietnamese control. Southwest Cay was their first target. Special forces landed on 13 April. After a short firefight some of the defenders realised their position was hopeless and surrendered. But one lieutenant, facing the prospect of a Communist prison camp, put his faith in capitalist camaraderie. He threw himself upon the good offices of the same Filipino soldiers his unit had so recently humiliated and swam the 3 kilometres across the lagoon to the safety of Parola. Luckily for him, the Filipinos were forgiving and gave him sanctuary. Meanwhile, the Communists pressed on – taking the remaining South Vietnamese-held islands even before the fall of Saigon.

Today, the garrisons of the twin islands are on speaking terms. Better still, they are now on sporting terms. In March 2012 the admirals in charge of the Vietnamese and Philippine navies agreed that, as a confidence-building measure, the two militaries would schedule a series of football and basketball games. The first matches were played in June 2014. For the visiting Filipinos, the contrast between their spartan accommodation on Parola and the increasingly comfortable facilities on Dao Song Tu Tay was stark. Just as they've done on Spratly Island, the Vietnamese have installed wind and solar power generators, radar towers and an artificial harbour. An elegant 40-metre-high lighthouse towers over the trees and the island's sporting facilities.

Back home on Parola, members of the Philippines' garrison live like smallholders on their desert island: tending vegetables, harvesting coconuts and fishing. Keeping busy is the best way to fight the boredom and loneliness in the months between the supply boat's visits. A broken-down bulldozer by the beach is a rusting testament to unfulfilled ambitions. For General Sabban, the situation on Parola is particularly depressing. He was its commander for six months in 1981 and remembers the days when his marines enjoyed a much better standard of living than their neighbours who, back then, were enduring the privations of state socialism. Since then Vietnam has liberalised its economy and generated the resources to develop its islands. In the Philippines, priorities have been different. Military budgets have been cut and the marines have had to cope with the consequences.

The consequences of the cuts can be seen on all the islands controlled by the Philippines. On Ayungin (known internationally as the Second Thomas Shoal) the marines live aboard the rusting hulk of the BRP *Sierra Madre*, a tank landing ship that was deliberately run aground on the reef in 1998. Even walking across the ship's main deck is dangerous. Years of sea salt and high winds have flayed the metal bare. In several large patches the deck is completely worn away and visitors have to literally 'walk the plank' to get across. The five marines and two sailors who guard the shoal have even less to amuse themselves than their counterparts on Parola. 'Life's quite hard here because there are no trees, no ground,' Petty Officer Third Class Benedicto de Castro told a visiting journalist in 2012. Their diet consists almost exclusively of the fish they catch. During 2013 their lives became even tougher as China Coast Guard ships laid siege to their outpost, turning away supply vessels.

Every three months or so the BRP *Laguna*, or another of the Philippine Navy's Second World War tank landing ships, sets off on the 'Log Run' – the logistical supply run around all nine features occupied by Filipino forces. It should be a seven-day trip but bad weather or mechanical problems frequently make it longer. None of the Philippine islands have harbours, or even jetties to receive larger ships, so supplies have to be loaded onto small boats and ferried to shore. At high tide on Rizal Reef (Commodore Reef on Western charts), the four-man garrison retreats to its stilt houses and plays cards until the water goes down again. How they envy their colleagues, just an hour's sail away, on Kota (Loaita Island) with their dry land and green trees.

One of the crew's duties on the Log Run is to inspect reefs and shoals that the Philippines claims but doesn't occupy. Increasingly, they discover evidence of foreign activity. It can start with something as apparently innocent as an orange buoy. The buoy might be just a mooring point for a fishing boat but General Sabban says that more often it is the first step in a surreptitious land grab. If the buoy isn't removed, he says, then within a few months it can evolve into a steel post. In mid-2011 his forces discovered one at Sabina Shoal that had evolved into a large commercial shipping container anchored to the reef. 'It's China, of course,' he says. Remembering the events of Mischief Reef in 1995, when the Philippines was caught napping, the sailors and marines have orders to remove everything they find. It's a game of cat and mouse, with the Chinese constantly testing the vigilance of the boys in blue and green.

The trip usually begins or ends on the main Philippine-held island: Thitu, or Pagasa as its inhabitants call it. Pagasa's name – 'hope' in

Tagalog – is appropriate, since hope is what sustains its small community. Thitu was one of the first islands to be occupied by Philippine forces and it's by far the largest at 37 hectares. It's big enough for a small settlement but not for the 1,260 metre-long runway that sticks out either side of it. The runway was built in the mid-1970s but is now only usable with the utmost care. In the words of Western Command's in-house magazine *Kanluran*, the 'runway is about to be completely detached due to erosion' by the sea. In early 2011 a Philippine Navy ship delivering materials to repair it ran aground on the surrounding reef. The armed forces declared they didn't have the resources or the skills to complete the job and appealed to the government to fund repairs by a civilian contractor. Pledges have been made but the waves are still eating away at the runway.

In 2001, the Philippines became the first country deliberately to settle civilians in the Spratlys but it requires a particularly tough constitution to stick out the conditions on Thitu/Pagasa. Officially, according to the 2010 census, the island has a population of 222. In reality, only around 60 live there at any one time. That's partly because the central government subsidy of $14,000 per year can only feed that many. Almost everything – except fish, salt and coconuts – comes by boat. Unlike the Vietnamese, the Filipinos haven't yet shipped in soil to make vegetable gardens. There's supposed to be a mobile phone station on the island but the signal is described as 'intermittent'.

The mayor of the island, in fact of the whole 'Kalayaan Island Group', is Eugenio Bito-onon. He was one of the pioneers, moving to Thitu/Pagasa in 1997 to work as a town planner for the hoped-for town. He's still planning, still hoping. Mayor Bito-onon dreams of a safe runway and a functioning harbour, of tourists flying in for infinity pools and pristine coral reefs, of yachts in a marina, of fishing boats stopping for supplies and a thriving community catering for all their needs. But nothing can move without an injection of central government funding and the government always has other priorities. In June 2012 Bito-onon opened the island's first school building with one teacher, three nursery children and five kindergarten pupils. It was just a single room with borrowed furniture but he hopes it will persuade more families to stay. Until then, children had been travelling 500 kilometres to Palawan, the nearest large island, for their education. He's pressing for the government to build a proper school with toilets and separate classrooms but is still waiting for the necessary $100,000 to get started.

China made diplomatic protests about the school opening, arguing it was a violation of its 'indisputable sovereignty' in the South China Sea. That seems to be the main reason why the Manila government's cheque-book remains closed. Its approach – policy might be too strong a word – has been to avoid giving China any reason to protest against activities on the Philippine-held islands and to hope thereby to maintain the status quo. The garrisons are clearly token forces and could be overrun within minutes by a determined enemy. Even on Thitu the defences consist of little more than a pair of 40-mm anti-air guns and the marines' personal weapons. In contrast to all the other occupied islands in the Spratlys, there are no anti-invasion obstacles in the water and almost no fortifications on land. An attempt to construct any would incur a protest from Beijing and, perhaps, repercussions. The Vietnamese just ignore such protests but the Filipinos take them more seriously.

One piece of construction that has been completed is a small statue of Tomas Cloma, the pioneer of Kalayaan. In a way, Mayor Bito-onon is Cloma's heir. He's responsible, in theory at least, for seven islands (Kota, Lawak, Likas, Pagasa, Panata, Parola and Patag) plus Rizal Reef, Ayungin Shoal, and dozens more unoccupied features and vast areas of sea in between. Thitu/Pagasa has a town hall but without a decent mobile phone signal it's hard to work from there. For most of the year, Kalayaan's local government operates from a small office in a dusty shopping development on the outskirts of Puerto Princesa, the capital of Palawan.

* * * * * *

By the time the People's Republic of China moved into the Spratly Islands in 1987–8, all the dry real estate had been occupied. Only barren reefs remained, clearly unable to sustain human life without the addition of hundreds of tons of concrete and steel and the provision of regular supply boats. Life has been particularly tough in these outposts. Although Chinese media reports always portray the occupants of the 'sea bastions' as ruddy-faced heroes brimming with patriotic zeal and socialist morals, sometimes they inadvertently reveal more of the truth. A March 2005 report in the *PLA Daily* newspaper, for example, hailed the inventiveness of one group of veteran soldiers stationed on Yongshu Jiao (Fiery Cross Reef) when trying to cheer up a newly arrived soldier, Chen Hao. Chen's birthday was approaching but 'there is neither butter nor eggs on the reef' so they made him a cake using bean curd. Chen's reaction to this confectionary delight was not recorded. In June 1994, Chinese radio reported that soldiers in the outposts 'once had sores in their mouths because of long periods without green vegetables' – an early symptom of scurvy – and described men stationed in 'lone pillboxes' for more than a year at a time.

More recent articles, while praising new developments, also tell us something of the continuing unpleasantness of life. A June 2012 report in the *PLA Daily* championed the delivery of kitchen equipment that is 'moisture and erosion-proof', 'sound-proof shields for generators' and glasses to protect against ultra-violet radiation. This seems to imply that metal fixtures are rusting away, that soldiers are living in close proximity to loud industrial machinery and suffering from sun-blindness. Almost every official picture of the reef forts is taken on a calm clear day when the sky is bright blue and the sea clear and calm. But for most of the year it's either 30°C and unbearably humid, or monsoon winds are blowing in one direction or another. From October to January there are periodic typhoons – with 200-kilometre-an-hour winds and waves occasionally large enough to break over the occupants' heads.

At the time of writing there are PRC-built blockhouses on eight reefs in the Spratlys: Cuarteron (Huayang Jiao), Fiery Cross (Yongshu Jiao), Gaven North (Nanxun Jiao) and Gaven South (Xinan Jiao), Johnson South (Chigua Jiao), Kennan (Dangmen Jiao), Mischief (Meiji Jiao) and Subi (Zhubi Jiao). Construction is also under way at a ninth, Eldad Reef (Anda Jiao). None were designed with aesthetics in mind: they're survival structures built to withstand waves, wind and military attack. Some have enough space for a basketball hoop or a table-tennis table and there's always the helipad for some *tai chi* but there's no chance of a game of football on any of them. Unlike the Philippine-controlled islands, which could be nature reserves, the clear purpose of the Chinese structures is to control the sea around them. They bristle with radar domes, satellite dishes and gun emplacements.

With no space to relax outside, the Chinese have turned inwards. Karaoke machines and video games have been available for some time but satellite connections now give soldiers access to the internet – officially for online learning but presumably for less high-minded purposes as well. For the past few years, all of the contending countries have been waging a logistical war – with each other and with the elements – to provide the best mobile phone coverage in the islands. Vietnam was the first to move, installing a base station in July 2006. Since then China has worked hard to catch up. Its first system in the Spratlys became operational in 2011 and in January 2013, China Telecom proudly announced that the largest outpost, Fiery Cross Reef, now has a working 3G mobile phone connection and it was busy rolling out coverage to the other garrisons. Across the archipelago soldiers and fishermen now have a choice of competing national phone companies. The Philippines is well behind the others, but at least the Filipino marines on Parola (Northeast Cay) can borrow the signal from their Vietnamese rivals on Dao Song Tu Tay (Southwest Cay) to call home.

* * * * * *

If it were ever asked to adjudicate the rightful ownership of the Spratly Islands, the International Court of Justice (ICJ) would have to unravel a very complex web of claims. Six states might try to pitch in: France – based on its discovery and occupation in 1933 and re-occupation in October 1946; the Philippines – based upon the proclamation of Vice-President Quirino in July 1946 (and possibly the activities of the United States as the colonial power during the 1930s); the (Taiwanese) Republic of China – based on its occupation in December 1946 and actions since (although since it's not a recognised member of the UN it wouldn't be able to present a case directly); the People's Republic of China – also based on the actions of the Republic of China and its claimed right to be the legitimate 'successor state'; and Vietnam – based upon its claim to be the successor state to French Indochina and its actions since.

The first thing the court would need to decide would be the 'critical date' – the moment at which the crucial events have all taken place and the dispute has 'crystallised'. The choice of date is usually critical to the outcome. For example, if the court had been asked to rule on Itu Aba's sovereignty in 1947, it would presumably have ruled in favour of France on the grounds that Paris had clearly asserted its claim and 'occupied' (in the legal sense) the island well before anyone else. But if asked the question now, the judges might decide to include more recent events – in particular the apparent failure of France to maintain its claim over the past 60 years – which would probably give an advantage to the Republic of China.

The 'critical date' has another related meaning: it's also the point after which actions taken by the parties in a dispute have no effect in the eyes of international law. Since the dispute has 'crystallised' – all sides have made their positions known – building a runway or incorporating islands into new provinces or drawing them on a new map will carry no weight at all with the judges at the ICJ. In the case of the South China Sea, the 'critical date' is certain to be a few decades ago. This basic piece of juris-prudence doesn't seem to be understood by the various claimants for the islands who persist in making irrelevant gestures and protesting about the irrelevant gestures made by others even though they are unlikely to have any bearing on the international legal situation. They are simply another bluffing strategy in their giant poker game.

If the parties chose to ask the question, the ICJ might be asked to rule on whether a claim to Itu Aba amounts to a valid claim on just one island, on the island's immediate surroundings or on the entire Spratly archipelago. There are precedents. For example, in a ruling on the status of eastern Greenland in 1933, the ICJ decided, in effect, that it was not necessary for a state to physically occupy every part of a remote and diffi-cult island to claim sovereignty over its entirety. If this precedent were followed, it's possible that a verdict on the sovereignty of Itu Aba would also apply to the other features of the coral atoll that it sits on – known as the Tizard Bank. They include the Vietnamese-occupied Namyit Island (Dao Nam Yet), Sand Cay (Da Son Ca) and Petley Reef (Da Nui Thi) and the Communist Chinese-occupied Gaven Reefs (Nanxun Jiao and Xinan Jiao) and Eldad Reef (Anda Jiao) which all lie within 40 kilometres of each other. However the court might also rule that these are separate islands carrying separate claims.

The more explosive question is whether a ruling on Itu Aba would apply to all the other islands in the Spratlys. Vietnam and both Chinas talk of their claims in this maximalist frame, declaring their sovereignty over the entire 'Truong Sa' and 'Nansha' archipelagos respectively. The Philippines speaks similarly, albeit for the subset of the Spratlys it calls the 'Kalayaan Island Group' (which includes Itu Aba). If all these states were to maintain their positions and ask a tribunal for a ruling on the islands as a whole, then the ownership of Spratly Island, Thitu and all the others would probably fall to whichever had the best claim to Itu Aba. Given that it has been in control of the island for most of the past 70 years, the winner is highly likely to be the Republic of China (Taiwan). The People's Republic of China (Beijing) would then need to argue that it has the legitimate right to succeed to the Republic of China's claim – opening a fresh can of worms.

Itu Aba would be the centrepiece of any South China Sea claimant's property portfolio and is clearly coveted by both Communist China and Vietnam. The occupants harbour a constant fear of invasion and an acute sense of vulnerability. Itu Aba is a dot in the ocean surrounded by hostile neighbours. The 1,400-kilometre sea journey from the nearest Taiwanese port, Kaohsiung, takes three days in good weather and much longer in a typhoon. Taiwanese governments have struggled to create an identity for the island that is both peaceful in intent but also resolute in defence. Unlike Spratly, Thitu or Woody islands there is little pretence about civilian life on Itu Aba: there are no children's schools or tourist hotels, for example.

In 1999, to try to de-escalate growing tension in the Sea, the government in Taipei announced that it was removing its marines from the island and replacing them with coastguards. But they are not ordinary coastguards: they are armed with 120mm mortars and 40mm cannon and trained by the military. In September 2012 they held live fire exercises to demonstrate how they would shoot up an invasion force. Like the two other largest islands in the Spratlys, Itu Aba's main feature is a runway, filling 1,200 metres of its 1,400 metre length. It was built in just 273 days and formally inaugurated with a flying visit from President Chen Shui-bian a month before the March 2008 presidential election. Chen declared the facility to be for 'humanitarian purposes' – to help in the rescue of stranded fishermen – but few believed him. The runway had been argued over for 15 years and stopped and started as relations with Beijing warmed and cooled. The opening was a gesture to demonstrate Chen's support for a more independent Taiwan. It failed to win Chen the election though.

The island is just 370 metres wide but it has its own supply of fresh water and a covering of natural vegetation. It's clearly able to support at least minimal human habitation, although the 120-strong garrison depend entirely upon supplies shipped from Taiwan. The strips of land either side of the runway host accommodation blocks, defensive emplacements, a solar power installation (to reduce the amount of diesel required to run the island's generators) and a conservation area for the island's population of endangered green sea turtles.

In short, Taiwan's position on Itu Aba is secure. It might therefore be better, in a legal sense, for Vietnam and the Philippines to modify their positions and no longer seek sovereignty over large groups of islands but over specific named features. Vietnam might then be able to demonstrate the strongest claim to Spratly Island (Truong Sa Lon) and potentially others, and the Philippines to Thitu Island (Pagasa) and potentially others, through long histories of occupation and use. The same might be possible between Vietnam and China for the Paracel Islands – with Vietnam's claim stronger to the Crescent group and China's claim stronger to the Amphitrite group. However, rolling back from their all-encompassing claims in the face of nationalist hypertension would require considerable political bravery.

* * * * * *

National pride is one reason why countries around the South China Sea expended blood and treasure to occupy the reefs and islands but right from the first claims on behalf of British guano-diggers in the 1870s, there have been economic motivations too. These days, with the bird droppings extracted and turned into fertiliser, the islands themselves contain almost nothing of value. Malaysia has turned Swallow Reef, which it calls Layang-Layang, into a diving resort with a hotel and swimming pool (next to the barracks, runway and naval harbour) but this is the only spot in the Sea that comes close to turning a profit. Apart from their somewhat overrated strategic importance (see Chapter 8), the rocks and islands are now only valuable because of the waters that surround them. That's the result of a new framework of international law that's grown up in the past half-century. This time, unlike the rules governing the grabbing of territory, none of the claimants can argue that they are victims of rules drawn up by medieval popes and nineteenth-century imperialists.

On 3 December 1973 members of the United Nations sat down in New York to draft a new Convention on the Law of the Sea. These heirs to John Selden and Hugo Grotius would spend the next nine years debating to whom the oceans belonged. The discussions were marked by the politics of the time. The war in Vietnam was in its final phase; the People's Republic of China was still a relatively new member of the UN; the Republic of China (Taiwan) had just lost its UN seat. The UNCLOS talks became a venue for Cold War arguments between capitalists and Communists but also between states that favoured freedom of the seas and those who wanted to keep others out – and away from 'their' resources.

As the UNCLOS negotiations dragged on, a compromise emerged around the concept of the 'Exclusive Economic Zone' (EEZ) and the ways it could be defined and claimed. An EEZ would not be 'territory' but coastal states would have the rights to exploit and regulate the resources flying over it, swimming within it, lying on the seabed and buried beneath it. As the diplomats debated, oil prices rose and governments grasped the implications. Whoever owned an island would own the rights to the fish, minerals and hydrocarbons surrounding it. As technology developed, governments issued offshore oil leases and exploration companies began to survey and drill further and further from land. UNCLOS had significantly raised the stakes in the South China Sea.

By the time the negotiations finally ended, at Montego Bay in Jamaica on 10 December 1982, the world's governments had agreed that coastal states could claim a territorial sea 12 nautical miles (22 kilometres) wide, an EEZ out to 200 nautical miles (370 kilometres) and perhaps an 'extended continental shelf' beyond that. They had also sketched out some broad principles for what does, and does not, count as territory. UNCLOS defines three kinds of maritime feature: 'islands' that can support human habitation or economic life; 'rocks' (including sandbanks and reefs above water at high tide) that cannot support either; and 'low-tide elevations' which, as the name suggests, are only dry at low tide. Although the exact definitions of 'human habitation' and 'economic life' were left unspecified, each type of sea feature was endowed with certain inalienable rights. Islands are regarded as 'land' and generate both a 12-nautical-mile territorial sea and a 200-nautical-mile EEZ. Rocks generate a 12-nautical-mile territorial sea, but no EEZ. Low-tide elevations generate nothing at all unless they are within 12 nautical miles of a piece of land or a rock, in which case they can be used as base-points from which the territorial sea and EEZ can be measured. As far as maritime resources are concerned, the difference between an island and a rock is vast. A rock generates a potential territorial sea of just 452 square nautical miles ($\pi \times 12 \times 12$). An island generates the same territorial waters but also a potential EEZ of at least 125,600 square nautical miles ($\pi \times 200 \times 200$).

On 22 January 2013 the Philippine government tried to change the terms of the South China Sea disputes by relegating traditional arguments about 'historic rights' over territory in favour of new arguments based upon UNCLOS. Rather than hold emotive debates about claims to wide areas of water, it tried to focus them onto designated pieces of sea based on distances from specific pieces of land. Its 20-page submission to the Permanent Court of Arbitration (PCA) in The Hague made clear that the Philippines wasn't seeking a ruling on the historical claims to the islands, or on any maritime boundaries, but purely on which features constituted islands and rocks and could thus be classed as 'territory', and on what kind of zones could be legitimately drawn from them.[10] The Manila government was hoping the PCA would rule that none of the features occupied by the People's Republic of China were islands capable of sustaining human habitation or economic life and were therefore unable to generate any EEZ whatsoever.

By forcing arbitration on these issues, the Philippines was explicitly seeking to have any historical claim to all the waters inside the 'U-shaped line' – based on a Chinese interpretation of the traditional model of international law – ruled invalid. Regardless of which country owned each rock, rights over the sea would be limited to – at best – a 12-nautical-mile radius around each feature. This would allow the Philippines to develop the oil and fish the seas within its EEZ, provided the resources lay outside the 12-nautical-mile potential territorial sea of each Chinese-occupied feature. A different court could make a ruling about ownership at a later date.

By the time the PRC joined the party in the Spratlys in the late 1980s, the best tables had been taken: only the cheap seats were left. Five of the eight PRC-occupied features are, at best, low-tide elevations (Mischief, Kennan, Subi, Gaven North and Gaven South Reefs). The remaining three, the Philippines case argues, are, at best, rocks that only generate a 12-nautical-mile territorial sea and no EEZ. UNCLOS is clear: it doesn't matter how large a fortress you build on a low-tide elevation; if the natural feature underneath would be under water at high tide then it doesn't generate any maritime territory. The same is true of all the features occupied by Malaysia (including Swallow Reef), most of those controlled by Vietnam and at least three of the Philippines' possessions. Constructed on low-tide elevations or reefs, they don't count as either islands or even rocks under UNCLOS.

The Philippines, Vietnam and the Republic of China (Taiwan) do control some features that might be classified as islands and therefore entitled to an EEZ. But to prove this to a tribunal they would need to establish that the islands can, in the words of UNCLOS, 'sustain human habitation or economic life of their own'. This is why all three go to such great lengths to develop civilian facilities wherever they can: houses and schools are clearly forms of human habitation and fishing depots and tourism plans are forms of economic life. All the children learning their multiplication tables on Thitu/Pagasa, and all the monks chanting their prayers on Spratly/Truong Sa Lon are, in their own small ways, helping to stake their country's maritime claims.

There are no children learning anything on the Scarborough Shoal but in April 2007 a group of grown men spent a week playing on it. They were amateur radio enthusiasts – 'DXers' – who compete to broadcast from the most extreme locations. They set off from Hong Kong on a chartered boat carrying all they would need: radio equipment and antennae of course – but also planks, sheets of wood, generators, umbrellas and life jackets. This was the fourth DXpedition to the Shoal since 1994 so the hams knew roughly what to expect. But when they arrived, they found almost nothing there. At high tide, just six rocks protrude above the sea: none more than two metres high and, at most, only three or four metres across. They set to work. In order to qualify for DX status, the transmissions had to take place on the rocks themselves but there wasn't a flat surface anywhere.

Using planks, they managed to construct a small platform on each one – just big enough for a table and chair, a generator, a radio and an umbrella. Working in shifts they then broadcast to fellow DXers around the world for five days.

To outsiders it may seem a bizarre and incomprehensible way to spend a holiday but the trip was the fruit of a long and emotionally charged battle with echoes of the geopolitical disputes in the South China Sea. There had been long arguments within the DX community about whether Scarborough Shoal qualified for 'new country status' – a marque that would unlock a flood of support from hobbyists keen to add another notch to their radio reception bedposts. In June 1995, a committee of the American Radio Relay League had tried to impose a minimum size rule for islands in order to disqualify Scarborough from consideration. It echoed the wording of UNCLOS, declaring that 'rocks which cannot sustain human habitation shall not be considered for DXCC country status'. However, the DX adventurers and their supporters lobbied to get the decision overturned – and seven months later they were successful. But, as the DXpeditioners conclusively proved, Scarborough Shoal is completely incapable of supporting human habitation. Even with timber, generators and umbrellas it was utterly inhospitable for more than a few hours at a time. There is a specific rule for this kind of feature in UNCLOS: it is a 'rock', so it generates a 12-nautical-mile territorial sea, but no EEZ or continental shelf whatsoever.

None of this deterred China's maritime authorities from expending an extraordinary amount of effort to wrest control of Scarborough Shoal from the Philippines during 2012. A standoff began on 10 April when Philippine coastguards tried to prevent eight Chinese fishing boats making off with a great hoard of coral, giant clams and even live sharks. Two large China Marine Surveillance ships then arrived to prevent the fishermen being arrested. The Philippines sent its biggest warship, the BRP *Gregorio del Pilar* (a former US Coastguard cutter built in 1965), before rethinking the decision and replacing it with coastguard ships. With a typhoon approaching, both governments agreed to withdraw their vessels – but only the Filipinos did so, leaving the Chinese in physical control of the shoal.

There is one other kind of feature that appears in Chinese territorial claims to the South China Sea but is conspicuously absent from the text of UNCLOS: the underwater feature. Under UNCLOS there are no grounds at all for any state to claim ownership of a shoal or a bank that is under water at low tide: they are simply a part of the seabed. Article 5 of UNCLOS declares that the usual baseline for measuring a territorial sea is the low-tide mark. Underwater features, by definition, have no low-tide mark and therefore cannot have a territorial sea of their own. But that hasn't prevented the Chinese asserting a territorial claim based on 'historic rights' to the Macclesfield Bank and to the James Shoal (Zengmu Ansha) – both of which lie well below the surface.

As we saw in Chapter 2, the highest point of James Shoal is a full 22 metres below the sea and its status as the 'southernmost point of Chinese territory' is probably derived from a translation mistake by a Chinese government committee in 1935. It lies 107 kilometres off the coast of Borneo and more than 1,500 kilometres from the coast of Hainan Island. It's well beyond any possible Chinese territorial waters claimable under UNCLOS. The weight of nationalist sentiment, however, prevents Beijing from making a sensible retreat from this nonsensical position. Even now, Chinese naval ships en route to anti-piracy patrols off the coast of Somalia still make a diversion to the shoal to demonstrate Chinese sovereignty over it. But since there isn't any dry land there on which to erect official monuments, they have to drop them over the side of their ships instead. There's now a small collection of Chinese steles lying on the seabed below. In March 2013 and January 2014 Chinese naval ships held military exercises at the shoal and added yet more rubble to the mound.

Interestingly, in another maritime dispute Beijing has rejected the idea that underwater features can have territorial status. Socotra Rock, also known as Ieodo or Suyan Rock, lies about 5 metres below the surface in the Yellow Sea, about halfway between the coasts of China and Korea. The South Korean government has built an ocean research station upon it, provoking protests from Beijing, but on 12 March 2012 China's Foreign Ministry spokesman asserted that 'China and the Republic of Korea have a consensus on the Suyan Rock, that is, the rock does not have territorial status and the two sides have no territorial disputes'. This consensus, however, doesn't seem to apply to the James Shoal or to another, much larger underwater feature: the Macclesfield Bank.

The Macclesfield Bank is much closer to China and considerably bigger than the James Shoal: about 140 kilometres long and 60 kilometres wide. It's also slightly closer to the surface: its shallowest point is only 9 metres below the waves. In the neat official nomenclature adopted in 1947, Macclesfield Bank is the 'central sands archipelago' – Zhongsha Qundao – to match the western sands (Xisha or Paracels), eastern sands (Dongsha or Pratas) and southern sands (Nansha or Spratly) archipelagos. But the Zhongsha 'archipelago' is a work of geographical fiction. In official Chinese parlance, it groups the Macclesfield Bank with several other underwater features between Helen Shoal in the north and Dreyer Shoal in the south. Most controversially it includes Scarborough Shoal to the east, the only part of the Zhongsha that protrudes above the surface. Maps of the seabed, however, make clear that there is no 'archipelago' in the accepted sense of the word: there is no chain of islands, just isolated underwater features separated by wide areas of some of the deepest sea on the planet. None of these underwater features can generate any EEZ whatsoever. Only Scarborough Shoal could generate, at best, a 12-nautical-mile territorial sea.

There are no grounds under UNCLOS for China to claim sovereignty over James Shoal, Macclesfield Bank or areas of water beyond 12 nautical miles from any land feature within the 'U-shaped line'. There is simply no mention of historic rights in UNCLOS, except in relation to areas within the territorial waters of an 'archipelagic state' – which China is not. By ratifying UNCLOS – which it did in 1996 – China signed away its right to claim 'historic rights' in other countries' EEZs – at least under UNCLOS. Instead, some Chinese state officials have been trying to argue a case based in the traditional form of international law: contending that Chinese explorers and fishermen have roamed the waters of the South China Sea for centuries and that those activities provide a basis to claim all the land – and all the sea – within the 'U-shaped line'. In other words, they are attempting to use an older form of international law to try to negate any rulings based upon UNCLOS. At its most extreme, the mobilisation of this argument appears to be an attempt to rewrite international law in China's favour and legitimise a territorial claim on everything within the 'U-shaped line'. Most scholars of the subject regard this argument as flawed on historical grounds and specious on legal ones but if the

Permanent Court of Arbitration rules in favour of the claim submitted by the Philippines in 2013, then it could become the mainstay of China's claim to the South China Sea. There is more on this in Chapter 9.

* * * * * *

So what would be the impact on the Sea as a whole if, by some unexpected alignment of geopolitical forces, the historical claims were to be taken to the International Court of Justice and all sides agreed to respect the result? Clearly we can't know for sure, but an excellent guide to the likely outcome is Professor Robert Beckman of the Centre for International Law at the National University of Singapore. He's been watching the disputes for a quarter of a century from his office next to the city-state's Botanic Gardens and has come to some conclusions. His review of previous ICJ judgments suggests that the effect of all the past half-century's island-grabbing might actually be surprisingly small. The ICJ has been generally sceptical towards large EEZ claims put forward on the basis of small rocks and islands when they overlap with claims from a mainland coast or larger island. In Beckman's words, 'it is not simply a question of drawing an equidistance line between the island and the mainland territory'. For example, in a 2009 judgment on a dispute between Romania and Ukraine over the alarmingly named 'Serpent's Island' in the Black Sea, the ICJ emphasised the relative lengths of the coastlines involved. In other words, they regarded the hundreds of kilometres of Romania's mainland coastline as much more significant than the 2-kilometre circumference of Serpent's Island. The resulting international boundary took no account of the island apart from giving it the standard 12-nautical-mile territorial sea. Another ICJ ruling, in November 2012, on a similar dispute over Colombian islands off the coast of Nicaragua, confirmed the principle that relative lengths of coastline are a key factor in judging maritime boundaries.[11]

The situation in the South China Sea is more complicated than in the Black Sea or the Caribbean because of the numbers of rocks, islands and claimants involved. However, it is entirely conceivable that the ICJ would take a similar approach. Even if we were to assume what, in the eyes of the Southeast Asian states, would be the worst-case scenario – that every rock and island in the sea is awarded to the Chinese – that wouldn't result in great chunks of each country's coastal EEZ being awarded to Beijing. It's more likely, according to Beckman, that EEZs drawn from the islands would extend the other way – into the centre of the sea and therefore 'reduce or completely eliminate the pocket of high seas in the middle of the South China Sea'. The result – in this 'Beijing-takes-all' scenario – would be a kite-shaped area of Chinese EEZ running southwest to northeast surrounded by the EEZs of all the other coastal states. A more limited ruling, awarding just Itu Aba in the Spratlys and the Paracel Islands to a 'combined China', would have a similar, though smaller effect.

However, taking the issue to the ICJ would require the consent of all disputing parties and since none could have confidence in the outcome, there's little incentive to agree. A government that 'lost' territory in an international judgment would formally cede the rights to the resources there and could expect to incur the wrath of angry sections of its population. The political risks are great. Nonetheless, there are signs of quiet compromise among the Southeast Asian claimants. In May 2009, Malaysia and Vietnam submitted to the UN a joint claim on their 'extended continental shelves' that ignored the question of which island belonged to which country and simply measured distances from their respective coastlines. Since 2009 the Philippines has modified its sweeping claim to a wide area of the Sea (the Kalayaan Island Group) into claims on specific islands (which are based on historic claims) and specific areas of sea measured from them according to the rules laid down in UNCLOS. But China has the most to lose from modifying its claim into one compatible with UNCLOS because the result would fragment the 'U-shaped line' into a series of smaller zones around particular islands. While the Chinese government as a whole continues to maintain 'strategic ambiguity' over what the line actually means, key elements within it (the military, the oil companies and southern coastal provinces) continue to act on the basis that China maintains a historic territorial claim to the whole Sea.

All the disputants assert a 'historic claim' to the reefs, rocks and islands they currently occupy and most of them (Vietnam, the Philippines and both Chinas – but not Malaysia or Brunei) claim all or some of the other features as well. These territorial claims are based upon the traditional norms of international law: occupation, prescription, cession and accretion. Before any resolution process could begin, the participants would have to decide whether the court should hear historic arguments first and make a judgment upon which rocks and islands rightfully belong to which country or whether to postpone those arguments and just make UNCLOS-based rulings on maritime zones and resolve ownership later. While the outcome of the former is highly uncertain, the latter would generally favour the Southeast Asian claimants over China. Hence Beijing increasingly talks about 'historic rights' while Southeast Asia increasingly talks about UNCLOS.

The rules of international law have long favoured the conquerors and explorers of previous centuries. The United Nations Convention on the Law of the Sea was an attempt to redress the balance and give coastal states more control over the resources that surround them. But the earth's geography is not equal. The arrangements of the continents and national borders have left some coastal states with access to great expanses of sea and others with much less. Japan's EEZ, for example, stretches into the Pacific Ocean whereas China's is blocked by Japan and, further south, by the Philippines and Vietnam. This sense of geographical injustice, exacerbated by nationalist anger at the 'century of humiliation', explains China's dogged pursuit of 'historic rights' in the South China Sea. China's diplomats have become expert in the use of opaque language to satisfy the minimum of its international obligations while keeping its future options as open as possible. China gains minimal legal advantage from the reefs it occupies but without a physical position in the Spratlys its territorial arguments would be purely theoretical. The outposts have given Beijing a seat at the head of a table where realpolitik has always been more important than international law.

Richard Spratly was free 170 years ago to hunt in whichever patch of sea he thought would bring the best returns. The lights and lips of America and Europe burned brightly with the oil and cosmetic ingredients he and the other rich-country whalers harvested. The result was the catastrophic decimation of the whale population. The search for a different kind of oil and the fear of a similar free-for-all eventually led the world's governments to agree to rules on how to divide up the world's maritime resources. But in the South China Sea the hunt for oil has continued to be an enduring source of instability . . . as we shall see next.

CHAPTER 5

Something and Nothing
Oil and Gas in the South China Sea

IN AUGUST 1990, Southeast Asia was getting very excited about the 'return of China'. It had been a year since the massacre in Tiananmen Square and many influential people thought it was time to get back to business. To much fanfare, one of the men behind the massacre, Premier Li Peng, embarked on a nine-day regional tour. His second stop was Singapore and after the usual civilities and state dinners, on 13 August he gave a news conference. Most questions focused on whether the two countries would resume diplomatic ties and few journalists noticed Li's apparently friendly announcement that China is 'ready to join efforts with Southeast Asian countries to develop the Nansha islands while putting aside, for the time being, the question of sovereignty'.[1] It wasn't an idle remark. It was the first public declaration of a policy originally advocated by Deng Xiaoping in talks with Japan over the East China Sea in October 1978, and subsequently raised with Philippine leaders in private meetings in 1986 and 1988: 'This generation is not wise enough to settle such a difficult issue. It would be an idea to count on the wisdom of following generations to settle it.' The statement has been the basis of Chinese state policy towards both the East and South China seas ever since.

In 1990 the Chinese leadership was fretting about energy. After 30 years in which China had been self-sufficient in oil, thanks to its inland field at Daqing, it was clear that the growing demand unleashed by

Deng's economic reforms would soon outstrip production. The country needed new sources of supply. In April 1987 Chinese scientists surveyed parts of the South China Sea and rapidly afterwards declared the existence of 'rich oil and gas reserves on the Zengmu [James] Shoal' off the coast of Borneo.[2] In December 1989, the *China Daily* reported official calculations that the Spratly Islands contained 25 billion cubic metres of natural gas and 105 billion barrels of oil and the James Shoal area a further 91 billion barrels.[3] Deng and other political leaders began talking about the Sea as the answer to the looming crisis. That theme was amplified by key voices in the energy sector and the military. *Jiefangjun bao*, the newspaper of the People's Liberation Army, published a series of articles between 1987 and 1990[4] linking the 'sacred' importance of defending national territory with pragmatic arguments in favour of harvesting the Sea's resources.[5]

These discussions were ignored in Southeast Asia. China was far away and lacked the means and expertise to develop anything more than a few miles from its shores. When Li Peng proposed joint development in the Spratlys, it was interpreted as empty posturing. Opinions would change. There was more to Deng's policy than simply postponing disagreements. Its full formulation had three elements: 'sovereignty is ours, set aside disputes, pursue joint development', of which the first was most significant. It meant, in effect, that any other country wanting to develop maritime resources within the 'U-shaped line' would either have to recognise Beijing's territorial claims or directly challenge Beijing's physical presence. Since none would recognise Chinese sovereignty, Li Peng's Singapore declaration has become the basis for the current disputes.

Until that moment, Beijing's interest appeared to be confined to the islands and reefs it had occupied in 1974 and 1987–8. After 1990 it became clear that many interest groups in Beijing wanted to enforce the 'sovereignty is ours' doctrine throughout the entire area within the U-shaped line. Chief among them was the China National Offshore Oil Company, CNOOC. But the person who pushed CNOOC to make its first move was an American.

* * * * * *

In 1992, a man from Colorado changed the game in the South China Sea by perfecting the art of modern alchemy: turning nothing into gold. He rewrote the rules of Southeast Asian oil prospecting, brought two countries to the edge of conflict and walked away with several million dollars. In the process, China made plain for the first time that its 'U-shaped line' claim wasn't just a historical relic but a statement of future intent and its neighbours came to learn that China's quest for energy security would threaten their own. But the story of Southeast Asia's resource wars has an unlikely beginning. It starts in 1969 with a young man walking several miles to the Denver Country Club to be interviewed for a golf caddy scholarship.

Randall C. Thompson's parents had divorced and neither could afford a car so Thompson made his own way to the interview. He flunked it, but one of the panel, impressed by the young man's grit, persuaded his colleagues to send him to the University of Colorado anyway, to study political science. The benefactor was Sonny Brinkerhoff, from the family that owned the Brinkerhoff Drilling Company. The following summer Brinkerhoff offered the 50 scholarship winners work on his oil wells in Wyoming; Thompson was the only one who applied. He liked the work and laboured for Brinkerhoff the next summer too. The summer after that, he graduated and went to see Brinkerhoff again. By the end of the day Thompson had a job as a landman with Amoco Corporation – searching out likely-looking oil prospects and negotiating the exploration rights.

Thompson learned the trade for six years and then moved on, got fired, quit another job, got fired again and quit a fifth job. He wasn't enjoying working for other people so, in 1980, he went back to see Sonny Brinkerhoff. He walked out of Brinkerhoff's office at the age of 31 with the rights to $1 million worth of oil-producing properties: Crestone Energy was born. It wasn't easy. With oil prices per barrel in the low teens, Crestone was just breaking even. But in 1989, Thompson took a call that would change his life. Edward Durkee was another Colorado oilman and one of the original 30 investors in Crestone. By 1989 he was working for the Swedish company Lundin Oil, which was looking to offload its interests in the Philippines. Durkee told Thompson it was a sure thing: 'Come here now or I'll never talk to you again.' The following day Thompson and his lawyer were on a plane to Manila.

Durkee lined everything up. Nine days later, on 4 September 1989, Crestone bought Lundin's exploration licence and immediately sold a 40 per cent stake in it to a consortium of seven Philippine companies. Thompson left Manila with a briefcase full of cash. Crestone now owned a majority stake in an exploration block, GSEC 54, off the island of Palawan. It covered about one and a half million hectares: from the existing Philippine fields all the way to the border with Malaysia. Crestone and its partners went over the old seismic data, searching for evidence of recoverable oil. It looked good. Just seven months later, in April 1990, they sold a 70 per cent stake in the block to British Petroleum (BP) for a few million dollars. Crestone had another briefcase full of cash. A year later, in April 1991, BP did find oil, but not in commercial quantities and a year after that it abandoned the Philippines altogether, returning the rights to Crestone's consortium. In oil industry terms there was nothing there, but Thompson had successfully turned it into gold anyway.

More importantly for the region, Thompson had discovered the South China Sea. At the party after the BP signing, in the home of the British ambassador to Manila, the beer flowed and tongues loosened. 'Alcohol was talking when it should have been confidential,' Thompson recalls, 'and everybody said Vietnam is going to be hot and the BP guys said, in so many words, it's the deep water in the Nansha islands.[6] The next day I went to the library to find out where the Nansha islands were.' In 1990 Vietnam was off-limits to American oil companies because the wartime US trade embargo was still in place. BP and some other European companies had started sniffing around but the only people actually pumping oil there were the Russians. Memories of a brief oil boom in the dying months of the Vietnam War lingered and that was all the incentive Thompson needed. He spent three weeks after the ambassador's reception scouring geological records and old surveys. He eventually settled on a patch of seabed between the Vietnamese coast and Vietnamese-occupied Spratly Island encompassing the Prince Consort Bank and the Vanguard Bank. But rather than head to Vietnam, Thompson learned all about the 'U-shaped line' and set his hopes on China instead.

In April 1991 Thompson travelled to the South China Sea Institute of Oceanography in Guangzhou to examine the seismic surveys that had been loudly trumpeted a few years before. 'They showed me some structures, I got excited about it and then I did some more research.' He pressed flesh and hosted dinners, trying to persuade the Chinese to take Crestone seriously until, in February 1992, after much deliberation at the highest levels in Beijing, he finally got to pitch his proposal to the board of CNOOC. Thompson took two advisors to precisely define the patch of seabed he wanted the rights to: his original mentor Ed Durkee and Daniel J. Dzurek, the former Chief of the Boundary Division of the US Department of State. The shape of the block they drew resembled a pistol with the handgrip pointing south and the barrel pointing east. The strange perimeter managed to include the likely oil prospects while touching, but not going over, the Indonesian, Malaysian and Brunei claim lines in four places. 'I took Ed Durkee to outline the block from a technical standpoint and Dan Dzurek to outline it from a political standpoint. We took great care to not get into Philippine waters, or Indonesian, Malaysian or Brunei waters,' Thompson remembers. If his block looked like a weapon, it was aimed only at the Vietnamese.

The same month that Thompson pitched his idea to CNOOC, the Chinese National People's Congress approved a 'Law concerning Territorial Waters and Adjacent Regions'. The Law formalised China's 1958 'Declaration on the Territorial Sea' (see Chapter 4), thereby claiming the Macclesfield Bank, the Paracels and the Spratlys and creating the legal basis – at least in Beijing's eyes – to lease out exploration blocks far from the mainland. The piece of seabed that interested Thompson was just 250 kilometres off the Vietnamese coast and more than 1,000 kilometres from the beaches of China. The audacity was breath-taking; even CNOOC was out of its depth – technically and politically. Thompson says he had to encourage CNOOC to give him the rights without a general auction, warning its executives that publicity would only cause problems with the Vietnamese.[7]

At this point Crestone had four employees: Thompson, a secretary, a receptionist and a part-time accountant. In the end he got his deal. CNOOC awarded one of the smallest oil companies in the world the rights to a huge area of sea: 25,155 square kilometres. It cost Crestone just $50,000. The Chinese called the exploration block 'Wan An Bei-21' (WAB-21). Under the deal, CNOOC would provide its existing geophysical data and retain the right to buy 51 per cent of the lease at a later date if it should prove profitable. Crestone would undertake more seismic surveying and cover the development costs. For the Chinese political leadership, Thompson was a dream come true. Here was a man, an American man, willing to physically assert China's territorial claim off the Vietnamese coast. Crestone would take all the flak while CNOOC could sit back and watch.

Thompson was bullish about the prospects and nonchalant about the political risk. When Crestone signed the lease on 8 May 1992, he told journalists he believed there was 'way in excess of 1.5 billion barrels of oil' in the block and that he would 'rather look for oil and gas in an area with high potential, low technical risk and bad politics than the other way round'. He was also happy with a pledge by the Chinese authorities of their 'full naval might' to defend his claim, if it came to a confrontation with the Vietnamese. The United States government kept clear. An American diplomat had attended the signing ceremony in Beijing but the embassy denied any involvement in Crestone's negotiations. Indeed, Thompson says that in the days after the signing both the US State Department and the CIA called him to try and find out what he was up to. The State Department in particular was concerned – warning Thompson to keep American personnel and equipment out of the block because of the risk of seizure by the Vietnamese.[8]

Because of the political sensitivity, Thompson could take his time: Crestone was not obliged to drill any wells for seven years. Meanwhile, the Vietnamese vented their anger, lodging official protests with the Chinese government and printing condemnatory newspaper articles. A verbal war continued for a year and a half. All the time Crestone continued its preparatory work. Then, in December 1993, Thompson was invited for talks in Hanoi with Dr Ho Si Thoang, the chairman of Vietnam's state-owned oil company, PetroVietnam. He was offered a deal: a joint venture, but only if he cancelled his existing agreement with CNOOC. Thompson declined, and the Vietnamese became even angrier. They prepared to deploy much bigger allies than Crestone.

For a few years American companies had been busy trying to line up deals in Vietnam. Among them was Mobil – itching to return to a prospect it had first identified just before the collapse of South Vietnam in 1975: an area it called 'Blue Dragon' inside what the Vietnamese, more mundanely, called Block 5.1b. Although it didn't overlap WAB-21, it was within the

'U-shaped line'. At the same time, PetroVietnam was also negotiating with another big American company, Conoco, about Blocks 133, 134 and 135 that definitely did overlap WAB-21. Nearby, Atlantic Richfield and British Gas were about to start drilling in another Vietnamese block claimed by China.[9] None, however, appeared concerned about the risk of alienating Beijing. On 3 February 1994 the day these companies had been waiting for arrived: the United States formally lifted its trade embargo on Vietnam and they rushed to sign contracts.

Crestone, however, was determined to be first to physically stake its claim. By April 1994, Thompson's friends in the South China Sea Institute of Oceanography were ready to go. The institute had been given the funding and the green light from Beijing to undertake a new round of seismic survey work in the northern part of the sea. Thompson persuaded them to change location – and head to WAB-21. As Mobil and its Japanese partners prepared to formally sign the Blue Dragon deal with PetroVietnam, Thompson and the institute were hard at work out at sea. On Tuesday 19 April, as the signing went ahead in the Military Guest House in Hanoi, Crestone announced it had begun seismic survey work in WAB-21 and was planning to drill its first exploratory wells, 'with China's full support'.[10]

Mobil clearly didn't take Crestone's activities seriously: at least not seriously enough to prevent it (and its Japanese partners) handing over $27 million for the rights to its block. According to Mobil's then communications manager, R. Thomas Collins, however, PetroVietnam specifically asked the company to announce that it was returning to an area it had previously explored under a licence from the previous South Vietnamese government in order to bolster its territorial claim.[11] Out at sea, things were about to get rough.

The Chinese ship never finished its survey. According to Thompson, after four days gathering data, three Vietnamese naval vessels appeared and fired across its bow. 'I was on a Chinese boat where no-one spoke English, being fired at by a Vietnamese boat where no-one spoke English,' he recalls. After a two-day standoff, Thompson and the ship's captain decided there was no point continuing and headed back to Guangzhou. Despite its earlier promises of full support, the Chinese Navy didn't show up. 'They didn't want a confrontation,' says Thompson. But Beijing was just biding its time.

Immediately after the Chinese had retreated, PetroVietnam rushed to assert its claim to the same piece of sea. On 17 May 1994, the *Tam Dao*, a drilling rig belonging to its Russian joint venture, VietSovPetro, moved onto the Vanguard Bank. This area, Block 135 to the Vietnamese, was the one Conoco was intending to lease, although it lay inside the southwestern corner of Crestone's WAB-21.[12] Now it was time for the Chinese to move. They deployed two ships but made no attempt to evict the rig. Instead they laid siege: blocking supplies of drilling mud and food. Details of what happened are sketchy but the rig's crew stuck out the siege for several weeks. According to Ian Cross, at the time a consultant with Integrated Exploration and Development Services in Singapore, they drilled down to about 3,000 metres but found no oil. According to Thompson, 'they didn't know what they were doing, the rig wasn't properly positioned. They just went to demonstrate sovereignty.' Certainly VietSovPetro never made any public announcement about what it found.

China's 1992 territorial law, its oil survey work, the Crestone contract and other displays of Beijing's seriousness about its 'U-shaped line' claim had deeply worried the governments of Southeast Asia. For some time, the six members of the Association of Southeast Asian Nations (ASEAN) had been discussing whether Vietnam should join their ranks. There were many factors to consider but as the oil confrontation escalated, the diplomacy accelerated. A flurry of visits and meetings in April and May 1994 led to an announcement on 11 July that Vietnam would be invited to join – even though it hadn't formally applied for membership. On 19 July, news of the *Tam Dao* standoff leaked to the outside world just as the final preparations were being made for the ASEAN foreign ministers' meeting at which the formal invitation would be extended to Vietnam. A week after the meeting, the Chinese military staged highly publicised exercises on Hainan Island demonstrating, in the words of the official media, 'almost the entire range of armaments, equipment and techniques'.[13] Such heavy-handedness only increased Southeast Asia's nervousness about China's intentions.

ASEAN's invitation may have been the trigger for a sudden change of tactics by Beijing. On 5 September 1994, after a month of closed-door discussions, it was announced that Jiang Zemin would make the first ever visit to Vietnam by a Chinese president. And by the end of the month, the Chinese had also offered to lend Vietnam $170 million to refurbish outdated manufacturing plants. Both sides were making a determined effort to repair relations. One reason may have been to smooth relations with ASEAN but another was probably that Beijing was already making secret preparations to occupy Mischief Reef (see Chapter 3). Around this time news had leaked from Manila that Alcorn Petroleum had begun survey work in another disputed area of the Sea, the Reed Bank off the Philippines. Perhaps the de-escalation with Vietnam was simply a ploy to divide potential opposition to the impending operation. This would also explain why, in January 1995, as the Mischief Reef incident unfolded, the Chinese authorities told Crestone to slow down its exploration work.

The situation was at stalemate. Thompson didn't have the funds to develop any prospects into commercial propositions. Crestone needed a company with an equally blasé attitude to political risk and much deeper pockets. What Thompson needed was a company like Benton Oil and Gas: a veteran of the rough and tumble of post-Soviet Russia. During 1996, on the back of the oil boom, Benton's share price tripled: it was ready for a piece of South China Sea action. On 24 September 1996 Benton agreed to buy Crestone for a cool $15.45 million. The deal was signed on 6 December with Benton noting that 'Crestone's primary asset is a petroleum contract with CNOOC'.[14] That was Block WAB-21, from which not a barrel of oil had yet been extracted. Once again, Randall C. Thompson had managed to turn a commercial nothing into a large pile of gold. Crestone's shareholders, of whom there were now around 130, made a tidy pile. Benton's fate wasn't so rosy. In 1998 and 1999, with the oil price crashing to $12 per barrel, the Benton Company was forced to write off a staggering $204 million. It survived by selling assets. But in mid-August 1999 the company's founder Alex Benton filed for personal bankruptcy and by September he'd been forced to resign as Chairman and CEO.

On 14 May 2002 Benton Oil and Gas changed its name to Harvest Natural Resources, making it sound more like a manufacturer of granola bars than an oil company with a penchant for political risk. It still owns the Chinese rights to Block WAB-21 though it now values them much less. In 2002 it wrote off their worth by $13.4 million dollars (almost 90 per cent of what it paid back in 1996). However, it still nurses the hope that one day they may come good. Between 2003 and 2008 it spent $661,000 on exploration and data acquisition in the block and presumably more since then, though it no longer itemises the expenses in its annual reports. Randall Thompson enjoys a fine life in Colorado, taking his grandchildren fishing. He's still active in the oil business and at the time of writing is seeking out new prospects off Italy, Morocco, New Zealand and South Africa. He still owns the rights to 4.5 per cent of the proceeds of Block WAB-21 – if it is ever drilled.

* * * * * *

The China National Offshore Oil Corporation's first foray into disputed waters failed to deliver any oil and, worse, united Southeast Asia in alarm. For 13 years Li Peng's offer of joint development was politely ignored: other governments weren't willing to 'put aside the question of sovereignty'. Vietnam, Indonesia, Malaysia and Brunei continued to lease their offshore waters to international oil companies and Crestone's block remained an anomaly. There was no need to seek any kind of joint development with Beijing. But in 2003 one government broke ranks. Surprisingly it was the country that, until then, had most strongly advocated a united ASEAN front towards Chinese encroachments: the Philippines. A small group at the top of Manila politics engineered the about-face, almost as a private initiative. They bypassed the established policy-making structures and set relations with China – and the region – on a radically different course.

In 2003, Jose de Venecia Jr was speaker of the House of Representatives, the lower house of the Philippine parliament, and president of the ruling party, the Lakas-Christian Muslim Democrats. As a young man, he'd made a fortune supplying Filipino labour to contractors in the Middle East and later he'd been involved in the first oil exploration off the coast of Palawan island. With money, family connections and political muscle he was a significant force in Philippine politics. He also made a point of developing close relations with China through, among other things, the International Conference of Asian Political Parties (ICAPP), which he launched in 2000, and the Association of Asian Parliaments for Peace (AAPP), of which he was president.

In 2003 Gloria Macapagal Arroyo had been Philippine president for two years, in which time trade with China – mainly exports of raw materials – had tripled: from $1.8 billion in 2001 to $5.3 billion in 2003.

With the US focused on its 'war on terror' in the Middle East, China saw an opening. In 2001, Beijing offered $400 million in soft loans for the 'NorthRail' project to link Manila to the former US airbase in Clark Economic Zone. When the project finally broke ground on 5 April 2004 the keynote speech, paying copious thanks to the Chinese government, was delivered by its main proponent: Jose de Venecia.[15]

Like de Venecia, Eduardo Manalac had been part of the team that drilled the Philippines' first offshore oil well in 1974. Unlike de Venecia, Manalac had stayed in the oil business, spending 28 years with the American company Phillips Petroleum, including seven as its China Exploration Manager. In 2000, he helped discover China's largest offshore field (in the Bohai Bay – far from any international boundary disputes) and was awarded both the Chinese government's 'Friendship Award' and CNOOC's 'Model Worker Award'. As a professional, Manalac knew exactly what was wrong with the Philippine oil sector. After retiring from Phillips, he offered his services to his homeland 'as payback for the cheap university tuition I once enjoyed' and in March 2003, was appointed Undersecretary of Energy. Although very different people with very different interests, Manalac and de Venecia would broker a deal between the Philippines and China that would startle the region.

Manalac knew China well but he wanted the Philippine oil and gas sector to stand on its own feet. He believed the real problem was internal: the small circle of local companies with access to the Ministry of Energy but not enough capital to invest in exploration. They were crowding out international players who might be ready to risk a few hundred million dollars to drill a well in untried waters. During 2003, Manalac organised the Philippines' first ever transparent bidding round to try and attract big companies to explore offshore. ExxonMobil took the rights to an area of the Sulu Sea but none was interested in the South China Sea. Manalac believed the prospects were good but, if the Philippines was ever to escape its near-total dependency on imported oil, it would need a different approach, one that took account of the geopolitical situation. 'My sense was that none of the big guys would dare enter that area as long as there are multiple [territorial] claims. Being as it's deep water it will entail a large amount of capital to drill and develop,' he recalls. 'I asked whether the President would support an idea where we go with the other countries that are claiming and do a joint development effort. And she said yes.'

Meanwhile de Venecia cultivated his links with the Chinese leadership. In April 2002 he organised the third annual meeting of his AAPP in Beijing and in March 2003 he was head of the government delegation to the first Philippine trade fair in Shanghai.[16] In September 2003 he hosted Wu Bangguo, who was both his counterpart as head of China's National People's Congress and also the chairman of the AAPP. While in Manila, Wu witnessed the signing of a $1 billion currency swap arrangement between the two countries' central banks (intended to defend the Philippines against a repeat of the 1997 Asian financial crisis) and addressed a meeting of congressional leaders. Afterwards de Venecia told journalists that 'Mr Wu proposed a joint exploration and development programme in the Spratlys'. De Venecia endorsed the idea, saying 'These areas are idle and we might as well let them bloom for joint profit sharing or multiple profit sharing by all.'[17] And it was agreed that 'a major Chinese oil exploration company' would send a delegation to Manila in November. On 10 November 2003 a letter of intent to 'engage in a joint programme to review, assess and evaluate relevant geological, geophysical and other technical data available to determine the oil and gas potential of the area' was duly signed between the Philippine National Oil Company (PNOC) and CNOOC.[18]

Quietly, Manalac and CNOOC executives drew up the boundaries of an exploration area. The western boundary had to avoid Malaysian waters but the northern and eastern limits were just a matter between the two sides. Ultimately it covered 143,000 square kilometres north and west of Palawan – including, but extending far beyond, the area of shallow sea known as the Reed Bank. Manalac knew the idea of sharing the resources was intensely controversial both at home and abroad but, as another PNOC manager explained later, '30 per cent of something is better than 100 per cent of nothing'. The question was how to structure the agreement to avoid all the potential pitfalls of Philippine politics and ASEAN diplomacy. Manalac asked to be transferred to the Philippine National Oil Company so the agreement with the China National Offshore Oil Company could be structured as a commercial rather than an inter-governmental arrangement. It was a thin ruse since both companies were state-owned enterprises.

In July 2004, when President Gloria Macapagal Arroyo (GMA to her friends and enemies) withdrew the small Filipino military contingent from Iraq, relations with Washington turned distinctly frosty. She responded by seeking 'comprehensive engagement' with China and the channel was Jose de Venecia. He had already arranged for the Chinese Communist Party to host the third congress of the International Conference of Asian Political Parties in Beijing in September 2004 and during August GMA was suddenly invited to give one of the keynote addresses. On 18 August, GMA reshuffled her cabinet and moved Eduardo Manalac from his job as Undersecretary of Energy to President of PNOC. Five days later de Venecia told reporters that GMA would lobby for joint exploration with China during her visit to Beijing. 'We should not allow regional differences to prevent us from developing,' he said after delivering a speech on the impact of high oil prices on the Philippine economy.[19] A week later, on 1 September, Manalac, now no longer a member of the government, signed what was called the Joint Marine Seismic Undertaking with his old friend, the President of the China National Offshore Oil Company, Fu Chengyu.

The Joint Marine Seismic Undertaking or JMSU was the brainchild of a small group around GMA. Professor Aileen Baviera, one of the Philippines' best-informed regional analysts, says the Department of Foreign Affairs and the National Security Council were 'largely excluded' throughout the negotiation process.[20] While some of the JMSU proponents, including Manalac, were motivated by a desire to improve the country's energy security and reduce its reliance on imports, others had less high-minded interests. De Venecia seems to have been keen to promote his own position as a power broker and gatekeeper for Chinese investment in the Philippines. (Such deals duly followed, particularly during the visits of President Hu Jintao in April 2005 and Premier Wen Jiabao in January 2007.) There was also a coterie of business people keen to conclude lucrative deals with Chinese companies. This ultimately included GMA's husband, Jose de Venecia's son and others in their circles. These elite cliques appear to have taken control of the country's foreign policy and bent it in their own interests.

Outside the mansions of Manila the reaction was astonishment. ASEAN diplomats wanted to know why the Philippines had undermined years of principled calls for regional solidarity. The Vietnamese were livid. For six months they hammered Filipino diplomats with protests but in the end decided it was better to be included in the survey than not. On 14 March 2005, PetroVietnam signed up to an expanded, three-year Joint Marine Seismic Undertaking. The China National Offshore Oil Company would handle the survey, PetroVietnam would process the data at a centre run jointly with an American company, Fairfield, and the Philippine National Oil Company, which had little else to offer, said it would organise the analysis. On 1 September an elderly CNOOC survey ship, the *Nanhai 502*, left Guangdong province with experts on board from all three countries. Over the next 75 days they gathered 11,000 kilometres of seismic data, covering the entire JMSU area. On 16 November the ship docked at PNOC's supply harbour in Batangas, south of Manila, where Eduardo Manalac declared that 'political tensions are history'.[21] Others would see it differently.

By January 2007 a few promising prospects had been identified, so a second phase of more detailed surveying was mooted. The Foreign Ministry was opposed and it wasn't until June that the President granted permission for Phase 2. Around the same time GMA was engulfed by a wave of corruption allegations involving her, her husband, the head of the Electoral Commission and projects funded by Chinese aid. Nonetheless, Phase 2 went ahead, gathering more detailed information about specific areas of the seabed. Plans were made for Phase 3: lining up locations for exploratory drilling. But then, in January 2008, the veteran journalist Barry Wain wrote an article for the *Far Eastern Economic Review* accusing GMA's government of making 'breathtaking concessions' in the JMSU and criticising its secret terms and conditions.[22] The article was seized upon by the growing army of GMA's critics and the JMSU became tarred by its association with China and corruption-tainted infrastructure projects.

As the allegations widened and the infighting worsened, the architects of the JMSU were pushed out. Manalac had continued his efforts to clean up the Philippine oil sector by cutting the cosy ties between local energy companies and the Ministry of Energy. He defied GMA by awarding an unrelated oil contract to the Malaysian company Mitra, rather than to one linked to her husband. Fed up with the ongoing corruption, he resigned from the Philippine National Oil Company in November

2006. De Venecia was deposed as speaker in February 2008 after his son accused GMA's husband of corruption over a Chinese-funded broadband infrastructure project. The JMSU agreement was dead in the water, the possibility of any renewal hopelessly lost amid the soap opera that passes for politics in the Philippines. It expired on 1 July 2008 with no-one in power prepared to argue for its renewal.

Manalac still regards the Joint Marine Seismic Undertaking as a success: it had allowed the Philippine National Oil Company to share costs on a survey it wanted to run anyway and without the risk of confrontation on the high seas. From China's perspective the success was partial. For the first time two ASEAN governments had 'put aside the question of sovereignty' and demonstrated a model of joint development. Once again, however, Southeast Asian opposition had thwarted the chances of CNOOC actually delivering any oil. It's not clear that permission for Phase 3 of the JMSU would ever have been granted.

Instead, other governments continued to ignore Li Peng's offer and lease out blocks to international companies inside the 'U-shaped line' on their own terms. But over the period of the JMSU, China's rocketing economic growth had begun to give it greater influence. If the JMSU was a Chinese carrot to promote joint development in the South China Sea, Beijing now had a stick to wield against companies that refused to comply.

* * * * * *

The centre of Vietnam's hydrocarbon industry is the city of Vung Tau on the country's southeastern coast. Once a French colonial resort, its grandeur has surrendered to industrial grit. One side of the long peninsula is a playground for Russian engineers with stout bellies and tiny swimming trunks. The other, facing the estuary, is dominated by storage tanks and welding yards. Between them lies a strip of unremarkable tower blocks and the optimistically named Grand Hotel where, on 4 June 2007, BP Vietnam formally welcomed its new director-general: Gretchen H. Watkins. Watkins had started out as an engineer with Amoco and, after the company was taken over by BP, moved through posts in London, the Netherlands and Canada. Young and ambitious, she now had a chance to prove herself on a wild frontier. What she didn't know was that her ultimate boss, BP's Chief Executive Tony Hayward, had already killed her chances. She would spend a year learning the hard way about the perils of trying to operate in the waters she could see from the Grand Hotel's windows.

BP had been in Vietnam since 1989 but had taken a decade to become one of the few international companies making good money there. In 2002 its *Lan Tay* platform in Block 6.1, which was 362 kilometres offshore, started pumping gas down the world's longest underwater pipeline to a power station up the estuary from the Grand Hotel. In 2006 BP's gas was generating over a third of Vietnam's electricity and there was more to come because the company had rights over two other exploration blocks. BP had sat on the blocks for years, waiting to be convinced that Vietnam's economy could generate sufficient demand to make it worth expanding the production of electricity, and therefore gas. In early 2007, with the country freshly enrolled as a member of the World Trade Organisation and big-name investors flooding in, BP was ready to commit. On 6 March it announced plans to develop two new gas fields in Block 5.2 and either link them to its existing pipeline or build another. A second power station would be built onshore to turn the gas into more electricity for the country and more cash for BP. The timescale was left vague but BP's partner PetroVietnam suggested the gas might come on-stream in 2011.

At around the same time, the Chinese ambassador to Australia, Madame Fu Ying, was making her own plans, preparing to move to a new post in London. Madame Fu had a bit of history with BP. In 2000, when BP announced its plans to develop Block 6.1, she had been director-general of the Department of Asian Affairs at the Chinese Foreign Ministry. According to a senior BP insider, she had made very strong representations to BP's management in Beijing and Southeast Asia demanding the company stop the project because it was infringing upon China's territorial claim. At the time, BP's CEO was John Browne, a veteran of many frontier battles. He simply shrugged off Madame Fu's objections and the project continued. But on 1 May 2007, Browne resigned from BP after a personal scandal and his place was taken by Tony Hayward.

Madame Fu arrived in London on 10 April, the same day that Beijing opened hostilities in a new battle with BP. In response to a planted question from a Chinese state TV journalist about the new gas project, the

Chinese Foreign Ministry spokesman Qin Gang declared, 'Vietnam's new actions [are] illegal and invalid . . . not beneficial to the stability of the South China Sea area'. Strangely, the block that Beijing was now taking exception to – Block 5.2 – was actually closer to the Vietnamese coast than BP's existing operation in Block 6.1. No matter: it was an opportunity for Madame Fu to have her revenge. One of the first things she did after unpacking in London was to request a meeting with the freshly installed Tony Hayward. The company had a good idea what was coming and called its top managers in Vietnam to London to prepare for the discussions. They outlined a robust case for BP to continue the project and then left matters to Hayward and his team.

By 2007, BP was one of the biggest foreign investors in China. Its $4.2 billion portfolio included stakes in petrochemical plants, offshore gas production, 800 petrol stations, a 30 per cent stake in the country's first liquefied natural gas terminal and several other businesses. Madame Fu knew this very well and on 18 May 2007 she made use of it in her meetings at BP's headquarters. She outlined her objections to BP's operations in the disputed waters and then, according to an insider, gave two specific warnings: firstly, that if the company went ahead in Block 5.2 the Chinese authorities would reconsider all the contracts they had awarded to BP, and, secondly, that China could not guarantee the safety of any BP staff working in the disputed area. It appeared to be a blunt threat to both the company's commercial life and to the lives of its employees involved in exploration and production. Lacking his predecessor's experience with roughhouse regimes, Hayward was taken aback. He made a deal with Fu – BP would continue to operate Block 6.1 but would suspend operations in Block 5.2. Fu had her revenge.

This was the mess that Gretchen Watkins inherited when she arrived in Vung Tau two weeks later. BP had signed contracts with PetroVietnam (acting for the Vietnamese government) and the American company ConocoPhillips committing it to survey and exploration work in Block 5.2. It appears from US diplomatic cables released by Wikileaks that BP didn't tell its partners of Hayward's commitment to Madame Fu until 8 June, when the company cancelled its work plan for 2007. Neither ConocoPhillips nor PetroVietnam was willing to let BP off the hook though. Watkins found herself out of her depth in the middle of a legal and geopolitical storm. On

13 June, news leaked that BP had suspended its planned seismic survey and over the following two days the American ambassador in Hanoi, Michael Marine, was visited by both his British counterpart and ConocoPhillips. In his account of the meetings (published by Wikileaks), ConocoPhillips complained that PetroVietnam was demanding that it fulfil their work contract despite BP's suspension. The British ambassador, Robert Gordon, told him that the UK was despatching a senior Foreign Office official for talks with the Vietnamese government.[23]

With BP having caved in to Chinese pressure, ConocoPhillips had little choice but to follow. It had smaller but still significant business interests in China, including the Xijiang field south of Hong Kong and the Peng Lai development in Bohai Bay. Scenting victory, Beijing widened the campaign. The same month, the Ministry of Foreign Affairs complained to the Japanese government about the activities of a consortium including Idemitsu, Nippon Oil and Teikoku Oil which was planning seismic survey work in Blocks 5.1b and 5.1c (next to BP's blocks). According to an account by the US ambassador in Tokyo released by Wikileaks, the Japanese government chose not to push the issue with Beijing and in July the Japanese consortium suspended its plans.[24] In early August 2007, executives from Chevron were summoned to the Chinese embassy in Washington DC and told to stop their company's exploration work in Vietnam's Block 122. The message was repeated more forcefully at another meeting in Beijing the following week. The demand was, on the face of it, outrageous. Block 122 lies immediately off the Vietnamese coast and firmly on its continental shelf. However, Chevron had just signed a very large agreement with PetroChina for a gas concession in Sichuan Province and had a lot to lose. It had suspended operations in Block 122 before the end of the month.[25] On 8 September, the Chinese consulate in Houston sent another oil company, Pogo, a letter telling them to stop work in Block 124, 50 kilometres south of Block 122.

Madame Fu was clearly very happy with BP because, on 31 August 2007, she made a special trip to the company's Wytch Farm onshore oil production site in southern England where she suggested that 'both sides could make more exchanges and cooperation'. Unusually for a visit to Dorset, her host was BP's Head of Asia Pacific, John Hughes. He made special mention of BP's hopes 'to carry out strategic cooperation with major

Chinese petroleum companies'.[26] But Beijing hadn't finished with BP. The next step was to try to use the company to manoeuvre the Vietnamese government into conceding sovereignty. According to a senior BP insider, the Chinese government 'suggested' the company facilitate discussions between the China National Offshore Oil Company (CNOOC) and PetroVietnam about joint development of Block 5.2 and its neighbour, Block 5.3. CNOOC's motives combined profit and politics: its president, Fu Chengyu, was known to have higher ambitions. CNOOC's head office in Beijing directly faces Fu Ying's employer, the Foreign Ministry, across the Chaoyangmen Road intersection. In 2007 and 2008, the Fu–Fu axis appeared to be two faces of the same policy.

This was actually the second time that CNOOC had compelled BP to play Cupid: there had been a previous attempt in 2003. Then, BP had introduced CNOOC to PetroVietnam and backed away. PetroVietnam had politely entertained some general discussions for a few months until it finally made plain that CNOOC was welcome to become a commercial partner but there was no way it was going to become the joint administrator of Vietnam's oil blocks. When CNOOC returned to the fray in 2007, Mr Fu had something more specific in mind: a stake in blocks 5.2 and 5.3. Just like the deal that Randall Thompson had proposed on behalf of Crestone 15 years before, it would have been a working arrangement that – under the cover of 'joint development' – would have implicitly recognised Chinese sovereign rights to the resources within the disputed territory. And this time BP wasn't going to be allowed to wash its hands of the discussions. It was going to be used, in effect, as an arm of Chinese foreign policy.

BP's senior management in London under Tony Hayward appears to have been blind to the history and geopolitics of the situation it now found itself in. The company continued to act on the basis that this could be just another joint venture, that CNOOC could be bought off with a commercial deal and that the sovereignty dispute could be left for the governments to handle. It didn't seem to realise that it *was* the sovereignty dispute. For more than a year Gretchen Watkins and other executives shuttled between Hanoi and Beijing passing messages between the two state oil companies. BP offered to develop projects in new areas, projects with reciprocal benefits for both sides, and convinced itself that a deal was on the cards. BP even changed Watkins' job title to Director-General for BP Vietnam and China Exploration and Production. Unsurprisingly there was no progress. Vietnam wouldn't budge on sovereignty and CNOOC wasn't interested in a commercial deal. But it took several months before Hayward and his team finally understood. They were much more interested in the huge prospects opening up in the Gulf of Mexico. For them, Southeast Asia was a sideshow.

Watkins and BP's regional management tried to find a way out. They knew they could not meet their contractual obligation to complete seismic surveys by the end of 2008. Instead, early in that year, BP and ConocoPhillips quietly turned over the operatorship of Blocks 5.2 and 5.3 to PetroVietnam. They continued to own the rights to the blocks but this arrangement meant they could avoid sending their own ships into the disputed waters. On 13 May 2008, Watkins briefed the newly appointed US ambassador to Hanoi, Michael Michalak, about the arrangements, telling him that BP and ConocoPhillips had no plans to tell the Chinese government about the change of operator.[27] Two weeks later the most powerful politician in Vietnam, Communist Party General Secretary Nong Duc Manh, visited Beijing for three days of talks. Accompanying him was the Chairman of PetroVietnam who held private discussions with Chairman Fu of CNOOC. Fu later visited Hanoi for talks with PetroVietnam but there was still no breakthrough. News of PetroVietnam's survey did leak out in July but the Chinese seemed too preoccupied by the impending Beijing Olympics to take any action.[28]

Watkins had had enough. The gas field development was stalled and her skill-set didn't include geopolitical negotiations. Her career was going nowhere with BP Vietnam so, in July 2008, she traded a medium-sized role with a mega-corporation for a bigger role with a relative minnow as Vice-President of International Production Operations for Marathon Oil, a company with fewer sovereignty disputes to deal with. Her successor was another American, Luke Keller, former president of BP's subsidiary Atlantic Richfield and possessed of years of experience with argumentative governments from Texas to Azerbaijan. By this time though, BP's management had realised the game was up and in late November 2008 they broke the news to PetroVietnam. BP wanted out. It quietly handed over its stakes in Blocks 5.2 and 5.3 to PetroVietnam for nothing and wrote off the

$200 million it had invested in them. The decision forced ConocoPhillips to do likewise in December. Madame Fu had won her ultimate victory.

Could BP have played it differently? The experience of another oil company – the world's biggest – suggests it could. ExxonMobil also received threats from the Chinese authorities – and ignored them. Over the years, ExxonMobil had been less successful in penetrating the Chinese market than BP. Its only sizeable investment was a 22.5 per cent stake in a refining and petrochemical project in Fujian. The local US consulate noted that this project had more to do with 'the relationships and potential political capital they give the Chinese government' than any vital contribution from ExxonMobil. Even the location of the project, just across the water from Taiwan, was seen as a means of gaining diplomatic leverage over the United States if there was ever another crisis between Beijing and Taipei.[29] The company had other cards to play too. China was desperate to increase its supplies of natural gas and ExxonMobil was developing a huge project just over its northeastern border on the Russian island of Sakhalin. Its Russian partner, Gazprom, wanted to sell the gas internally but ExxonMobil wanted to export it. Beijing couldn't afford to alienate Exxon too much. Equally importantly, and in stark contrast to the British and Japanese companies, ExxonMobil could rely on the US government to press its case with the Chinese authorities.

In January 2008 a new head of exploration arrived in Vietnam: Russ Berkoben. He'd been with ExxonMobil for 32 years, including a stint as head of exploration in China. Shortly afterwards the company signed a Memorandum of Understanding with PetroVietnam to explore Blocks 156 to 159. The blocks were by far the furthest offshore that Vietnam had ever leased. The southeastern corner of Block 159 was more than 500 kilometres from the Vietnamese coast – well into disputed waters. ExxonMobil was also in serious talks about leasing Blocks 117, 118 and 119 just off Vietnam's central coast. On 20 July 2008, Greg Torode of the Hong Kong-based *South China Morning Post* reported that Chinese diplomats in Washington had warned ExxonMobil that its business prospects in mainland China were at risk.[30] Torode's source was a senior Obama administration official who'd been briefed by an ExxonMobil executive.

At the end of August it looked as if the Chinese were getting serious. ExxonMobil's planned joint venture to build a $1 billion liquefied natural gas facility in Hong Kong was unexpectedly cancelled. Company executives told American diplomats they didn't think the Vietnam dispute was the reason – the deal was strongly opposed by local environmental activists – but it appeared that the Chinese were making good their threats. Then, ironically, ExxonMobil got punished by the Vietnamese because they were being punished by the Chinese. The company had negotiated with PetroVietnam for over a year about four blocks (Blocks 129 to 132, between Blocks 156–9 and the coast) but in October 2008 PetroVietnam awarded them to Gazprom of Russia instead. Berkoben told Ambassador Michalak that PetroVietnam feared that ExxonMobil would buckle under pressure from Beijing.[31] In July 2008, Russian diplomats had told their American counterparts that China hadn't put any pressure on Russian companies – and presumably the Vietnamese authorities were aware of that too.[32]

ExxonMobil wasn't the only company to shrug off Chinese coercion. The Indian energy company ONGC Videsh (which was a partner with BP in Block 6.1 and also the leaseholder in Blocks 127 and 128), KNOC of Korea and some smaller companies without significant interests in China – such as Premier of the UK and Talisman of Canada – also ignored it. Beijing tried other ways to exert pressure. In October 2007, Mike Bruce, Chief Financial Officer for Pearl Energy in Singapore, received a call from the Chinese embassy. The diplomat told Bruce that his company was illegally prospecting in Chinese waters and invited him to the embassy for discussions. Bruce declined and instead invited the Chinese to visit him. A few days later a delegation duly arrived and informed the Pearl managers they knew that the company had a survey ship at work (in Block 6.94, which almost surrounds BP's Block 6.1). According to Bruce, they 'threatened to put pressure on the Singapore government because Pearl was listed on the Singapore stock exchange'. But when Bruce informed them that Pearl was no longer listed in Singapore, having been bought by Aabar Energy of Abu Dhabi a year before, their faces fell. 'Oh, that's different,' said the woman leading the group and Pearl never heard from them again.

By early 2009, the only company with interests in China still exploring off Vietnam was ExxonMobil. On 30 June it signed a production-sharing contract with PetroVietnam for two sets of blocks (Blocks 156 to 159 in the wild southeast and Blocks 117, 118 and 119 off Danang), making it the largest offshore acreage holder in Vietnam. A week beforehand Russ

Berkoben had been to the US embassy in Hanoi to explain that the ceremony was going to be held 'quietly' to avoid upsetting the Chinese. He
admitted being uncertain about their likely reaction but said ExxonMobil
was 'ready if China reacts'. Berkoben's reward came just over a year and
a half later, in October 2011, when the company found potentially huge
gas reserves in Block 118. Exploration work continues in the other blocks.

With the exception of ExxonMobil every oil company has had to make
a choice between operating in China or in the waters claimed by one of the
other countries. ConocoPhillips had left Blocks 5.2 and 5.3 in December
2008 but retained stakes in two other blocks just next to the Vietnamese
coast, far from any trouble with China. In February 2012 it left the country
completely to concentrate on more profitable ventures. Chevron retained
its 20 per cent stake in Block 122 but suspended all activities there until it
finally sold out in early 2013. That seems to have pleased Beijing because,
in 2010, Chevron was awarded stakes in three fields in the northern part
of the South China Sea, off Hainan Island.[33] At the time of writing, in
mid-2014, Chevron was reported to be trying to offload its remaining
Vietnamese interests – two blocks off the southwest coast, close to the
maritime borders with Indonesia and Malaysia.

BP remained in business in Vietnam, running its original gas-to-power
operation from Block 6.1. But then, in July 2010, Tony Hayward's Gulf of
Mexico bonanza turned into a disaster. The company suddenly needed $30
billion to pay compensation after the Deepwater Horizon explosion and
spill. On 18 October 2010 BP sold its interests in Vietnam and Venezuela
to its Russian joint venture, TNK-BP, for a total of $1.8 billion. Perhaps it
felt the Russians would be able to take the heat. BP had another mission
for Luke Keller's steady hands. He was appointed Executive Vice-President
of BP's Gulf Coast Restoration Organization – helping to clean up the
mess. A few weeks before the sale, on 21 September 2010, Tony Hayward
met Madame Fu Ying again. After her successes in London, she had been
appointed China's Vice-Foreign Minister. Hayward brought his successor
Bob Dudley. It was one of Hayward's last official duties for BP. Nine days
later he was no longer Chief Executive.

Fu Chengyu's fate was neither high office nor disgrace. In spite of all
its arm-twisting, the China National Offshore Oil Corporation had once
again failed to gain access to the potential oil resources around the far

reaches of the South China Sea. There was to be no political reward for its ambitious boss. His consolation prize, in April 2011, was a move to CNOOC's sluggish rival Sinopec, Asia's biggest oil refiner. Fu's business abilities were clear: CNOOC's profits had quintupled during his reign; the Communist Party of China felt he would be more valuable as an industrial rather than a geopolitical fixer.

* * * * * *

By late 2010 Beijing's campaign had forced BP and ConocoPhillips to cease exploration inside the 'U-shaped line' and the Joint Marine Seismic Undertaking had established a precedent for China's preferred alternative. However, a new government in the Philippines and the same old governments in Vietnam, Brunei and Malaysia were not budging on sovereignty and the lure of potential profit remained strong enough to attract other companies, less worried by Chinese pressure, to try their hand in the contested waters. Beijing had exhausted its commercial leverage; asserting its territorial claims would now require less subtle techniques.

On Wednesday, 2 March 2011, the seismic survey ship MV *Veritas Voyager* (owned by the French geophysics company CGG Veritas) was firing its powerful airguns over the Reed Bank, an area of shallow sea about 160 kilometres off Palawan. Four 'streamers' – hydrophone cables – extending 2,700 metres behind, picked up sound waves reflected back from layers of rock thousands of metres below the sea floor. Sitting in his combat operations centre in the Palawan provincial capital, Puerto Princesa, Lieutenant General Juancho Sabban, Chief of the Western Command of the Armed Forces of the Philippines, was waiting for something to happen. The *Voyager* had been surveying for nearly two months and notices warning of its activities were posted on the coast-guard website. The crew had sighted a Chinese ship on 28 February and the following day had acquired an unwanted escort. A China Marine Surveillance (CMS) vessel had come within 100 metres of the *Voyager* and ordered it to leave.

The *Voyager* was on contract to a British-registered (though Filipino-controlled) company, Forum Energy. In 2005, just as the above-mentioned JMSU survey was about to begin, Forum had taken over an exploration block from another British company, Sterling Energy – right in the middle of the JMSU area. Eduardo Manalac had assured his Chinese counterparts that Forum's exploration lease would be allowed to lapse but others in the Philippine government had been swayed by Forum's lobbying. On 10 February 2010, the lease was upgraded to a full Service Contract, SC-72. Manalac was furious, Forum was buoyant. Earlier surveys had suggested the Sampaguita prospect inside the block contained 3.4 trillion cubic feet of gas. Now it just needed to work out exactly where to drill.

As the *Voyager's* survey continued, Forum's President Ray Apostol was in daily contact with General Sabban. On 2 March he called Sabban in a panic. Two CMS ships (numbers 71 and 75) had sailed across the *Voyager's* bows and ordered it to leave the area. 'We're packing up,' he told the general. Sabban told him to order the crew to stay put and scrambled a pair of unarmed OV-10 spotter planes. By the time they reached the area, two hours later, the Chinese ships had gone. He then deployed the BRP *Rizal*, a minesweeper built in 1944, and the BRP *Rajah Humabon*, built in 1943. The ships were elderly but effective enough to keep the CMS vessels away from the *Voyager* for a further seven days, enabling it to complete the survey ahead of schedule.

Twelve weeks later, CMS tried a more aggressive tactic on the other side of the sea. The survey ship, the *Binh Minh 02*, owned by a joint venture between PetroVietnam and CGG Veritas, was working in Block 148, 120 kilometres east of the Vietnamese port of Nha Trang. In the early morning of 26 May 2011 three CMS ships, numbers 12, 17 and 84, appeared on the horizon and then closed in. A pair of fishing trawlers were guarding the *Binh Minh 02* but they couldn't protect the entire 17,000-metre cable trailing behind it. CMS ship number 84 cut across the cable, deliberately severing it. Fortunately for the Vietnamese, the multi-million dollar streamer was equipped with emergency floats that brought it to the surface for recovery. The damage was repaired and the *Binh Minh 02* returned to sea the following week, accompanied by eight escorts.

Two weeks after that, another seismic vessel, this time contracted jointly by PetroVietnam and the Canadian company Talisman, was intercepted in Block 136-03, in the extreme southeast of Vietnam's claimed Exclusive Economic Zone. The block was just south of the three that ConocoPhillips had abandoned in 2008 and included part of Randall Thompson's

WAB-21. Once again CGG Veritas owned the ship, the *Veritas Viking 2*. This time, however, the attackers weren't from China Marine Surveillance but from the Fisheries Law Enforcement Command (FLEC). And this time the Chinese put on an elaborate charade to justify the cutting of the cable. A small flotilla of Chinese fishing boats appeared in the survey area and remained, despite warnings from a Vietnamese Coastguard ship to leave. The next day, 9 June, while FLEC vessels 303 and 311 sailed in front of the *Viking*, trawler number 62226 sailed across its streamers behind. The trawler snagged its net and was dragged backwards through the sea. The FLEC ships then rushed to help the trawler cut the streamers in what the Chinese authorities would later claim was an act of self-preservation.

These three incidents in the first half of 2011 provoked angry criticism of Chinese 'bullying' around Southeast Asia and beyond. Four more followed: the *Binh Minh 02* had its cables cut a second time on 30 November 2012 in Block 113 (near the Paracel Islands and leased to Gazprom) and there were two incidents in the Malaysian EEZ off Borneo on 21 August 2012 and another on 19 January 2013 where Chinese government vessels blocked oil survey work.[34] Some seized upon the actions of China's maritime agencies as proof of Beijing's hostile intentions. They also provided yet more evidence that parts of the Chinese state – the China National Offshore Oil Company, China Marine Surveillance and the Fisheries Law Enforcement Command – regarded the 'U-shaped line' as a real claim to 80 per cent of the South China Sea. All the incidents took place far from any Chinese-claimed land feature and therefore seemed incompatible with any claim based on UNCLOS. As the criticism mounted, the Beijing leadership seems to have recognised that CMS and FLEC went too far. In March 2013 the government announced plans to bring all the different maritime agencies (the State Oceanic Administration, including China Marine Surveillance, under the Land and Resources Ministry; the China Coast Guard, under the Public Security Ministry; the Maritime Safety Administration, under the Transport Ministry; the Fisheries Law Enforcement Command under the Ministry of Agriculture; and the General Administration of Customs) under a single management. Since then, at least until the time of writing, there have been no more such incidents.

How successful was the strategy? Off Vietnam it failed: the cable cuttings didn't prevent continued exploration and Talisman is expected to drill in Block 136–03 in late 2014. However, off the Philippines it was much more effective. Forum has been unable to begin drilling on the Reed Bank and, given the Philippines' inability to physically defend its claims with its ageing warships, China has now, in effect, established a veto over development there. Forum's management has been involved in lengthy discussions with CNOOC but, at the time of writing, there is no sign of a breakthrough. Filipino politicians have a choice: will they back down on sovereignty in order to improve energy security? Is it better to defend the territorial claim in the hope of gaining 100 per cent of the resources in the future, but in the meantime getting nothing, or is it wiser to compromise now in the hope of gaining a partial share of something more rapidly?

* * * * * *

CNOOC and Beijing's other agencies have gone to extraordinary lengths to try and win access to the hydrocarbon resources around the South China Sea. But what are they likely to receive in return for all their efforts? One of the best places for a genuinely unbiased assessment of the oil and gas potential of the Sea is the Penny Black pub on the old waterfront in Singapore. It's a noisy, beer-guzzling place dominated by discussions of all kinds of sport. But the rumbustiousness overlaps with a deep knowledge of geological structures. The Penny Black is a watering hole for the small group of geological and geophysical consultants who've spent decades surveying Southeast Asian waters. Most of them are Brits in their forties and fifties, members of the Southeast Asia Petroleum Exploration Society (SEAPEX), and between them they have probably worked for everyone who has ever tried to find hydrocarbons in the region. They've seen dozens of companies jump into the region and most of them limp out again. They've helped some to make money and others to realise there was none to be made. Their livelihoods depend upon keeping commercial confidences and with many billions of dollars at stake they can't be too specific but hints can be dropped and eyebrows raised.

The collective wisdom is surprising. These experts are convinced that the disputed areas of the South China Sea actually contain relatively little oil and gas. The vast majority of the Sea's resources lie outside the 'U-shaped line'. There are some good fields and interesting prospects within the Chinese claim, but the geoscientists of the Penny Black believe the possibilities aren't worth the fuss the area generates. A proper understanding would require a degree in geology but the over-a-pint explanation is that seismic surveys are looking for three things: source rock for hydrocarbons, a reservoir where they can accumulate and a seal to make sure they don't disappear. There are only a few places in the Spratly Islands where these three exist. During the Miocene era, 30 million years ago, large reefs formed in the sea and, as the earth's crust moved and sea level changed, these reefs have grown steadily taller, forming thick banks of carbonate rocks. These carbonate rocks are porous and the oil and gas that might have formed in earlier eras has probably evaporated or slipped away. With the carbonate layer up to 3,000 metres thick, it's very hard to get accurate surveys of what lies beneath. Without an accurate survey, who would risk the millions of dollars required to drill a well?

There is even worse news in the centre of the disputed area. At the end of the continental shelf the seabed drops sharply from 200 metres to 2,000 metres and to as deep as 6,000 metres in places. Jon Savage knows the South China Sea almost as well as the Penny Black, having worked on dozens of projects over the years, including Forum's 2011 interrupted survey. His verdict on the deep water? It's mostly oceanic crust, there's no source rock for oil and gas, no reservoirs in which it might accumulate and no seal to prevent it leaking away. In short, there's 'no hydrocarbon potential', he told a conference in Ho Chi Minh City in November 2013.[35] That opinion is shared by almost everyone in the industry. So why do Chinese sources continue to trumpet the opposite?

The answer seems to lie in a combination of dogma and opportunism. After the fanfare that greeted the original Chinese surveys in the 1980s and the tasking of key state agencies to secure new energy supplies for the country, too many people have had an interest in promoting the Sea as an energy panacea. In September 1994, for example, the Minister of Natural Resources, Song Ruixang, declared that the Spratlys 'promise an oil potential of 30 billion tons' (about 220 billion barrels).[36] Once these official sources had declared the numbers to be true – and the solution to a national crisis – it was very hard for any other official to declare them nonsense. The China National Offshore Oil Corporation was given the task of developing these vast reserves and became another powerful voice within the system amplifying the Sea's potential. The bigger the reserves appeared to be, the stronger its case for winning more funding from the state.

But there is a huge difference between 'resources' – what lies underground – and 'reserves' – the proportion that can be extracted. Usually around a third of the 'resources' can be brought to the surface technically whereas only around a tenth can be brought to the surface commercially. The most authoritative and transparent recent estimates of the hydrocarbon potential of the Sea have come from the US Geological Survey (USGS) in June 2010 and the US Energy Information Administration in February 2013. The Energy Information Administration estimated the Sea contained just 11 billion barrels of oil and 190 trillion cubic feet of gas as commercially viable reserves. That's about the same amount of oil as in Mexico and the same amount of gas as in Europe (excluding Russia).[37] Based on what is known about the region's geology, the USGS estimated yet-to-be-discovered resources at around 11 billion barrels of oil (with low and high estimates of 5 and 22 billion barrels) and 4 billion barrels of 'natural gas liquids' – making a combined total of 15 billion barrels. The USGS estimated that undiscovered gas resources could be more significant – somewhere between 70 and 290 trillion cubic feet. So, undiscovered resources could be about the same as the current level of reserves.[38]

These figures, however, refer to the whole Sea region, including areas firmly within the different countries' Exclusive Economic Zones. Only a fraction of the headline figures lies in the disputed territory and only one-tenth of that fraction would be commercially recoverable. These prospects could make a sizeable impact in the economies of smaller, poorer economies such as the Philippines or Vietnam. But given that China consumes about 3 billion barrels of oil and about 5 trillion cubic feet of natural gas each year, the reserves and resources of the South China Sea are hardly worth all the *Sturm und Drang* expended on them. Even if every drop and bubble were sent to China, they would power the country's economy for a few years at best. The geology is difficult, the region is prone to typhoons and the supporting infrastructure poorly developed. Tony Regan, a former Shell executive, now a Singapore-based energy consultant, is blunt about the commercial prospects for the South China Sea. 'The region has never been of significance to the oil majors and they don't believe it's the next big thing now. There are far more attractive areas out there – Western Australia and East Africa for example and of course unconventional gas from coal seams and shale.'[39] In other words, there are cheaper and more reliable ways for China to ease its fears about energy security than stirring up the South China Sea.

All countries in the region are concerned about their energy security. Demand is surging while production is falling. Offshore development is being delayed by the territorial disputes and not enough new Southeast Asian fields are being discovered to replace those that are declining. The result is ballooning imports from outside the region. The South China Sea is now far more important for the hydrocarbons that sail through it than for those that lie beneath it. In 2013 the Energy Information Administration calculated that a third of the world's oil and half the world's liquefied natural gas passed through the Straits of Malacca heading for China, Taiwan, Korea and Japan. On average two very large crude carriers, each carrying 2 million barrels of oil, and two large liquefied natural gas carriers, each carrying 200,000 cubic metres, must arrive in Japan every day, just to keep the lights on.[40] All of the countries in East and Southeast Asia are vulnerable to disruptions in supply. In 2008 oil made up 22 per cent of China's total energy consumption, half of that oil was imported and 85 per cent of those imports came through the Straits of Malacca. In other words, almost 10 per cent of China's energy supplies crossed the South China Sea. All these numbers have risen since 2008 and look set to rise further still.[41]

In the quarter-century since Li Peng's made his remarks in Singapore, the Chinese leadership's approach to its energy problem has assumed that the country must physically control the resources in order to rely on them. This has been the pattern from the Crestone concession to the JMSU to the battles inside the 'U-shaped line'. There are alternatives. Reducing the tension over maritime claims could give governments greater confidence that freedom of navigation would be protected. A more cooperative regional approach to energy supplies might allow all countries to develop the resources in their own EEZs and companies to sell to wherever demand is greatest. Governments would then be more willing to trust others to guarantee the safe arrival of their energy supplies rather than trying to monopolise them through force of arms. But passions about the South China Sea have been rising in the countries around its shores and compromise is appearing less and less likely.

CHAPTER 6

Drums and Symbols
Nationalism

THE CROWD GATHERED near the Hanoi Opera House was small but angry. It was remarkable that it had gathered at all. In the days beforehand, Facebook had been buzzing with outrage but the Vietnamese authorities had been busy too. It had been just over a week since Chinese vessels had, for a second time, cut the seismic cables of the *Binh Minh 02* and a month since Beijing had unveiled new passports bearing a map of its 'U-shaped line' claim in the South China Sea. But there are many constraints upon public expressions of anger in Vietnam. Neighbourhood wardens keep eyes on the back streets, editors-in-chief keep eyes on their newspapers and 'supervisory bodies' watch over all civic organisations. People chat, people grumble, but people, generally, don't challenge the rule of the Communist Party in the street.[1]

Online is a different world. Facebook, in particular, allows grievances to multiply. The Party watches this world too but it draws a clear distinction between talk and action. On 9 December 2012, that line was crossed. The bloggers and chatters agreed that something public needed to be done. Almost exactly five years after Vietnam's first ever public protests about the South China Sea, they decided to take to the streets again. They had wanted to hold their protest on the steps of the old French-built opera house but a Communist Party Youth League event had been organised, at remarkably short notice, for the same location. With a stage being constructed in the square, they were forced to gather around the corner, along the old colonial boulevard now called Trang Tien Street. In the cooler temperatures of December, it's a pleasant walk past the little shops and cafes, the shore of Hoan Kiem Lake and the big old mansions of Dien Bien Phu Street – all the way to the Chinese embassy.

As a crew, they were motley but well organised. Two hundred people is a good turnout for any kind of protest in Vietnam. They carried large professionally made banners bearing slogans in Vietnamese and English, many wore T-shirts displaying a large X over a map of the 'U-shaped line' and they were in good voice. Some were supporters of 'No U FC', a group of anti-China activists who, weary of harassment by the authorities, had formed a football club so they could meet legitimately. The club's name is an attack on the 'U-shaped line' with 'FC' an acronym for both 'Football Club' and 'Fuck China'. While some banged drums, one supporter, 74-year-old violinist Ta Tri Hai, entertained his compadres with patriotic protest songs. Some well-known faces weren't able to make it, however. The anti-corruption activist Le Hien Duc, for example, had received an early-morning house call from officers of the Ministry of Public Security and been obliged to stay and entertain them.

More officers were on hand along Trang Tien Street to prevent any outbreaks of anti-social activity. Many wore their bright green uniforms but others were in plain clothes. A police car tried to push through the crowd but the marchers held firm. They chanted against Chinese aggression, declared that 'the Paracel and Spratly islands belong to Vietnam' and insisted their government do more to protect the country's territorial rights. A small crowd of foreign journalists was on hand to amplify their voices to the world but it became clear that the protestors weren't going to be allowed to complete their Sunday stroll.

The police insisted the marchers disperse. The marchers insisted the police disperse but the police were stronger. While the men in uniform stood aside, the men in plain clothes forced around 20 marchers onto a commandeered city bus and drove them off to the Loc Ha detention centre 15 kilometres outside the capital. The rest of the marchers got the message. The Chinese embassy would remain untroubled by nationalistic noise. News and images of the protest, and a similar one in Ho Chi Minh

City in the south, were carried around the world. It was, as an editor might say, a good 'picture story'.

The following Tuesday morning, at their regular weekly meeting with the Ministry of Information and Communications, Vietnam's editors-in-chief were berated for their coverage of the country's relations with China. They were told they had injected 'anti-China sentiment' into their reports about the *Binh Minh* incident – ignoring earlier instructions to 'stick to the facts'. It was entirely their fault that the country was getting stirred up. The problem for the Vietnamese authorities is that regardless of how many newspapers they muzzle or dissidents they detain, anti-China sentiment appears to be growing. It's impossible to openly or accurately measure such things in Vietnam but the South China Sea has brought small crowds onto the streets of Hanoi and Ho Chi Minh City at least a dozen times since 2007. If a few people are willing to risk arrest and punishment, it's certain that many more share the sentiment but lack the courage to join an organised protest. The fate of the 'East Sea', as the Vietnamese call it, and allegations of Chinese plots to undermine the country frequently provoke online outbursts of nationalist fury.

More than 30 years ago, the historian of Southeast Asia, Benedict Anderson, offered us an explanation for the emergence of nationalism in the nineteenth and twentieth centuries. He talked of the creation of 'imagined communities' in which newly conscious national citizens began to feel a bond with compatriots they had never met, a bond so strong that they were prepared to kill and die to protect it. He attributed the rise of these imagined communities to economic development and the possibilities of individual self-definition that it created, to the invention of national media and to the solidification of feelings of difference from others speaking different languages and following different customs.

In the early twenty-first century around the coast of the South China Sea a new wave of nationalism is creating new imagined communities. Economic development, new media technologies, new desires for self-expression – the same driving forces behind the anti-colonial nationalisms of the last century – are propelling renewed nationalisms. This time, however, the 'others' against which these communities define themselves are not imperialists from far away but neighbours in a region which has been connected since ancient times. Netizens proclaim their willingness to

die for the glory of their country and the fate of a few almost uninhabitable rocks. Across the region millions of people have come to believe that
their identity as a human being can only be complete if the imagined
community to which they feel they belong appears stronger than its rivals.
Nationalism is undoubtedly strong – but how much is it actually driving
the disputes? An examination of these expressions of populist passion
suggests the picture is more complex.

* * * * * *

Modern Vietnamese nationalism more or less defines itself in opposition
to China. Most of the main streets of Vietnamese towns and cities are
named after people (real or mythic) who fought against people from what
is now called 'China': Hai Ba Trung, the Trung sisters who led a rebellion
in 40 CE; Ngo Quyen, whom Vietnamese regard as the first ruler to separate the country from 'China', in 938; Ly Thuong Kiet, who fought the
Sung in 1076; Tran Hung Dao, who defeated the Mongols in 1284; Le Loi
(also known as Le Thai To), who defeated the Ming in 1428; and Nguyen
Hue (also known as Quang Trung), who defeated the Qing in 1789. Most
of this is anachronistic myth. The first time that two countries with the
present borders of Vietnam and China went to war was 1979. The earlier
conflicts were between regional rulers, rebels, warlords, protégés and
upstarts. The languages they spoke were neither the same as their modern
equivalents nor, necessarily, that different from their enemies'. And yet
all these great battles are now taken, in Vietnam, as proof of a long and
glorious history of successful resistance to the imperialist designs of 'Trung
Quoc' – the 'central kingdom' to the north.

From architecture to cuisine the cultural connections between the
two countries are obvious; yet at the grassroots, suspicion of the people
still referred to as 'Tau' – a derogatory word that could be translated into
English as 'Chink' – is strong. The prejudice comes from fear. Vietnamese
see themselves as more creative and cultured than the Chinese but unable
to compete with the impenetrable network of Chinese business interests.
This seemingly closed community with its alleged tentacles stretching all
around East Asia appears destined to take over the country and the whole
region.

A less prejudiced view of Vietnamese history might acknowledge the importance of links with 'China' from the time of the first Nusantao, through the arrival of sea traders from Fujian and right up to the first investments by ethnic Chinese from around Southeast Asia in the 1980s as Vietnam started to dismantle Stalinism. The Vietnamese Communist regime owes its existence to the sanctuary and succour it received from China throughout most of the twentieth century. Ideological inspiration, rockets and rice flowed south from Beijing: Chinese supplies built the foundation for Hanoi's victory over Saigon in 1975.

That political debt to Beijing is a key part of the appeal of the 'anti-China' message to many Vietnamese: it is implicitly 'anti-Party'. To demonstrate openly against the Communist Party in central Hanoi would invite a lengthy prison sentence. By criticising China's actions, however, protestors can appear patriotic while indirectly questioning the legitimacy of a Communist Party that came to power through Chinese support and still shares strong ideological and practical links with its bigger brother in Beijing. But many otherwise loyal Party members are also strongly critical of China's influence. For some, it is a matter of patriotism, but playing the 'China card' can also be a way of undermining rivals. By criticising China they are criticising those sections of the Party which have the strongest ideological links to Beijing and which also favour tighter social control, continuing dominance of the economy by state-owned enterprises and a more hostile attitude to the West.

In 1968 the Vietnamese Communist Party leadership fought a vicious internal battle that was retrospectively framed as an argument over whether the country should lean towards China or the Soviet Union. Dozens of senior figures were purged or imprisoned. But the geopolitical fight was a cover for other arguments: about war strategy, the pace of socialist changes and a host of domestic issues. Ever since then, 'China' has been a live issue in all the major debates about the future of Vietnam – a cypher through which other battles are fought. Even before Hanoi had parked its tanks on the lawn of the presidential palace in Saigon, the Communist Party leaderships in Beijing and Hanoi had begun to fall out. In Chinese eyes, the Vietnamese were ungrateful brats who failed in their duties of filial loyalty to their benevolent parent. For the Vietnamese leadership, which had just liberated the country from foreign aggression, Chinese attitudes smacked of imperial hauteur. They had no wish to become a vassal state. Relations deteriorated so badly that, in February 1979, China (with political and intelligence support from the US) decided to 'teach Vietnam a lesson' and invaded. Their troops got a mauling but several Vietnamese border towns were smashed. The two leaderships weren't reconciled until 1991.

These battles within battles are still being fought today – something that became brutally obvious just a few days after the attempted march down Trang Tien Street, when a rambling hour-long recording of what was supposed to be a secret speech found its way onto YouTube. The hapless star of this recording was Colonel Tran Dang Thanh, an instructor on the South China Sea issue at the Political Academy of the Vietnamese Ministry of Defence. The occasion was a gathering of Communist Party members who were senior administrators at universities in Hanoi (it's hard to become a senior anything in Vietnam without being a Party member). Colonel Thanh had a blunt message: there have been too many demonstrations and they must stop. 'The Party expects you to manage your kids. If we find that students from your school are taking part in demonstrations, you can be sure there will be a black mark on your record,' he admonished the deans and professors.[2]

The transcript provided a unique insight into the inner thinking of those parts of the Vietnamese security establishment that normally keep well away from the media. He began with a warning: if the Communist regime goes down, he told the professors, so will your living standards. 'Defending our nation and socialist ideology covers a lot of things and among these is the very practical fact that we are protecting our own pensions and the pensions of those that will come after us.' After this appeal to basic self-interest he outlined a straightforward case for not antagonising China – there are 1.3 billion of 'them', he noted, and only 90 million of 'us'. While we must never forget that they've invaded us over and over, he went on, 'we must not seem ungrateful' for China's great sacrifices for Vietnam in more recent times. He blamed China's recent actions on the legacy of Deng Xiaoping's 'burning desire' for mastery of the South China Sea, on China's need for maritime defence and on the lure of oil and gas. Vietnam's task now, he said, was to preserve the country's independence but also preserve peace and stability. The only way to do that, he argued, was to avoid confrontation and preserve feelings of solidarity between the people of Vietnam and China.

For a leadership most concerned about creating a million new jobs a year to satisfy the rising aspirations of a growing population, the sovereignty disputes are a maddening distraction. The Party goes to great lengths to avoid provoking antagonism with Beijing. A few weeks after Colonel Thanh's lecture, on 6 January 2013, a national hero was reburied in his home province of Thanh Hoa, just south of Hanoi. The national press covered the story in detail but, strangely, none of them was able to say just how the martyr had died; his killers were described simply as 'hooligans' – nationality unknown. Le Dinh Chinh was actually killed by Chinese border guards on 25 August 1978 as post-war tensions between the two countries were starting to escalate. Vietnam was in the process of expelling tens of thousands of ethnic Chinese, resulting in confrontations at a border crossing inaptly named 'Friendship Gate'. Fights broke out between militias armed with sticks and knives. Four Chinese and two Vietnamese were killed, including 18-year-old Le Dinh Chinh.

Over the following decade, with relations between the two countries veering between bad and worse, Le Dinh Chinh was made into a folk hero in Vietnam. Four months after the clash, the state publishing house issued a book eulogising his heroic life and patriotic death. Schools and streets were named after him and children were encouraged to emulate his example. But as relations between Hanoi and Beijing improved after 1990, the story of Le Dinh Chinh became less useful for popular mobilisation and gradually more embarrassing for the Hanoi government. The nationality of his killers was erased from official memory.

It's quite normal for the dead to be reburied in Vietnam. A few years after burial, the bones are disinterred, cleaned and reburied in an ossuary with appropriate ceremonies. It's very rare, however, for a reburial to take place 35 years later. With the newspapers clearly instructed not to include the word 'China' in accounts of his death, rumours and conspiracy theories began to circulate online about why Le Dinh Chinh was being reburied. They were amplified by a story that had begun circulating 18 months earlier about the defacing of a war memorial near Khanh Khe in the border province of Lang Son. The memorial, a large block of stone, carried an inscription dedicated to the soldiers of 337 Division who 'firmly stopped the Chinese invasion' in 1979.

In August 2011, bloggers circulated a picture of the memorial in which the words 'Chinese invasion' appeared to have been chiselled off. But the picture was heavily cropped. The full image showed the stone sitting in the middle of a civil engineering project – a new road and bridge were being constructed around it. It's quite possible that the memorial could have been damaged during the construction works. But since the authorities would make no official comment, it was confidently asserted online that a craven Vietnamese government, beholden to Beijing, had ordered the vandalism.

The reburial of Le Dinh Chinh, hundreds of kilometres south of his original grave site near the border, led one of the country's best-known bloggers, a former security agent called Nguyen Huu Vinh who uses the nom-de-plume Anh Ba Sam, to allege that the state was gradually removing all potential symbols of Vietnamese nationalist protest away from the border area. This may, in fact, be the case. Or it may not. The problem for the Vietnamese authorities is that, when it comes to relations with China, few people believe them any more. Their orders to newspapers and professors to prevent discussion of the issue have only increased the spread of conspiracy theories. Nefarious motives are attributed to everything they say and do regardless of their intent.

The Party, although sophisticated and intelligent in many ways, appears unable to respond to these challenges except in its time-honoured fashion. It has passed new laws to control blogging (though just as ineffective as the old ones) and cracked down on activists who make common cause with overseas-based anti-Communist organisations. There have been dozens of 'show trials' over the past few years. The security establishment seems happy to weather the inevitable international criticism – using the trials *pour encourager les autres*. Some argue that 'pro-China' forces in the Party are actually quite happy with this criticism since it deters Western governments from becoming too close to Vietnam and helps them to keep the country under their control.

As the world saw clearly in May 2014, when protests against a Chinese oil-drilling expedition near the Paracel Islands turned to rioting, there are certainly nationalistic, anti-China passions in Vietnam that cause difficulties for the Communist Party leadership. They are not, however, forcing it towards confrontation with China. Rather, they are forcing the Party into confrontation with a segment of its own population. The Party fears the protests because of their implicit anti-Party message and the possibility that they could escalate into something that might threaten its rule. Its priority is stability in both domestic and international affairs rather than freedom of expression. But those in favour of free expression and personal liberty at home are also those most vocally in favour of confrontation abroad. One side favours peace, the other freedom. Neither offers both.

* * * * * *

Another city, but this time two noisy crowds and opposing agendas. In the early morning of Monday, 16 April 2012, a 'lightning rally' hits Manila's seafront promenade, Roxas Boulevard, named after the first president of an independent Philippines. Around 70 supporters of the League of Filipino Students rush at the wall of the United States embassy. The compound is stoutly built on land reclaimed from Manila Bay, the piece of water where in 1898 the United States became a world power by defeating the Spanish Navy. The activists find the policeman supposed to be on duty outside fast asleep in his patrol car and, amazed by their luck, set to work on the symbols of imperialism. They hurl red and blue paint bombs at the wall, spray slogans on the stucco and perform the traditional rite of burning the American flag. A few militants jump the railings and work on the embassy's bronze signage. By the time the riot police show up, the building has been renamed the '.m.as.. of the .ni.ed S.ates of .merica'. The protestors flee into the side streets unhindered by the forces of law and order – presumably to argue over the maximum Scrabble score they could achieve with their eight stolen letters. The sleeping policeman doesn't wake up until it's all over; he drives away, apparently unaware that anything has happened at all.[3] He and his superintendent are later charged with misconduct.

Six hours later and 7 kilometres distant, in the shining, moneyed surroundings of the Makati business district, an equally noisy but better-behaved crowd gathers outside the Chinese consulate. Here the police are awake and forewarned and the protest is marshalled safely away from vulnerable walls, signs and plate-glass windows. There's been a bit more organisation here – or at least more money. Rather than home-made banners and a crowbar, the few dozen demonstrators are wielding neatly designed placards in the shape of STOP signs – demanding that 'China – back off!' and end its 'Poaching in Phil Waters'. The contrasts continue. Rather than wild-eyed revolutionaries, photographers pick out sweet-faced girls to grace the next day's pages, offering their editors a straight choice between contrasting images of protest and radically different worldviews.

That morning in Manila two Filipino nationalisms asserted themselves. The numbers involved were tiny: just a few busloads from a metropolis of 12 million people. But for the drum-bangers and symbol-shakers, the actions were vital assertions of national feeling in the face of apparently threatening displays of state power. The students at the embassy had timed their assault to coincide with the start of the annual US–Philippine military exercises known as *Balikatan* – Tagalog for 'shoulder-to-shoulder'. In a conspicuous display of unity, over 6,000 marines, soldiers, airmen and sailors from both countries were about to practise the arts of war and humanitarian intervention on beaches and military bases around the country. The sweet-faced girls with the STOP signs, on the other hand, were incensed by the Chinese authorities' efforts to annex the Scarborough Shoal, 230 kilometres off the coast of Luzon. A Philippine operation to detain eight Chinese boats suspected of illegal fishing, eight days before, had turned into a rout. Chinese Marine Surveillance ships had shown up, preventing the Philippine Navy and Coastguard taking any action against the fishermen who had collected hundreds of giant clams and large amounts of coral in defiance of conservation regulations. The impotence of the Manila government in the face of Beijing's might had been brutally exposed.

But for the defacers of the American embassy, Manila's impotence was the result of a century of domination by the United States. In the eyes of Bayan – a coalition of the radical left which includes the League of Filipino Students – US domination poses a much bigger threat to the country's future than the Chinese ships offshore. The word *bayan* means 'nation' in Tagalog and, when asked to describe what his movement stands for, its Secretary-General Renato Reyes is clear: 'left, nationalist, anti-imperialist'. I met Reyes in a slice of Americana, the Yellow Cab Pizza

Parlour on the Manila seafront. He chose the location: conveniently close to the site of yet another demonstration outside the embassy and not far from the hospital where he was about to go and support striking healthcare workers.

As our conversation progressed it became clear how, for Reyes, socialism and nationalism are intertwined. There's a sense of violated pride, the feeling that the country cannot stand tall so long as it lives in the United States' shadow, and that this second-class status is – or should be – felt as a personal humiliation for each individual Filipino. 'A senator long ago characterised it as a "mendicant foreign policy". You're always begging for scraps, always asking for help from your big brother, the United States, and over the past half-century we haven't really developed or modernised because of that.' As he tucks into another slice of Italian-American-Filipino pie, Reyes develops his point: this dependency is a continuation of the colonial strategy to maintain the Philippines as a captive market for American goods in which the Filipino elite reap the rewards of maintaining the economic and political status quo.[4] 'We are opposed to Chinese incursions but we feel that short term and long term the bigger threat would be the United States. If you're going to rank the bullies in this region, the bigger bully would be the United States.'

The organiser of the anti-China protest, on the other hand, is a reluctant nationalist. For decades Walden Bello has been known as a vocal opponent of Western neo-imperialism. But now his Akbayan party is often on the streets to condemn the People's Republic of China and its Communist leadership. (Akbayan plays on the word *bayan*, but *akbay* literally means to put one's arms around someone's shoulders, either in affection or solidarity.) 'I'm not exactly sure whether you can call ours a nationalist position,' he ponders, 'given the fact that nationalist positions have often been associated with irrational nationalism.' Bello denies that he has changed sides. 'No, I think that it's just a bit more of a complex situation. I think that the biggest destabiliser in the area at this point is really the US pivot to Asia. But at the same time the US is making use of China's aggressive moves in the West Philippines Sea to make it appear like it's a balancer.'

The two leaders are bitter political rivals. Reyes' party has described Bello as a 'special agent of the Aquino regime' and Bello describes Reyes as being stuck in the politics of the 1960s. Both, though, share similar views on the role of the United States in world politics. As Reyes explained, 'we don't really see China at this point as having the same imperialist intentions as the United States. Of course it may be headed there, it may want to expand its economic and military force and influence but it hasn't reached the level of the United States wherein the US is prepared to wage war, to colonise and occupy other countries just so they could advance their economic interests.'[5] But in espousing an 'anti-China' position, Bello is also trying to keep the United States out of Filipino affairs: 'if you bring in one superpower to oppose the other, then superpower dynamics begins to push the issue and marginalises a peaceful settlement. I think that balance of power politics is really dangerous because it often ends up with people running out of control, with arms races just like the First World War in Europe.' What appear to be clear 'anti-US' and 'anti-China' positions in the Philippines are not contrasting attitudes to the great powers but something different, rooted in the country's hybrid history.

By the late nineteenth century, two different nationalisms were challenging Spanish rule in the Philippines: one from the elite, the other from the middle class. For centuries Spanish rulers had discriminated against Chinese immigrants and their descendants. The details are long and inglorious but, broadly, the immigrants had a choice. Those who converted to Catholicism were allowed to take up permanent residence, marry and travel around the Philippines – but not back to China. Those who didn't convert were able to travel back and forth to China but the only place they could live in the Philippines was the Manila ghetto known as the Parian. They were barred from either marrying or permanently settling in the Philippines. Until the late 1880s the Spanish officially classified the children of those who converted and married as *mestizo* – 'mixed race'. *Mestizos* took Spanish names, spoke Spanish (unlike 95 per cent of the inhabitants[6]) and adopted Spanish ways, but no matter how wealthy or educated they became, they could never advance to the top of society. From their ranks sprang the 'Ilustrados' – the 'enlightened ones'. José Rizal, the author of the seminal nationalist novel *Noli Me Tángere*, was the paramount example. They began to call themselves 'Filipino' – a term previously reserved for the 'full-blooded' Spanish – and demanded equality.

A different movement emerged from the urban middle classes, partly in response to Spain's brutal response to the Ilustrados – Rizal was executed in 1896, for example. The leadership of the 'The Highest and Most Respectable Society of the Sons of the People', better known as the Katipunan, came from the ranks of office workers and shopkeepers and was predominantly *indio* – native – rather than *mestizo*. Whereas the Ilustrados wanted to be accepted as equals by Spain, the Katipunan fiercely rejected Spanish rule and set out to consciously formulate an alternative national identity. But this national project was also based on chauvinism. Coming mainly from Manila, the Katipunan elevated Luzon culture, in particular the language of Tagalog, to the status of national culture and sought to impose it on the rest of the country. In many places it was – and still is – resisted as an alien intrusion into local life.

When the Katipunan revolted against the Spanish in 1896 many of the Ilustrados fought with them against their common enemy. They sought support from another country that had also thrown off the chains of colonisation. But after the United States had won the battle of Manila Bay, American commanders went on to strangle the infant Republic of the Philippines at birth with a vicious counter-insurgency campaign. Many Ilustrados, alarmed by the rise of the Katipunan and other militaristic groups, abandoned the 'national' interest in favour of their own: they entered a symbiotic relationship with the country's new colonisers.[7] Being highly educated, these Ilustrados (mainly, though not exclusively, descendants of *mestizos*) were well placed to assist the Americans and equally well placed to receive the rewards as the vast 'friar estates' of the Catholic religious orders were expropriated and redistributed. Election laws were written to benefit those with property and education.[8] For half a century American administrators ruled the islands, crushed the opposition and built up the power of the elite. A fraction of the Philippine population – no more than 5 per cent – went on to dominate the entire society. It still does. Presidents Roxas, Laurel, Quirino, Magsaysay, Marcos, Cory Aquino and Benigno Aquino were (or are) all descendants of *mestizos*, for example, as are many of the country's richest families such as the Ayalas, the Aboitiz and the Razons.

But their ascendancy is bitterly opposed by the many groups who claim to be political descendants of the Katipunan. They exist across the political spectrum: from Communist revolutionaries to disillusioned army officers. What they have in common is the belief that members of an elite that 'sold' the country to the United States in exchange for personal gain have no right to call themselves leaders of the nation. In rural areas there has long been a tradition of militancy against landowners and the state they control, dating from the independence war and through the Hukbalahap guerrilla movement of the 1940s and 1950s. The rapid expansion of education in the Philippines in the 1960s helped spread this anger to urban areas. As migrants flocked to the cities, their children grew up politicised by the injustices they saw around them: monstrous social inequality, rampant corruption and ruthless political brutality.

Following the cue of leftist thinkers, such as the historian Teodoro Agoncillo, this radical generation argued that the only true Filipinos were the masses – those at the bottom.[9] Those at the top – members of an elite who had acquired their position from an alliance with the American colonisers – were not truly 'of the nation'. In a country that had only become independent in 1946, comprising a disparate collection of islands forced into a unitary state with little in the way of a 'national' culture, they argued that it was suffering that united the people of the Philippines. The radical left, the forebears of both Bayan and Akbayan, based their appeal to the masses on the argument that the people as a whole were suffering because of abuses being committed by a foreign-backed and, to a degree, alien elite. It was, at its heart, a nationalistic message. They tried to create a national identity for the people – 'Filipino' – out of an economic identity – poverty. For them, to be 'Filipino' was to be anti-American. It was a popular argument that reached deep into the urban slums and the rural plantations. But whereas the political ancestors of Akbayan sought to wrest control of the state through politics, the ancestors of Bayan decided there could be no compromise with a state controlled by the elite and took up arms against it – eventually forming the Maoist New People's Army.

Their different positions on the South China Sea are therefore only the latest in a long series of disputes between opponents of the Filipino elite. From time to time these groups have been able to forge a narrative that unites them and also wins support from the wider population. But the power of anti-American or anti-Chinese rhetoric is inconsistent. At certain moments it can bring huge numbers to the streets but the huddled masses of the Philippines generally pay more attention to religious festivals and escapist soap operas. The story of the suffering of Jesus Christ has more resonance with most Filipinos than the argument that their country is being crucified by a modern-day Pontius Pilate. Three months before the events of April 2012, the procession of the Black Nazarene at the Basilica of Quiapo on the outskirts of Manila drew a crowd estimated at between 6 and 8 million – numbers the left can only dream about.

These personal narratives of suffering and redemption are much more important to most Filipinos than a national narrative of oppression and liberation. That's reinforced by a school curriculum which tells children that their history only began when Magellan arrived in 1521 and which often teaches by using the United States as an ideal against which the Philippines must try to measure up. Seen in this light it's less surprising that, despite a century of colonialism and unequal relations, repeated surveys indicate that Filipinos are the most pro-American people on the planet. Polls by the Pew Global Attitudes Survey and BBC/Globescan from 2002 to 2013 consistently found 85 to 90 per cent of the Filipino population holding positive attitudes towards the US. The 2013 Pew Survey also found that 85 per cent of Filipinos believe the United States takes the Philippines' interests into consideration when formulating its policies.[10] There is a general assumption that the US will be there to support them in any future hour of need.

This lies behind what may appear to be a general passivity in the population about the South China Sea – or the West Philippine Sea as it has been officially known in the country since 5 September 2012.[11] While the 2013 Pew Survey suggested that 90 per cent of the population regarded the dispute with China as a 'big problem' there is little demand for action. 'It's not that Filipinos don't care about the West Philippine Sea, it's just that they know that it belongs to us – by sheer proximity,'[12] argues Jose Santos Ardivilla, a weary observer of these trends as both a cartoonist for the *Manila Star* newspaper under the pen-name 'Sic N Tyred' and a humanities lecturer at the University of the Philippines. 'They're not immediately affected by it and they have other pressing issues. But they do care about sovereignty and ownership because we've heard that the islands are quite mineral rich.' In the days after the Scarborough Shoal incident began, hackers from both the Philippines and China waged an online war to deface each other's websites. There were signs that popular nationalism was being stirred into life over the rocks but it dissipated within days. In short, there is little pressure from below to push the elite into taking action over the territorial disputes. Such pressure that does exist comes from a thin stratum of political activists and commentators but it has little effect: the elite is almost incapable of consensus, let alone concerted action.

One of the most striking features of Philippine politics is just how little agreement there is about the 'national interest'. There is plenty of rhetoric about the nation, particularly at election time, but regional identities are often stronger. As a collection of islands divided internally by steep mountain ranges it's not surprising that people look inwards towards their local ruler rather than outwards to a faraway national capital. Both Spanish and American colonisers found it convenient to rule through these local bosses, cementing both the families' hold on power and their own. For the Philippines as a whole, the result has been local strength and national weakness. Manila is weak, local rulers frequently act with impunity and, even at the national level, powerful families can run private policies purely in their own interests. Since they control the commanding heights of the economy and politics, individuals' influence can be profound and destabilising. The scandals over the NorthRail and Joint Marine Seismic Undertaking projects (see Chapter 5) exposed the way national figures have, time and time again, leveraged the national interest and bargained with foreign governments for their own personal gain.

Very occasionally elite nationalism plays a role in international politics. In 1991 the Senate stunned Washington by voting against the renewal of the 1947 Military Bases Agreement, forcing the closure of the vast American naval base at Subic Bay. But those were special circumstances. Some of the 12 dissident senators were old-school nationalists who felt the country's development had been stunted by its reliance on Uncle Sam. But their numbers were swelled by popular anger against Washington's earlier role in supporting the dictatorship of Ferdinand Marcos (which had, at least in its early years, attempted to reduce the power of the old elite families). Others didn't want the Philippines to host American nuclear weapons and some were angry about the abuse of local women by US servicemen.

Yet 1991 was an exception. The ties that bind the Filipino elite to the United States – the shared language, history and outlook – are tight. But they lull its members into unwarranted comfort based on their assumption that the feeling is mutual. This fraction of society, that has rendered such great service to Washington over several generations, has convinced itself, just as General MacArthur did in 1944, that America 'shall return' in the hour of need and naturally take the Philippine side in any disputes. This exaggerated sense of their own importance blinds policy-makers to changing realities in the region: Washington's relationship with Beijing is now far more important than its obligations to Manila. The result has been dangerous for the country as a whole and it has blundered into foreign policy crises, such as the standoff at Scarborough Shoal in 2012, full of bluster but without the muscle to back it up. This failure of belief in the United States may have wider consequences in the future. The elite may decide that its interests are better served by closer relations with Beijing, or it may stick with Washington and lose its legitimacy in the eyes of the wider population if Washington fails to deliver in crisis after crisis.

But there is another strand to Filipino nationalism that plays on another antipathy – towards the more obviously 'Chinese' minority. In contrast with the *mestizo* elite that sought to hide their Chinese origins, twentieth-century immigrants had little choice but to remain publicly identified as such. For centuries the Fujianese were kept outside Filipino society. The Spanish classified them as 'Sangleys' and then 'Chinos', the American administration passed a 'Chinese Exclusion Law' to control their immigration and a 1947 treaty placed them under the jurisdiction of the Republic of China – a situation that was only ended in 1975 as Manila switched its diplomatic recognition to Communist China and made the 'Chinos' full citizens. As a community they have prospered. Nineteen of the 40 richest Filipinos on the 2013 *Forbes Magazine* list had obviously Chinese surnames: Henry Sy owns shopping malls, Lucio Tan owns beer and tobacco businesses, John Gokongwei owns an airline and real estate, George Ty owns financial services companies – and so on.[13] Some of these fortunes have been bolstered through cooperation with old *mestizo* families – Sy with the Ayalas and Gokongwei with the Lopezes, for example.[14] But prejudice against people with 'short names' lingers. It's common to hear ethnic Chinese referred to as 'intsiks' (insects) by other Filipinos, although the word has now been taken up in an ironic way by some Chinese to refer to themselves. They sometimes refer to new arrivals from

China as 'genuine intsiks'. Today the accepted term for Chinese-Filipinos is 'Tsinoy' – a play upon 'Pinoy', the Tagalog word for Filipino.

The Tsinoy community is most obvious in the Manila district of Binondo, which was originally a piece of land given to Chinese who had converted to Catholicism and their offspring – the original *mestizos*.[15] Binondo became home for the wider Chinese population in the late eighteenth century after the destruction of the Parian 'ghetto' in which the non-converted Chinese had originally been obliged to live (within easy range of the Spanish guns on the city wall). Binondo is also just a cannon shot away from the old city but today the risks to life and limb don't come from gunfire but from the stinking waterways feeding the Pasig River and the miasmas of exhaust fumes that fill the narrow streets. On first sight it appears run down but behind the decay, the district remains a key hub of the national economy. Its small shops are often fronts for much larger trading or distribution businesses. Large tower blocks are going up on the spaces in between.

Partly through heritage and partly through administrative fiat Binondo retains a distinct hybrid character. Binondo was remade in the early 1970s after the mayor of Manila decided that it wasn't 'Chinese' enough. In an effort to attract tourists, ornate pagoda gates were erected at the entrances to the district and the community was ordered to display Chinese signs over their businesses.[16] Incense sticks are lit before Catholic altars, Hong Kong and Hollywood DVDs mingle on the shelves and English mixes with Hokkien, the language of Fujian province on the other side of the sea. As tensions have grown between the Philippines and China, attention has again focused on the loyalties of the Tsinoy population. Are these people any more pro or anti the US or China than the rest of the population?

In the shops of Binondo the overwhelming sentiment is a desire to avoid any kind of trouble. Few will be openly quoted but one print-shop owner typifies the district: 'business is business, politics is politics'. There's wariness though. 'The people in the middle of society don't have a problem with the Chinese but the uneducated ones and those with vested interests might,' he cautions, blaming the media for stirring up antipathies. On a different street Ka Wilson Ng, successful baker and past president of the local Lions Club, personifies Tsinoy hybridity. 'If they attack us, I will defend this country. But if we attack them, I will side with China.' He clearly identifies with 'us' – the Filipinos – but ties still bind him to the other country. Wilson's family came from Fujian three generations before him. He married a Filipino woman and they spoke Hokkien at home but he doubts if his grandchildren can muster more than a few words of the language. It's a story of irresistible integration.

Across the population as a whole, attitudes towards China have been generally positive for many years, albeit less so than towards the United States. In 2005, 54 per cent of Filipinos had a positive view of China and 30 per cent a negative one. By 2011, with trade between the two countries rocketing, the positives were up to 62 per cent with the negatives still on 31 per cent. However, in 2013, in the wake of the Scarborough Shoal standoff, the positives fell back to 48 per cent, according to the Pew Global Attitudes Survey, with 39 per cent now regarding China as more of an enemy than a partner. It seems unlikely that this will translate into popular calls for action, however. Despite rising levels of concern about China's intentions, periodic 'flame wars' between online bloggers and the volubility and pictorial appeal of Manila's street protests, none of the major players in Philippine politics has yet managed to link the struggles over sovereignty and offshore energy resources with the masses' daily struggle for survival. Whether from left or right, the argument is still couched in the high-falutin language of national sovereignty and, in the Philippines, rhetorical battles come a distant second behind the daily struggles to put food on tables.

* * * * * *

Around the coast of the South China Sea other 'Chinese' communities, descendants – in the main – of other Fujianese sojourners, are bedevilled, always to their great irritation, with recurring questions about their loyalties. The stakes are perhaps highest in Indonesia where, during the May 1998 riots in the wake of the Asian financial crisis, Sino-Indonesians were specifically targeted – partly by agents provocateurs from the military who were looking for an excuse for a coup – but also by street mobs. Several hundred ethnic Chinese were killed in the rioting and many thousands more fled the country – taking around $20 billion worth of investment with them. But in the years since, the position of those who stayed and survived has improved dramatically. Chinese culture is celebrated, discrimination has declined and prosperity has returned. The disputes in the South China Sea are virtually irrelevant to them despite the Chinese claim to part of Indonesia's claimed Exclusive Economic Zone near the Natuna Islands. Ever since Indonesia's display of offshore military might in the summer of 1996 (see Chapter 3) Beijing has been circumspect about overtly pursuing the issue. As a result, the issue raises no great passions in the country at all. The 2013 Pew Survey suggested 70 per cent of Indonesians had a favourable view of China, compared to 61 per cent with a positive view of the US. Just 3 per cent saw China as an enemy.

On the map, and occasionally in the sea, Malaysians might have more reason to be concerned about the disputes. The country claims 12 features in the Spratly group and occupies five of them – all within the 'U-shaped line'.[17] Well within its EEZ lies the James Shoal – the Beting Serupai in Malay, Zengmu Ansha in Chinese – which Beijing has officially declared the southernmost point of its territory, although it's 22 metres below the sea surface and over a 1,500 kilometres from China 'proper'. Chinese vessels disrupted oil survey work off the coast of Sarawak, well within Malaysia's EEZ, twice in August 2012 and again on 19 January 2013. But even when Chinese naval vessels stopped at the shoal in March 2013 to try to reinforce their claim, the incident failed to stir emotions. Given that this was just a month before a hotly contested general election this could have been a moment when the issue could potentially have been exploited for political ends – but it wasn't.

'Malaysians are much more occupied with "bread and butter" issues like social justice, corruption, governance, accountability, identity politics and public safety,' says Cheng-Chwee Kuik, a lecturer in Strategic Studies at the National University of Malaysia and an expert on relations with China. In recent years an increasingly assertive civil society has taken to the streets to demand a greater say in national politics but the question of the South China Sea has not been on their lips or placards. In fact Malaysians became more outspoken over a government agreement in June 2012 to rent of a pair of pandas – Feng Yi and Fu Wa – from China for the seemingly extortionate fee of 20 million Ringgit ($6 million) to celebrate 40 years of diplomatic relations. But the resulting abuse poured onto the head of the prime minister, not Beijing.

It's highly unlikely that the question of relations with China will feature in political campaigning for one simple reason: cash. Since 2009, China has been Malaysia's largest trading partner.[18] Two-way trade was worth $90 billion in 2011 with a $30 billion surplus in Malaysia's favour.[19] Neither government nor opposition has any interest in upsetting that. Since the end of the Cold War, Malaysia's governing elite has courted China both economically and diplomatically – and entered a mutually fulfilling relationship. China has opened its doors to Malaysian companies and Malaysian companies have repaid the favour with investment and job creation. China has even provided development aid despite Malaysia being far wealthier than it on a GDP per head basis. In Putrajaya, the federal administrative centre, the net result is a desire to handle relations with Beijing quietly and without popular pressure. Outside government there's little desire to stoke anti-China feeling either: there are few votes to be won in attacking the country's main source of export earnings. There's no urge to bang drums on streets in protest at intangible violations of national sovereignty in which no territory was lost nor blood shed. In the 2013 Pew Survey, Malaysia was (with Pakistan) the world's most pro-China country, with 81 per cent of the population having a positive view (compared to 55 per cent for the US).

The result is good news for the quarter of Malaysia's population with Chinese ancestry. For decades after independence, the ethnically Malay elite regarded the Chinese community as either economically over-dominant or subversively Communist. Members of the Chinese minority resent the regulations and practices that still confine them to second-class citizenship. Relations between the communities were tested again following the 2013 elections when some figures in the governing party referred to the narrow result as a 'Chinese tsunami' after the opposition won every single majority-Chinese constituency. However, a closer look shows the opposition Pakatan Rakyat coalition actually won support from across the ethnic spectrum. Although hostility lingers in some quarters, the ethnic Chinese are now generally championed as both an integral part of Malaysian society and a cultural bridge to the mega-market across the sea.

Singapore is unique in Southeast Asia for having a Chinese majority, making up three-quarters of the population. That was the main reason behind its exit from the Malaysian Federation in 1965. Ever since,

Singapore's ruling party has strived to create its own 'imagined community' – one that citizens of a city state, the offspring of a match between British free trading and Chinese entrepreneurship, could take into their hearts. It found one in its tiny size. Indonesia's former president B.J. Habibie once referred to the country as 'that little red dot' and others have called it 'the nut in the nutcracker' between two much larger majority-Muslim neighbours. It gives the entire country a sense of being a minority and makes survival a national imperative. The parallel with Israel's self-image is clear and, right from independence, the two have shared military expertise and a defence doctrine based upon conscription and reserve duty.

How 'Chinese' is Singapore? At one of the many conferences on the South China Sea that have proliferated in the past few years, one former very senior Singaporean diplomat confided to me that 'this is the only other country run by Chinese', deploring the involvement of Singapore and other Southeast Asian countries in American-led efforts to force a legalistic solution to the disputes. 'China is not interested in these games,' he insisted. Younger diplomats at the conference were adamant that these were the views of an older generation, dismissing his thinking as outdated. But another former Singaporean diplomat, Kishore Mahbubani, now an academic and polemicist for our present 'Asian Century', believes that it does capture an essential truth about Singapore. Of Indian descent, Mahbubani is from a minority in a minority state and he understands the dilemmas that that brings. Although firmly rooted in Singapore he recognises the imagined communities that still exist within its hybrid society. 'If there's ever an outright war between America and China there's no way that Singapore can join a war against China – the population won't support it. But at the same time, in terms of diplomatic posturing, Singapore's certainly very careful and very nuanced. We're neither pro-American nor pro-Chinese. We're pro-Singapore.' At another conference in another luxury hotel, the chairman of the Singapore Institute of International Affairs, Simon Tay, shared the new word he had just coined to describe the political location where he thinks Singapore should position itself: 'equiproximate' to both China and the US.

* * * * * *

Three weeks after Bayan and Akbayan rallied their supporters on the streets of Manila an opposing force mobilised outside the Philippine embassy in Beijing. China's notorious 'angry youth' gathered to defend their country's rights over the Scarborough Shoal or, as they proclaimed it, Huangyan. The protest, on Saturday, 12 May 2012, was passionate – and quickly squashed by the authorities. It didn't take long because just five people had turned up (out of Beijing's population of 20 million).[20] Despite the pathetic attendance, *Xinhua* thought the event deserved coverage not just in print but on its television service CNC too. But why had the protestors turned up on the leafy street outside the embassy, so many days after the incident had started? Was it purely a spontaneous outburst of assertive nationalism?

On the Tuesday before the protest, the Chinese Foreign Ministry had published the full text of its dressing-down of the Philippine ambassador, in which it blamed his government for 'making serious mistakes and . . . stepping up efforts to escalate tensions'.[21] The same evening the Foreign Ministry warned Chinese citizens in the Philippines to stay indoors and avoid 'anti-Chinese protests', and China Central Television reported a warning from the Chinese embassy in Manila about large-scale anti-China marches expected in the city at the end of the week. The day ended with every Chinese nationalist's favourite tabloid newspaper, *Huanqiu Shibao* or *Global Times*, publishing an editorial stating it would be 'a miracle if there is no conflict' between the two countries. On Wednesday, the Manila warning was the top story on four of the five main online news sites and number one on the Twitter-like *weibo* microblogs.[22] Given the authorities' propensity to block *weibo* content they don't like, this could only have happened with official approval. And to cap it all, the Foreign Ministry spokesman warned, during his regular press conference, that the issue 'has already led to a strong reaction and attention from the Chinese masses at home and abroad'.

What could explain this deliberate campaign to provoke nationalist outrage? Two answers emerge from the evidence. Firstly, the campaign exactly coincided with the period when the blind human rights activist, Chen Guangcheng, was seeking asylum inside the American embassy in Beijing. That embarrassment came a month after the scandal-tainted former mayor of Chongqing, Bo Xilai, had been publicly sacked from the Politburo Standing Committee for wrongdoing. In contrast to the Scarborough Shoal standoff, coverage of these two episodes had been strongly suppressed, both in the Chinese media and on social networking sites. The media campaign against Manila was, in part, probably a good way to distract attention from an internal problem but doesn't explain everything.

Perhaps the most remarkable thing about the episode, given concerns about the influence of populist nationalism in China, was the smallness of the public reaction. Despite two more days of high-profile coverage – including a TV reporter being allowed through the Chinese blockade of the shoal to plant a flag there on Thursday and *Xinhua's* republishing of foreign media reports that the southern military region had moved onto a war footing on Friday – only five people turned out in front of the Philippine embassy on the Saturday. There was plenty of online outrage but nothing that would disturb the social peace. In several previous periods of international stress the Chinese authorities have allowed, and sometimes encouraged, street protests. There were demonstrations against the attacks on the ethnic Chinese in Indonesia in 1998, after the American bombing of the Chinese embassy in Belgrade in 1999, following the revision of Japanese history textbooks in 2005, after pro-Tibetan protests against the Olympic Torch relay in Europe in 2008, and during the standoff with Japan at the Senkaku or Diaoyu Islands in 2010 and 2012. In each case officials permitted protests. But in April 2012 there were none.

The lack of street protests did not reflect a low level of interest in the issue. In late 2013 Andrew Chubb, an Australian researcher of Chinese foreign policy-making, commissioned a commercial survey of public attitudes to the South China Sea. The results suggest 53 per cent of the Chinese population pay 'close' or 'very close' attention to developments, only slightly less than the 60 per cent who say the same about the East China Sea disputes, which had provoked severe rioting the year before. This is a population that could, potentially, take to the streets over issues in the South China Sea. Yet it doesn't. Chubb believes that the deliberate stoking of outrage over Scarborough Shoal immediately followed by the firm suppression of street protest shows that nationalist feeling was being deliberately manipulated.

The period was marked by frequent hawkish, and sometimes threatening, commentaries in the Chinese media by a small group of serving or retired military officers. In an article on 26 April 2012 about the Scarborough Shoal standoff, Major General Luo Yuan declared that the Philippines 'has "fired the first shot" strategically. It must pay a price for this and we cannot let this example be set as though after it has finished provoking us it can go back to square one via negotiations.'[23] Hundreds of thousands of *weibo* and news website users commented on this one article alone. Another well-known television pundit is Air Force Colonel Dai Xu. On 28 August 2012, the *Global Times* published an article of Dai's calling Vietnam, the Philippines and Japan 'the three running dogs of the United States in Asia'. 'We only need to kill one, and it will immediately bring the others to heel,' he claimed.[24] Dai has produced even more blood-curdling articles under the pseudonym Long Tao. In one, he warned unspecified Southeast Asian countries extracting hydrocarbons from inside the 'U-shaped line': 'when those towering oil platforms become flaming torches who will be hurt most?'[25]

These officers have spent almost their entire careers in military academies ensuring the armed forces toe the Party line. In an interview with the *Southern Weekend* newspaper in April 2012, Major General Luo explained his job: 'This army was created by our Communist Party, and ever since we were born each one of us has had to know what we live for, why we exist.'[26] Luo is part of the Communist aristocracy: his father, Luo Qingchang, was the former head of the Party's foreign intelligence service. Colonel Dai also has interesting connections. When writing as Long Tao, Dai frequently described himself as a strategic analyst for an obscure think-tank called the China Energy Fund Committee (CEFC). The CEFC is headed by Ye Jianming. Between 2003 and 2005, Ye was deputy head of the Shanghai branch of the China Association for International Friendly Contacts (CAIFC). The CAIFC is considered by China watchers, such as the Washington-based think-tank Project 2049 Institute, to be a front organisation for a key part of military intelligence: the Liaison Department of the General Political Department of the People's Liberation Army.[27] Andrew Chubb believes Ye is probably the grandson of the former head of the People's Liberation Army-Navy, Ye Fei, or perhaps even the son of a former director of the Liaison Department, Ye Xuanning.[28]

In other words, at least two of China's best-known 'military hawks' have direct personal connections into the heart of Chinese military intelligence and propaganda. By their own admission,[29] these 'hawks' are operating within military and Communist Party discipline and, given their easy access to the media, their role appears to be to strengthen the image of China as a threat. Why would the Beijing leadership want to amplify such voices? The most likely answer is that they serve two useful purposes: domestic and international. They promote patriotic feelings among the populace and also encourage the 'angry youth' to let off steam online. That allows the leadership to claim it is under domestic pressure to take a hard line – something that strengthens its hand in dealings with other countries. They also create an impression that 'hawks' represent a genuine constituency among the military, which may be wresting control of policy-making. If other governments, notably in Manila and Washington, become fearful of provoking irrational action by these 'hawks', their political resolve is likely to be undermined. In other words, one of the roles of the 'media hawks' is to intimidate rivals in the region and make up with bluster what China lacks in actual military power. They also make China's overall strategy less obvious and therefore harder to counter. The media jingoism, then, is not necessarily a sign that the Beijing leadership is struggling to contain waves of extreme nationalism, but rather shows the careful use of nationalist sentiments as a diplomatic tool. If it were to allow street protests, the Party leadership would face the same problem as its Vietnamese counterpart: the risk of them running out of control. Aggressive online punditry is more easily turned off once its usefulness is exhausted. Beijing would prefer the appearance of public pressure without the threat of public disorder.

Just as in Vietnam, there is clearly a substantial section of the population which feels passionately about the South China Sea, but that isn't what's driving Chinese policy. In both countries it's not the masses pushing governments into confrontation but rather governments using nationalism to further their own agendas. The Communist parties of China and Vietnam seek two kinds of legitimacy: material and psychological. Both leaderships need to deliver rising living standards to their populations and also demonstrate their 'moral' fitness to rule. Both parties face similar existential threats – the ebbing of popular support if they fail to deliver prosperity and the existence of rival claimants to their thrones. A strong position in the South China Sea will, they hope, provide access to the resources to fuel economic growth and also demonstrate their superiority over their critics. To buttress their right to rule, both parties promote official versions of history that frame them as the saviours of the nation.

In 1991, two years after the crushing of the Tiananmen Square democracy protests, the Chinese Party leadership promulgated a 'patriotic education' campaign, 'to boost the nation's spirit, enhance cohesion, foster national self-esteem and pride, consolidate and develop a patriotic united front to the broadest extent possible, and direct and rally the masses' patriotic passions to the great cause of building socialism with Chinese characteristics.'[30] Twenty years later, on 1 March 2011, the National Museum of China in Tiananmen Square unveiled its grand new permanent exhibition, 'The Road to Revival'. Spread over two floors of the northern end of the museum, high-definition displays and panoramic projections tell the story of that humiliating century from the first 'Opium War' of 1840 up to the victory of the people's revolution in 1949 and beyond. The exhibition's curator Cao Xinxin told journalists its purpose was 'to show visitors the real scenes that happened in history'.[31] Eighteen months after that, the freshly appointed leader of the Communist Party, Xi Jinping, chose the exhibition as the venue to launch his big idea – the 'Chinese Dream'.

From local schoolroom to national museum the leadership has worked to instil the notion that China's modern history was shameful until the Party took over. While much of the message is about taking pride in the country's contemporary achievements, it's underpinned by a sense of personal violation at the dismemberment of the country's national territory and the collective violation of the Chinese people at the hands of foreigners. This narrative, in turn, now underpins mainstream discussion of territorial issues. Any questioning of it provokes a stern response. In 2006, the Communist Youth League's weekly magazine *Freezing Point* was closed for two months after it printed an article by a retired philosophy professor, Yuan Weishi, in which he said that the version of history taught in the country's schools was akin to 'drinking wolf's milk'. 'If these innocent children swallow fake pills, then they will live with prejudices for their own lives and go down the wrong path', he argued. The Party didn't agree and only allowed the magazine to reopen if it printed a long article putting the professor back in his place.

The result is that discussions of the South China Sea, whether elite or popular, nationalist or liberal, now take place within a discourse that begins by assuming that the islands are naturally 'ours' – an inseparable part of the motherland since ancient times – and that foreigners have wrongfully taken them from 'us'. This provides the foundation for both online angry youth and elite policy-making. More importantly it creates a national narrative that, in effect, stakes the legitimacy of the ruling elite upon their performance over these tiny islands. When the Norwegian researcher Leni Stenseth finished her thesis on the subject in 1998 she could argue that 'the Spratly conflict was only to a limited extent embedded in an official nationalism discourse', because of the relative absence of articles on the subject in official newspapers.[32] Sixteen years on, the situation has changed significantly: multiple articles flow forth daily in newspapers, web pages and the broadcast media. In the rhetorical competition with the rival claimants to its throne in Taipei there is no way that Beijing can make an orderly retreat from its South China Sea position without suffering some kind of crisis in legitimacy.

Zha Daojiong, the urbane but steely professor of International Political Economy at Peking University, reinforces the case that China's stance in the South China Sea is driven not by mass nationalism but by the leadership's need for credibility – abroad and at home. 'It's about standing firm, rather than stamping your feet and throwing your arms in the air while doing nothing,' he told me. For him, the crucial transition came in September 2008, a month after the triumph of the Beijing Olympics, when 40,000 Hong Kong investors collectively lost $2.5 billion in the collapse of the American bank, Lehman Brothers. Although almost all their money was repaid three years later, the shock did irreparable damage to the Chinese elite's faith in the American way of running the world. Before then, according to Professor Zha, Chinese policy-makers were happy to use Western vocabulary and thinking. Afterwards, there was a reassessment.

It was during this period that the notion of an alternative 'China Model' began to take off. David Bandurski of the Hong Kong University-based China Media Project calculates the phrase was used in around 500 online headlines in 2007, around 800 in 2008 but, after a push by the official *Xinhua* news agency, the figure quadrupled to 3,000 in 2009.[33] The phrase has since dropped in popularity – replaced by President Xi's 'Chinese Dream' – but the sense of specialness has endured. Bandurski calls it a 'discourse of greatness', or *shengshi huayu*. The trouble-making Professor Yuan traces its roots back to the original nineteenth-century burst of nationalism, arguing that 'a sense of righteousness was passed on like a spiritual birthright from generation to generation'.[34]

In one crucial aspect China's rhetorical development is mirroring that of the United States: both now share a semi-official discourse, a national ideology, of 'exceptionalism'. The American national belief – shared by both elite and popular opinion – in their country's 'manifest destiny' to spread liberty around the world is increasingly matched by an official Chinese discourse of 'righteousness' in its international affairs. This sense of righteousness – combining victimhood with superiority – increasingly appears like arrogance to smaller countries on the receiving end. And in the end, this uncritical self-view may be the undoing of the entire project. It may provoke the other countries of the region to resist Beijing's advances.

For now, the 'angry youth' of the countries around the South China Sea are fighting their battles in the comment sections of English-language news websites. When tensions rise out at sea, passions boil over online. New imagined communities are being forged in the posting and flaming, and new divisions entrenched. The drum-beating and the symbol-waving are manna for editors eager to render the disputes interesting to uncomprehending audiences but they are a poor guide to reality. The governments in China and Vietnam are rarely swayed by public opinion on matters of foreign policy, the chances of a coherent nationalist movement becoming influential in the Philippines are remote, and elsewhere in the region there is little public concern about the disputes. It is in the interests of all these governments to make it look as if they are under attack from hotheaded nationalists, to the extent that they might even be forced to take what appears to be foolhardy action if it improves leverage against their rivals. These displays of power certainly carry the risk of provoking conflict by mistake. However by far the greatest risk to peace and security in the South China Sea is not angry street nationalism but the interplay of these regional disputes with the growing confrontation between the two great powers in the region.

CHAPTER 7

Ants and Elephants
Diplomacy

DUSK IN PHNOM PENH, Friday, 18 December 2009. Twenty members of China's Uyghur minority are resting in an apartment provided by the United Nations High Commission for Refugees (UNHCR). They fled the eastern province of Xinjiang following clashes between Muslim Uyghurs and Han Chinese the previous July in which at least 200 people had been killed. After tense journeys through Vietnam and Laos the Uyghurs might have felt safe. The day before, Cambodia's Prime Minister, Hun Sen, had signed a sub-decree committing his country to international standards in dealing with refugees and asylum seekers. This was a surprise: the decree had been delayed for several years and diplomats didn't expect it to be signed for several more months. Why the urgency?

The Uyghurs' presence in the city had become common knowledge two weeks earlier after the World Uyghur Congress had publicised their plight to the *Washington Post*. Unusually, the Chinese government made little public comment about the issue – despite regarding Uyghur activists as 'splitists' and religious extremists. When asked about the group on 8 December, the Foreign Ministry spokeswoman noted China's friendly relationship with Cambodia and called for 'enhanced cooperation to fight terrorism' – but her comments were omitted from the official transcript.[1] On 15 December she said only that members of the group 'were involved in crimes' and were being investigated by Chinese authorities. She warned that 'the international refugee protection system should not be a haven for criminals to evade legal sanctions', but said little else.[2]

In private, Beijing was more voluble. On 14 December, Cambodia's Foreign Ministry acknowledged receiving a diplomatic note about the Uyghurs from the Chinese embassy. But the same day, according to US cables released via Wikileaks, UNHCR's Cambodia director told the American ambassador that discussions with the Cambodian government about the Uyghurs were positive and the cases would be resolved within a few weeks.[3] Over the following three days everything changed. The sub-decree the Prime Minister signed also ended an agreement with UNHCR under which the two shared responsibility for refugees and asylum seekers. Immediately the ink had dried, Cambodia's Acting Interior Minister, Em Sam An, ordered the Uyghurs to be deported, claiming they had violated the country's Immigration Law.

In the evening of 18 December, police raided the UNHCR 'safe house' and took away the occupants, including a mother and two children, at gunpoint. The following evening they were put on board a private jet that had just arrived from China and flown off into the darkness.[4] International protests – both to the Cambodian and Chinese governments and to the UNHCR – were swift and loud but useless. Later reports suggested that four of the group had been sentenced to life imprisonment, four to 20 years, four to 17 years and four to 16 years. The woman and her two children were released.[5]

The day after that plane took off from Cambodia, a different one arrived. This one bore the then Vice-President of China, Xi Jinping, ending a four-country tour of Asia. Two days later, headlines proclaimed a mightily successful visit: 14 agreements signed and, according to the Cambodian side, promises of $1.2 billion in aid. Dams would be built, roads constructed and ancient temples restored. Cambodian diplomats insisted the fate of the Uyghurs didn't feature on the agenda at all[6] but the linkage between the two seemed clear to most outside observers. And according to another American cable, Cambodia's Deputy Prime Minister Sar Kheng had told UNHCR's regional representative that his government was in a 'difficult position due to pressure from outside forces'.

That private admission demolished Hun Sen's public narrative of his country's relations with China. Speaking the previous September at the construction site of the third of eight 'Cambodia–China Friendship' bridges, the Prime Minister had lauded the Beijing leadership for providing aid without strings. 'They are quiet, but at the same time they build bridges and roads, there are no complicated conditions'[7] – such as observing international human rights conventions, for example.[8]

Human rights groups continued to criticise the Phnom Penh government over the Uyghur deportation and, as a result, four months later, on 1 April 2010, the US government announced it was suspending a shipment of 200 surplus military trucks and trailers to Cambodia.[9] Meant as a slap on the wrist from Washington, it became an opportunity for Beijing. Just a month later, the Chinese government announced that it would provide 256 trucks – brand new, not surplus – and 50,000 uniforms on top. When the vehicles arrived at the end of June, the photo-op featured the tall and athletic-looking political commissar of the General Armaments Department of the People's Liberation Army, General Chi Wanchun, placing a giant key into the grasping hands of the short, portly and over-eager Cambodian Deputy Minister of Defence, Moeung Samphan. Coming less than a month after the formal opening of that third 'Cambodia–China Friendship Bridge', the moment seemed to symbolise the future of Cambodia's foreign relations.

But the US wasn't going to be outplayed by a giant key and some long bridges. Three weeks after the big Chinese truck handover, Washington's man was in Phnom Penh with his own gift: a crate-full of antiquities. Under secretary of State for Political Affairs William J. Burns made a special trip to mark the 60th anniversary of diplomatic ties between the two countries, taking the opportunity to hand over seven looted Cambodian statues and carvings seized by customs authorities in Los Angeles. The relics had been transported aboard a US Navy medical ship that sailed into town to win hearts and minds with free healthcare. Elsewhere in the country, other hearts and minds were being wooed with the renewing of military ties – only two months after their supposed suspension.

As the statues were being handed over, American and Cambodian troops were taking part in the first ever multilateral peacekeeping training on Cambodian soil, dubbed Angkor Sentinel 10. It was part of the US State Department-funded 'Global Peace Operations Initiative' which has facilitated cooperation between American forces and many other armies since 2006. Human rights groups, though, were continuing to criticise the choice of Cambodia for the 2010 exercise – partly because of the Uyghur deportation but mainly because, they alleged, some of the Cambodian military units taking part were guilty of forced evictions of farmers, torture and summary executions. That was denied by the US embassy which said its staff had 'rigorously vetted' the participants in the exercise – all several hundred of them. Unusually the peacekeeping exercise involved a combined parachute jump for Cambodian paratroopers and US special forces.[10] If the US government had had doubts about supporting the Cambodian military a few weeks before, they had disappeared.

In fact, Cambodian defence cooperation with the United States goes much deeper than a couple of hundred second-hand trucks. In 2013, Carl Thayer, an expert on Southeast Asian militaries, estimated the annual value of US military assistance to Cambodia at over $18 million.[11] Exercise Angkor Sentinel is now an annual event. So are the CARAT – Cooperation Afloat Readiness And Training – exercises at sea. The third pillar of US military aid (after peacekeeping and military education) is counter-terrorism. Cambodia doesn't have a terrorism problem but the country's counter-terrorism force is, at the time of writing, commanded by Lieutenant General Hun Manet, the prime minister's eldest son. He and his unit are directly advised by a small team of American special forces based out of the US embassy. In fact, for all the talk of strengthening Cambodia's ability to take part in international peacekeeping, American military aid seems deliberately targeted at areas likely to deliver political influence. All three of Hun Sen's sons have received American military training. Manet went to West Point in 1999, Manith to the George C. Marshall European Center for Security Studies in 2010 and the youngest, Many, attended the National Defense University in 2011.[12] At the time of writing, Manith is Cambodia's Deputy Chief of Intelligence, with the rank of Brigadier General, and 30-year-old Hun Many is his father's Deputy Chief of Cabinet, head of his party's youth wing[13] and, since the July 2013 elections, a member of the National Assembly.

We can't know to what extent the Hun dynasty feels beholden to the United States for this largess, but we do know that the Chinese authorities are prepared to spend plenty of cash trying to sway the Huns in their direction. Beijing has a key advantage: a dearth of domestic human rights activists prepared to criticise its military aid policies. A year after the truck delivery in 2010, China loaned Cambodia $195 million to buy 12 new Chinese-built Zhi-9 military helicopters. In May 2012 the two countries' defence ministers agreed a further $17 million training arrangement, augmented in January 2013 with commitments to provide yet more training and equipment.[14] The Chinese embassy didn't need to investigate whether the beneficiaries were guilty of torturing farmers before committing to the deal.

There has been consternation in Phnom Penh, and also in American policy circles, about the extent to which Cambodia has been 'bought' by Beijing. Very large figures have been quoted for the amount of aid now being provided by China – such as the much-trumpeted $1.2 billion that followed Xi Jinping's visit. A more thorough look at that figure, however, shows a less impressive reality. The Chinese side gave no information at all and the Cambodians couldn't provide a detailed breakdown of the figures – just a list of 14 agreements mainly covering loans to build roads and other infrastructure. Shortly afterwards, the Cambodian ambassador to China, Khek Caimealy Sysoda, told American diplomats in Beijing that the figure was 60 per cent loans and 40 per cent grants and included hydro-electric projects.[15] There was no way that the money could be disbursed in a single year. In short, the $1.2 billion included agreements made earlier and delayed so they could coincide with Xi's visit, commercial investments which were not aid and commitments that would take many years to fulfil.[16] The headline announcement was just the kind of political spin designed to make American observers sit up and get nervous.

In 1964 the then Cambodian leader Norodom Sihanouk advised a *National Geographic* reporter, Thomas S. Abercrombie: 'When two elephants are fighting, the ant should step aside'.[17] Ten years later Sihanouk's country was crushed in the conflict between American capitalism and the Russian and Chinese variants of Communism. Nowadays, the Cambodian government, and particularly the military, regard playing the 'elephants' off against each other as good politics and good business. Their priority is to stay in power and continue to enrich themselves and fellow members of what local wits have dubbed the 'Khmer Riche'. Having two wealthy rivals prepared to subsidise their political projects and personal lifestyles can only be a good thing. The trick is to keep both of them in a permanent state of anxiety about whether they are losing out to the other. Hun Sen is a master of the diplomatic equivalent of 'treat 'em mean to keep 'em keen'.

But Cambodia's foreign dealings are not simply about playing off the two rivals. The legacy of the country's bitter history is uneasy, sometimes hostile, relations with its two most significant neighbours: Thailand and Vietnam. Cambodia has active border disputes with both countries and nationalist feelings have been quick to surface during, for example, clashes with Thailand about which country owns the land around the highly symbolic Preah Vihear temple. Vietnam may have overthrown the Chinese-backed *génocidaires* of the Khmer Rouge in 1979 and installed Hun Sen in power but popular animosity towards the Vietnamese is widespread and fervent. In the Cambodian narrative of 'national humiliation' the 'Yuon' wrongfully seized Khmer lands in the Mekong Delta and are responsible for two centuries of atrocities and injustices since. There is little sense of regional solidarity and most Cambodians would relish a chance to get back at the foreigners who stole 'their' territory.

The battle for the loyalties of little Cambodia exemplifies the bigger struggle for influence across Southeast Asia. Like the monsoon winds, pressure and persuasion blow alternately from different points of the compass. Like the monsoon, these global, regional and local currents can bring good and ill: aid, trade and investment but also corruption and militarisation. Delegations sweep in from east and west and local elites seek to harness the forces they represent for their country's (or simply their own) benefit. American anxiety about China's rise and Chinese anxiety about American encirclement combine with long-standing local grievances and regional power struggles to create crises and opportunities.

The Southeast Asian 'ants' still fear the consequences of a rumble in the jungle. None of them wishes to make a choice between the US and China. The US is the region's largest investor and China is its main trading partner. Southeast Asian governments know that their rapid economic growth is based upon the stability created by American military dominance and most have some form of defence arrangement with the US. They are also well aware that China is close, and getting closer. The rivalry between the two has created new opportunities for the ants. In the half-century since Sihanouk used his animal metaphor they have learnt how to make the most of the elephants, bringing them on side when it's in their interests, rebuffing their demands if they become too assertive. At the same time they can't avoid being caught up in big-power battles. The disputes in the South China Sea have caused local, regional and global battles to become interlinked in a way not seen in the region since the end of the Indochina wars in 1975.

* * * * * *

'Southeast Asia' is a relatively new part of the world: it only broke away from the 'Far East' in the mid-twentieth century with the encouragement of German academics and Japanese strategists. But while anthropologists such as Robert Heine-Geldern discussed the culture of 'Sudostasien' and Japanese generals plotted to invade it, the rest of the world – including 'Southeast Asia' itself – remained largely oblivious to its existence. The Japanese authorities coined the term 'Nanyo' to describe a region stretching from Taiwan to Papua New Guinea within their 'Greater Asian Co-Prosperity Sphere'. It wasn't until 16 November 1943, however, when the wartime Allies created 'South East Asia Command' to fight the Japanese, that the term properly entered the English language.[18] But South East Asia Command (SEAC) was responsible for the war only in India, Burma, the Malay Peninsula and Sumatra. The Philippines, Borneo, the rest of the Dutch East Indies and Papua New Guinea remained in South West Pacific Command and the position of French Indochina was left vague until the Allies' conference in the Berlin suburb of Potsdam in July 1945. At that meeting 'South East Asia' took on its modern shape: Borneo and Java were transferred to SEAC and, in an eerie precursor of later events, Indochina was partitioned between SEAC in the south and the China Command in the north. South East Asia Command was abolished in November 1946 but the term, or rather the vision of a coherent region called 'South East Asia', stuck around – and became a weapon in another kind of war.

Once again it was a military vision – and one imposed from outside. At its foundation in Manila in September 1954, only two of the members of the South East Asia Treaty Organisation (SEATO) were actually from the region: Thailand and the Philippines. The others – the US, the UK, Australia, France, Pakistan and New Zealand – had other reasons to join. Britain still had colonies in what are now Brunei, Malaysia and Singapore, and France, although it had withdrawn from northern Vietnam, still had a presence in southern Vietnam, Laos and Cambodia. The US wanted to create an anti-Communist alliance but SEATO lacked credibility. It slowly withered until 1977 when it was finally put out of its misery following the Communist victories in Cambodia, Laos and Vietnam. Its influence lingers in the security treaties between the United States and Thailand and the Philippines.

By 1958 fear of domestic Communist subversion and of Chinese regional domination were motivating more home-grown initiatives, including an abortive 'South-East Asia Friendship and Economic Treaty' (SEAFET) promoted by Malaya. The wreckage of that effort led, in July 1961, to the foundation of the Association of Southeast Asia (ASA), which combined the region's three most dynamic economies: Malaya, Thailand and the Philippines. ASA was publicly 'non-political' but, in the context of the Cold War, it clearly had an anti-Communist purpose.

The first challenge facing the members of ASA was to convince sceptics that a regional organisation had any role at all. Indonesia's nationalist government regarded it as a front for American policy: its Foreign Minister Subandrio told visitors the idea was 'without substance' and 'useless'.[19] It was also hard to see a coherent regional identity emerging when individual countries were unable to agree where their shared borders lay. Four months after ASA's foundation, a new Filipino president, Diosdado Macapagal, renewed his country's claim to North Borneo – which was due to become the province of Sabah in newly independent Malaysia. In the wake of the claim ASA withered too.

Indonesia was simultaneously asserting its own claim to Sabah, along with the rest of northern Borneo. In 1963 the Sukarno government initiated *konfrontasi* to try to force Malaysia to give up the territory. It took a military coup in Indonesia to reanimate the idea of Southeast Asia. General Suharto deposed Sukarno in March 1966 and a few months later, on 1 June 1966, Indonesia agreed to end *konfrontasi*. It was the turning point. Two days later Malaysia and the Philippines established full diplomatic relations. With the 'American War' now raging in Vietnam and Chinese-sponsored Communist movements causing trouble at home, Southeast Asian elites came to the view that closer relations between countries would enhance their ability to rule within them. By banding together they could

promote trade and economic growth to satisfy the needs of growing populations and also keep others out of their domestic affairs and foreign policies. The result was the foundation, in Bangkok on 8 August 1967, of
the Association of South-East Asian Nations (ASEAN), bringing together
the three members of ASA with Indonesia and Singapore. Southeast Asia
finally had a regional organisation worthy of the term.

ASEAN had a slow beginning. It was almost killed within a year when
the Philippines once again renewed its claim on Sabah and the mutual
mistrust lingered. It took the Communist victories in Indochina in 1975
to spur ASEAN into action. Its leaders (anti-Communist strongmen like
Suharto, Ferdinand Marcos and Lee Kuan Yew) held their first summit in
Bali in February 1976 and signed the Treaty of Amity and Cooperation
– in which they pledged to 'refrain from the threat or use of force and
. . . settle such disputes among themselves through friendly negotiations'.
They pioneered the 'ASEAN Way': pledging to work by 'consensus' and
turning a blind eye to unpleasant events in each other's countries. Two
decades of 'Asian Tiger' growth followed, but Southeast Asian crony capitalism crashed in the 1997 Asian financial crisis. Since then, the desire
to compete in the globalised economy – and also to keep the big powers
at arm's length – has obliged the region's ruling elites to form closer ties.
ASEAN has doubled in size (from five to ten members) and tripled in
aspiration. ASEAN is becoming a 'community' modelled on the European
Union (EU) and based on three pillars: political-security, economic, and
social-cultural. The region has travelled a long way from the days when
neighbours threatened to invade each other.

* * * * * *

In early 2008, Derek J. Mitchell was having trouble raising money. His
employer, the Center for Strategic and International Studies (CSIS), is one
of Washington's best-funded think- tanks but its usual donors weren't interested in Southeast Asia. Instead Mitchell had to turn to the embassy of
Thailand for his programme's core funding. In September 2008, Mitchell
organised a conference on 'The United States and Southeast Asia' with
several contributors from Thailand and a few from elsewhere. All said similar
things: Southeast Asia felt ignored by Washington. Professor K.S. Nathan

of the National University of Malaysia complained that the ten ASEAN countries combined received just a tenth of the attention given to Japan. The director of the Diplomatic Academy of Vietnam called for the United States to be a greater contributor to regional security and the Singaporean ambassador said the Western financial crisis had reinforced the impression that the United States was 'a distracted power'. Panitan Wattanayagorn, an advisor to the Thai Ministry of Defence, talked of a prevalent sense in the region that 'China is too near and the United States is too far'.

The delegates complained that the Bush administration just wasn't visible enough in Asia. 'There was talk of China eating our lunch,' Mitchell recalls. President Bush had skipped the 2007 ASEAN–US summit and his Secretary of State, Condoleezza Rice, had missed two of her three ASEAN Regional Forum meetings. This wasn't an entirely fair picture. While most of the Bush administration were busy with the 'War on Terror', some had already begun looking at other priorities. As one former Pentagon policy-maker explains, 'the work had been done back in 2007–8. The big pivot point was the ASAT test in January 2007.' The 'ASAT test' was an unannounced Chinese missile firing that destroyed a defunct orbiting satellite and startled the American military. The Pentagon began to change tack. In May 2008, Defense Secretary Robert Gates stood up at the annual Shangri-La Dialogue in Singapore and reminded everyone that the United States was still 'a resident power in Asia' and, in a first for a senior American official, mentioned the South China Sea and the importance of freedom of navigation.[20] American diplomats were still very active in the region and the US military retained hundreds of thousands of military personnel based around the continent, it was just that, with all the attention given to Iraq and Afghanistan, people had stopped noticing.

Mitchell's final work for CSIS was a report on 'US Alliances and Emerging Partnerships in Southeast Asia' with the pointed subtitle: 'Out of the Shadows'. It made four main recommendations: the US should reinvigorate its alliances, cultivate relationships with emerging powers, develop relationships with regional multilateral bodies and work closely with leading Southeast Asian countries on economic issues. By the time it was published in mid-2009 Mitchell had joined the new Obama administration as Principal Deputy Assistant Secretary of Defense for Asian and Pacific Security Affairs. Another think-tanker, Kurt Campbell, had just moved from the Center for a New American Security to become Assistant Secretary of State for East Asian and Pacific Affairs. Both had worked in the Pentagon's Asia team during Bill Clinton's administration in the 1990s. They took up their new jobs at a time of great pessimism, in the wake of the worst economic crisis for decades. According to Campbell, 'Most of our assessments suggested that our Chinese friends generally viewed the United States as being in a deep and irreversible decline and that we would be out of Asia over the course of a few decades.'[21] Mitchell borrowed a line from Woody Allen to describe his strategy: '90 per cent of life is just showing up'. The United States would become more visible in Asia.

The new Secretary of State, Hillary Clinton, was briefed and ready. Her first trip in office, in February 2009, took her to Japan, South Korea, Indonesia and China. In Jakarta she announced that the US would sign the ASEAN Treaty on Amity and Cooperation. This was a strategic move that the then Australian Prime Minister, Kevin Rudd, had been pushing the United States to make for some time. It gave the United States member-ship of the East Asian Summit, which brings ASEAN leaders around the table with counterparts from China, Japan, Russia and India among other countries. Clinton signed the treaty on 22 July. In between, on 7 May, the Chinese government had alarmed the entire region by appending a map of the 'U-shaped line' to its submission on the United Nations' Commission on the Limits of the Continental Shelf. It was the first time it had used the line in an official international context and, in so doing, appeared to be laying claim to almost the entirety of the South China Sea. The game changed.

Until this point, and as far back as the Second World War, the United States had consistently refused to take sides in the sovereignty disputes in the South China Sea. But under Hillary Clinton the intra-regional conflicts over territory and the wider issues between the US and China began to interlink. According to Mitchell's successor at CSIS, Ernie Bower, this was the point at which the Obama administration came to recognise that 'the Chinese are reading their own press releases and actually do believe that it's their time. They've dropped the Deng doctrine of "hide your capabilities, bide your time" and they're responding to a domestic political push for the Chinese to assert themselves.'[22] This was compounded by what was, from an American point of view, a disastrous visit to China by President

Obama in November 2009. 'Obama tried a new approach, proposing a world where the US and China would work together,' Bower remembers, 'but that was seen as weakness in Beijing. That was when the Campbells and Mitchells asserted themselves and said "we need to broaden the chessboard here" and define a return to Asia, using ASEAN-based architecture that will force the Chinese to come to the table because ASEAN is hard-wired for regional balance.'

So Clinton kept on showing up at ASEAN events, and getting more deeply involved in regional politics. Several ASEAN members, concerned by China's new-found assertiveness, were now keen to play the 'American card'. The result was a showdown in Hanoi at the ASEAN Regional Forum or ARF – another venue where ASEAN meets its neighbours and the world's major powers. In July 2010 Clinton told the annual meeting that:

> The United States supports a collaborative diplomatic process by all claimants for resolving the various territorial disputes without coercion. We oppose the use or threat of force by any claimant. While the United States does not take sides on the competing territorial disputes over land features in the South China Sea, we believe claimants should pursue their territorial claims and accompanying rights to maritime space in accordance with the UN Convention on the Law of the Sea. Consistent with customary international law, legitimate claims to maritime space in the South China Sea should be derived solely from legitimate claims to land features.[23]

Part of this was a restatement of an American position first announced in May 1995 but the emphasis on 'collaborative diplomatic process' was new and a public statement of support for the ASEAN claimants' strategy. Her comments about the threat of force, accordance with UNCLOS and the derivation of claims solely from land features were clear rebukes to the Chinese position. Following her speech, 11 other countries commented on the Sea disputes. This was the first time they had been raised at a meeting of ARF: American forthrightness had given ASEAN members and other countries the political cover they needed to speak up. The Chinese government accused Washington of making trouble but, according to Derek Mitchell, Clinton only spoke as she did because of requests from the region. 'There is no doubt. The issue was Southeast Asia pushing us. The Chinese like to have a narrative of victimisation but that wasn't how it was.' However, ASEAN didn't want to push this assertiveness too far. Exactly two months later, at the second US–ASEAN summit in New York, the final communiqué made no mention whatsoever of the South China Sea.[24] The 'ants' had made their point and now wanted to calm the waters to avoid upsetting the other elephant in the region.

After 2010, American calls for 'ASEAN unity' and 'ASEAN centrality' became louder. The phrases sound benign but in the context of the South China Sea they aren't neutral: it's an attempt to corral all ten member states into standing behind, in particular, Vietnam and the Philippines in their territorial disputes with China. But a former ASEAN Secretary-General, Rodolfo Severino of the Philippines, gave me a pessimistic assessment of the chances of American success: 'I don't think you can get ASEAN to agree to anything, because each country has a different perspective on it. It's all national interests – or what they think are their national interests. Very few leaders are willing to take a long view on this because the next election is only two or three years away.' The Chinese understand this very well and have worked doggedly to frustrate any combined ASEAN activity on the disputes. Some ASEAN states have little interest in the Sea, few obligations to the claimant countries and enjoy the benefits of Chinese investment and largess. ASEAN is already being pulled in different directions.

* * * * * *

Another evening in Phnom Penh: two and a half years after the Uyghur deportation. The venue is grander but the issue is the same: to whose tune does Cambodia dance? This time it's not refugees and humanitarian groups asking the question but the foreign ministers of ASEAN. It's almost exactly 45 years since their predecessors signed the Bangkok Declaration and the organisation has come a long way. The meetings in Phnom Penh are being held under the official slogan of 'One Community, One Destiny'. And yet, in one of the many grandiose meeting rooms inside the optimistically named Peace Palace, ASEAN is in crisis over the South China Sea.

The story can begin when ASEAN first took a united position on the Sea, with the 'Manila Declaration' of July 1992; or with the first attempts to draft an enforceable 'Code of Conduct' for the Sea, which began in March 1995 immediately after the Chinese occupation of Mischief Reef (see Chapter 3); or with the adoption by ASEAN and China of a 'Declaration on the Conduct of Parties in the South China Sea' (DOC) in November 2002; or with the agreement of 'Guidelines to Implement the DOC' in July 2011. The issue has been the same for more than two decades: some members of ASEAN want to bind China to a set of rules limiting its actions in the Sea, in particular to prevent it occupying any more land features. It clearly helps Vietnam and the Philippines, and to a lesser extent Brunei, Malaysia and Indonesia, if they can face China with the backing of all ten members of ASEAN. It's clearly to China's advantage if it can negotiate with each country separately. The struggle has been interminable.

In March 2012 I met the Filipino Foreign Secretary, Albert del Rosario. The huge windows in his giant office at the top of the Department of Foreign Affairs provided a panoramic view over Manila Bay and the Sea beyond. Del Rosario knew very well what was at stake out there. Before taking up his position he had been a director of both FirstPacific and Philex: companies that own controlling stakes in Forum Energy. Just as he was moving between jobs, a year before our conversation, the *Veritas Voyager*, contracted by Forum to survey the Reed Bank for gas deposits, had been obstructed by ships from China Marine Surveillance (see Chapter 5). China seemed determined to stop Forum from developing the field. Del Rosario said the Philippines wanted a set of rules, a Code of Conduct, to resolve the problem: 'We realise that the hydrocarbon deposits there are very important to our future. We need those resources for our economic development as quickly as possible. It could be the game-changer for us.'

There was another, symbolic, reason to push ahead with the Code of Conduct. November 2012 would be the tenth anniversary of the signing of the DOC. The issue had been drifting for a decade. ASEAN, which was then being chaired by Cambodia, had assigned the job of drawing up yet another draft of the code to the Philippines but del Rosario revealed that he was working on something even more ambitious. 'You're catching us at a time when we're trying to begin an initiative which we feel is the way to move forward,' he told me. 'There are four claimants from ASEAN. What we think we ought to be doing, and we've started this process, is to get together with the country that is closest to ourselves in terms of thinking how we may be able to settle these issues [Vietnam]. We will, on a bilateral basis, work with this country in terms of settling issues between us quietly. Then the two of us will go to the third country [Malaysia] and say would you like to do this with us and then if we get that done then the three countries will go to the fourth country [Brunei] . . . And then we turn around and we say to Cambodia: "look we've done this by ourselves but you can take credit for it as Chair so that this could be an ASEAN initiative." We've actually embarked on the initiative already.'

In other words, del Rosario was hoping to agree a draft Code of Conduct that would contain a mechanism to resolve all the maritime disputes between the Philippines, Vietnam, Malaysia and Brunei (and ultimately China too) in just nine months. It appeared wildly ambitious – the timetable one might expect in a business deal, not an international negotiation. The mechanism – a 'Zone of Peace, Freedom, Friendship and Cooperation' in which all sides would agree which areas are disputed and then focus their efforts accordingly – looked good on paper (see Chapter 9 for more). The problem was that Philippine diplomacy lacked the capacity to bring it to fruition. ASEAN only moves forward when all ten of its members agree and there was no sign that the Philippines was putting in the necessary behind-the-scenes diplomacy to bring the other capitals on board. Even del Rosario admitted that the plan had been received poorly when he tabled it at an ASEAN Foreign Ministers meeting in January, 'essentially because there wasn't much time given for ASEAN to be able to digest the concept'.

The Philippine approach had two fundamental flaws. Firstly it was presenting a fully formed plan to official meetings without the necessary preparation and secondly Manila wanted to bind the Beijing authorities with a set of enforceable rules – the 'Code of Conduct' – but was not prepared to engage its Chinese counterparts in talks about those rules until all ten ASEAN countries had agreed them first. China could argue that it should be at the table from the start and several ASEAN countries were likely to agree. Beijing was working hard on its counter-strategy: focusing on the country where it had most leverage. At the end of March, four days before an ASEAN leaders' summit, President Hu Jintao made an official visit to Cambodia, meeting Hun Sen, announcing a new $70 million tranche of aid and pledging to double trade between the two countries to $5 billion in five years.[25] After the meeting, one of Hun Sen's advisors, Sri Thamrong, told journalists that Hu had said China wanted to move towards finalising a code of conduct in the South China Sea but not 'too fast'. Hun Sen had responded that he shared China's belief that the Sea issue should not be 'internationalized'.[26] Indeed, the Cambodians initially left the issue off the official agenda of the ASEAN summit, only reinstating it after protests from the Philippines and other countries. In late May China offered Cambodia a further $20 million in military aid[27] and in mid-June another loan – of $430 million.[28] As ever, both sides insisted that there were no strings attached.

On Monday, 9 July 2012, Albert del Rosario was in Phnom Penh making another attempt to persuade his ASEAN colleagues to take a tough line on Beijing. In the four months since he had outlined his strategy to me, Chinese ships had taken control of the Scarborough Shoal and the Chinese National Offshore Oil Company (CNOOC) had tendered exploration blocks inside Vietnam's Exclusive Economic Zone. In late May, the Philippines and Vietnam had asked their ASEAN colleagues to issue a statement condemning what they saw as violations of the spirit of the DOC. But, said the Cambodian Foreign Ministry, there was no consensus on the matter.

There was slightly better news for Manila on the Code of Conduct. Del Rosario's draft had been eviscerated during the ASEAN discussions – the elegant mechanism for deciding which areas were in dispute had gone – but the dispute resolution process was still intact.[29] It was a good enough result, particularly when the foreign ministers formally adopted the text that morning and agreed to pass it to the Chinese for the next stage of the negotiations. The ministers' plenary session ended and they moved on to the less formal part of the discussion – known as the 'retreat'. But far from being a quiet chat, the retreat pitched ASEAN into one of the worst crises in its history.

The retreat was supposed to agree the final communiqué to be issued after a week of meetings that would include ASEAN discussions with Australia, Canada, China, the European Union, India, Japan, New Zealand, Russia, South Korea and the US – individually, in different combinations and finally altogether as the ASEAN Regional Forum (ARF). The work of drafting the communiqué had been delegated to del Rosario and his counterparts from Indonesia, Malaysia and Vietnam: all countries with direct interests in the South China Sea. Their draft text had 132 paragraphs. Paragraphs 14 to 17 referred to the South China Sea, and one, Paragraph 16, specifically mentioned both Scarborough Shoal and the Vietnamese complaint. Communiqués are the bread and butter of such gatherings. They're usually drafted in advance, issued once the formal business is complete and almost immediately forgotten. It wouldn't happen like that in Phnom Penh.

We know some of what took place next because the notes of one delegation were leaked to the Australia-based academic Carl Thayer.[30] Albert del Rosario made an impassioned call for support, asking his ASEAN colleagues why they had stayed silent as the Philippines lost control of the Scarborough Shoal. Was China's move not a violation of the 'need to promote a peaceful, friendly and harmonious environment' as laid down in the DOC? He listed other examples of Chinese 'expansion and aggression' over the years and accused Beijing of 'bad faith' in failing to withdraw its ships from the Shoal. Then, in a final flourish, del Rosario deployed the words of Pastor Martin Niemöller's anti-Nazi recitation: 'First they came for the communists but I didn't speak out because I wasn't a communist. Then they came for the trade unionists . . .' But since most ASEAN states (including the Philippines) have actively persecuted Communists in the past and some of the others still ban independent trade unionists today, this didn't cut much ice. More to the point, few felt that there was any risk of China 'coming for them' after the Philippines. Some, in fact, blamed the Philippines for escalating the dispute at Scarborough Shoal by deploying its naval flagship, the *Gregorio del Pilar*, early in the standoff. Others were concerned that Manila had been openly appealing for United States support – violating ASEAN's cherished neutrality.

One by one, the other ministers spoke. Surapong Tovichakchaikul of Thailand was equivocal but spoke of the need to preserve ASEAN unity. Pham Binh Minh of Vietnam wanted support against 'serious violations of sovereignty' by China. Marty Natalegawa of Indonesia insisted that ASEAN should stand together, and mentioned the latest developments in the South China Sea, as did Anifah Aman of Malaysia. Prince Mohamed Bolkiah of Brunei said little but indicated that he could support the communiqué. He was followed by the ministers from Laos and Myanmar who said nothing against the text and then by K. Shanmugam of Singapore who noted that 'recent developments were of special concern'.

Up until this point (according to the account that we have), every foreign minister had either spoken in favour of the text or said nothing against it. But then the Cambodian Foreign Minister Hor Namhong took the microphone, declared 'there is no consensus' and announced that paragraphs 14 to 17, and particularly 16, should be bracketed rather than adopted straightaway. The four drafting ministers were aghast and immediately asked to settle the matter then and there. But Hor maintained that 'now or in the near future we can't expect to resolve these disputes. Not ASEAN'. The first suspicions began to rise – had Cambodia been bought? Was it prepared to fracture ASEAN in order to please Beijing?

Natalegawa of Indonesia then read out a compromise version of Paragraph 16 – which mentioned 'the situation in the affected Shoal/ disputed area, exclusive economic zones and continental shelves' – but Hor insisted that there was no need to mention any specific incidents and went on a rambling diversion about whether it was possible to tell the difference between a shoal and an island or identify whom it belonged to. He finished by proposing to delete Paragraph 16 altogether. Del Rosario pointed out that the text said nothing about who owned the Shoal.

The argument then moved to whether the phrase 'disputed area' could be used instead. Natalegawa and Aman of Malaysia suggested the idea but Pham Binh Minh insisted that Vietnam's Exclusive Economic Zone could not be called a 'disputed area' and del Rosario said the same about Scarborough Shoal. Pham Binh Minh proposed a short break in the discussions – at which point our record of the event ceases. But the arguments over how precise the communiqué could be about the recent troubles in the Sea continued for four days, alongside all other scheduled bilateral and multilateral meetings.

At press briefings in Beijing and Phnom Penh on the following day, Tuesday, 10 July 2012, Chinese diplomats continued to warn that the meetings were not the 'appropriate place to discuss the South China Sea issue', noting that 'the Chinese side appreciates the long-standing, firm support of Cambodia for China on issues that concern China's core interests'.[31] Although journalists were kept cooped in the official media centre, safely away from the spectacle of ministers and officials racing up and down the echoing corridors, the first hints of trouble inside the Peace Palace started to reach the outside world. An emergency meeting of ministers on the Wednesday morning was described as 'sharp' and 'intense'. ASEAN's Secretary-General, Surin Pitsuwan of Thailand, decided to play Pollyanna, however, telling journalists the discussions were 'going well'.

By Thursday, Surin was prepared to concede that there was a 'hiccup' in proceedings. Marty Natalegawa, meanwhile, was trying to cure the problem – while declaring the behaviour of some of his colleagues 'utterly irresponsible'. He offered at least 18 different drafts of Paragraph 16 but to no avail. There was another emergency meeting. One Cambodian diplomat complained that his country was being 'bullied'. Unnamed diplomats told journalists that Hor Namhong repeatedly took the drafts out of the room to consult with unseen advisors. There were suggestions that these texts were being shared with Chinese officials.[32] Although this allegation was later criticised by Cambodian diplomats (for example in a letter to the *Phnom Penh Post*) it was never actually denied.[33]

It was now Hillary Clinton's turn to have a go. The American Secretary of State arrived in Phnom Penh with a beaming smile but a recognition that discussions were 'intense'. She reminded everyone that it was US policy not to take sides in the Sea disputes – before taking sides in the disputes by criticising 'confrontational behavior' at the Scarborough Shoal, 'worrisome instances of economic coercion' and 'national measures that create friction'.[34] No-one doubted which country she was referring to. She called on ASEAN to 'speak with one voice'. It sounded like an attempt to unite ASEAN behind the communiqué.

On Friday morning Surin Pitsuwan was still talking about a 'hiccup' in the Peace Palace. Shanmugam was about to get on his plane home to Singapore when he received a desperate call from Natalegawa calling him back: the Philippines and Vietnam had agreed a compromise wording. There was a final emergency meeting. During the discussions Hor cut off Surin's microphone mid-sentence.[35] Despite further entreaties for compromise, Hor picked up his papers and stormed out of the room.[36] It was no good. For the first time in its 45-year history a meeting of ASEAN foreign ministers ended without an official communiqué. Natalegawa expressed his 'deep, profound disappointment'. Surin upgraded his assessment of the situation to a 'major hiccup'. Other participants were calling it a different kind of 'up'. As the questions poured in on Friday, Cambodia's Foreign Minister offered the bizarre explanation that 'the meeting of the

ASEAN foreign ministers is not a court, a place to give a verdict about the dispute'.[37] No-one had asked the meeting to do such a thing.

Few were surprised that Cambodia had acted in sympathy with the Chinese position but most were taken aback by the brazen way it had done so and the fact that it been prepared to damage ASEAN so badly in the process. The Cambodian government didn't appear to care very much. After all, why should Cambodia act in the interests of ASEAN as a whole? The only thing that matters to Hun Sen is the future of Hun Sen. In blocking the statement he had simultaneously pleased Beijing and annoyed Hanoi – a double win. There was no down side. The Americans weren't going to break off relations. In fact they were going to redouble their efforts to keep him from sliding any further into the Chinese camp – a triple win.

But for others with a stronger interest in regional unity, Phnom Penh was a disaster. Only Marty Natalegawa had the initiative and the authority to try to repair the damage. Five days after the summit he sped from Jakarta to Manila, Hanoi, Phnom Penh, Bangkok and Singapore. His mission was hailed as a triumph, although its only achievement was to get ASEAN to reiterate the six points it had iterated many times before: support for the DOC, for the Guidelines, for having a Code of Conduct, for international law, self-restraint and the peaceful resolution of disputes. The words 'Scarborough Shoal' or 'Exclusive Economic Zone' were not mentioned. However, after the failure in Phnom Penh, the only thing that mattered was having a single piece of paper with all the foreign ministers' names on it.

But the issue kept on rumbling, amplified by vituperative newspaper articles penned by undiplomatic diplomats. Albert del Rosario's senior assistant, Erlinda Basilio, fired the opening shot with a lengthy account of the summit in two Philippine newspapers. Cambodian diplomats sent emotive rebuttals to articles printed in the *Bangkok Post*, *The Nation*, the *Phnom Penh Post*, the *Cambodia Daily*, the *Japan Times* and the *Philippines Star*. In the latter, the Cambodian ambassador in Manila, Hos Sereythonh, accused the Philippines of 'dirty politics'. Del Rosario's office summoned him to a meeting with a notice posted on the front gate of his embassy and the front page of a newspaper. Hos claimed he was too ill to attend and sent a deputy instead. Ten days later, in what the Cambodian embassy in Manila said was an attempt to repair relations, Hos was recalled to

Phnom Penh and replaced. After that things quietened down a bit. In December, Erlinda Basilio was appointed the Philippine ambassador to China – a sign that Manila would continue to take a tough stance. But to what end? At the time of writing, well after the showdown in Phnom Penh, the Code of Conduct is still no closer to being agreed and the Zone of Peace, Freedom, Friendship and Cooperation has been consigned to the filing cabinet.

* * * * * *

In 2011 the Asia team in the State Department were, in the words of Ernie Bower, 'absolutely panicked that Beijing would read the impending withdrawals from Iraq and Afghanistan as additional weakness'.[38] They looked for a way to describe the developments in a positive light. They initially settled on the phrase 'the turn to Asia' but Ben Rhodes, the Deputy National Security Advisor for Strategic Communications, had a better idea. In November 2011, in the pages of *Foreign Policy* magazine, Hillary Clinton unveiled the rebranding of the end of the United States' entanglements in Iraq and Afghanistan. It wasn't a retreat; it wasn't even a 'turn'. It was a 'pivot'. Her article outlined six 'key lines of action' – four taken from Derek Mitchell's CSIS report of 2009 (reinvigorating alliances, cultivating relationships with emerging powers, developing relationships with regional multilateral bodies and working closely with Southeast Asian countries on economic issues) plus two more: the US would forge a broad-based military presence in Asia and advance democracy and human rights.

As a strategic marketing exercise the pivot was staggeringly successful. No-one could now claim the United States was ignoring Asia. The choice of word had the desired effect. The problem was that it became associated with just one of the six 'lines of action'. The first practical result of the pivot came just days after Clinton's article when President Obama flew to Australia to announce an agreement for 2,500 US marines to be semi-permanently based in Darwin. Only afterwards did he fly on to Bali and become the first US president to attend the East Asia Summit. Even Derek Mitchell, who had just left the Pentagon, admits 'the message wasn't initially rolled out so well'.[39] The pivot became too closely associated with military deployments. 'Pivot' also sounded impermanent. If the

US could pivot towards Asia, perhaps it could pivot away again just as easily. Washington needed something that sounded longer-lasting. Within six months 'pivot' had become 'rebalance'.

Most of the governments in Southeast Asia have welcomed the US 'rebalance'. It allows them to balance their relationship with China and enjoy greater freedom of action. Some, like Cambodia, have deliberately played one power off against the other. Others, mainly the maritime states, have tried to use the rebalance to bolster their positions, particularly in the South China Sea. The disputes there have made it easier for the US to strengthen relations with the countries involved. Two agendas have developed symbiotically: the regional anxiety about China's growing assertiveness and the US's concerns about its global strategic role. Gradually the two sets of issues – the regional disputes over territory and the 'global' differences between the US and China – have become interlinked. It's what makes the South China Sea such a potentially dangerous place. In the words of Derek Mitchell, there's a risk of 'the tail wagging the dog'.

'It's not just about China' is the mantra Mitchell and other American diplomats must chant every time they mention the 'rebalance'. That's true – it's about reinvigorating ties with Japan, Korea, ASEAN and South Asia. But all those places form an arc around . . . China. Clinton's six lines of action form rhetorical arcs around China too. Each one is associated with a key phrase that reveals its underlying focus. When she wrote of engaging emerging powers, she asked them 'to join us in shaping and participating in a rules-based regional and global order'. The 'rules-based order' is the international system that underwrites American global primacy through such traditions as the UN Security Council veto, the Bretton Woods institutions, the hegemony of the dollar, the principles of free trade and the doctrine of freedom of navigation. Future American security and prosperity will depend upon new global powers abiding by the norms of the existing international system. From a strategic perspective, American primacy depends, in particular, upon access to all the world's seas. In the words of the United States' 2011 National Military Strategy, 'assured access to the global commons and cyberspace constitutes a core aspect of U.S. national security . . . The global commons and globally connected domains constitute the connective tissue upon which all nations' security and prosperity depend.'

The South China Sea is a crucial link in the 'global commons', connecting the Pacific to the Indian Ocean, Persian Gulf and Europe. Right now, along with the East China Sea, it is the most contested piece of sea in the world and one of the main reasons for the current anxiety over China's intentions. As one former Pentagon policy-maker explained, 'we're happy to have a lot of countries out there steaming around. What is not on is proprietary behaviour which, in a direct assertive way or in a subtle suffocating way, wants to crowd other players out.'[40] When Americans talk about China working within the international system, they mean that, among other things, China must agree to keep the South China Sea open to the US Navy.

Great efforts are now being made to encourage China to desist from 'proprietary behaviour' and fully engage with the existing system – in other words, play the game on Western terms. From state visits to military discussions to phytosanitary working parties, Beijing is being 'love-bombed' by diplomats and strategists. As Kurt Campbell told an Australian audience in 2013, 'What we are seeking is for China to integrate into the global community in such a way that there are shared norms, values and procedures that we work on to define together, that are in all of our best interests.'[41] All this effort is being expended because those diplomats and strategists believe that the Beijing leadership is not convinced of the merits of the current international system and will seek to challenge its tenets in the decades to come.

Clinton's emphasis on alliances gives us our second phrase. The pivot has introduced a new geographical area to the world: the 'Indo-Pacific'. Although anthropologists and zoologists have used the term for years, supporters of the 'rebalancing' have given it new meaning – a loose alignment of countries concerned about the rise of China. The Indo-Pacific is now a strategic region, just as 'Southeast Asia' was during the Second World War and the Cold War. It forms a giant quadrilateral stretching from India to the United States, via Japan and Australia, the country where beaches are washed by both the Indian and Pacific oceans and where the phrase first surfaced. Australia, Japan and the US have had a 'Trilateral Security Dialogue' since 2005. In 2006 the then Japanese Prime Minister Shinzo Abe proposed inviting India to join a 'Quadrilateral Security Dialogue' but the idea was extinguished by the ambivalence of the then Australian

Prime Minister Kevin Rudd. In the wake of that episode, Rudd's predecessor as Labor Party leader, Kim Beazley, introduced the 'Indo-Pacific' to the public in a November 2009 article warning of future rivalry between China and the US.[42] Rory Medcalf of the Sydney-based Lowy Institute for International Policy pushed the concept along until Hillary Clinton gave it an American stamp of approval in an October 2010 speech in Hawaii. The political centre of the Indo-Pacific quadrilateral is the South China Sea.

The phrase describes a strategic vision – to 'bring in' India to the region previously known as the Asia-Pacific. In her pivot article Clinton declared: 'the United States is making a strategic bet on India's future, that India's greater role on the world stage will enhance peace and security'. In Kurt Campbell's words, 'India is the linchpin of this system, and will have a large and important role in East Asia'.[43] India has long shunned any role in American-led military alignments, but in the face of China's rise (and developments in Pakistan and Afghanistan) it agreed to a regular 'India–US Strategic Dialogue' in 2009. Since then India has bought about $13 billion worth of American military equipment, including helicopters, transport aircraft and artillery, much of it intended to support new mountain units defending the country's Himalayan frontier with China.

Australia has been working hard to further embed the 'Indo' into the 'Pacific'. The two countries agreed a 'Joint Declaration on Security Cooperation' in 2009 and talks in June 2013 produced agreements on joint naval exercises and regular consultations about regional security issues.[44] India is developing other relationships too: a 'strategic partnership' with Vietnam, a 'Defence Policy Dialogue' with Japan, and a 'trilateral dialogue' with Japan and South Korea. It has provided Vietnam with $100 million in cheap loans to buy patrol boats to protect Indian-operated oilfields off the Vietnamese coast and holds joint exercises with Malaysia, Singapore, Thailand and Japan.[45] However, Indian political culture still espouses 'strategic autonomy' and the country is unlikely to join any formal alliance with the US.

Inside the quadrilateral, Australia, New Zealand, Japan, Korea, Taiwan, the Philippines and Thailand have had defence treaties or agreements with the US for decades. More recently, seven ASEAN members have agreed some form of military partnership with Washington (the exceptions are

Myanmar, Vietnam and land-locked Laos – and the first two are moving cautiously towards some kind of engagement). China's list of military friends, on the other hand, is more limited: North Korea, Cambodia, Laos, Myanmar, Bangladesh, Sri Lanka and Pakistan. None can be described as allies and all except North Korea like to play their suitors off against one another. Myanmar is currently opening to the West mainly because it wants to be less reliant on China. Laos balances China against Vietnam, Cambodia plays everyone off against each other and Sri Lanka does the same. If there is to be a strategic competition between the two powers, the United States starts with an overwhelming advantage. The question in Southeast Asia is whether it can sustain that position.

In 2013, American spending on intelligence alone was over $50 billion – more than the total military spending of all the members of ASEAN combined.[46] That was in addition to the official military budget set at $625 billion for 2014.[47] Defence makes up over a fifth of US federal government spending – 22 per cent in 2014. With the national debt standing at $17 trillion at the time of writing,[48] cuts will have to be made. Worries about how long the US can remain committed to the region are encouraging countries to hedge their bets and build up their relations with China, creating a vicious circle for the US: having to increase spending to counteract this impression; coming under renewed budgetary pressure at home; thereby increasing the likelihood that it really will have to draw down its military presence; thus giving countries inside the quadrilateral even more reason to toe Beijing's line. This is a narrative that Beijing has been keen to amplify – the more it looks like the US is struggling to support its Asian commitments, the more likely Asian states are to look elsewhere for support.

Hence the third key phrase, 'burden-sharing', which overlaps with the pivot's emphasis on regional multilateral institutions. Washington is actively encouraging 'China-concerned' countries to build their own 'peer-to-peer' military links. Japan is providing the Philippines with ten coastguard vessels, each worth about $11 million, and training Vietnamese coastguards. South Korea has donated a warship to the Philippines and Australia is providing equipment and training. Australia also signed a Defence Cooperation Arrangement with its neighbour Indonesia in 2012. Australia has also started working together more closely with Japan – for example with Exercise Nichi Gou Trident in June 2012.[49] The 'Five Power Defence Arrangements', agreed in 1971, still link Australia, New Zealand, Singapore, Malaysia and the UK.

But does all this activity add up to anything more than a sea of beans? Korea and Japan are still at odds over disputed islands and Vietnam is unlikely to join any American-led defence arrangement without some mortal threat from China. The rest of ASEAN is happy to shelter under an American military umbrella – and indeed use it to keep a lid on some of the intra-ASEAN disputes – but has no interest in trying to resurrect anything like SEATO. This is not an alliance, a coalition or even a partnership. One description that might come close could be borrowed from physics. It's a 'flux' – a series of particles and forces in constant realignment. But that, according to the former Pentagon official we heard from before, is not necessarily a bad thing. 'In a diplomatic sense, our biggest advantage over the Chinese isn't ships and planes and stuff that can go boom. It's that the Chinese still haven't worked out how to play a multilateral game. We know how to do it. And as we get weaker we're going to have to do it better which, luckily, we know how to do. We're just rediscovering stuff we used to do a long time ago – pre-Second World War. A lot of countries there, I can tell you as a fact, want us there. Not in force, not assertively, but at the tactical level.'[50]

So how can these particles be persuaded to align themselves along Washington's axis? In short, through the fourth line of action: expanding trade and investment. The key phrase here is the 'Trans-Pacific Partnership'. One of the major motivations behind the pivot was the fear that the US was being squeezed out of its markets in eastern Asia. In 2004 the US was ASEAN's largest trading partner. By 2010 it was the fourth largest, after China, Japan and the EU. The China–ASEAN Free Trade Area came into force that year and China was pushing for a wider East Asian Free Trade Area to include Japan and South Korea in which it could wield considerable influence over Northeast and Southeast Asia. According to Ernie Bower, 'there was a real question about Asian economic integration and the Chinese running away with the store. They had started to dominate the "ASEAN Plus Three" structure in the sense that they were the ones setting the agenda. If you talked to the Japanese and the Koreans there was real worry and the Australians and the Kiwis were apoplectic because

Asian integration was starting to roll on without them. So there were a lot of warnings to the Americans.'

In January 2008, while George W. Bush was still president, his administration adopted an obscure group of four oddly matched countries – Brunei, Chile, New Zealand and Singapore – calling themselves the 'Trans-Pacific Partnership' (TPP) and pushed it to the front of American economic planning for Asia. The Obama administration was initially less keen. When Obama boarded Air Force One to make his first official trip to Asia in November 2009 he had no plans to make any announcements on trade. But during the flight, after conversations with Hillary Clinton and Kurt Campbell, he was persuaded and, to the surprise of everyone, announced in Japan that the US would join the TPP process. In the years since, the TPP has grown to comprise 12 countries, including two more members of ASEAN (Vietnam and Malaysia) and Japan. South Korea may join too. Ultimately Washington would like to see the TPP expand to become a 'Free Trade Area of the Asia-Pacific' but there's widespread scepticism about whether the TPP can even reach its first objectives. These include stipulations on labour rights, environmental protection, intellectual property and government contracts – rich-country issues that are way down the agenda in Asia.

ASEAN has pushed ahead with its own acronym: RCEP, the Regional Comprehensive Economic Partnership. It's a framework with much lower standards, primarily focused on unifying ASEAN members' existing Free Trade Areas, including with China. There has been much talk of rivalry between the American-backed TPP and the China-inclusive RCEP but it's worth noting that ASEAN deliberately chose to push RCEP (and not the East Asian Free Trade Area) because it included India, Australia and New Zealand along with Japan and South Korea – making it much less China-focused. But all the same ASEAN is voting with its feet, integrating with its most significant markets.

Aside from a programme to help ASEAN states work towards the standards of the TPP (the Expanded Economic Engagement initiative), however, Washington has offered little in the way of official economic incentives to pull the Indo-Pacific in its direction. This reflects the power of domestic lobbies more worried about unfair competition from Asian manufacturers than about America's strategic position in Asia. Instead, the private sector has been told to get on with it. In 2012 the US–ASEAN Business Council and the US Chambers of Commerce organised a US–ASEAN Business Forum in Cambodia at the same time as the ASEAN foreign ministers were haggling over their communiqué but this wasn't repeated in 2013. The pivot still seems much more focused on guns than on butter.

But what kind of guns? Chinese officials have proposed interpretations of international law that would potentially close the South China Sea to the US Navy. China is simultaneously developing weapons with the capacity to 'deny' the Sea to American fleets. Washington sees those developments as fundamental threats, not just to its navy but also to its global position. The fifth element of the pivot announced by Hillary Clinton is 'a broad-based military presence' but, as we will see in the next chapter, it's become associated with the phrase 'air-sea battle'. Could there be a war? There certainly doesn't have to be. The US Navy has made room for an emerging power in the past and could do so again. In the decades after 1962, the Soviet Union developed a 'blue water' navy and its Far Eastern fleet sailed far and wide from Vladivostok. But back then, both powers were disciples of Hugo Grotius. It suited them to be able to sail through the South China Sea, and everywhere else, at will. What is different now is Beijing's apparent desire to overturn centuries of convention and deny that right to military vessels.

The final strand of the pivot was 'advancing democracy and human rights' under the rubric of 'universal values'. This is its least-developed element. Successes have been trumpeted in Myanmar, where Derek Mitchell is, at the time of writing, US ambassador, but disagreements over human rights have slowed down the development of relations with Vietnam. Ultimately they are what defines the difference between the US and China, with the Beijing leadership convinced that the promotion of individual rights will undermine its political system and lead to another round of imperialist domination. It's likely that human rights considerations will play a relatively minor role in the unfolding strategic contest.

Two strategic imperatives and many regional interests collide in the South China Sea. The dispute is so dangerous because it crystallises two nations' ideas of who they are. Both the United States of America and the People's Republic of China are founded upon, and their elites are imbued with, a mighty sense of purpose. For China's Communist Party rulers, legitimacy comes from a history of anti-imperialist struggle and an ongoing campaign to recover territories hacked from the national corpus by colonists and traitors. However historically mistaken the belief, those territories include the Sea. The United States' elite has an implicit belief in its manifest destiny too: America as an 'exceptional country', the world's 'last best hope', an 'indispensable power', an upholder of the norms and rules of the international system. The South China Sea is the first place where those norms and rules are being challenged. If the United States loses access to those waters it loses its global role and becomes just another power. The shock would be profound and the consequences for American identity, prosperity and security devastating. It could be something worth fighting for. And, as we shall see, plans are already being made.

CHAPTER 8

Shaping the Battlefield
Military Matters

IT LOOKS LIKE a giant grey box, its top speed is just 10 knots and like most good spies it hides behind a dull job title. As an 'ocean surveillance ship' the USNS *Impeccable* usually keeps out of the spotlight. It works alone, far out to sea and right at the edge of international law. Although owned by the US government and controlled by the Department of Defense it's operated by a private company, the more glamorously named 'Special Mission Division' of the shipping giant Maersk. The *Impeccable's* job, and the reason for its boxy shape, is to tow expensive cables through stormy seas. Its 'special mission' is to hunt Chinese submarines with the 1,500-metre-long Surveillance Towed Array Sensor System (SURTASS) it pulls in its wake.

On Thursday, 5 March 2009, the *Impeccable* was ploughing its lonely furrow about 140 kilometres southeast of the Yulin submarine base on Hainan Island when a Chinese frigate suddenly sailed across its bow. Two hours afterwards a Chinese spotter plane made 11 low-level passes and the frigate crossed its bow again. On Saturday, 7 March another Chinese naval ship, an 'Auxiliary-General Intelligence' (AGI, the euphemism for spyship), ordered the *Impeccable* to leave the area or 'suffer the consequences'. The *Impeccable* didn't leave and the next day the consequences arrived.

We know some of what happened because the US Department of Defense released a video shot by one of the *Impeccable's* crew – identified as 'Bobby' by his shipmates. We join the scene under a clear

blue sky and atop a flat calm sea. The *Impeccable* is already surrounded by
a motley flotilla. Two civilian trawlers, apparently bored of fishing, sail up
behind the *Impeccable*. Shadowing them are one ship from the Fisheries
Law Enforcement Command, one from China Marine Surveillance and
the original AGI. Neither of the trawlers is towing nets but both are flying
large Chinese flags fore, middle and aft. One, with a battered but newly
painted red hull, comes close enough for several faces to be made out
pressed against the windows of the bridge. Two other men stand at the
bow, one waving a flag. Then the trawler makes a move: black smoke
spurts from the funnel as it rushes across the stern of the *Impeccable*,
apparently trying to sever the SURTASS. The crew is standing to, ready
to repel boarders but taking the whole thing as a bit of a joke. Bobby the
cameraman describes the scene: 'Lou and Wilson man the hoses while the
Chinese irritate us to tears'.

Having failed to cut the cable with the keel, one of the two men on
the bow of the red trawler reaches into the water with a long pole to try
and snag the cable. This amuses the crew even further since the SURTASS
weighs 155 tons. 'He won't be staying on that deck if he does grab it – he'll
be gargling sea water,' says one. At some point, though it's not shown on
the video, Lou and Wilson are ordered to turn on the *Impeccable*'s fire
hoses to try and dissuade the two 'fishermen' with water power. The men
aren't dissuaded. They strip off to their underwear and keep on probing
with the pole. But after many minutes of futile fishing, the trawler captain
changes tactics. With more great black belches, the boat lurches up the
port side of the *Impeccable* and then stops right in front. The blue-hulled
trawler does the same on the starboard side. The government ships are still
loitering nearby – keeping their distance but presumably ready to defend
the fishing boats should they be 'threatened' by the *Impeccable*. With
everyone now stationary the two trawlers gradually move directly towards
each other – completely blocking the *Impeccable*'s way forward. Then the
white-painted Fisheries Law Enforcement ship moves in close, just behind
the blue trawler. Unable to move forward and unable to turn around
because of the SURTASS still extended from the stern, the *Impeccable*'s
officers consult their superiors.

Outside on the decks, crew members who had been larking around at
the beginning of the confrontation fall silent. In the final few seconds of

the video one can clearly be heard telling a colleague: 'We got the word for emergency destruct.' The Pentagon could not risk the ship's ultra-sophisticated intelligence-gathering facilities falling into Chinese hands. If there had been an attempt to board the *Impeccable*, a pre-planned operation would have destroyed documents and equipment. But the procedure is kept on hold. Over the radio, the *Impeccable*'s captain announces that he's leaving and requests a safe path out of the area. The Chinese ships oblige and the *Impeccable* beats a slow retreat to the horizon.

In the very public recriminations that followed, each government loudly accused the other of violating international law. The Chinese Foreign Ministry spokesman, Ma Zhaoxu, asserted that the US had 'conducted activities in China's Exclusive Economic Zone in the South China Sea without China's permission' and demanded that the United States 'take effective measures to prevent similar acts from happening'. The White House spokesman Robert Gibbs was adamant, however: 'We're going to continue to operate in those international waters, and we expect the Chinese to observe international law around that'. But Gibbs' loose use of the phrase 'international waters' went right to the heart of the problem. It may seem arcane but the legal debate over what one country's military vessels can do in another country's offshore Exclusive Economic Zone (EEZ) has already brought the US and China to the edge of conflict. It's a battle between American demands for access to the 'global commons' and China's search for security. It's a struggle that will define the future of Asia, and possibly beyond.

* * * * * *

The rules about EEZs are laid down in the United Nations Convention on the Law of the Sea (UNCLOS), agreed in 1982, as we saw in Chapter 4. China is one of 163 UN member states to have ratified UNCLOS. The United States is one of the 30 that have not (of which 16 are land-locked). The US Senate won't ratify the convention because a large number of senators believe UNCLOS would undermine American sovereignty – despite arguments from every relevant arm of American government that it would not. The absence of ratification clearly damages Washington's credibility when it urges others to act in line with UNCLOS. Nonetheless, successive US administrations have argued that all countries are bound by the convention anyway since it now forms part of 'customary international law'. For its part, the US Navy says that it always operates in accordance with UNCLOS, regardless of the lack of ratification.

Among the hundreds of articles in UNCLOS are a few stipulating what can and can't be done in another country's Exclusive Economic Zone. The Chinese authorities have seized upon three in particular to argue that the work of the USNS *Impeccable* is illegal: Article 56 – which gives the coastal state jurisdiction over 'marine scientific research' in the EEZ; Article 58 – which obliges other countries to 'have due regard to the rights and duties of the coastal State and . . . comply with the laws and regulations adopted by the coastal State'; and Article 246 – which states that 'marine scientific research in the exclusive economic zone and on the continental shelf shall be conducted with the consent of the coastal State'. Since the United States has neither sought nor been granted permission for its research activities they must, according to Beijing, be illegal.

According to Washington, however, all this is completely irrelevant. The *Impeccable* and its sister ships aren't engaged in marine scientific research – they're simply spying. If the *Impeccable* was engaged in peaceful research – such as oil prospecting – then its activities would be illegal under UNCLOS. But since there's no commercial or scientific point to her work, the *Impeccable* can make use of the established rights of any ship to travel through the sea outside the 12-nautical-mile territorial limit. And since, under UNCLOS, states don't have sovereignty beyond their 12-nautical-mile territorial sea, all the laws that China has passed attempting to regulate what can be done in its 200-nautical-mile EEZ are, in the view of Washington, themselves illegal.

UNCLOS was the result of nine years of legal argument between coastal states that wanted to control everything that happened off their shores and maritime states that wanted freedom of navigation. The man who presided over the final debates, Tommy Koh of Singapore, later summed up the compromise: 'The solution in the Convention text is very complicated. Nowhere is it clearly stated whether a third state may or may not conduct military activities in the exclusive economic zone of a coastal state. But, it was the general understanding that the text we nego-tiated and agreed upon would permit such activities to be conducted.'[1] But several countries disagree with that 'general understanding' and are actively seeking to change it. China is the most prominent but Brazil, India, Malaysia, the Maldives, Vietnam and a few others all demand that foreign warships seek permission before sailing through their EEZs. The problem – for China and the world – is that changing the nature of the EEZ in this way would fundamentally alter the rules of the global system. It would also constitute a full-on challenge to the military primacy of the United States by cutting off its direct access between the Pacific and the Middle East.

Moving warships and forces between the western United States and Asia requires freedom of navigation through the Pacific, the South China Sea, the Malacca Straits and the Indian Ocean. Going through Indonesia's internal waters, or between Indonesia and Australia, is navigationally and politically challenging, and heading south, around Australia, adds weeks to the journey to the Persian Gulf and, for a large fleet, tens of millions of dollars in extra fuel costs. If EEZs were closed to military vessels the US would lose access to its bases and allies around Asia. With the US Navy at bay, Taiwan's defensive position would be severely weakened. Other East and Southeast Asian countries might feel similarly compromised. US influence in Southeast Asia could drain away. Even more worryingly, in the eyes of the Pentagon, without guaranteed military access there is no guarantee of civilian access either. A hostile power could cut off the flow of goods, commodities and energy upon which the American economy depends. That's why, since 1979, the United States has pursued its little-known Freedom of Navigation (FON) Program to actively challenge any attempts to close off EEZs.[2] FON combines diplomatic discussions with brute force. Sometimes the State Department just sends a protest letter. From time to time, however, the US Navy simply shows up in another country's EEZ to prove that it can. It's modern gunboat diplomacy, and Washington would say that everyone benefits from its efforts to make sure the seas are open for global trade and security.

Washington is equally forceful in dismissing the validity of Article 301 of UNCLOS, which says: 'State Parties shall refrain from any threat or use of force against the territorial integrity or political independence of any State'. It argues that simply collecting information doesn't amount to a threat of force. China, on the other hand, is adamant. It believes the data are being collected in order to prepare for a possible future conflict and that American military activity as close as 12 nautical miles to its shores is an existential threat.

Looking out from Hainan Island, China's dilemma seems acute. Ever since Deng Xiaoping ordered the creation of his country's first special economic zone in Shenzhen in 1980, national prosperity has depended upon an arc of cities around the coast, and the movements of imports and exports that sustain them. China has been a net importer of food since 2007 and in September 2013 China surpassed the US to become the world's largest net oil importer just as the shale-fracking boom was starting to lead the US in the direction of energy self-sufficiency.[3] Foreign trade makes up more than half the value of Chinese GDP (compared to less than a third in the United States) yet the country has no clear access to the open sea. The forces of geophysics have thrown up islands all around its coast and the forces of geopolitics have turned them all into potentially hostile neighbours. In the view of Wu Shicun, President of China's National Institute for South China Sea Studies, the number one reason for China's stance on the South China Sea is to ensure strategic access through it to the world's oceans. And a country serious about maintaining that access – and fearful of the intentions of the United States – must necessarily develop the capabilities to protect it. The logic is towards conflict in the South China Sea.

In April 2013 the Ministry of Defence in Beijing issued a White Paper making its objectives plain. 'With the gradual integration of China's economy into the world economic system, overseas interests have become an integral component of China's national interests', it said. 'Security issues are increasingly prominent, involving overseas energy and resources, strategic sea lines of communication (SLOCs), and Chinese nationals and legal persons overseas. Vessel protection at sea, evacuation of Chinese nationals overseas, and emergency rescue have become important ways and means for the PLA to safeguard national interests and fulfil China's international obligations.'[4] The contradiction that will shape the future of Asia is this: if China chooses to protect its coastal cities and lengthy supply lines through military means it will inevitably develop the capacity to confront the current naval hegemon. But the American naval hegemon fears that this policy is motivated not by self-defence but by a determination to achieve regional hegemony – and will therefore oppose it. For the

USA, 'access' underpins everything. Which is why so much effort – and cash – are now being expended in Washington think-tanks and military headquarters to ensure continued American 'access' to every part of the ocean – but particularly the South China Sea.

* * * * * *

In January 2012, the US Department of Defense released its 'Joint Operational Access Concept', setting out the task in blunt terms: 'As a global power with global interests, the United States must maintain the credible capability to project military force into any region of the world in support of those interests.'[5] The Joint Operational Access Concept sits in the middle of a hierarchy of strategy documents. Beneath it are more detailed plans setting out how 'access' will be won, the most important of which is the 'Air-Sea Battle Concept'. The Air-Sea Battle Concept was actually drawn up before the others: contemporary US strategy towards China was more or less written around it.

The origins of the Air-Sea Battle Concept can be traced back to the 'Taiwan Crisis' of March 1996 when President Bill Clinton's deployment of two US aircraft carrier groups forced the Chinese military to end a series of intimidating exercises being staged in the run-up to Taiwan's general election. That deployment was the trigger for the Chinese People's Liberation Army Navy (PLAN) to begin developing the means of preventing it happening again. In the years after 1996 Chinese military spending shifted significantly towards the navy, air force and missile units and a new phrase, *shashoujian* – assassin's mace – began to enter military documents. *Shashoujian* describes a strategy to use relatively inexpensive weapons to surprise and disable a much more sophisticated adversary.[6] As the PLAN's capabilities grew it was given a new mission. In 2001, President Jiang Zemin called on the navy to enhance its 'far-seas defence' capabilities and the message was reinforced the following year by his successor, Hu Jintao.[7] Then, in January 2007, the Chinese military successfully tested a missile that could destroy an orbiting satellite. The assassin's mace appeared to be getting sharper. The implications for the US military, with its satellite communications and guided weapons, were obvious.

In simple terms, the assassin's mace is the ability to prevent American air bases and aircraft carriers in the Western Pacific and South China Sea launching their planes and missiles against Chinese targets. The primary reason for it, Western analysts assume, would be to halt or delay a future United States intervention in support of Taiwan. If a future Taiwanese government made any moves towards independence, the Chinese Navy would be expected to lead some kind of blockade or invasion and fend off the US Navy. The assassin's mace wouldn't necessarily have to be used; it would just have to create sufficient uncertainty in the minds of American admirals to stop them deploying their most powerful assets. The US military has a more prosaic name for the tactic: 'Anti-Access' or 'A2'. When a similar method is used closer to the target area it's called 'Area Denial' and the two in combination have become known as 'A2/AD'. China's A2/AD tactics might use mines or submarines armed with torpedoes and cruise missiles or cyber attacks but most attention has been focused on a new weapon – the Dong-Feng-21D anti-ship ballistic missile. With a range of over 1,500 kilometres and the ability to manoeuvre as it descends, the Dong-Feng-21D could, theoretically at least, hit large ships from bases on the mainland.

In mid-2007 information about the development of the new missile began to reach the public and by October 2008 the US Pacific Air Forces were already war-gaming their response: an 'operational concept with long-range conventional threats to surface ships and land bases' is how the US Pacific Air Forces spokesman, Lieutenant Colonel Edward Thomas, described it.[8] Two desktop simulation exercises, entitled 'Pacific Vision' 1 and 2, tested how the US would respond to a challenge from an unnamed 'near-peer competitor' in the Asia-Pacific region in 2028. By the end of the exercise, the response had a name: Air-Sea Battle.

Pacific Vision was part-funded by the Pentagon's internal research group, the Office of Net Assessments. Since its creation in 1973, the office's job has been to imagine worst-case scenarios for the United States and then imagine ways to avoid them. The office has only ever had one boss: Andrew Marshall, 92 years old at the time of writing. Marshall lives in a highly secret world of potential dangers to American security: some clear and present, others distant and hypothetical. Unlike most horror writers he has a budget of more than $13 million a year to amplify his fears among the Washington security community.[9] Marshall is routinely described as 'highly influential' by policy-makers and pundits alike. His sage-like pronouncements have led others to call him the Jedi Master.

One of the staff working on the exercises was Jan van Tol, a former US Navy captain who had spent several years working in the Office of Net Assessments before transferring to its favourite think-tank, the Center for Strategic and Budgetary Assessments. He says the exercises dramatically illustrated how new Chinese technologies could radically alter the balance of power in East Asia: 'The big thing about Pacific Vision was that it pointed out that if the Chinese move to longer and longer range ballistic missiles, then fixed bases in the Western Pacific would become highly vulnerable. And that basing underpins all our strategies for how we would fight a war. That was the real shocker that caught attention at quite a senior level.'[10]

In the weeks after Pacific Vision, the results were passed up the military chain of command to the Air Force Chief of Staff, General Norton Schwartz, and the Chief of Naval Operations, Admiral Gary Roughead. During the same period the think-tank delivered its recommendations to Washington policy-makers. And it was at almost exactly this time that the Chinese maritime authorities chose to blockade the USNS *Impeccable* and deliver – as if on cue – a textbook example of the threat to freedom of navigation in the South China Sea. With all of Washington's defence thinkers now alert to the issue, the Office of Net Assessments and the Center for Strategic and Budgetary Assessments were pushing at an open door. By the time the Air-Sea Battle concept arrived at the Pentagon, there was a tsunami of support behind it. In July 2009, Secretary of Defense Robert Gates directed the navy and air force to address the challenge and in September General Schwarz and Admiral Roughead signed a still-secret memorandum to develop Air-Sea Battle into an operational concept.

The discussions went on until December 2010 when Bryan Clark, a retired nuclear submariner turned Special Assistant to the Chief of Naval Operations, was ordered to collate the ideas into a coherent document. 'The concept was intended to guide service force development activities,' he says. 'What we buy, what we train to do, the doctrine that we use, all of the things that the services do to prepare forces to hand over at some future date to the combatant commanders.' According to Clark, the concept that he authored was directly informed by the work of the Center for Strategic and Budgetary Assessments (CSBA): 'The work that Jan and everybody at

CSBA did was very useful and I incorporated a good portion of that into the classified DoD [Department of Defense] concept.' Clark's 44-page document was completed in February 2011 and approved by service chiefs that April. By the autumn of that year the Department of Defense had begun, in Clark's words, 'deliberately applying the concept to our investments . . . using it to guide their budget development, exercise development, the training they do and their doctrine'.

Outside the Pentagon, however, the concept of Air-Sea Battle had become highly controversial. The only public explanation of it had been released by CSBA in May 2010. Despite early caveats asserting that the United States did not seek to confront or contain China, the entire document was a blunt warning of the threat posed by the Chinese 'assassin's mace'. 'The United States will find itself effectively locked out of a region that has been declared a vital security interest by every administration in the last sixty years', it intoned. Chapter 3 of the document described how the US might fight back. It called for 'kinetic and non-kinetic' (in other words both explosive and electronic) strikes against inland command centres, radar systems and intelligence gathering facilities, raids against missile production and storage facilities and 'blinding' operations against Chinese satellites. It also said that China's 'seaborne trade flows would be cut off, with an eye toward exerting major stress on the Chinese economy and, eventually, internal stress'. The paper was intended to stimulate discussion. It succeeded far beyond its authors' expectations, causing outrage all the way to Beijing.

It took until May 2013 for the US government to release an unclassified summary of Air-Sea Battle and only 16 of Clark's original 44 pages survived the censor. The essence of Air-Sea Battle was given an ungainly acronym: NIA/D3 – 'networked, integrated forces capable of attack-in-depth to disrupt, destroy and defeat adversary forces'. It's the 'in-depth' part that has given most cause for concern. The word 'China' doesn't appear but other key aspects of van Tol's paper were there: in order to overcome the A2/AD threat – the 'Anti-Access' and 'Area Denial' tactics of China's 'assassin's mace' or its anti-ship ballistic missile – the US would have to attack command and control systems located far from the battlefield. As Clark explains, 'you've got to go in and do surgical operations to take out specific elements of the A2/AD network'. But he's keen to assert that 'attack' doesn't have to mean death and destruction: 'it might also be a non-kinetic attack where I turn some piece of equipment off or deny it the ability to see me or make its communications not work, that's all a fairly deep attack'.

He also insists that it's not aimed at China. During his last weeks working in the Pentagon, Clark discussed Air-Sea Battle with Admiral Wu Shengli, the head of the Chinese Navy, who was visiting Washington DC. 'We explained that it's much more about an Iran-type situation . . . or Syria. It's not just about China; we've already seen how these capabilities are getting out there. Other countries want to stop the world intervening in the bad things they do.' But the message is falling on deaf ears. Everything China's top brass have heard about Air-Sea Battle has confirmed their worst fears and hardest prejudices about US intentions.

The problem for the region is that both powers are basing major decisions upon fear and prejudice. Neither trusts the other. The crystal ball-gazers at the Office of Net Assessments and its favoured think-tank have done what they're paid to do and imagined future threats to the United States' global supremacy. It doesn't really matter to them whether the threat is likely; the point is that it is possible. 'To those who would argue that a Sino-US conflict is "unthinkable",' wrote Jan van Tol in his May 2010 paper, 'it should be emphasized again that the purpose of "thinking about the unthinkable" is that by doing so, ways can be found to sustain and enhance a stable military balance in the Western Pacific, thus keeping conflict in the domain of the "unthinkable".' In other words, the United States' military dominance in the South China Sea and its environs must remain so overwhelming that no other country would dare to challenge it. And put like that, once a possible threat to US primacy has been articulated, the only politically acceptable response is to commission new strategies and weapons systems to defeat it.

* * * * * *

How real is the 'China Threat' to American access in the South China Sea and beyond? The bare numbers appear dramatic. China now has the world's second-largest naval fleet and its second-largest military budget. (The US is, of course, first in both leagues.) The Stockholm International

Peace and Research Institute estimated China's 2012 defence spending at $166 billion – a 12 per cent rise on the year before.[11] The naval modernisation programme begun by Admiral Liu Huaqing (see Chapter 3), which began with the import of Russian-made submarines and destroyers in the early 1990s, is now at a stage where China can design and build its own warships and weapons systems. By 2014, according to the report on the Chinese military that the Pentagon must deliver to Congress each year, the Chinese Navy possessed '77 principal surface combatants, more than 60 submarines, 55 medium and large amphibious ships, and roughly 85 missile-equipped small combatants' and, since September 2012, its first aircraft carrier, the *Liaoning*.[12]

The ship numbers appear even more dramatic when compared to the US Navy, which has around 96 large combatants, 72 submarines, 30 large amphibious ships, 26 small combatants and 10 aircraft carriers.[13] And unlike the Chinese Navy, whose ships are concentrated in one area, US Navy ships are spread around the globe. But the bald numbers tell us almost nothing about the relative strength of each force. Gary Li is one of the best-informed independent observers of the Chinese Navy. As a former analyst for the International Institute for Strategic Studies in London, now working for the shipping intelligence service IHS Maritime in Beijing, he closely observes the capabilities of the ships now serving with the navy of the People's Liberation Army and he isn't impressed. 'The Chinese are about two or three generations behind compared to the Americans. The American Arleigh Burke class of destroyer can take care of a small navy by itself. Yes, the Chinese are building ships like crazy, but they are barely reaching the level of America in the 1990s. The naval force is probably 20 years off reaching the state of America and the Americans are still edging forwards – even with all the budget cuts.'[14]

Even the much-discussed aircraft carrier, the *Liaoning*, has no catapults to launch its planes and uses a 'ski jump' instead. This means the J-15 jets that it hosts can only carry lighter, shorter-range missiles and no electronic counter-measures pod when taking off fully fuelled.[15] A rare critical article in the Chinese media in 2013 warned that the ship and its planes would be vulnerable to attack even by Vietnamese forces. As Gary Li puts it, 'Every single new bit of kit that the navy adds makes it look a little closer to a modern navy. But that doesn't mean it is a modern navy.' Basic problems continue to hamper the fleet. A December 2013 article in Chinese in the *People's Liberation Army Daily* observed that, during one recent naval exercise, sailors on the four participating ships had been able to hear one another but could not transmit combat data because their information systems weren't compatible.[16] The fleet also lacks the unglamorous but vital logistics ships that keep navies afloat, and this prevents the carrier and other ships from operating far away from port.

There are further problems when it comes to actually using the equipment. Most military personnel arrive poorly educated: junior ranks are mainly from peasant families and few are educated beyond the age of 14; fewer than a third of officers have a university degree.[17] Recruitment is still by conscription and conscripts only serve for two years, giving them little chance to learn advanced skills. In May 2013 the Chief of the PLA General Staff Fang Fenghui told an audience at the Nanjing Army Command College that it is essential for military academies 'to cultivate talents in line with actual combats, battlefields and combat requirements', suggesting that up until that point they had been failing to do so.[18] The PLA Navy lacks experience in all areas of modern warfare. 'The last major sea battle they had was in the Paracels in 1974,' notes Li. 'The British and the Americans have had almost a century of experience with aircraft carriers. The Chinese have had about a year. They have no experience with anti-submarine warfare or long-range missile attacks, they don't even have enough mine countermeasures vessels. The Americans could bottle up the whole PLAN North Sea Fleet just by mining the Bohai Bay.' Furthermore, in any direct confrontation between the two, it's likely that US forces would be supported by highly capable navies from Japan, South Korea, Taiwan and possibly elsewhere.

Even the author of the Air-Sea Battle concept, Bryan Clark, concedes that the Chinese Navy currently poses little threat to the United States: 'Right now the US can – through electronic warfare or direct kinetic attack or other procedures – defeat all the A2/AD capabilities that are out there.'[19] At the time of writing, the Dong-Feng-21D anti-ship ballistic missile still has not been tested against a moving target at sea and there's doubt about whether the PLA has the capacity to deploy and integrate the immensely complex sensors and guidance systems – the 'kill chain' – that it will depend upon.[20] The Pentagon is confident it can already combat such systems. 'We've taken

[China's] kill chains apart to the "nth" degree,' Lieutenant General Herbert Carlisle, the then US Air Force Deputy Chief of Staff for Operations told *Aerospace Daily* in September 2011.[21] In January 2014 it emerged that when China sold a different version of the missile to Saudi Arabia in 2007, US intelligence analysts dismantled and thoroughly examined it.[22]

So while the dominant narrative in foreign capitals is about the growing strength of the Chinese military, within the Chinese military the narrative is more about its relative weakness. As one Chinese academic with access to policy-makers told me in Beijing, 'China doesn't want to see the US block its sea transport lanes but it doesn't have a clear strategy about how to respond. It doesn't know what to do.' China's leaders are well aware, however, that they are profoundly lucky. Their unprepared military faces no immediate mortal threats and the country has time to build up its economic and military strength to face the challenges ahead. It's enjoying what its ideologues call 'the period of strategic opportunity' – our current era of relative peace, stability and prosperity.

In the eyes of the Chinese leadership – civilian and military – the country's entire development depends on extending that period for as long as possible. Hints of this emerge from time to time. On 4 February 2013, at a time when China and Japan appeared on the verge of conflict over the Diaoyu or Senkaku Islands, that message was openly spelled out in black and white in a surprising place. The *Global Times* newspaper is usually full of verbal attacks on the United States, Japan, the Philippines and Vietnam and demands for tough action against those who violate China's sovereignty. So when General Liu Yuan used its pages to tell warmongers to shut up, it caused a stir. 'China's economic development already has been shattered by war with Japan twice before', he wrote, and it 'absolutely must not be interrupted again by some accidental incident'. He hammered home the point in TV interviews too.

General Liu is no dove. He's the son of Communist China's first president, the revolutionary hero (and main victim of Mao's Cultural Revolution) Liu Shaoqi. He's known to be very close to President Xi Jinping and has been tipped for promotion to China's highest military body, the Central Military Commission. He's better known for 'speeches and essays pushing a form of militant Chinese nationalism that rejects Western notions of political openness and civil liberties', in the words of one Western news agency report. In other words, he appears to represent the authentic voice of the Communist military. Why is a man of such apparently hawkish credentials advocating such a dovish approach? The clue lies in the title of his *Global Times* article: 'Protect the Period of Strategic Opportunity, War is a Last Resort'. Liu's argument is that China's enemies have nefarious plans to lure it into conflict in order to keep it weak. There is little doubt, in the minds of China's military leadership, that if the country were to fight the United States in the next decade or two its armed forces would be humiliated and its economy blockaded and strangled. Even a small setback could cause major problems for a government craving public legitimacy. In the view of the Beijing academic, 'the Chinese government can't afford even a minor failure in a confrontation'.

But this gives China a major problem. If its neighbours around the South China Sea believe that Beijing will never fight a war, then its strategic influence will be greatly reduced. Somehow the rival territorial claimants must be encouraged to believe that the country might opt for war – regardless of how apparently irrational that might appear. This is the strategic role that China's 'media hawks' play. As well as boosting domestic nationalism (as we saw in Chapter 6) they serve a very subtle but critical function in China's strategic manoeuvring. Australian researcher Andrew Chubb has intensively analysed the belligerent language and the timing of statements by the country's best-known military analysts, including Major General Luo Yuan, Rear Admiral Zhang Zhaozhong and Air Force Colonel Dai Xu. He believes they help to inculcate 'national defence awareness' among the people (something that has been mandated by law since 2001) but just as importantly they keep up the pressure on China's rivals. By creating the idea of a 'hardline faction' demanding ever stronger action from civilian leaders they help reinforce the negotiating position of those leaders. At the same time their rhetoric magnifies the country's capabilities and gives the impression that China is ready to attack. The overall purpose comes straight from Sun Tzu: 'The supreme art of war is to subdue the enemy without fighting.'

The result is an unholy triangle linking the Chinese hawks delivering their sabre-rattling quotes as part of the PLA's political warfare, international media outlets who know that bellicose talk of confrontation attracts valuable audiences and American hawks who seize upon each piece of new evidence of the 'China Threat' to justify increased spending on the armed forces and the targeting of China. That, in turn, gives the PLA hawks more evidence of the nefarious plans of the United States and bolsters their position with their domestic audiences. As the Beijing academic confided with a smile, 'So many people believe in conspiracy theories in China that we just assume they are acting deliberately to lure us into a trap.' Another Chinese academic, Professor Zha Daojiong of the Center for International and Strategic Studies at Peking University, told me that his biggest worry is that 'the Chinese military could believe the American rhetoric and embark upon an arms race and follow the Soviet Union to the same end. I try to advise them against that. The risk is that the military will grow too big, get too much budget and too much power within China.' The battle for access to the EEZs of the South China Sea is fundamental to the global balance of power. The world could end up with security policies determined by the most hawkish sectors of the US and Chinese political classes in a self-perpetuating and potentially self-destructive struggle for supremacy.

For the time being there is very little chance that China will deliberately seek open military conflict: the consequences for itself would be too costly. A defeat by the US could irreparably destabilise the leadership. China may have the ambition to drive the United States away, but does not have the military capacity to do so – for now. Gradually, however, the gap between the two sides will narrow and the chances of conflict will grow. In the meantime each military will play up the threat from the other and enjoy the benefits of budgetary support that follow. The danger is that the two confrontations taking place in the South China Sea – one between China and the United States over access and the other between China and its neighbours over territory – will interact in unpredictable ways.

It's unlikely that China will pick an overt fight with a Southeast Asian military. Even if the Chinese prevailed, the country's diplomatic legitimacy would be destroyed: its professed policy of peaceful coexistence would be proved a lie. But all options short of conflict remain on the table. Some incidents, such as the Philippines losing Scarborough Shoal or the confrontation in mid-2014 when China placed an oilrig inside Vietnam's claimed EEZ near the Paracel Islands, get wide publicity. Others, involving Indonesia and Malaysia for example, are kept quiet. In each case China used force but not direct military force. As Huang Jing, the director of the Center on Asia and Globalization of Public Policy in Singapore, told the *New York Times* in 2013, 'What China is doing is putting both hands behind its back and using its big belly to push you out, to dare you to hit first'.[23] But the net result is the same: Southeast Asia isn't prepared to take Beijing's soothing words on trust. They are preparing for the worst, just in case.

* * * * * *

A company of US marines crouched in the tree line: partly for camouflage, partly for shade. The dry season temperature was building and, weighed down by their battlefield burdens, they were glad of the chance to rest. Thai marines, more used to the heat and dust of this part of Southeast Asia, took cover nearby. From high above, the valley looked green but down below the landscape was parched. A few tall trees disguised the desiccation. Beneath their branches, last season's grasses had turned to tinder. Cracked paddy fields awaited the rains, their farmers long gone. Even the birds had fled, alarmed by the tactical movement on the ground. They flapped up to the high limestone crags that dominated the flat valley floor. All was silent.

A pair of planes screamed over the heads of the marines: Thai F-16s. Their target lay at the base of those cliffs. Forward air controllers guided them in, painted their objective with lasers and waited as the 500-pound bomb fell away from the belly of the jet. Everyone in the valley was about to learn the real meaning of the word 'impact'. A brief flash of orange flame and for a few seconds it wasn't clear if the strike was a success but when the sound of the explosion arrived, it was immense: ear-splitting even for those well outside the safety perimeter. As the column of smoke grew taller, the second plane delivered its bomb, even closer to the cliffs: another flash and another clap of deafening thunder. Then two US marine FA-18s joined in: two more 500-pounders. The targets were obliterated.

Far out of sight, howitzers roared. Half a minute later shells slammed into the ledges half-way up the cliff, sending fragments of rock and hot shrapnel ripping through the forest. Aim was adjusted and more shells arrived: more shrapnel and more smoke. Then the bombardment ceased and the marines got the order to move. The Thais took the lead, moving cautiously through the trees and fields behind a creeping barrage of mortar shells. They reached a pre-planned firing position and let rip with auto-matic fire. The Americans moved a few hundred metres to one side and joined battle. A pair of armoured vehicles blocked their progress but the marines swung their AT-4 rockets onto their shoulders. Two rockets into each target and the marines could move past the blazing hulks, firing into the vegetation as they manoeuvred towards their ultimate objective. Mission accomplished. High on the hill opposite, shaded in their obser-vation post and well supplied with chilled bottled water, the audience of assorted commanders applauded the efforts of their grunts on the ground.

The battle had lacked only one thing: an enemy. No-one had fired back, the cliffs had been empty of insurgents and the 'armoured vehi-cles' had been a couple of old saloon cars. But everything that had been dropped or fired was deadly real, for this was a CALFEX – a Combined Arms Live Fire Exercise – a chance to practise what marines call 'warheads on foreheads'. A CALFEX is, by definition, a demonstration of immense trust. Commanders place the lives of their units in the hands of pilots and gunners from each other's militaries. A misplaced bomb or shell could be catastrophic. Those few hours in a remote stretch of Lop Buri Province represented the glue that holds together the military alliance between the US and Thailand.

The combined assault was the finale of the 2012 iteration of 'Cobra Gold' – Asia's largest multinational exercise. Seven countries had contrib-uted over 9,000 personnel: 5,300 from the US, 3,600 from Thailand and 300 from South Korea. In a demonstration of the ways that regional tensions are forcing Southeast Asian countries to hedge their security bets, Malaysia and Indonesia were fully participating for the first time, albeit in small numbers. They, Singapore and Japan had each sent about 70 troops. Cobra Gold started as a bilateral US–Thailand event in 1982 but has grad-ually drawn in more countries from around the region and beyond. In 2012 there were observers from as far away as Sri Lanka and Mozambique. The Chinese military had also accepted an invitation to come and watch. There was a reason why the Americans wanted them to be there.

Cobra Gold has three distinct three parts: on-the-ground training such as the CALFEX, a 'command post exercise' or CPX for senior officers, and a 'hearts and minds' programme for local communities. What's most remark-able about Cobra Gold is that it's unremarkable. Every year thousands of

American troops turn up in parts of Thailand, practise fighting wars with allies and partners, blow things up and nobody bats an eyelid. The media turn up for the annual beach assault and take snaps of marines drinking snake-blood during jungle training. The US embassy issues press releases about how many schools, orphanages and hospitals the hearts-and-minds forces have built or rehabilitated and then everyone goes home again until the following February. What's it all for?

The CPX was taking place 150 kilometres from the mock battle, in the much more comfortable surroundings of Camp Suranaree, on the outskirts of the unremarkable city of Nakhon Ratchasima. I was prepared to rough it but discovered that these warriors fought with computers and telephones, stayed in hotels and ate in restaurants. The common language was English, which meant everyone could socialise, and after a day of war games there were plenty of other ways to keep playing. Not for nothing have some veterans dubbed the exercise 'Cobra Golf': there's one course on the army base and another at the air base right next door.

The work of the CPX was done inside the white two-storey officers' mess building. Downstairs, a lecture theatre had been turned into the COC – the Combat Operations Centre – with over a hundred work places: white plastic chairs and folding tables in front of laptops plugged into COWAN – the Combined Operations Wide Area Network that under-pins the entire operation. All military exercises have a scenario but Cobra Gold's are among the most elaborate. They take place on an imaginary island in the middle of the Pacific Ocean, exactly the same size and shape as the American west coast. The towns and cities are in the same loca-tions and even have the same names. The island of Pacifica stretches from just north of Seattle to just south of San Diego and inland as far as Salt Lake City and Albuquerque. The main difference is that Pacifica is divided between the evil-doers of the northern state of Arcadia, the good folks of neighbouring Kuhistan and four smaller countries: Isla del Sol (a severed Baja California), Mojave, Sonora and Tierra del Oro. Complicating the situation are the ethnic Arcadians living in Kuhistan and a host of other regional difficulties.

The scenarios vary. In 2012, Arcadia had attacked Kuhistan and the multinational force was intent on driving them back. It was, in the words of the acting Chief of Staff of the CPX, US Army Colonel Dave Parker, 'a high-end war-fighting scenario – peace-enforcement'. Parker's talk was as straight as his crew cut. I put to him questions Chinese journalists had raised about whether the exercise was aimed at their country. 'Of course they have to be concerned when they come into a Joint Operations Centre and they see Malaysians sitting next to Singaporeans, sitting next to Thais, Indonesians, Koreans and Americans – obviously they're going to have some concern that we have a relationship together and that we are all able to come together as one multinational force – and maybe they should be concerned about that. But I think that speaks volumes that we get that many nations to be able to form a multinational force.'

The Cobra Gold command post exercise is not always about war. That of 2011 had been about humanitarian assistance and disaster relief, and 2013 would be too. But as Parker explained, the scenario is almost unimportant. What matters is the way the different national contingents work together. 'We're operating off one Standard Operating Procedure – the Multinational Force SOP – that was developed here in the Pacific. The organisation that maintains it – the Multinational Planning Augmentation Team – resides at US Pacific Command and they facilitate all the 34 nations that have a part of this SOP. It is a huge task and an ongoing process.' The MNF SOP governs the way information is shared between the different cells within the command team and how it is delivered to on-the-ground commanders – from the design of the computer system to the order in which meetings take place. In his regular job Colonel Parker was head of the Planning Directorate of Pacific Command (PACOM), so he knew this process well.

The importance of Cobra Gold is the way it allows the different militaries of the region to practise working as a single unit towards a common goal – using the MNF SOP under PACOM's umbrella. The lessons learnt have been used several times in the real world: notably after the tsunamis in 2004 around the Indian Ocean, and in 2011 in Japan, and after Typhoon Haiyan in the Philippines in 2013. According to Parker, 'the most important thing about this is the relationships that we build with the militaries of the other nations. Let's just say that we have to respond to another natural disaster in Indonesia. Well, there are several key individuals that were part of this exercise here that are going to help us start the process a lot quicker because of the relationship that we have.' But as Parker says, the scenario is unimportant – those contacts would be just as useful in a future conflict situation as in a natural disaster.

PACOM has a strange existence. In contrast to all the other American regional commands around the world, it has done almost no war-fighting in its operational area since the fall of Saigon. In fact Parker struggled to remember the last time it had been involved in a real military operation: the modest intervention in East Timor in 1999. Instead PACOM spends considerable time and effort on humanitarian relief: 'You see how many earthquakes, tsunamis there are in this region. It's not a matter of "if", it's a matter of "when",' says Parker. But PACOM isn't just a well-endowed relief agency. It spends most of its time preparing for potentially cataclysmic confrontations with North Korea or, increasingly, China. These two aspects of its work – aid and assault – are not separate functions; they are integral to PACOM's mission: to deter a confrontation by preparing for one. The strategy is built on three declared pillars: 'building strong relationships', 'maintaining an assured presence in the region' and 'effectively communicating intent and resolve'. Cobra Gold ticks all three boxes. That's why the Chinese were invited to observe. In 2014 they were even allowed to take part – but only in the humanitarian operations, not in the war-fighting.

This approach was put front and centre in the US 'Joint Operational Access Concept', released in January 2012, as we saw earlier. It defines 'Operational Access' as 'the ability to project military force into an operational area with sufficient freedom of action to accomplish the mission'. As the first page of the concept makes clear, the battle to defeat A2/AD (China's tactical assassin's mace) begins many years beforehand:

The challenge of operational access is determined largely by conditions existing prior to the onset of combat operations. Consequently, success in combat often will depend on efforts to shape favorable access conditions in advance, which in turn requires a coordinated interagency approach. The joint force will attempt to shape the operational area in advance of conflict through a variety of security and engagement activities such as multinational exercises, access and support agreements, establishment and improvement of overseas bases, prepositioning of supplies, and forward deployment of forces.

In other words, everything that PACOM does – from exercises and port visits to relief operations, academic seminars and golf tournaments – is a part of the strategy to counter any attempt to close the seas to American forces. It's called 'shaping the battlefield' in advance and it's all about relationships.

PACOM takes the same approach at sea too. In 1995 it launched CARAT – the Cooperation Afloat Readiness And Training programme, which now conducts annual naval exercises with seven of the ten members of ASEAN. Only land-locked Laos, previously isolated Myanmar and cautious Vietnam have yet to take part. But Vietnam now hosts frequent port visits by American ships and has begun taking part in what are described by analysts as 'CARAT-type' activities. Slowly it is deepening its engagement with PACOM. In June 2012, US Defense Secretary Leon Panetta flew to Vietnam to make a speech aboard an American logistics ship, the USS *Robert Byrd*, which was making use of the ship repair facilities at the immense natural harbour at Cam Ranh Bay. Many of the facilities in the harbour were originally built by US engineers during the Vietnam War when the bay was a huge American logistical hub. Panetta spoke warmly of his hopes for deeper cooperation in the future.[24]

PACOM doesn't need big bases to begin to shape the battlefield; it just needs access. American commanders have learnt the hard way that having large numbers of military personnel based in Asian societies can be problematic. Local resistance to the aircraft noise generated by the Marine Corps Air Station at Futenma on Okinawa is a permanent thorn in their sides, the killing of two schoolgirls by an American armoured vehicle in Korea in 2002 led to widespread protests, and anger at the treatment of local women by American servicemen based in the Philippines was a key argument behind the closure of Subic Bay Naval Base. Memories run deep. In October 2013, a proposal to build a new base at Oyster Bay on Palawan in the Philippines – to which the US Navy would have access – was made public. The immediate reaction from four out of the five local village chiefs was opposition because they expected it to lead to a rise in prostitution. Local anti-Americanism seems to rise when there are more uniformed Americans around. A smaller military 'footprint' helps keep these incidents to a minimum while also saving billions of dollars.

Even where the US does have a base, it will be a different kind of presence. In Singapore, PACOM's Logistics Group, Western Pacific – the hub for the CARAT exercises and a key element of the American rebalancing – is based inside the civilian cargo terminal at Sembawang within a secure zone administered by New Zealand forces under the 'Five Power Defence Arrangements'. Only around 150 military personnel and 150 civilian contractors are permanently based there.[25] Singapore's naval harbour at Changi is the regional hub for two (ultimately four) of the new generation of Littoral Combat Ships, designed to show the Stars and Stripes in Southeast Asian waters, but the ships' sailors aren't allowed to live on shore. Even when in port they sleep on their ships (although they are free to leave the base when off duty). There may be no major bases in the Philippines anymore but the 'Mutual Logistics Support Agreement' provides for refuelling, resupply, billeting of troops and transport arrangements. In Darwin in northern Australia, the presence of 2,500 US marines is not described as 'permanent' because contingents rotate through the base on six-month assignments. As a result the base will not develop the kind of infrastructure for a settled community that used to exist in the Philippines and still exists in Japan, Korea and Guam. But in a time of crisis warships, planes, ammunition, supplies and personnel would flow through these hubs to enable the US to project power directly into the heart of the region. That's why 'access' is so critical.

Southeast Asian governments welcome this lighter American 'footprint' in the region. It's large enough to demonstrate Washington's continuing political commitment but small enough to reduce the risk of political embarrassment. Logistics hubs draw less attention than military bases and are less likely to provoke criticism from jealous foreign powers or domestic opposition movements. But the lighter presence is also a cause for nervousness. For decades, the countries of Southeast Asia relied upon the United States to maintain maritime security in their neighbourhood. The Philippines did so explicitly and the others implicitly – even Vietnam, after the demise of the Soviet Union. As budget cuts loom in Washington the region's governments have realised that they can't expect the US Navy to do as much as it once did. It certainly won't defend their territorial claims in the South China Sea. They have to make alternative arrangements – and that means boom time for weapon makers.

* * * * *

When James Hilton published his novel of Himalayan heaven in 1933, we can be sure he had no idea it would give a name to a canapé-packed gathering of Asia's military-industrial complex. But 69 years after Hilton's *Lost Horizon* first introduced us to his verdant mountain paradise, generals and diplomats seeking the path of enlightenment gathered for the first time at the 'Shangri-La Dialogue'. The name invites a vision of a transcendental meeting of minds, a murmuring of pilgrims in a heady atmosphere of mind-expanding aromatics.

But Shangri-La has travelled a long way since Hilton first conjured it up from his Himalayan wanderings. It began its journey in the late 1960s when the Chinese-Malaysian businessman Robert Kuok made a killing in the global sugar markets. With anti-Chinese sentiment rising at home in Malaysia, Kuok sought a safer haven for some of his fortune, buying real estate in neighbouring Singapore. And in 1971, Shangri-La took on concrete form for the first time, not in the shape of a Tibetan monastery but in the form of a 24-storey deluxe hotel. So many sought his vision of beauty that he rolled out the concept continent-wide. There are now 72 Shangri-La hotels across Asia: nirvana on tap for executives on business.

The next step in Shangri-La's transformation emerged from a discussion between a British security think-tank, the International Institute for Strategic Studies, and the Singaporean government. Asia, they felt, needed a venue where nation could speak peace (or its opposite) unto nation in comfort – the Shangri-La hotel. The IISS would handle the guest list, the Singapore government would sort out the security, and the sponsors would pay for everything else. Singapore and the IISS would get the kudos; ministers would get a few minutes in the spotlight; and the sponsors plenty of opportunities to press the flesh.

So, each June since 2002, the Shangri-La Dialogue has come to Singapore. It's all very tasteful. There are no blaring sirens or multi-car convoys and almost no road closures. The only other clues that an international gathering is taking place are little rubber seals on the manhole covers and the shrink-wrapped postboxes – both intended to prevent anyone depositing explosives within a block of the hotel. Inside the building, security is just as low-key. Once through the metal detectors, guests are free to network with ministers in suits and generals in braid. It's easy to miss the steely-eyed Gurkhas blending into the background in their charcoal business suits. Only their over-large attaché cases mark them out, just the right size to conceal their submachine guns: it's security for gentlemen. This is a twenty-first-century Shangri-La, where the men from the Himalayas take care of the close protection.

For those in search of bigger guns, the 2012 Dialogue had plenty, courtesy of its sponsors: Boeing (makers of the Apache helicopter, the F/A-18 fighter, the C-17 transporter and the Harpoon anti-ship missile among other products), EADS (whose own portfolio includes the Cougar helicopter, the Typhoon fighter, the A400M transporter and the Exocet anti-ship missile), Mitsubishi (taking part five months after the Japanese government relaxed its blanket ban on military exports), Singapore-based ST Engineering (makers of the Bronco all-terrain vehicle, the MATADOR anti-tank missile and the *Fearless* patrol ship) and two non-defence-industry contributors: Japan's *Asahi Shimbun* newspaper and the fabulously well-endowed John D. and Catherine T. MacArthur Foundation. Given that the six sponsors had equal billing on the publicity and the MacArthur Foundation declared that its support amounted to $250,000, it seems reasonable to assume that the overall budget for the two-day event was well in excess of $1.5 million. One insider thought it might be closer to $4 million.

Boeing clearly feels that it gets good value from its contribution: 2012 was its eleventh year as a sponsor. It's not hard to see why. With so many key players staying in the same hotel, the networking opportunities are immense. During the 2012 Dialogue, the head of Boeing Defense, Space & Security, Dennis Muilenburg, managed meetings with 13 different defence ministers: all potential customers. They're vital conversations for his company. In interviews with journalists he revealed that overseas sales now make up a quarter of his unit's revenues. With US and European defence spending being cut, Asia is becoming a vital market. In June 2012 Boeing Defense only had one customer in Southeast Asia: Singapore. But with all countries in the region getting richer and more worried about security, this is where threat meets opportunity.

Which is why so many people come to the Dialogue each year. The public focus may be the big-name speeches but, as a member of the

Canadian delegation confided in the lift, the bilateral meetings are 'really where the action's at'. Not many people came to the 2012 gathering to hear the Indian Defence Minister discuss the 'para-diggim' shift in Asia's strategic thinking or his Cambodian counterpart devote just 60 words to his country's border dispute with Thailand (which had brought the two countries to the point of war the previous year) in a speech on regional stability. No, the point of the Dialogue, as far as most of its attendees are concerned, is what goes on in private.

The game was partly given away at the end of Leon Panetta's address. It was the speech that everyone wanted to hear. The room was packed, over 500 people sat in attentive rows and more stood around the walls as the US Secretary of Defense explained what the US 'pivot' to Asia really meant. It would make headlines far and wide. But just before his session concluded, two groups of uniformed men got up and left. The German and Vietnamese delegations had timetabled a bilateral meeting to discuss military cooperation – and that was more important than hearing the last few minutes of Mr Panetta. Off they trooped for their off-the-record chat. It was only the first. In all, according to a member of their delegation, the Vietnamese managed 12 official bilateral meetings during their weekend stay.

The year 2012 was significant for East Asia's militaries. For the first time in recent history, their budgets were larger than the European members of NATO.[26] This was mainly because of cuts in Europe but also because East Asian countries spent 7.8 per cent more on their armed forces than in 2011: a total of $301 billion, according to the Stockholm International Peace and Research Institute. China made up 55 per cent of that total. Japan, South Korea and Taiwan collectively accounted for a further 33 per cent. By comparison, the smaller, poorer economies in Southeast Asia are spending very little on their own defence. The combined military budgets of the five Southeast Asian claimants to the South China Sea – Brunei, Indonesia, Malaysia, the Philippines and Vietnam – make up just 6 per cent of the East Asian total: around $18 billion. That's about the same as Turkey.

The two most sophisticated militaries in the region, Singapore and Thailand, make up almost all the remainder. But spending is growing rapidly. In 2012, Vietnam's rose by 20 per cent, the Philippines' by 10 per cent, Indonesia's by 16 per cent and Singapore's by 5 per cent. It fell slightly in Malaysia and Brunei, but only because they had high figures in 2011. These are interesting markets for arms makers looking to recover from the 11 per cent spending cut among European members of NATO since 2006.

After hours at the Shangri-La's many bars, representatives of weapons makers jokingly toast the Chinese leadership for helping them to meet their sales targets. If the US concern for access is firing Chinese concern for security, then the Chinese push for security is stoking everyone else's fears about insecurity.

In late 1992, shortly after China passed its territorial law laying claim to the island groups in the South China Sea and awarded Crestone its oil concession off the Vietnamese coast (see Chapter 5), Indonesia conspicuously purchased one-third of the former East German Navy: a total of 39 ships including frigates, landing ships and minesweepers.[27] Those ships are now obsolete, as are the country's six largest warships: 60-year-old former Dutch frigates. Indonesia's navy is becoming less and less capable of defending the country, even as incursions by Chinese ships increase. Its only modern craft of any size are four Dutch-built corvettes and five Korean-built amphibious landing vessels. The rest of its navy comprises around 50 patrol boats and four small missile craft. For a country of 13,000 islands, Indonesia seems to place a relatively low priority on its maritime forces. The country has no airborne early warning systems, no in-flight refuelling to assist long-range patrols over the sea and only rudimentary command and control systems.[28] The only reason that it has an 'Integrated Maritime Surveillance System' of coastal and ship-based radars is because the United States paid for it, ostensibly to combat 'piracy, illegal fishing, smuggling, and terrorism', in the words of the US State Department.[29]

The Indonesian military is notoriously corrupt and its weapon purchases don't correlate very well with the likely challenges it might have to face. In August 2013 it agreed to buy eight Apache attack helicopters (from Boeing) at a cost of $500 million. In 2012 it bought 103 surplus main battle tanks from Germany. It's not clear what either of these systems is intended for. They certainly won't help protect maritime claims. Plans to invest in large-scale modern naval hardware have been repeatedly delayed or halted by budget problems. Indonesia had intended to buy new Russian submarines but was forced to buy cheaper Korean ones instead. Three are under construction at the time of writing and there is talk of buying more. Plans to buy a second-hand Russian destroyer and three offshore patrol vessels from Brunei were cancelled. However, the fears about Chinese ambitions in the sea have finally prodded the Indonesian government into action and it is now starting to purchase some smaller boats and arm them with new anti-ship missiles, including the Exocet (built by EADS), the Russian Yahont and, ironically, the Chinese-designed but locally built C-802.

The Philippines is, once again, talking about modernising its military, as it does every few years only to discover that the money has been squandered. The armed forces of the Philippines are currently in a worse situation than they were in 1995 when the Chairman of the Senate National Defence and Security Committee, Orlando Mercado, told the *Far Eastern Economic Review*, 'we have an air force that can't fly and a navy that can't go out to sea'.[30] The navy's two largest vessels are former US Coastguard cutters, the next largest date from the Second World War and most of the remainder are small patrol vessels retired from service in the UK or South Korea. Debates about purchasing amphibious ships and new frigates have been going on for years but without resolution at the time of writing. Japan has lent the Philippines $184 million to buy ten new coastguard vessels, but they will be civilian, not military. The air force consists of a few helicopters and transport aircraft; its last jet fighter was retired in 2005. A $415 million plan to buy 12 new FA-50 fighter jets from Korea has been announced but it will be years before pilots will be ready to fly them on combat missions. In May 2014, as a coda to that deal, Korea announced it was donating a small 30-year-old corvette to the Philippines.

Malaysia has been spending money more strategically over a longer period and has built up a fleet of patrol boats for its coastguard and larger ships for its navy. It now possesses two French-built submarines based at Kota Kinabalu on Borneo near its offshore oilfields. In October 2013, seven months after a major Chinese naval exercise near the James Shoal, Malaysia announced plans to create a new marine corps to be based down the coast from the submarines, at Bintulu, the port nearest the shoal. The marines will need an armoury of new equipment, including at least one new amphibious ship, landing vehicles and helicopters. Malaysia faces another potential threat in the region: the lingering territorial claim on Sabah from the descendants of the Sultan of Sulu, who launched a mini-invasion in early 2013, killing 15 Malaysians, but that doesn't explain why it's buying submarines.

Vietnam spends much less on its military than Malaysia but has concentrated on its own version of the 'assassin's mace': cheaper equipment with the potential to inflict damage on a much stronger opponent. In early 2014 Vietnam received the first of six new Russian submarines. It has also bought two batteries of Russian shore-based anti-ship missiles and Israeli-made ballistic missiles with a range of 150 kilometres, and will locally produce the Russian Uran anti-ship missile. If it came to a major shooting war in the disputed areas the Vietnamese are probably in the strongest position, argues Gary Li. 'There's no way the Chinese Navy can do it. It's far too risky. If they sail a fleet down past the coast of Vietnam it's basically a shooting alley. The Vietnamese have their brand new Bastion missiles, Kilo submarines and their little attack boats. If the Vietnamese sustain damage they just pop back to base. If a Chinese ship is damaged, it's a thousand miles away from home and they don't have a major naval base down there.'[31]

The relatively small weapon purchases in Southeast Asia don't count as an 'arms race'. There's no way any of the countries could compete with Chinese military spending. But they are clearly trying to deter unwelcome naval activity by acquiring the kind of weapons that could inflict damage on a stronger fleet. Their ability to resist a concerted Chinese naval operation in the South China Sea is limited but in operations where neither side wants to open fire first, the simple deployment of sufficiently threatening forces might be enough to tip the balance against, for example, a Chinese Coastguard ship attempting to prevent an oil rig drilling in an area within the 'U-shaped line'. The unknown factor is, of course, how the Chinese Navy would react to a threat to a coastguard ship. It could be the beginning of a rapid escalation towards open conflict.

The United States takes no official position on the territorial disputes. It shares the same view of the islands that British chiefs of Staff had in 1950. 'The Spratley [sic] Islands are of no appreciable strategic value . . . Enemy occupation in war would not, so long as we retain control of the South China Sea, be a serious strategic threat.'[32] If it ever came to a conflict, the lonely blockhouses would be sitting ducks for guided missiles fired from far away. The issue for the US is for how long it can 'retain control of the

South China Sea'. At present, despite all the bluster about China's growing capabilities, its position seems secure. In time, however, Chinese capabilities will grow and there may come a time when the Beijing leadership will want to push the imperialist aggressors out of its backyard, just as the US pushed Great Britain out of the Caribbean a century ago.

In the meantime conflict is more likely to emerge from a miscalculation in a confrontation between China and one of the regional claimants. Will the Chinese authorities use military force to physically prevent oil development and fisheries protection off the coasts of Vietnam, Indonesia, Malaysia, Brunei and the Philippines? Will those countries use military force to defend their claims? Will a Chinese government and populace, inculcated since primary school with the belief that the 'U-shaped line' is indisputably theirs and locked into a rhetorical commitment to confrontation, decide that they have no choice but to open fire? Will Southeast Asian countries try to draw in the United States? Will the US regard developments as a threat to its 'freedom of navigation' and intervene? There are many choices still to be made but the battlefield of the South China Sea is already being shaped.

CHAPTER 9

Cooperation and its Opposites
Resolving the Disputes

THE *SARIMANOK* IS said to grant wishes but it didn't grant many to Eric Palobon during this voyage. On a good trip his boat can bring home 30 tuna with the largest weighing 100 kilos. This time he caught just six and the largest weighed 60 kilos. The mythical bird painted on the whitewashed bow couldn't compensate for the ravages being wrought upon the tuna population out at sea. Eric is a modern heir to the Nusantao way of life and his *banca* is little more than a high-sided canoe with long, thick bamboo outriggers to keep it upright in the rolling waters of the South China Sea. The wheel-house looks just big enough to shelter three people but Eric said he'd had a crew of 12 on board for the past two weeks, living off rice and some of what they'd caught. A central spar overhead supported tarpaulins that could be rolled down like a giant tent to shelter the whole creaking craft from the sun and the rain but pulling into Manila Bay the crew had rolled them back and festooned the rigging with laundry instead.

As they watched the boat glide into the dock, a handful of eager boys back-flipped off the quay into the murky waters in expectation of a tip or two for helping to land the catch. Traders gathered around the doorway to the giant shed in anticipation of some haggling. A rope was thrown ashore and the first of the tuna was lowered onto a raft made from old polystyrene boxes lashed together with netting. Standing astride the huge yellowfin, one of the boys pulled the precious cargo, hand over hand, towards the cavernous halls of the Navotas fish port; 80 per cent of the fish eaten by the 12 million people living in Metro Manila comes through these buildings. It's by far the biggest fish port in a country that eats a great deal of fish.[1] Eric was expecting to get somewhere between 200 and 300 pesos per kilo for each of his 60-kilo tuna: between $1,600 and $2,000 to be shared between 12 people for 14 days' work – $10 a day each. Not a bad living – about double the national average.

The Philippines is a great place to catch yellowfin tuna. They migrate from the South China Sea into the Sulu Sea from June to August and back again between August and October, passing through a small number of relatively narrow gaps in the island chain. The country provides a quarter of the tuna on American supermarket shelves.[2] And that market has tempted in some very big fish indeed. Around the dock from Eric's outrigged *banca* sat a very different kind of tuna enterprise. The *Lake Lozada* was much bigger but less seaworthy. It was possible to tell that the hull had once been blue, though it was now almost entirely rust-coloured. In places, just above the waterline, the rust had eaten great holes through the metal. Judging from the harpoon platform on the prow, the ship had once been a Japanese whaler but it didn't look capable of catching anything now. According to its crew, the *Lake Lozada*'s job had been to sit out at sea, for up to a year at a time, hauling in 300 to 500 tuna per day. On a good day, that number could rise to 2,000. Carrier boats met the ship every other day to transport its catch to the canning plants on shore so there need be no let up in the harvesting process.

No-one knows the exact state of the tuna stocks in the South China Sea because the countries around its rim can't agree to cooperate on a proper investigation. In their eyes, allowing another state to jointly administer fish stocks carries the risk of bolstering a rival claim to sovereignty. In the meantime, the situation appears to be heading for catastrophe. The best estimates have been provided by the Southeast Asian Fisheries Development Center, an inter-governmental organisation created in 1967 to try to resolve exactly these kind of problems. They can only measure what's caught, not what's still in the sea. In 2001 fishermen in the region recorded a total tuna catch of 870,000 tons. By 2008 that figure had more than doubled to 1.9 million tons. This represented about 14 per cent of all the fish caught in Southeast Asia.[3] But by 2010 tuna were becoming harder to find and the catch had fallen to 1.6 million tons.

It's not just tuna: all species are under pressure. Some 500 million people live around the shores of the South China Sea and as rural people migrate to cities and become richer, their demand for fish is rocketing. As more fish are pulled out of the sea, it becomes harder to catch those that remain. In 1980 there were 584,000 fishing operators registered in the Philippines. By 2002 there were 1.8 million. Over the same period, the average catch of a small-scale inshore fisherman fell from 20 kilos to 2 – barely subsistence level.[4] In China, as incomes rose between 1970 and 2010, the proportion of fish in the national diet quintupled to 25 kilos per person per year. As the country gets richer it will rise further: in Indonesia the figure is 35 kilos, in Taiwan it's 45 kilos and in Japan it's 65 kilos. Exacerbating the problem, China became a major fish exporter over the same period. Although 70 per cent of China's fish supply comes from aquaculture, the total sea catch quadrupled from 3 million tonnes in 1978 to 12 million tonnes in 1998 and remains at that level, according to official Chinese statistics.[5] The steadiness with which the annual catch matches the declared target has led some experts to doubt the truth of the figures, particularly since a 2008 report by the State Oceanic Administration estimated the sustainable level of the catch at just 8 million tonnes. As the catch has increased, the stocks have decreased.

Zhang Hongzhou of the Rajaratnam School of International Studies in Singapore has studied the development of the problem. He found that official attempts to reduce the size of the Chinese fishing fleet through legislation and compensation have failed. Not only are there now more boats than when the policy started in 1998, they are bigger and more powerful. As a result they are heading further and further out to sea. In 1988, 90 per cent of the Chinese industry fished inshore. By 2002 that had dropped to 64 per cent, with over a third of the fleet heading offshore. The trend has continued. By 2006, 60 per cent of the catch in Guangdong province was offshore. Overall, according to official statistics, the total catch landed in China has not increased – but the proportion of the catch obtained far from the Chinese mainland has tripled. As Chinese boats have fished further away from their home ports they have encountered other countries' coastguards and rival crews. Chinese media have documented thousands of cases of alleged harassment of Chinese fishing boats over the past two decades.[6]

The same is true for other countries' fishing crews. Since 1999, in an effort to try to let fish stocks recover, China has imposed an annual ten-week fishing ban between May and August in the area north of the Spratly Islands (defined as beyond 12° N). While the ban itself may make sound conservation sense, its unilateral imposition has prevented other countries from joining it because they fear that acquiescence could be interpreted as recognition of Chinese sovereign rights. The result, each year, is an increasing number of clashes between fishermen from Vietnam and the Philippines sailing into the closed area and Chinese maritime authorities determined to enforce their regulations in the name of both sovereignty and spawning fish. The Chinese authorities loudly advertise the impact that their ban has on the home fishing fleet. In 2013, according to the official media, it affected around 9,000 boats registered in Hainan province and 14,000 in Guangdong province. Compensation was paid to those who lost incomes by staying in port but, of course, not to crews from other countries.[7]

The ban doesn't apply to Chinese boats with official licences to fish in the contested waters around the Spratlys, however. The message to them is clear – head off to the disputed areas, fly the flag and bring home the tuna. Subsidies are given to Chinese fishermen who upgrade their boats in order to travel the longer distances to the islands – the bigger the engine, the more they get – and boat owners get additional payments for every trip they make there.[8] One report in the *Straits Times* newspaper from August 2012 described how Chinese officials visited the port of Tanmen on Hainan Island to encourage fishermen to voyage down to the Spratlys.[9] During the 2012 ban, the Hainan Province Department of Ocean and Fisheries organised the largest-ever Chinese fishing fleet to reach the islands: 30 vessels including a 3,000-ton supply ship. Journalists were taken along just to make sure that the message reached the world. In 2013 another 30 ships were sent during the ban and the head of the Fisheries Office, Huang Wenhui, told *Xinhua* news agency that the ultimate aim was to 'explore ways to exploit high-seas resources in a systematic manner'. Clashes over fishing around the Spratlys are the result of overfishing around the Chinese coast combined with a deliberate policy of developing new sources of supply.

The policy, however, ignores the obvious reality that other fishing fleets are already overfishing the Spratlys in order to feed their own growing populations. As long ago as 1994, researchers found it difficult to catch adult fish on some of the reefs off the Malaysian and Philippine coasts.[10] Even where catches remain steady, the amount of effort to bring them in has increased. Between 1995 and 2005, fish stocks off Sabah collapsed by 70 per cent. The Gulf of Thailand provides a sobering warning of what may ensue. As early as 1990, after two decades of overfishing, crews were reporting that 85 per cent of what they were catching was 'trash fish'. With no reliable income in their home waters Thai fishermen became known as the region's biggest trespassers, with thousands arrested each year while trying to make a living in other countries' EEZs.[11] The South China Sea is heading for a similar fate, threatening the food supplies of half a billion people. Macro-scale statistical models suggest the stocks of larger species fell by more than half between 1960 and 2000. Fish were once plentiful right across the Sea, except in the very deepest areas. Large areas are now commercially empty. The only part of the region where stocks remain in better condition is off Brunei – where the presence of so many oil rigs has prevented large-scale destructive fishing. What can be done? Can the disputes be resolved before it's too late to save the fish?

Professor John McManus has spent two decades studying the aquatic life of the region and is now Director of the National Center for Coral Reef Research at the University of Miami. McManus believes the contested islands play a vital role in keeping the whole South China Sea alive. Fish breed there and then ocean currents spread their larvae far around the region. 'The coral reefs of the Spratly Islands have among the world's highest species diversities,' he told me. 'The surrounding coastlines are heavily over-exploited, and it's likely that local population collapses of certain species are being prevented by occasional influxes of larval fish from the Spratlys and other remote reefs in the Sea.' For years McManus has argued that the Spratlys should be turned into a marine conservation park for the benefit of the whole region. By preserving what is, in effect, a giant fish nursery, a 'peace park' could provide the stock to allow fish populations elsewhere to recover, provided that fishing elsewhere becomes more sustainable.

There has been one attempt in the recent past to try to create something similar. In March 2001 all the South China Sea claimants agreed to put aside their differences and cooperate in a $32 million United Nations Environment Programme-led project on 'Reversing Environmental Degradation Trends in the South China Sea and Gulf of Thailand'. The project ran for six years from 2002 until 2008 and chalked up a number of successes. However, its final evaluation concluded ruefully that 'in the end, there still was no success in getting China and Malaysia involved in issues that would involve multilateral agreements, notably in the case of trans-boundary fish stocks'.[12] McManus confirms that. 'The participation of the People's Republic of China ensured that the issue of the Spratly Islands would not be taken up officially in that project,' he told me. The United Nations team found it almost impossible to develop projects involving more than one country at a time and none were undertaken in the disputed areas of the Sea. The planned objective – to create 'refugia' in the sea to protect sites where fish spawn and grow – came to nothing.

The International Union for the Conservation of Nature has voted in favour of the 'peace park' idea and, according to McManus, 'many regional scientists and conservationists in all the claimant countries are very supportive, especially in the Philippines, Taiwan, and Vietnam'. The problem lies at the official level. Only one of the claimants, the government in Taiwan, is officially in favour although President Ramos of the Philippines once gave it his backing too. 'Most political leaders have been reluctant to open a dialogue on this with the PRC [People's Republic of China],' laments McManus. 'The potential for oil in the basin has also complicated the issue, although it is well known that oil is more abundant and much less expensive to access along the continental shelf areas of the South China Sea than within the deep waters amid the Spratly reefs.' As a result, it's hard to be optimistic about the possibility of countries working together to prevent a total collapse of the South China Sea fisheries.

Fish stocks should, in theory, be easier to manage than oil and gas for two reasons: they are renewable and they move. It doesn't make sense for one country to try to manage migratory fish. All around the world, regional fisheries management organisations have been created so that countries can cooperate in overseeing the stocks upon which they all depend. In Southeast Asia the organisation with the best record of researching and acting to protect the region's fish stocks is the Southeast Asian Fisheries Development Center. China could easily join, but it has chosen not to. Given its unwillingness to join similar regional initiatives in the past, it seems unlikely that it will do so in the future. Beijing isn't opposed to fisheries agreements in principle. It has concluded them with Japan in 1997, with South Korea in 2000 and with Vietnam, also in 2000. It held one round of talks in the 'Philippines–China Joint Commission on Fisheries' in 2005 but then no more.[13] The sticking point is its refusal to deal with any issue in the South China Sea on a multilateral basis. The Vietnam deal only applies in the Gulf of Tonkin, an area of sea that was only disputed between those two countries. But tuna don't respect international boundaries, so bilateral arrangements are unlikely to solve the problem. All countries around the Sea depend upon cheap supplies of fish to feed their populations. In the absence of any agreement to safeguard the stocks, increasing short-term exploitation is putting all countries in the region at risk of a major food crisis. If China and its neighbours can't agree on basic steps to avoid the risk of starvation, how likely are they to reach agreement on the wider issues of sovereignty and territory?

* * * * * *

A lasting agreement on sovereignty and territory would answer many prayers around the region, not least in the Philippines. As Secretary-General of the Commission on Maritime and Ocean Affairs, Henry Bensurto is the brains behind the Philippines' policy in the South China Sea disputes. His soft voice and dark eyes camouflage a steely resolution. The battles he has fought to persuade the Philippine establishment to bring the country's maritime claims into line with international law, and then to defend those claims at innumerable international workshops, have introduced grey flecks into his formerly jet-black hair. On the day we met they matched his forehead, streaked grey by the Catholic rite of Ash Wednesday. Bensurto has faith in international law too: he believes it can resurrect the chances of peace in the Sea. Under his guidance Manila has switched the basis of its territorial claim from the earlier premise that the Philippines inherited it from 'Admiral' Tomas Cloma who 'discovered' the islands (see Chapter 3) to one grounded in the United Nations Convention on the Law of the Sea

(UNCLOS). In 2009, he pushed for a new Philippine Baseline Law that ended the country's claim to Cloma's huge polygon of the 'Kalayaan Island Group' and brought it into line with UNCLOS. Then in 2011, Bensurto offered a new hope. He called it the Zone of Peace, Freedom, Friendship and Cooperation.

The essence of the zone is that claimants should first clarify which areas of the Sea are disputed and which are not and only then move on to resolving the disputes. The disputes come in two kinds. One set is 'territorial disputes' – the question of the legitimate 'ownership' of each land feature in the South China Sea. The other set is 'maritime boundary disputes' – what size 'zones' are generated by each feature under UNCLOS. If a tribunal rules that a particular island can sustain human habitation or economic life they would award it an Exclusive Economic Zone (EEZ) of up to 200 nautical miles radius; if they rule it is just a 'rock' that cannot sustain human or economic life then it would only generate a 12-nautical mile territorial sea and no EEZ; and if in its natural state it would be under water at high tide it generates no territorial sea or EEZ at all.

Unlike his predecessors, Bensurto decided to tackle the second problem first. He proposed 'enclaving' the disputed area by first identifying which features might possibly generate a 12-nautical mile territorial sea and then drawing the relevant boundaries around them. He then tried to draw likely EEZ boundaries. Using the precedent set by the International Court of Justice (ICJ) in its 2012 ruling on the island dispute between Colombia and Nicaragua, he assumed that a court would be very unlikely to grant the disputed islands an EEZ 'outwards' – in other words, in the direction of the coasts of the surrounding countries. This would then narrow the 'disputed area' to just that part of the Sea near the islands. This could be 'enclaved' – set aside for further discussion – thus allowing the Philippines and all the other littoral countries to get on with developing the oil and gas fields off their coasts. The disputants could then try to reach some kind of settlement or cooperative arrangement in the 'enclaved' area. If, however, a tribunal ruled that any of the islands were entitled to a full EEZ, it would swallow up most of the enclaved area.

On the face of it, the the Zone of Peace, Freedom, Friendship and Cooperation presents an entirely reasonable and rational route forward. The only problem is that – it's proposed by the Philippines. The country's relations with China gradually soured after Benigno Aquino became president, nose-dived during the Scarborough Shoal confrontation in mid-2012 and hit rock bottom on 22 January 2013 when Manila announced that it was, in effect, going to put Bensurto's plan to an international court. The Philippines has asked the Permanent Court of Arbitration in the Hague to rule on key elements of the plan: whether the 'U-shaped line' is compatible with UNCLOS; whether five of the eight features occupied by China should be considered 'submerged' and therefore unable to generate either territorial sea or EEZ; whether the remaining three features occupied by China are just rocks without claim to an EEZ; and whether the Philippines is entitled to a full 200-nautical-mile EEZ, regardless of the existence of other occupied features offshore.

China has refused to take part in the proceedings but the court has begun the legal process anyway and could issue a judgment as early as 2015. The court has no power to enforce its rulings, however. The Washington-based lawyer acting for the Philippines, Paul Reichler, knows this well. In 1986 he helped the government of Nicaragua win a case against the United States at the ICJ. The court ruled that US support for the Contra rebels fighting the left-wing government of Nicaragua, and the placing of anti-ship mines in its harbours, was illegal. The United States simply ignored the ruling. Instead, it funded the right-wing political alliance that won power in Nicaragua in 1990 and two years later cancelled the country's demand for compensation. A Philippines victory in the case could be equally pyrrhic, although Henry Bensurto would at least be able to wield a newly sharpened sword of righteousness in future discussions with his Chinese counterparts. However, even as the Philippines tries to clarify the international legal situation through its legal case, on the other side of the South China Sea Chinese thinkers are trying to change the questions.

* * * * * *

Some of those questions are being developed in a substantial campus of red-brick buildings on Hainan Island, about half an hour's drive east of the city of Haikou. The complex feels like a cross between a university and a beach resort and it's only a short walk from the real beach resorts that fringe the tree-lined shore of the South China Sea. The neighbourhood could be a metaphor for China's approach to the Sea itself. Virgin territory has been surveyed and developed and turned into living space for a population with new aspirations and wider horizons. A landscape of luxury apartments, second homes for those with plenty of disposable income, has emerged from the sand dunes and paddy fields. And in the middle of this state-sponsored real estate boom stands the National Institute of South China Sea Studies and in one of its two towers sits the institute's president, Dr Wu Shicun.

In recent years Dr Wu has become the public face of China's South China Sea diplomacy. His immaculate coiffure and sunny smile grace workshops in Washington and seminars in Singapore. He presents a firm line in defence of China's 'indisputable' sovereignty in the Sea but his speeches also reveal nuances in official thinking. He has an immaculate political background for the job, having worked his way up the Communist Party system, from Deputy Secretary of the Youth Committee of Nanjing University, to the Hainan Provincial Party Committee and then News Director for the Hainan Provincial Foreign Affairs Office. He was clearly trusted to present the Party's official views to overseas audiences. In 1996 Hainan province created a new organisation, the Hainan Research Institute of the South China Sea, to promote its interests and Dr Wu became its first boss. In 2004 the Ministry of Foreign Affairs in Beijing decided it could also make use of Dr Wu's skills and provided the extra money and official sponsorship for the organisation to become the National Institute. In 2011 it moved from a grim office block in Haikou, to its new campus by the beach.

The institute is not the only Chinese body looking at the South China Sea. The China Institute for Marine Affairs (sponsored by the State Oceanic Administration, which oversees the China Coast Guard) also looks at legal and historical justifications for China's claims as well as maritime development more widely. The China Institute for Contemporary International Relations (affiliated with the Ministry of State Security) focuses on other countries' approaches to the issue. Both organisations are relatively reclusive. The National Institute of South China Sea Studies, on the other hand, is hospitable in the extreme. The vast majority of its campus is dedicated to delivering China's message in generous comfort. It has a 200-seat auditorium and a 100-seat meeting room plus several

smaller seminar rooms, classrooms, VIP rooms, protocol rooms, a publications room and several exhibition rooms. The top floor has well-equipped
offices for visiting academics (and writers). An annexe houses large and
small dining rooms, 13 well-appointed bedrooms for guests (complete
with flat-screen televisions, bathrobes and L'Occitane toiletries in the
bathrooms) and, on the top floor, the Ambassadorial Suite with separate
entrances for the wife and the mistress. The institute's 40 research staff, on
the other hand, work in three large offices and journey to and from the
campus in a shuttle bus.

Dr Wu's office is on the fourth floor but four is an unlucky number in
Chinese culture (it sounds like the word for death) whereas six is auspi-
cious (it sounds like the word for wealth). So there is no fourth or fifth
floor in the building and Dr Wu works on the sixth. This card-carrying
but superstitious Communist enjoys a semi-detached status. He has the
ear of the Ministry of Foreign Affairs but he doesn't represent it. He has,
in effect, a licence to test out new ideas and explore possible ways forward
in the disputes without committing his government to anything. His may
be only one voice in the discussion but it does give us some idea about the
range of options that the Beijing leadership is considering. Dr Wu's smile
rarely fades but his demeanour is more determined than optimistic. 'There
is no way to solve the sovereignty issue in the near future,' he states baldly
– an acknowledgement that other countries are not swayed by China's
historical and legal arguments.

Ever since 7 May 2009, when the Chinese government appended
a map of the 'U-shaped line' to its submission to the United Nations'
Commission on Limits of the Continental Shelf, it has come under pressure to clarify what it is the line represents exactly. Different parts of
the Chinese state have treated it differently. In April 2011, the Chinese
Foreign Ministry submitted another official letter to the UN referring to
'indisputable sovereignty over the islands in the South China Sea and the
adjacent waters'. It made no reference to the 'U-shaped line'. However, the
actions of the former China Marine Surveillance organisation and Fisheries
Law Enforcement Command (which were merged into the China Coast
Guard in 2013) in the waters off the Philippines, Vietnam, Malaysia and
Indonesia's Natuna Islands in 2011, 2012 and 2013, and the decision by
the China National Offshore Oil Company to offer exploration blocks

off the Vietnamese coast in June 2012 suggest that all these organisations interpret the line as a territorial claim on the whole area.

Public declarations by other parts of the Chinese state apparatus have made the situation more vexed: the line has taken on a life of its own. For example, every map published in China must be approved by the National Administration of Surveying, Mapping and Geoinformation. Even a small non-governmental organisation wanting to illustrate where in China it is working can't publish that map unless it includes the 'U-shaped line'.[14] A map of the line has been printed in every Chinese passport issued since April 2012. Although the exact meaning of the line has not been explicitly stated, many Chinese have simply assumed that it delineates a territorial claim. A retreat from that position could provoke furious domestic criticism. The institute, however, seems to be testing the waters with foreign organisations and governments to see what overseas reactions might be to different ways forward. The current starting point is to state China's claim firmly within the language of UNCLOS, just as Henry Bensurto is doing in the Philippines. 'From my perspective, the nine-dash-line should be the line of the ownership over all the features inside the line and adjacent waters,' says Dr Wu. 'At international conferences I also explain that China never claims the whole South China Sea inside the line as its historic waters.'

For some time there has been a concern among outside observers that Chinese policy-makers might reach the conclusion that if China could not successfully defend its claims within the norms of international law it might opt out of UNCLOS altogether. But the idea of China 'going rogue' alarms Chinese policy-makers too. It would destroy decades of careful diplomacy based around the rhetoric of 'peaceful rise'. The institute appears to be part of a concerted national effort to try to square the South China Sea claims with international law. Certainly that is now the language that Dr Wu uses when he speaks publicly. It is a tough task and now there is a considerable risk that, if the Philippines case at the Permanent Court of Arbitration succeeds and China's UNCLOS-based claims are ruled minuscule or non-existent, that strategy could be completely undermined.

So the institute has begun investigating more sophisticated but also more arcane legal alternatives. In October 2013 the institute convened an international conference investigating whether China could use the legal concept of 'historic rights' to claim the resources within the line even without a claim of sovereignty. Dr Wu admits that it is contentious. 'It's arguable. It's hard to reach a common consensus on this issue. Some scholars say that historic right is only the right of fishing activity in those areas. It needs to be further studied, this area: fishing rights, navigation rights, natural resources exploration. China should have sovereignty over the islands and also enjoy historic rights on a cumulative basis.' There is no mention of 'historic rights' in UNCLOS at all. The concept was deliberately kept out of the text. In order to develop the case, the Chinese government will have to step into the wilder fringes of international law.

The institute is not alone in this effort. In January 2013 the Executive Director of the China Institute of Marine Affairs, Gao Zhiguo (who is also a judge at the International Tribunal on the Law of the Sea), and Jia Bing Bing, Professor of International Law at Tsinghua University, published a lengthy academic article arguing that the 'U-shaped line' does have a foundation in international law.[15] Rather than focusing on the 'historic rights' that the institute is investigating, it used a different set of arguments to claim that China has 'historic title' to the waters. In the words of the authors, 'the nine-dash line does not contradict the obligations undertaken by China under UNCLOS; rather, it supplements what is provided for in the Convention' – in other words, even if the 'U-shaped line' is ruled incompatible with UNCLOS, it can still have a basis in other aspects of international law. One Chinese legal expert in Beijing, who preferred not to be named, explained the thinking. 'The preamble to UNCLOS states that the convention is not intended to be exhaustive. Reference still has to be made to customary law and state practice.' This could be a problem for the Philippines' case. 'The premise of the Philippines case is that the international law of the sea is only UNCLOS. But whatever the definition of an island, there is still a question of title – first.' The expert's view is that the Permanent Court of Arbitration would need to decide whether a different court needed to rule on the question of sovereignty before it could rule on the status of the features. This would completely upend Henry Bensurto's strategy.

These arguments are, to say the least, controversial. They are also based upon an understanding of the history that owes more to nationalist feeling than historical evidence. For example, Judge Gao's article includes the statement that 'the South China Sea had been known to Chinese fishermen and seafarers from time immemorial', without further explanation. Yet the efforts being expended are a sign of how seriously parts of the Chinese state are thinking about defending the country's interests in the Sea while simultaneously remaining inside the framework of current international law.

Broadly speaking, there are four main strands to China's interests: a sense of historic entitlement to the South China Sea combined with a desire for national prestige, the need for 'strategic depth' to protect China's coastal cities, the desire to guarantee strategic access to the open waters of the Indian and Pacific oceans, and the wish to have access to the resources of the Sea itself – particularly its fish and hydrocarbons. These four agendas are being sponsored by different power bases within China and while the Foreign Ministry, for example, might be willing to recognise the strength of the legal case against it, the military, the State Oceanic Administration, the Chinese National Offshore Oil Company (CNOOC) and provinces with large fishing industries are more likely to disagree. The Foreign Ministry does not sit at the top table in China's political system, but much lower down the hierarchy. One expert judged it to be only the 40th most important state body (out of 50).[16] In practical terms the Foreign Ministry appears to have less influence at the highest levels of decision-making in Beijing than its bureaucratic rivals.

These ministries and state organs maintain their power within the Chinese political system through constant lobbying, whether for state funding, the opportunity to make larger profits or local employment. They all have long experience of framing their arguments within the narratives likely to win favour with the central leadership. It's not hard to dovetail their cases with the 'national imperative' for China to gain unchallenged access to the resources of the Sea. When CNOOC launched its ultra-deepwater drilling rig, the HS981, in May 2012, the company chairman Wang Yilin declared it to be part of 'China's mobile national territory and a strategic weapon for promoting the development of the country's offshore oil industry'.[17] He didn't mention the amount of state subsidy that had gone into the nearly $840 million cost of the rig or the effect it was likely to have on the firm's profits, though these were probably more important to him. Chinese policy is less likely to be the result of a considered summation of reasoned arguments than the unpredict-able result of an agglomeration of lobbying campaigns. When they work together, the power of these interest groups is immense. One thing they can all agree on, whether for reasons of nationalism, security, profit or jobs, is that China must have access to the resources of the South China Sea. The areas off its own coast have been so thoroughly exploited for both fish and hydrocarbons that domestic lobbies are insisting on looking further afield. Early on, Chinese leaders were realistic enough to understand that this would provoke resentment and opposition. China's 'offer' to Southeast Asia has remained the same for a quarter of a century. In the words of Dr Wu, 'the reasonable, pragmatic way is to go for joint development'.

Chinese policy has been consistent on this point ever since Deng Xiaoping first proposed it to other regional leaders in the 1980s and Li Peng announced it to the world in Singapore on 13 August 1990: 'China is ready to join efforts with Southeast Asian countries to develop the Nansha islands while putting aside, for the time being, the question of sovereignty' (see Chapter 5).[18] For years, however, the policy remained largely rhetor-ical. In 2003, for example, Wu Bangguo, then chairman of the National People's Congress, proposed it in the Philippines and in 2005 he offered it in Malaysia. The same year Hu Jintao suggested it in Brunei. In the Philippines, the proposal led to the Joint Marine Seismic Undertaking, which ended in political scandal, killing any chances of development work. None of the other countries took up the offer and the idea languished. But on 6 September 2011, perhaps as a response to international criti-cism over the various 'cable-cutting' incidents of that year, China's State Council Information Office released a 'White Paper on China's Peaceful Development', emphasising Deng's guidance on joint development.[19] In December 2012 the National Institute of South China Sea Studies helped to give it new impetus with an international conference on the subject. Since then Beijing has been pushing it harder than ever, with a mixture of public diplomacy and hype.

In October 2013, the Chinese media loudly proclaimed that Brunei and Vietnam had agreed to work with China on 'joint development' in the Sea and editorials urged 'other countries' – presumably the Philippines, Malaysia and Indonesia – to also 'take up the magic wand'.[20] But the trum-peted agreements were much less than they appeared to readers of Chinese

websites. The deal between China and Brunei was actually a commercial joint venture between CNOOC and the Brunei National Petroleum
Company to provide services to oilfields. It had nothing to do with sharing
the hydrocarbon reserves in disputed areas of the Sea.[21] The agreement
with Vietnam was even less concrete. It merely set up a working group to
study maritime cooperation, yet the Chinese news agency *Xinhua* described
it as a 'breakthrough'.[22] The same article quoted Dr Wu: the agreement
'undoubtedly sends a clear message to other claimants that putting aside
bickering on sovereignty and sitting at the table for joint development is a
pragmatic choice'.

Joint development does indeed sound reasonable and there are many
examples where it has worked, both in Southeast Asia and more widely.
But the sticking point in the South China Sea has always been deciding
where it should take place. In his conversation with me, Dr Wu emphasised only two areas: 'The Reed Bank area, which the Philippines claims,
and the Vanguard Bank where Vietnamese claim they exercise jurisdiction.
So, from China's perspective, the whole Spratly area could be possible for
joint development. Some foreign scholars even suggested that the Paracels
or the Scarborough Shoal area would be another case for joint development.' Both Reed Bank and Vanguard Bank have been surveyed recently
and both are thought to hold viable oil or gas fields but both are long
distances from China and neither the Philippines nor Vietnam appears
willing to concede its sovereign rights to their resources. I asked Dr Wu
whether joint development might be easier in an area north of the Spratlys
that is less contested. 'I'm not sure whether the northern part of the Spratly
area is rich in oil. It is not a political problem, it is a commercial or a technical problem' was his deadpan reply. While there may be some support
for joint development in principle, the problem is that no-one is willing
to take up China's offer. It takes two to tango and at present China doesn't
yet have any dancing partners.

* * * * * *

Ernie Bower is on first-name terms with most of those who might
consider taking up a Chinese offer. Bower directs the Sumitro Chair for
Southeast Asian Studies at the Center for Strategic and International

Studies in Washington DC. Government officials regularly consult him on aspects of US policy, as do businesses through his private consultancy BowerGroupAsia. His work has won him honours from the king of Malaysia and the president of the Philippines and plaudits from well-placed people with direct interests in the South China Sea. The advisory board of the Sumitro Chair includes Richard Armitage, former Deputy Secretary of State, now a director of the oil company ConocoPhillips; William Cohen, former US Secretary of Defense and now head of his own defence consultancy; Hashim Djojohadikusomo, the former boss of the Indonesian oil company PT Pertamina; Admiral Timothy Keating, the former head of US Pacific Command; Melody Meyer, President of Chevron Asia-Pacific; Edward Tortorici, Vice-Chairman of First Pacific Corporation, which owns a controlling stake in Forum Energy, the company attempting to develop gas reserves on the Reed Bank; James Blackwell, an Executive Vice-President of Chevron; 'Skip' Boyce, President for Southeast Asia at Boeing; and George David, former Chairman of United Technologies Corporation, an aerospace contractor.

Bower talks to so many key figures that his views on resolving the South China Sea disputes probably reflect an emerging consensus in Washington policy-making circles. 'At the core of the US understanding of what it takes to have a secure Asia-Pacific is the fact that you don't have stability and security unless China feels secure in terms of its energy, water and food,' he says. 'We can go around a lot of semantics but in essence there's no way to have a stable, secure Asia unless the Chinese find a way with their neighbours and with the encouragement of the United States to find a way towards joint development in the South China Sea. Eventually, that's what has to happen.' Remarkably, the US and China find themselves agreeing on a route out of the disputes. But there is a major problem.

In parallel with Dr Wu's efforts in Haikou, Western think-tanks have also been investigating possible ways forward. The John D. and Catherine T. MacArthur Foundation's Asia Security Initiative funded a three-year study by the National Bureau of Asian Research,[23] for example, and the Centre for International Law at the National University of Singapore has been exploring potential legal frameworks. All these researchers have generally come to the same conclusion. Joint development will only be possible once there is consensus on the territorial and maritime claims. We are back at the beginning again. The irony for China is that 'setting aside claims and pursuing joint development' will only be possible once it has formalised its claims – the very thing that it does not wish to do because of the internal disputes that this would generate between different parts of the state bureaucracy.

The Indonesian diplomat Hasjim Djalal has lived these arguments for more than a quarter of a century. Quietly and patiently he has tried to help the different sides find common ground. He was one of the negotiators who drew up UNCLOS in the 1970s and 1980s and was also, for a time, ambassador to the United Nations. When he heard about the battle of Johnson Reef in 1988 (see Chapter 3) he understood exactly what the implications could be for Southeast Asia. 'I felt somewhat uneasy as the South China Sea continued to gain more strategic interest in the eyes of China, the United States, Japan, ASEAN countries and even India and Russia.'[24] For Djalal, it was crucial that the region should try to resolve the disputes without the involvement of outside powers. He feared that tensions and rivalry within the region, as countries competed to grab sea resources, would stymie the possibilities of economic growth.

He reached the conclusions that formal negotiations would get nowhere, even in the medium term, and that countries didn't want outsiders to try to broker a solution. Instead he saw an opportunity in UNCLOS, particularly its stipulations that countries around enclosed and semi-enclosed seas were obliged to cooperate. Djalal had been a leading member of the Fisheries Taskforce of the Pacific Economic Cooperation Council, which had succeeded in getting governments in Southeast Asia, the Pacific islands, and Pacific Latin America to work together, where previous official initiatives had failed. Then, while attending a workshop on the joint development of oil reserves in Southeast Asia in early 1989, he met Ian Townsend-Gault, a law professor at the University of British Columbia in Canada. The two men found they had reached the same conclusion: the South China Sea also needed an informal venue to nurture practical cooperation. Townsend-Gault pitched the idea to the Canadian Department of Foreign Affairs, which agreed to fund the initiative for five years.[25]

Towards the end of 1989 Djalal persuaded the Indonesian Foreign Minister, Ali Alatas, to send him and Townsend-Gault on a tour of embassies and ministries around ASEAN. They concluded that everyone wanted something to be done, that an informal approach would be best and that ASEAN states should coordinate their positions before engaging others. Djalal and Townsend-Gault set themselves two aims: to manage the potential conflicts by seeking an area in which everyone could cooperate and to develop measures to build trust between the rival claimants. Indonesia had two major cards to play: it didn't claim any features in the contested zone and it had a number of luxurious hotels on tranquil beaches where delegates could dialogue in peace. The first 'Workshop on Managing Potential Conflicts in the South China Sea' took place shortly afterwards, in January 1990, in Bali, for delegates from the then six ASEAN countries only. The following year other countries were invited too. Informality allowed many difficult issues to be side-stepped: both China and Taiwan could take part, territorial issues could be on the agenda and policy options considered. According to Djalal, the Chinese were initially reluctant to take part because they didn't want the issues 'regionalised' but eventually did so.

The discussions started well. Some of the ideas even filtered directly into the formal realm with the signing of ASEAN's 'Manila Declaration' on the South China Sea in 1992 (which was itself a response to China's new Law on the Territorial Sea announced a few months before). That year the informal workshops agreed to form technical working groups to look at specific issues. They eventually included: resources, scientific research, environmental protection, safety of navigation and legal matters. Progress was slow but by 1995 they had approved two scientific research projects: one on sea level change and one on sharing data. Canada approved another five years of funding. But then, according to Djalal, the problems began: 'China wanted only national institutions to do the implementation', not regional ones. In 1998, for example, Beijing opposed an Indonesian suggestion to study hydrocarbons, a Thai plan to study fish stocks and even a plan to create a regional database on geoscience.[26]

In 1993 Djalal had suggested a specific area where a preliminary effort at genuine joint development might take place. The location was kept confidential to prevent negative public reactions. Most countries supported the idea, some had reservations but one 'did not want to talk about the proposed "zone" at all'. The idea languished until Djalal submitted a revised proposal in 1998. The workshops created a 'Study Group on Zones of Cooperation' to try to push the idea forward. The group identified four problems that needed to be overcome: where the development would be located, which resources would be developed, what kind of organisation would manage the development and which countries would take part. Discussions continued for three more years but nothing concrete could be achieved. Although the discussions were themselves confidence-building measures, in the end the only practical project to come out of the South China Sea Workshops was a joint expedition, in March 2002, to investigate bio-diversity, and even that took place around the undisputed Indonesian island of Anambas. By then the Canadians had decided to end their funding and the workshops slipped into inactivity.

In Djalal's eyes, this was a victory for Beijing, since China 'seems to feel that the process has gone too far, too fast and has discussed too many topics. Therefore it seems that it would like the Workshop process to slow down.' Looking back over the ten years of discussions about joint development, Djalal had this to say: 'It appears that what China means by joint development is that China would like to jointly and bilaterally develop – with the other claimants concerned – the resources of the South China Sea in the area claimed by the other and China.'[27] In other words, China is not interested in joint development except in other countries' claimed EEZs.

This is still the fundamental dispute that prevents joint development in the Sea. When Dr Wu talks about joint development, he says openly that it only applies to areas within other countries' EEZs, not China's. Ernie Bower of the Center for Strategic and International Studies in Washington says no other country is likely to join such an initiative. 'The bottom line is that everyone other than China will reject joint development under the terms that China is the biggest player in the region and will define and dictate the terms. The big question is whether and when China will have the confidence to negotiate terms as a crucial partner but not trying to dictate the terms.'

In November 2011, at the ASEAN–China Summit in Bali, Premier Wen Jiabao announced the launch of a 3 billion yuan ($470 million) 'China–ASEAN Maritime Cooperation Fund'. Senior officials have promoted the fund on many occasions since. In September 2013, Wen's successor, Li Keqiang, told the launch of the ASEAN–China Expo: 'We are doing researches in carrying on a series of cooperation projects, giving priorities to construction of fishery bases, environmental protection for maritime ecology, seafood production and trade, navigation safety and search and rescue, and facilitation of maritime transportation.' These are almost the same issues on which Beijing had vetoed cooperation during Hasjim Djalal's workshops. 'We are expecting the active participation of the ASEAN countries,' he continued.[28] But the ASEAN countries are not participating – they assume there will be political strings attached that could compromise their territorial claims. At the time of writing not a single yuan has gone to a project involving ASEAN. Only one project has been touted – and that would benefit a state-owned Chinese company, Guangxi Beibu Gulf International Port Group, which is expected to buy a stake in Kuantan port in Malaysia during 2014 and then upgrade its facilities. It sounds like another neat coincidence between national rhetoric and Chinese corporate interest.[29]

* * * * * *

There is an apartment in London overlooking the River Thames, a couple of miles upstream from Captain Richard Spratly's birthplace and a few miles downstream from where he died, where an alternative way forward is being nurtured. It's a very grand apartment, in the heart of the Whitehall political district, trimmed with works of art, antiques and curios from all around East Asia. It frequently hosts members of the trans-Atlantic elite hopping between homes in old and New England and it's also home to an organisation that considers itself a potential solution to the South China Sea disputes. The 'Kingdom of the Colonia of Saint John' may sound like a Ruritanian fiction but its supporters claim that it is the legitimate heir to the empire of the Filipino 'admiral', Tomas Cloma, and to Cloma's claim in the South China Sea. The administrator of the claim goes under the pseudonym Thomas de Lys: banker, former associate of the Marcos family and once a financial advisor to Madame Chiang Kai-shek, the 'Dragon Lady' wife of the Kuomintang leader.

De Lys showed me a document, a Decree of the Supreme Council of State of Freedomland, apparently signed by Tomas Cloma on 24 August 1974, in which the name of Freedomland was changed to 'Colonia' and Cloma resigned as head of state in favour of a British property developer called John Barnes (who subsequently changed his name to John de

Mariveles). The signing was witnessed by Tomas' brother, Filemon Cloma, and an associate of Barnes, a former U-boat commander called Eric Sroka. It was later notarised by a Manila lawyer, Rufino A. Sanic. According to de Lys, insiders had warned Cloma that President Marcos was about to force him to hand over the claim to the Philippine government so he tried to outsmart them. When Cloma eventually did sign the government's document, on 4 December 1974 after nearly two months in jail, he used the words 'whatever rights and/or interests they might have acquired over said islands called Freedomland', implying that there actually weren't any interests left, although Marcos wasn't to know that.

De Lys' argument is essentially this: under the 1951 Treaty of San Francisco, the Japanese state renounced its claim to the Spratlys. They therefore became, in legal terminology, unoccupied – *terra nullius* – allowing Cloma to legitimately claim them for himself. Readers who've made it this far will know that there was a pre-existing French claim on six islands dating from 1933, renewed in October 1946, and a Chinese claim to Itu Aba, dating from December 1946. But in de Lys' view, Cloma avoided these problems. 'In deference to this French claim, Cloma partitioned off the southwest corner of the territory that included Spratly Island, which had the effect to give the Cloma claim its current trapezoidal shape. Specifics related to ROC [Republic of China] claims could be considered "extinguished" as the ROC is arguably not considered a "state" in international law and specifics related to PRC [People's Republic of China] claims have not to date ever been proposed or clarified by China, other than the so-called "nine-dash line". The Vietnam claim is based on the contention that they are successor to the French claim but the French dispute this.'

Over the years many entrepreneurs have attempted to set up their own countries: the Brooke family managed it in Sarawak, for example. Most, however, were of dubious integrity. US authorities have had to deal with a number of fraudsters who claimed to be representing countries based on coral reefs and wanting access to the international banking system. There have been several in the South China Sea. In 1971 an American, Morton Frederick Meads, announced himself the ruler of the Kingdom of Humanity–Republic of Morac-Songhrati-Meads based in the 'Meads Islands' and managed to fool the Malaysian government for a while. Unfortunately for the Kingdom–Republic, its supporters were reported drowned during a typhoon in June 1972. A rival 'Principality of Freedomland' was apparently announced by a French conman in 1974 – with no known connection to Tomas Cloma – and the Republic of Thaumaturgy, with a declared capital on Louisa Reef, attempted to sell government bonds to gullible investors in 2004. In fact there's an entire international sub-culture of groups and individuals claiming to represent atoll-based nation states, chivalric orders and defunct royal families.

The Kingdom of the Colonia of St John, however, appears different. It has a real address, with real people behind it and real documents to support its claim. More importantly it has real access to influential people and real money behind it. Thomas de Lys is part of an east coast American dynasty, which made its money building power stations in Asia and later provided the United States with a treasury secretary and Yale University with some fine new buildings. De Lys' chums include many who know the corridors of power – from buccaneering capitalists to hot-shot lawyers.

Virginia Greiman specialises in designing novel solutions to old problems. She was a lawyer on the 'Big Dig' – the massive tunnelling project under Boston – and now teaches at Harvard Law School. Her case for Colonia begins with exactly the same argument as the Gao Zhiguo and Jia Bing Bing article – that UNCLOS isn't everything and a country can assert 'historic title' to territory, but that Colonia is the rightful successor to Freedomland's claim from 1956. Over lunch in central London she outlined her proposed development model, a 'hybrid institution' based on her experience with mega-projects. Her approach would try to answer the four questions identified by Djalal and Townsend-Gault but with a private sector rather than an inter-governmental model. A Joint Study Group from all the claimants would develop a framework for dialogue and negotiate an agreement. The agreement would define a 'Spratly Island Concession Area' (SICA) and the allocation of assets within it. It would be open to all claimants, with disputes referred to the area's own arbitration court. The area would have its own authority that would allocate concessions to extract resources.[30]

'It could be a bridge between China and the Philippines,' she argues. 'The key is to keep it in the private sector and prevent countries going to international tribunals.' She is confident that both China and the Philippines would gain from the arrangement. But what about Colonia?

Under the SICA model Colonia would receive a share of the revenues and it would be up to Colonia's 'rulers' to decide what to do with them. She says some would go to good causes. 'Colonia wants to share resources for the benefit of the world so it's building links with churches and others to form a possible trust to benefit, for example, poverty alleviation.' The most obvious challenge to this grandiose plan is the considerable doubt about whether any of the claimants will take Colonia seriously. The next will be whether the claimants will be any more likely to find agreement in Greiman's 'Joint Study Group' than in the existing structures open to them through informal workshops and international arbitration. It might sound crazy, but is it any less realistic than expecting China to abandon its 'indisputable claim' to the South China Sea?

* * * * * *

Weary readers of this book might, at this point, be wishing for a sizeable dose of climate change to raise sea level and submerge the features of the South China Sea altogether. Even the conservative prediction of a 39 to 58 centimetre rise by 2100 could put some of the existing features below water. Sadly it's less likely to reduce the problem than unleash yet another round of instability. Future rises in sea levels weren't a major concern when UNCLOS was drafted and so the convention provides no explicit guide as to how they should be dealt with. Hypothetical arguments have already begun, with scholars arguing either that the correct interpretation of international law would maintain the status of land features as they existed in 1982 or that boundaries could move. Even if they fall far below the waves, states would probably continue to make claims on them. Japan has already spent huge sums to try and prevent the rocks on Okinotorishima, an atoll far into the Pacific Ocean, being eroded away in order to preserve its case that it is really an island entitled to a full EEZ.

So with that 'solution' unlikely, what else is possible? The good news and the bad news were displayed during the month of May 2009. When Malaysia and Vietnam made their joint submission to the United Nations' Commission on the Limits of the Continental Shelf, they only measured their claims from their mainlands and not from any of the disputed islands.[31] But that was the cause for China to issue the 'U-shaped line' map a few days later – apparently changing the terms of the argument. All the countries, with the exception of China, have gradually brought their claims broadly into line with UNCLOS. Southeast Asian countries may not recognise the validity of each other's claim, but they are starting to agree a basis to resolve their disagreements. Little by little some of the disputes in the Sea are being untangled.

Vietnam, Malaysia and Indonesia have settled their seabed claims in the area where they meet and the three countries are working towards delimiting their EEZs. In the meantime they are pursuing joint development in the overlapping zone. The boundaries between Malaysia and Brunei were initially settled by British colonial administrators in 1958 and then extended by a bilateral agreement on 16 March 2009. There is still a latent dispute over Brunei's extended continental shelf, which would run into the Malaysia–Vietnam joint development area but this seems unlikely to provoke confrontation. At the time of writing Vietnam, the Philippines, Malaysia and Brunei have still not clarified their full continental shelf claims.

The biggest intra-ASEAN problem is the Philippines' continuing claim on the Malaysian province of Sabah – derived from the British North Borneo Company's initial agreement to cede or lease (the exact translation is critical to the dispute) the area from the Sultan of Sulu in 1878. As the putative 'invasion' of Sabah in February 2013 by supporters of the then Sultan demonstrated, the claim remains a highly sensitive issue. Although that Sultan died in October 2013, his final wish was that the claim should be upheld.[32] As a result the Philippines cannot agree even the starting place for its boundary delimitation with Malaysia, since one side would first have to recognise the legitimacy of the other's claim to Sabah. When Henry Bensurto of the Philippines presented the idea of the Zone of Peace, Freedom, Friendship and Cooperation to the Malaysian government's Institute of Maritime Affairs in December 2011 he used a slide showing the Philippine boundary emanating from the border between Malaysia and Brunei. It was perhaps not the most diplomatic way to present the plan. Unsurprisingly, the Malaysians later declined to support the initiative.

Law is unlikely to provide the final answer to the disputes. Even if the Permanent Court of Arbitration rules in favour of the Philippines, no global policeman is likely to enforce the verdict. However, should

China ever attempt to restrict US military access through the Sea, we can be sure that international law would be invoked to justify Washington's response. In the meantime, the threat of force is working the other way. The Philippine government argues that if it could develop the hydrocarbons in the Reed Bank the living standards for millions of its people would improve. Turning the argument around, it might argue that the government's inability to develop those resources is keeping levels of malnutrition and infant mortality in the Philippines unnecessarily high: people are dying because of the South China Sea disputes. If Forum Energy, or another company, attempts to survey or drill on the Reed Bank without Beijing's consent, Chinese vessels will block it. In the long term Manila might build up sufficient naval strength to be able to protect a drilling rig, but that seems far away. In the meantime, the Philippines does not have the military capacity to assert a credible defence, so it will either have to delay development or submit to China's demands. Will Manila get sufficiently desperate to do a deal? Will China come to some arrangement either before or after a verdict by the Permanent Court?

There are no easy alternatives to continuing strife in the South China Sea. No side wishes to provoke a conflict but none is willing to reduce tension by moderating its territorial claims. With every rock now either occupied or under the control of one or other country, the stress has shifted to the spaces in between and the resources that may, or may not, lie beneath. There is, unfortunately, plenty of opportunity for conflict to emerge and escalate. The merging of the territorial disputes with the wider struggle between the US and China over access and security only makes the situation more dangerous. Given that governments are refusing to work together on an issue as critical as food supply, it's hard to see any likelihood of progress towards regional cooperation. Joint development sounds like a good idea but won't be practical until China clarifies its position. Which brings us back to its historical territorial claim.

Chinese officials privately recognise the legal absurdity of maintaining a claim to places like the James Shoal, which lie under water and within the EEZ of another country. Chinese diplomats are also reported to have given assurances to Indonesia that Beijing has no claim on the waters around the Natunas, even though they are partly enclosed within the 'U-shaped line'. But those same officials say they cannot formally adjust the 'U-shaped line' for political reasons – the domestic criticism would be too great – so they must continue to maintain their claim. Some of this is the calculated result of political propaganda: deliberately bolstering the government's position abroad by spreading the message that it is under pressure at home. But it's clear that some of the risk is genuine. A 'retreat' from China's current position would provoke a howl of popular criticism. How then could a Chinese population be persuaded to take a different view of the history of the South China Sea?

Perhaps one answer lies in Taiwan. The chances of a freer debate on Chinese history are much greater in Taiwan than on the mainland. There are already a number of 'dissident' academics rethinking aspects of twentieth-century history. Taiwan is also where the archives of the Republic of China, the government that first drew up the 'U-shaped line', are stored. An open and thorough examination of the haphazard process through which the line came to be drawn might convince opinion-formers to re-examine some of the nationalist myths they have long declared to be gospel truth. Perhaps the strongest reason for starting in Taiwan is that the authorities in Beijing fear that any concession they might make would be loudly criticised in Taipei. As Professor Zha Daojiong of Peking University explained, 'it's simple, it's the Communists versus the KMT'. If the Kuomintang or KMT government, the rulers of Taiwan, were to de-escalate the historiographical conflict in the South China Sea, it would be much easier for the Beijing government to do the same. The key to a peaceful future could lie in an honest and critical examination of the past.

Epilogue

In March 2014, immediately after the disappearance of Malaysian Airlines Flight MH370, vessels from Vietnam, China, the Philippines, Singapore, Indonesia, Thailand and the United States scoured parts of the South China Sea for survivors. It was an unprecedented example of maritime cooperation. If the presumed crash site had been further south and east, however, the world might have been treated to an unseemly international argument as China insisted that it must lead any search and rescue mission within the 'U-shaped line' and other countries refused to cooperate for fear of legitimising the Chinese sovereignty claim. Instead, in a part of the Sea where territorial claims have been largely resolved, all sides worked together harmoniously.

Optimists might hope that such episodes could lead to a new era of cohabitation within the South China Sea: a virtuous circle of growing trust and building confidence. Practical cooperation is always welcome and would certainly be a step in the right direction but so long as the underlying disputes remain unresolved, the territorial question will continue to threaten peace. Within two months of MH370's disappearance, however, cooperation had turned to conflict as Vietnam resisted China's efforts to drill for oil off the Paracel Islands. The region again seemed to be headed towards potentially catastrophic confrontation. The threat stems both from the possibility that one claimant might use force to evict another from some remote atoll and also from the chance that strategic jostling between China and the United States could create enough friction to ignite an unexpected blaze. The consequences of conflagration in one domain would quickly spread to the other and turn a virtuous circle into a vicious one.

If there were no islands in the South China Sea there would be no issue. There would be no land territory to occupy, no sense that this land belonged to anyone, no basis upon which to claim large areas of sea, no means to potentially close a vital international sea lane or trigger a contest over strategic access. But these specks of land, from which flow historical arguments and modern maritime zones, form the stage for an international chest-beating contest in which the status of a country, or rather the elite that runs that country, will be judged, abroad but more importantly at home, upon its public performance. We have entered a world in which psychology and perception trump any material calculations about the practical benefits and costs of owning these maritime features.

Some observers view the Chinese claim in the South China Sea as simply a huge bluff in a game of strategic poker that has enabled Beijing to get a seat at the table and impress the watching audiences. I believe the problem runs deeper than that. From primary school to politburo, the 'U-shaped line' has become a secular religion. This myth, with its origins in China's confused transition from empire to republic, will be difficult to dispel. While the fates of faraway rocks can be the perfect foil for leaders in need of distractions from domestic problems, the higher that governments raise the rhetorical stakes the more difficult they will find it to climb down and reach a settlement. The 'U-shaped line' will continue to poison relationships in Southeast Asia. The politicised map-making of nationalist cartographers over the last century has become a threat to the chances of a new 'Asian Century' bringing rising prosperity to billions of people.

There are clearly some within the Chinese leadership who would like to change the terms of the dispute and reach an accommodation based upon the principles of UNCLOS. But there are more powerful lobbies that, for reasons of prestige or profit, insist upon the maximalist claim. These domestic interests, particularly the military, oil companies and a few coastal provinces, pursue actions that pose threats to Southeast Asia's food, energy and political security. These actions threaten the credibility of Beijing's professed policy of 'peaceful rise' yet the central leadership seems unwilling to rein in its subordinates. For the time being, the legitimacy of the Communist Party leadership depends more upon the approval of these lobbies than on the approbation of the outside world. Yet the further the lobbies lead Chinese policy down this road, the stronger will be the perception among neighbouring countries of a 'Chinese threat' and the greater their desire to take counterbalancing steps – whether through an indigenous military build-up or closer links with the United States or both. China's overall strategic interests are being jeopardised by junior actors within its Party-state.

All could yet be well: China could rise peacefully, Southeast Asia could look northeast without fear and the US and China could reach an accommodation about maritime access – if only China could abandon its claim to the whole of the 'U-shaped line'. If, however, the Chinese military starts to believe its own propaganda and attempt to enforce a territorial claim within the 'U-shaped line', the result would be a head-on confrontation with the US. For the time being, given their relative strengths, that's highly unlikely. But how long will it be before the Chinese military leadership begins to think that it might be able to prevail? For the sake of world peace, the disputes in the South China Sea need to be resolved before then.

China is a relatively new actor on the international stage. For decades it chose isolation over engagement and its foreign policy was more often an extension of domestic power battles than the fruit of a coherent conception of the outside world. That changed under Deng Xiaoping and, to the surprise of many sceptics, since the 1980s China's leadership has pursued integration with the wider world on terms it would once have regarded as imperialist or, at the very least, bourgeois. China is still learning how to play this new role and the South China Sea is where it must make some hard decisions about the relative importance of domestic and international priorities. Adjusting its sense of entitlement to fit modern norms will not be easy.

I started writing this book because I believed, like many other people, that some kind of conflict in or around the South China Sea was imminent. In the very last phase of my research I changed my mind. I became convinced that the Chinese leadership understands that it can only lose from a shooting war, although it views everything short of war as a useful policy tool. I expect that, from time to time over the coming decades, low-level confrontation will escalate into periods of diplomatic and military crisis and perhaps even superpower confrontation. During the course of my research I have seen a new world being forged around the South China Sea. China is emerging, the United States is retrenching and Southeast Asia is adjusting to the new realities. Reams of analogy have been mobilised to describe this new world. In particular, there's been much talk about the ancient Mediterranean and the inevitable confrontation between a declining Sparta and a rising Athens, analogous to the new world of the South China Sea.

However, there is nothing inevitable about the next phase in the history of the South China Sea. For all the bluster – on both sides of the Pacific – about China's growing capabilities, a cold empirical analysis of the relative strengths of the two militaries, and the societies behind them, makes the United States the dominant power into the foreseeable future. Instead I offer an alternative Mediterranean analogy: one that offers a richer prospect. It's a semi-enclosed Sea with a shared history and a connected present whose whole is greater than the sum of its parts. It will be a Sea with agreed boundaries based upon universal principles and governed by shared responsibilities to use its resources most wisely, a Sea where fish stocks are managed collectively for the benefit of all, where the impacts of oil exploration and international shipping are alleviated and where search and rescue operations can take place unimpeded. It could happen – if a line is redrawn.

Notes

Introduction

1. United Nations Convention on the Law of the Sea, Article 121.

Chapter 1: Wrecks and Wrongs: Prehistory to 1500

1. Atholl Anderson, 'Slow Boats from China: Issues in the Prehistory of Indo-Pacific Seafaring', in Sue O'Connor and Peter Veth (eds), *East of Wallace's Line: Studies of Past and Present Maritime Cultures of the Indo-Pacific Region* (Rotterdam, 2000) (*Modern Quaternary Research in Southeast Asia*, vol. 16), 13–50, plus personal communication.
2. 'Historical Evidence to Support China's Sovereignty over Nansha Islands', Ministry of Foreign Affairs, People's Republic of China, 17 November 2000. Available at <http://www.coi.gov.cn/scs/article/z.htm
3. Pierre-Yves Manguin, 'Trading Ships of the South China Sea', *Journal of the Economic and Social History of the Orient*, vol. 36, no. 3 (1993), 253–80.
4. Michael Churchman, 'Before Chinese and Vietnamese in the Red River Plain: The Han–Tang Period', *Chinese Southern Diaspora Studies*, vol. 4 (2010), 25–37.
5. Pye, Lucian W. "China: Erratic State, Frustrated Society." *Foreign Affairs*. 1 Sept. 1990. Web. 17 July 2014. <http://www.foreignaffairs.com/articles/45998/lucian-w-pye/china-erratic-state-frustrated-society>.
6. Wilhelm Solheim, *Archaeology and Culture in Southeast Asia: Unraveling the Nusantao* (Quezon City 2007), 74.
7. Derek Heng, *Sino-Malay Trade and Diplomacy from the Tenth Through the Fourteenth Century* (Athens, Ohio, 2007).
8. Personal interview. Singapore 1 June 2012.
9. Kate Taylor, 'Treasures Pose Ethics Issues for Smithsonian', *New York Times*, 24 April 2011.
10. Personal interview. Singapore 1 June 2012.
11. The origins of the word 'China' seem to come from Southeast Asia. See Chapter 3 of Anthony Reid, *Imperial Alchemy: Nationalism and Political Identity in Southeast Asia* (Cambridge, 2011), and Geoff Wade, 'The Polity of Yelang and the Origins of the Name "China" ', *Sino-Platonic Papers*, no. 188 (May 2009). Available at <http://www.sino-platonic.org>.

12. Geoff Wade, 'An Early Age of Commerce in Southeast Asia, 900–1300 CE', *Journal of Southeast Asian Studies*, vol. 40 (2009), 221–65.
13. Personal email. 12 December 2013.
14. Quoted in Geoff Wade, 'The Zheng He Voyages: A Reassessment', *ARI Working* Paper, no. 31 (October 2004). Available at <http://www.ari.nus.edu.sg/docs/wps/wps04_031.pdf>.
15. Ibid.
16. Zhang Wei, 'The Problems Encounter [*sic*] in the Protection of UCH [underwater cultural heritages]', paper delivered at the 15th ICOMOS General Assembly and Scientific Symposium in Xi'an, China, 17–21 October 2005. Available at <http://www.international.icomos.org/xian2005/papers/4-45.pdf>.
17. Jeff Adams, 'The Role of Underwater Archaeology in Framing and Facilitating the Chinese National Strategic Agenda', in Tami Blumenfield and Helaine Silverman (eds), *Cultural Heritage Politics in China* (New York, 2013), 261–82.
18. 'China Starts Building Base for Researching Underwater Relics', *Xinhua*, 17 March 2012.
19. 'On China's Sovereignty over Xisha and Nansha Islands', *Beijing Review*, 24 August 1979, 24.
20. Chi-Kin Lo, *China's Policy Towards Territorial Disputes: The Case of the South China Sea Islands* (London, 1989), 94.

Chapter 2: Maps and Lines: 1500 to 1948

1. Robert Batchelor, 'The Selden Map Rediscovered: A Chinese Map of East Asian Shipping Routes, *c.*1619', *Imago Mundi*, vol. 65 (2013), 37–63. For an alternative account of how the map might have reached England, see Timothy Brook's *Mr Selden's Map of China: The Spice Trade, a Lost Chart and the South China Sea* (Rotterdam, 2014).
2. David Sandler Berkowitz, *John Selden's Formative Years: Politics and Society in Early Seventeenth-Century England* (Cranbury, New Jersey, 1988).
3. Roderich Ptak, 'Ming Maritime Trade to Southeast Asia 1368–1567: Visions of a "System" ', in Claude Guillot, Denys Lombard and Roderich Ptak (eds), *From the Mediterranean to the China Sea* (Wiesbaden, 1998), 157–92.
4. Roderich Ptak, 'Portugal and China: An Anatomy of Harmonious Coexistence (Sixteenth and Seventeenth Centuries)', in Laura Jarnagin, *Culture and Identity in the Luso-Asian World: Tenacities & Plasticities* (Singapore, 2012) (*Portuguese and Luso-Asian Legacies in Southeast Asia, 1511–2011*, vol. 2), 225–44.
5. Léonard Blussé, 'No Boats to China. The Dutch East India Company and the Changing Pattern of the China Sea Trade 1635–1690', *Modern Asian Studies*, vol. 30 (1996), 51–76.
6. Ibid.
7. Angela Schottenhammer, 'The Sea as Barrier and Contact Zone: Maritime Space and Sea Routes in Traditional China', in Angela Schottenhammer and Roderich Ptak (eds), *The Perception of Maritime Space in Traditional Chinese Sources* (Wiesbaden, 2006), 3–13.
8. Dennis O. Flynn and Arturo Giráldez, 'Born with a "Silver Spoon": The Origin of World Trade in 1571', *Journal of World History*, vol. 6 (1995), 201–21.
9. Léonard Blussé, 'Chinese Century. The Eighteenth Century in the China Sea Region', *Archipel*, vol. 58 (1999), 107–29.
10. Cornelis Koeman, *Jan Huygen van Linschoten* (Coimbra, 1984).
11. Peter Borschberg, 'The Seizure of the *Sta Catarina* Revisited: The Portuguese Empire in Asia, VOC Politics and the Origins of the Dutch–Johor Alliance (1602–*c.*1616)', *Journal of Southeast Asian Studies*, vol. 33, no. 1 (2002), 31–62; Peter Borschberg, *Hugo Grotius, the Portuguese and Free Trade in the East Indies* (Singapore, 2011); Martine Julia van Ittersum, *Profit and Principle: Hugo Grotius, Natural Rights Theories and the Rise of Dutch Power in the East Indies, 1595–1615* (Leiden, 2006).
12. Bardo Fassbender *et al.* (eds), *The Oxford Handbook of the History of International Law* (Oxford, 2012), 369.

13. Edward Gordon, online notes for the exhibition curated by Edward Gordon and Mike Widener, *Freedom of the Seas, 1609: Grotius and the Emergence of International Law*, at Yale Law School in autumn 2009.

14. Roderich Ptak, 'The Sino-European Map (*Shanhai yudi quantu*) in the Encyclopaedia *Sancai Tuhui*', in Angela Schottenhammer and Roderich Ptak (eds), *The Perception of Maritime Space in Traditional Chinese Sources* (Wiesbaden, 2006), 191–207.

15. Léonard Blussé, 'No Boats to China. The Dutch East India Company and the Changing Pattern of the China Sea Trade 1635–1690', *Modern Asian Studies*, vol. 30 (1996), 51–76.

16. Hydrographic Office, The Admiralty, *The China Sea Directory* (London, 1889), vol. 2, 108.

17. David Hancox and Victor Prescott, *Secret Hydrographic Surveys in the Spratly Islands* (London, 1999). Spanish cartographers already knew Scarborough Shoal as the Maroona Shoal and later the Bajo de Masingloc.

18. Edyta Roszko, 'Commemoration and the State: Memory and Legitimacy in Vietnam', *Sojourn: Journal of Social Issues in Southeast Asia*, vol. 25, no. 1 (2010), 1–28.

19. David Hancox and Victor Prescott, 'A Geographical Description of the Spratly Islands and an Account of Hydrographic Surveys Amongst those Islands', *Maritime Briefings*, vol. 1, no. 6 (1995). Available at <https://www.dur.ac.uk/ibru/publications/view/?id=229>.

20. Wang Wen Tai, *Hong mao fan ying ji li kao lue* [*To Study the Foreigners*], 1843, quoted in Han Zhen Hua, Lin Jin Zhi and Hu Feng Bin (eds), *Wo guo nan hai shi liao hui bian* [*Compilations of Historical Documents on our Nanhai Islands*], Dong fang chu ban she, 1988, 163, quoted in François-Xavier Bonnet, 'Geopolitics of Scarborough Shoal', Irasec's Discussion Papers, no. 14 (November 2012), 13. Available at <http://www.irasec.com>.

21. Ibid.

22. James Horsburgh, *The India Directory Or, Directions for Sailing to and from the East Indies, China, Australia, and the Interjacent Ports of Africa and South America*, 6th edn (London, 1852), vol. 2, 346.

23. Dennis Owen Flynn and Arturo Giráldez, 'Cycles of Silver: Global Economic Unity through the Mid-Eighteenth Century', *Journal of World History*, vol. 13 (2002), 391–427.

24. David P. Chandler *et al.*, *In Search of Southeast Asia: A Modern History*, rev. edn (Honolulu, 1987).

25. Carl A. Trocki, *Prince of Pirates: The Temenggongs and the Development of Johor and Singapore, 1784–1885* (Singapore, 2007).

26. Hydrographic Office, The Admiralty, *The China Sea Directory* (London, 1889), vol. 2, 103, quoted in François-Xavier Bonnet, 'Geopolitics of Scarborough Shoal', Irasec's Discussion Papers, no. 14 (November 2012). Available at <http://www.irasec.com>.

27. Eric Tagliacozzo, 'Tropical Spaces, Frozen Frontiers: The Evolution of Border Enforcement in Nineteenth-Century Insular Southeast Asia', in Paul H. Kratoska, Remco Raben and Henk Schulte Nordholt (eds), *Locating Southeast Asia: Geographies of Knowledge and Politics of Space* (Singapore, 2005).

28. Edward J. M. Rhoad, *China's Republican Revolution: The Case of Kwangtung, 1895–1913* (Cambridge, Massachusetts, 1975).

29. *Straits Times*, 21 October 1907, 5.

30. *Straits Times*, 23 July 1909, 3.

31. *Straits Times*, 29 March 1909, 7.

32. *Straits Times*, 28 October 1909, 7.

33. *Straits Times*, 23 December 1910, 7.

34. Guangdong dong tu [General map of Guangdong Province], 1866, in Wan-Ru Cao and Zheng Xihuang (eds), *An Atlas of Ancient Maps in China* (Beijing, 1997), vol. 3, no. 196; Guangdong Yudi Quantu [Atlas of Guangdong Province], 1897, in Ping Yan, *China in Ancient and Modern Maps* (London, 1998), 247.

35. P. A. Lapicque, *A propos des Iles Paracels* (Saigon, 1929), quoted in Monique Chemillier-Gendreau, *Sovereignty over the Paracel and Spratly Islands* (Leiden, 2000), 101.

36. Guangdong yu di quan tu [New map of Guangdong Province], 1909, in François-Xavier Bonnet, 'Geopolitics of Scarborough Shoal', Irasec's Discussion Papers, no. 14 (November 2012), 15. Available at <http://www.irasec.com>.
37. William A. Callahan, 'The Cartography of National Humiliation and the Emergence of China's Geobody', *Public Culture*, vol. 21, no. 1 (2009), 141–73.
38. Han Zhenhua (ed.), *A Compilation of Historical Materials on China's South China Sea Islands* (Beijing, 1988), quoted in Zou Keyuan, *Law of the Sea in East Asia: Issues and prospects* (Abingdon, 2005), 28.
39. Han Zhenhua (ed.), *A Compilation of Historical Materials on China's South China Sea Islands* (Beijing, 1988), quoted in Zou Keyuan, 'The Chinese Traditional Maritime Boundary Line in the South China Sea and its Legal Consequences for the Resolution of the Dispute over the Spratly Islands', *International Journal of Marine and Coastal Law*, vol. 14, no. 1 (1999), 27–55.
40. William Callahan, 'Historical Legacies and Non/Traditional Security: Commemorating National Humiliation Day in China', paper presented at Renmin University, Beijing, April 2004. Available at <https://www.dur.ac.uk/resources/china.studies/Commemorating%20National%20Humiliation%20Day%20in%20China.pdf>.
41. Stein Tønnesson, 'The South China Sea in the Age of European Decline', *Modern Asian Studies*, vol. 40 (2006), 1–57.
42. François-Xavier Bonnet, 'Geopolitics of Scarborough Shoal', Irasec's Discussion Papers, no. 14 (November 2012), 15. Available at <http://www.irasec.com>.
43. Stein Tønnesson, 'The South China Sea in the Age of European Decline', *Modern Asian Studies*, vol. 40 (2006), 24.
44. *Wai Jiao bu nan hai zhu dao dang an hui bian* [*Compilation by the Department of Foreign Affairs of all the records concerning the islands in the South Sea*] (Taipei, 1995), vol. 1, 47–9, quoted in François-Xavier Bonnet, 'Geopolitics of Scarborough Shoal', Irasec's Discussion Papers, no. 14 (November 2012), 15. Available at <http://www.irasec.com>.
45. Zou Keyuan, 'The Chinese Traditional Maritime Boundary Line in the South China Sea and its Legal Consequences for the Resolution of the Dispute over the Spratly Islands', *International Journal of Marine and Coastal Law*, vol. 14, no. 1 (1999), 27–55.
46. François-Xavier Bonnet, 'Geopolitics of Scarborough Shoal', Irasec's Discussion Papers, no. 14 (November 2012), 18. Available at <http://www.irasec.com>.
47. Li Jinming and Li Dexia, 'The Dotted Line on the Chinese Map of the South China Sea: a Note', *Ocean Development and International Law*, vol. 34 (2003), 287–95.
48. William A. Callahan, *China: The Pessoptimist Nation* (Oxford, 2009).
49. Wu Feng-ming, 'On the New Geographic Perspectives and Sentiment of High Moral Character of Geographer Bai Meichu in Modern China', *Geographical Research*, vol. 30 (2011), 2109–14.
50. Han Zhen Hua, Lin Jin Zhi and Hu Feng Bin (eds), *Wo guo nan hai shi liao hui bian* [*Compilations of Historical Documents on our Nanhai Islands*], Dong fang chu ban she, 1988, 353, quoted in François-Xavier Bonnet, 'Geopolitics of Scarborough Shoal', Irasec's Discussion Papers, no. 14 (November 2012), 22. Available at <http://www.irasec.com>.
51. United States Pacific Fleet, Patrol Bombing Squadron 128, Action report 3 May 1945, available at <http://www.fold3.com/image/#295881925>. United States Pacific Fleet Commander Submarines, Philippines Sea Frontier War Diary, 11/1–30/45. Available at <http://www.fold3.com/image/#301980047>.
52. A.B. Feuer, *Australian Commandos: Their Secret War Against the Japanese in World War II* (Mechanicsburg, Pennsylvania, 2006), Chapter 6.
53. US Navy Patrol Bombing Squadron 117 (VPB–117), Aircraft Action Report No. 92, available at <http://www.fold3.com/image/#302109453>.
54. US Navy, USS Cabrilla Report of 8th War Patrol. Available at <http://www.fold3.com/image/#300365402>.
55. Quoted in Kimie Hara, *Cold War Frontiers in the Asia-Pacific: Divided Territories in the San Francisco System* (Abingdon, 2006), 146.
56. Ibid., 147.

57. Ulises Granados, 'Chinese Ocean Policies Towards the South China Sea in a Transitional Period, 1946–1952', *The China Review*, vol. 6, no. 1 (2006), 153–81, esp. 161.

58. Yann-Huei Song and Peter Kien-hong Yu, 'China's "historic waters" in the South China Sea: An Analysis from Taiwan, R.O.C.', *American Asian Review*, vol. 12, no. 4 (1994), 83–101.

59. Zou Keyuan, 'The Chinese Traditional Maritime Boundary Line in the South China Sea and its Legal Consequences for the Resolution of the Dispute over the Spratly Islands', *International Journal of Marine and Coastal Law*, vol. 14, no. 1 (1999), 27–55, esp. 33.

60. Li Jinming and Li Dexia, 'The Dotted Line on the Chinese Map of the South China Sea: a Note', *Ocean Development and International Law*, vol. 34 (2003), 287–95, esp. 290.

61. *Wai Jiao bu nan hai zhu dao dang an hui bian* [*Compilation by the Department of Foreign Affairs of all the records concerning the islands in the South Sea*] (Taipei, 1995), vol. 2, 784–88, quoted in François-Xavier Bonnet, 'Geopolitics of Scarborough Shoal', Irasec's Discussion Papers, no. 14 (November 2012), 22. Available at <http://www.irasec.com>.

62. Zou Keyuan, *Law of the Sea in East Asia: Issues and Prospects* (Abingdon, 2005), 83.

63. Euan Graham, 'China's New Map: Just Another Dash?', *Newsbrief of the Royal United Services Institute*, 3 September 2013. Available at <https://www.rusi.org/downloads/assets/201309_NB_Graham.pdf>.

Chapter 3: Danger and Mischief: 1946 to 1995

1. Spencer Tucker, 'D'Argenlieu, Georges Thierry', in Spencer Tucker (ed.), *The Encyclopedia of the Vietnam War: A Political, Social and Military History*, 2nd edn (Santa Barbara, California, 2011).

2. Quoted in Stein Tønnesson, *Vietnam 1946: How the War Began* (Berkeley, 2010).

3. Stein Tønnesson, 'The South China Sea in the Age of European Decline', *Modern Asian Studies*, vol. 40 (2006), 1–57.

4. Michael Sullivan, *The Meeting of Eastern and Western Art*, rev. edn (Berkeley, 1997), 99.

5. Ulises Granados, 'Chinese Ocean Policies Towards the South China Sea in a Transitional Period, 1946–1952', *The China Review*, vol. 6, no. 1 (2006), 153–81.

6. Stein Tønnesson, 'The South China Sea in the Age of European Decline', *Modern Asian Studies*, vol. 40 (2006), 1–57, esp. 33.

7. Ibid., 21.

8. Daniel J. Dzurek, 'The Spratly Islands Dispute: Who's On First?', *Maritime Briefings*, vol. 2, no. 1 (1996), 15. Available at <https://www.dur.ac.uk/ibru/publications/view/?id=232>.

9. Personal interview with Ramir Cloma, son of Filemon Cloma, on 22 July 2012.

10. Ibid.

11. A.V.H. Hartendorp, *History of Industry and Trade of the Philippines: The Magsaysay Administration* (Manila, 1958), 209–30; Jose V. Abueva, Arnold P. Alamon and Ma. Oliva Z. Domingo, *Admiral Tomas Cloma: Father of Maritime Education and Discoverer of Freedomland/ Kalayaan Islands* (Quezon City, National College of Public Administration and Governance, (University of the Philippines, 1999), 36–7.

12. Monique Chemillier-Gendreau, *Sovereignty over the Paracel and Spratly Islands* (Leiden, 2000), 42.

13. Stein Tønnesson, 'The South China Sea in the Age of European Decline', *Modern Asian Studies*, vol. 40 (2006), 1–57, esp. 50.

14. Monique Chemillier-Gendreau, *Sovereignty over the Paracel and Spratly Islands* (Leiden, 2000).

15. Stein Tønnesson, 'The South China Sea in the Age of European Decline', *Modern Asian Studies*, vol. 40 (2006), 1–57, esp. 50.

16. Rodolfo Severino, *Where in the World is the Philippines?* (Singapore, 2010).

17. A.V.H. Hartendorp, *History of Industry and Trade of the Philippines: The Magsaysay Administration* (Manila, 1958).

18. Rodolfo Severino, *Where in the World is the Philippines?* (Singapore, 2010).

19. Daniel J. Dzurek, 'The Spratly Islands Dispute: Who's On First?', *Maritime Briefings*, vol. 2, no. 1 (1996), 19. Available at <https://www.dur.ac.uk/ibru/publications/view/?id=232>.

20. Marwyn S. Samuels, *Contest for the South China Sea* (London, 1982).

21. Robert S. Ross, *The Indochina Tangle: China's Vietnam Policy 1975–1979* (New York, 1988).

22. Chinese amphibious assaults in the Paracel Archipelago SRD-SR–44–74. US Army Special Research Detachment, Fort Meade, January 1974. Available from US Army Military History Institute.

23. US Embassy Saigon, Weekly Roundup January 10–16 1974 US Embassy Saigon. Available at http://aad.archives.gov/aad/createpdf?rid=10696&dt=2474&dl=1345. See also RVN Captain Ha Van Ngac, *The January 19, 1974 Naval Battle for the Paracels against the People's Republic of China's Navy In the East Sea* (Austin, Texas, 1999), 40.

24. Ho Van Ky Thoai, *Valor in Defeat: A Sailor's Journey* [*Can Truong Trong Chien Bai: Hanh Trinh Cua Mot Thuy Thu*] (Centreville, Virginia, 2007, self-published).

25. US Embassy, Saigon, telegram GVN/PRC DISPUTE OVER PARACEL ISLANDS, 17 January 1974. Available at http://aad.archives.gov/aad/createpdf?rid=4752&dt=247 4&dl=1345.

26. Kiem Do and Julie Kane, *Counterpart: A South Vietnamese Naval Officer's War* (Annapolis, Maryland, 1998).

27. *Foreign Relations of the United States 1969–1976*, vol. 18, China, 1973–1976, Document 66. Available at <http://history.state.gov/historicaldocuments/frus1969–76v18/d66>.

28. *China: People's Liberation Army* (Washington, JPRS Report, Foreign Broadcast Information Service, JPRS-CAR–90–005, 22 January 1990).

29. Garver, John W., 'China's Push through the South China Sea: The Intersection of Bureaucratic and National Interests', *China Quarterly* 132 (December 1992) 999–1028.

30. You Ji, 'The Evolution of China's Maritime Combat Doctrines and Models: 1949–2001', *RSIS Working Papers*, no. 22 (Singapore, May 2002). Available at <http://dr.ntu.edu.sg/handle/10220/4422>.

31. Yang Guoyu (ed.), *Dangdai Zhongguo Haijun* [*The Modern Chinese Navy*] (Beijing, 1987), cited by John W. Garver, 'China's Push through the South China Sea: The Interaction of Bureaucratic and National Interests', *The China Quarterly*, no. 132 (1992), 999–1028.

32. For more on this see Chapter 9 of my *Vietnam: Rising Dragon* (New Haven, Connecticut, and London, 2010).

33. M. Taylor Fravel, *Strong Borders, Secure Nation: Cooperation and Conflict in China's Territorial Disputes* (Princeton, New Jersey, 2008), 292.

34. Chen Hurng-Yu, 'The PRC's South China Sea Policy and Strategies of Occupation in the Paracel and Spratly Islands', *Issues & Studies*, vol. 36, no. 4 (2000), 95–131.

35. John W. Garver, 'China's Push through the South China Sea: the Interaction of Bureaucratic and National Interests', *The China Quarterly*, no. 132 (1992), 999–1028.

36. David Hancox and Victor Prescott, 'A Geographical Description of the Spratly Islands and an Account of Hydrographic Surveys Amongst those Islands', *Maritime Briefings*, vol. 1, no. 6 (1995). Available at <https://www.dur.ac.uk/ibru/publications/view/?id=229>.

37. Two of the ships were American-built Second World War tank landing craft left behind at the end of the Vietnam War. HQ–505 was formerly the USS *Bulloch County*, built in 1943. The third was a freighter.

38. 'Chinese Navy Detains Filipino Fishermen in Spratlys: Report', *Agence France Presse*, Manila, 24 January 1995; *Lianhe zaobao* [*United Morning Post*], Singapore, 25 January 1995, 34, quoted in Chen Hurng-Yu, 'The PRC's South China Sea Policy and Strategies of Occupation in the Paracel and Spratly Islands', *Issues & Studies*, vol. 36, no. 4 (2000), 95–131.

39. Liselotte Odgaard, 'Between Deterrence and Cooperation: Eastern Asian Security after the "Cold War" ', *IBRU Boundary and Security Bulletin*, vol. 6, no. 2 (1998), 73 (map). Available at <https://www.dur.ac.uk/ibru/publications/view/?id=131>.

40. 'Philippines Orders Forces Strengthened in Spratlys', Reuters News Service, 15 February 1995, quoted in Ian James Storey, 'Creeping Assertiveness: China, the Philippines and the South China Sea Dispute', *Contemporary Southeast Asia*, vol. 21 (1999), 95–118.

41. 'Dragon Flexes its Muscles in Islands Dispute', *Independent on Sunday*, 19 March 1995, quoted ibid.

42. 'Spratlys Tension Helps Push Forces Upgrade', *Jane's Defence Weekly*, 25 February 1995, quoted ibid.

43. Renato Cruz de Castro, 'The Aquino Administration's 2011 Decision to Shift Philippine Defense Policy from Internal Security to Territorial Defense: The Impact of the South China Sea Dispute', *Korean Journal of Defense Analysis*, vol. 24 (2012), 67–87.

44. *East Asia Today*, BBC, Interview with Lee Kuan Yew, broadcast 6 June 1995.

45. Ian James Storey, 'Creeping Assertiveness: China, the Philippines and the South China Sea Dispute', *Contemporary Southeast Asia*, vol. 21 (1999), 95–118.

46. 'China Accepts Natunas Drill, Says Indonesia', AFP report, *Straits Times*, 12 September 1996, 21.

Chapter 4: Rocks and Other Hard Places: the South China Sea and International Law

1. Geoffrey Marston, 'Abandonment of Territorial Claims: the Cases of Bouvet and Spratly Islands', *The British Yearbook of International Law 1986* (Oxford, 1986), 337–56.

2. Letter of 16 June 1955 from General Jacquot, General Commissioner of France and Acting Commander-in-Chief in Indochina, quoted in Monique Chemillier-Gendreau, *Sovereignty over the Paracel and Spratly Islands* (Leiden, 2000), Annex 40.

3. Ulises Granados, 'As China Meets the Southern Sea Frontier: Ocean Identity in the Making, 1902–1937', *Pacific Affairs*, vol. 78 (2005), 443–61.

4. 'Truong Sa Lon: Growing Town at Sea', Vietnam News Agency, 18 May 2011.

5. 'Spratlys to Become Self-sufficient in Food', *Viet Nam News*, 19 July 2011.

6. 'Vietnam Navy Commemorates Soldiers Killed in 1988 Clash with China', VoV [*The Voice of Vietnam*], 8 January 2012.

7. Rommel C. Banlaoi, *Philippines–China Security Relations: Current Issues and Emerging Concerns* (Manila, 2012).

8. The atoll is known as the Tizard Bank after the second officer of the British naval ship that surveyed it in the 1860s. David Hancox and Victor Prescott, 'A Geographical Description of the Spratly Islands and an Account of Hydrographic Surveys Amongst those Islands', *Maritime Briefings*, vol. 1, no. 6 (1995). Available at <https://www.dur.ac.uk/ibru/publications/view/?id=229>.

9. General Juancho Sabban, personal interview on 5 March 2012 in Puerto Princesa, Philippines.

10. 'Notification and Statement of Claim', Republic of the Philippines, Department of Foreign Affairs, 22 January 2013. Available at <http://www.dfa.gov.ph/index.php/component/docman/doc_download/56-notification-and-statement-of-claim-on-west-philippine-sea>.

11. The full judgment is available at <http://www.icj-cij.org/docket/files/124/17164.pdf>.

Chapter 5: Something and Nothing: Oil and Gas in the South China Sea

1. Nayan Chanda and Tai Ming Cheung, 'Reef Knots: China Seeks ASEAN Support for Spratly Plan', *Far Eastern Economic Review*, August 1990, 11.

2. 'Oil Discovered on Nansha Islands', *Xinhua*, 24 July 1987.

3. *China Daily*, 24 December 1989.

4. John W. Garver, 'China's Push through the South China Sea: the Interaction of Bureaucratic and National Interests', *The China Quarterly*, no. 132 (1992), 999–1028.

5. Knut Snildal, *Petroleum in the South China Sea – a Chinese National Interest?*, Thesis, Department of Political Science, University of Oslo, 2000.

6. Personal interview by telephone. 2 December 2013.
7. 'Benton, Successful in 2 International Ventures, Plunges into Disputed China Play', *Oilgram News*, 13 December 1996. See also John R. Engen, 'Where Hope and Risk Go Hand in Hand', *World Trade Magazine*, February 1996.
8. *World Trade Magazine*, February 1996.
9. 'British Gas, Arco Begin Drilling in Area Claimed by Vietnam', *The Oil Daily*, 7 June 1994.
10. 'Crestone Begins Project in South China Sea Despite Dispute over Sovereignty of Area', *The Oil Daily*, 20 April 1994.
11. R. Thomas Collins, *Blue Dragon: Reckoning in the South China Sea* (Vienna, Virginia, 2002), 116.
12. 'Heat Builds and Vietnam and China Begin to Drill', *Offshore*, August 1994.
13. Chan Wai-fong, 'PLA Flexes its Muscles for Vietnam's Benefit', *South China Morning Post*, 3 August 1994.
14. 'Benton Oil And Gas Company Completes Acquisition of Crestone Energy Corporation', PR Newswire, 5 December 1996.
15. 'North Rail Project Launched; RP, China Start Building Rail Project from Manila to Ilocos', *Manila Bulletin*, 6 April 2004.
16. See <http://www.asean-china-center.org/english/2010–07/12/c_13395670.htm>.
17. 'RP, China to Push Formation of Asian Anti-Terror Alliance', *Philippines Star*, 1 September 2003.
18. 'Oil Giants to tap Ocean Resources', *Xinhua*, 13 November 2003.
19. Maria Eloise Calderon, 'Government Mulls Oil Search at Spratlys with China', *Business World*, 24 August 2004.
20. Aileen S.P. Baviera, 'The Influence of Domestic Politics on Philippine Foreign Policy: The Case of Philippines–China Relations since 2004', *RSIS Working Papers*, no. 241 (Singapore, June 2012). Available at <http://www.rsis.edu.sg/publications/WorkingPapers/WP241.pdf>.
21. 'China, Philippines, Vietnam Get Seismic Data from South China Sea', *Xinhua*, 19 November 2005.
22. Barry Wain, 'Manila's Bungle in the South China Sea', *Far Eastern Economic Review*, January/February 2008.
23. US State Department Cable 07HANOI1119, 'Conoco Phillips and BP Concerns About Projects in the South China Sea', 15 June 2007. Available at <http://www.wikileaks.org/plusd/cables/07HANOI1119_a.html>.
24. US State Department Cable 08TOKYO544, 'Japan Plans No Action in South China Sea Dispute', 29 February 2008. Available at <https://www.wikileaks.org/plusd/cables/08TOKYO544_a.html>.
25. US State Department Cable 07HANOI1599, 'Sino-Vietnam Territorial Dispute Entangles Multiple Multinational Energy Firms', 7 September 2007. Available at <https://www.wikileaks.org/plusd/cables/07HANOI1599_a.html>.
26. 'Fu Ying Visits Wytch Farm Oilfield of the [sic] British Petroleum', Chinese Embassy, London, 25 September 2007. Available at <http://www.chinese-embassy.org.uk/eng/EmbassyNews/2007/t377632.htm>.
27. US Embassy Cable 08 HANOI579, 'BP Transfers Operatorship of South China Sea Blocks to Petrovietnam; Exploration Work Resumes', 16 May 2008. Available at <https://www.wikileaks.org/plusd/cables/08HANOI579_a.html>.
28. 'Petrovietnam Surveying Oil Block Eyed by China-BP', Reuters, 22 July 2008.
29. US State Department Cable 07GUANGZHOU317, 'The Tiger Sprints Ahead: Exxonmobil First Western Oil Major to Launch Fully Integrated Joint Venture in China', 9 March 2007. Available at <https://www.wikileaks.org/plusd/cables/07GUANGZHOU317_a.html>.
30. Greg Torode, 'Oil Giant Is Warned over Vietnam Deal', *South China Morning Post*, 20 July 2008.
31. US State Department Cable 08HANOI1241, 'Vietnam Negotiates Deal with Gazprom, Bypasses ExxonMobil', 6 November 2008. Available at <https://www.wikileaks.org/plusd/cables/08HANOI1241_a.html>.

32. US State Department Cable 08HANOI897, 'Russian Concern about Chinese Pressure on ExxonMobil', 4 August 2008. Available at <http://wikileaks.org/cable/2008/08/08HANOI897.html>.

33. Chevron Corporation, *2010 Supplement to the Annual Report*, March 2011. Available at <http://www.chevron.com/documents/pdf/chevron2010annualreportsupplement.pdf>.

34. Buku Bertemu Ruas, 'The RMN Against China Maritime Surveillance Agency', Malaysia Flying Herald blog, 16 April 2013. Available at <http://malaysiaflyingherald.wordpress.com/2013/04/16/buku-bertemu-ruas-the-rmn-against-china-maritime-surveillance-agency/>.

35. Jon Savage, 'Oil and Gas Potential of the Area, Seismic Activities to Date and the Delays to Hydrocarbon Exploration Caused by Disputes'. Copy of presentation available at <http://cil.nus.edu.sg/wp/wp-content/uploads/2011/06/Session–1-Jon-Savage-South-China-Sea-Conference-June–20111-pdf.pdf>.

36. 'Minister Reveals Spratly Islands' Oil Potential', *Xinhua*, 5 September 1994.

37. US Energy Information Administration, 'South China Sea Energy Brief', 7 February 2013. Available at <http://www.eia.gov/countries/regions-topics.cfm?fips=scs>.

38. US Geological Survey, 'Assessment of Undiscovered Oil and Gas Resources of Southeast Asia', Fact Sheet 2010–3015, June 2010. Available at <http://pubs.usgs.gov/fs/2010/3015/pdf/FS10–3015.pdf>.

39. Personal interview. Singapore 4 June 2013.

40. Japanese energy imports, 2012 figures: liquefied natural gas: 108.87m^3 / 365 days / average LNG carrier size of 200,000 m^3; oil: 3.65 million barrels a day / average VLCC of 2-million-barrel capacity. See <http://www.reuters.com/article/2013/04/04/lng-gas-japan-idUSL5N0CR3XZ20130404>.

41. Jian Zhang, 'China's Energy Security: Prospects, Challenges and Opportunities', *Working Papers by CEAP Visiting Fellows*, Brookings Institution Center for East Asia Policy Studies, no. 54, July 2011.

Chapter 6: Drums and Symbols: Nationalism

1. I have written a fuller account of political and social life in Vietnam in my book *Vietnam: Rising Dragon* (New Haven, Connecticut, and London, 2010).

2. David Brown, 'State Secrets Revealed in Vietnam', *Asia Times*, 22 December 2012.

3. 'Police Caught Napping while Vandals Attack US Embassy', *Philippine Daily Inquirer*, 17 April 2012.

4. For more on US economic policy towards the Philippines, see David Joel Steinberg's *The Philippines: A Singular and a Plural Place*, 4th edn (Boulder, Colorado, 2000), 22.

5. Personal Interview. Manila 23 February 2012.

6. Benedict Anderson, 'Cacique Democracy in the Philippines: Origins and Dreams', *New Left Review*, 169 (May–June 1988), 3–31.

7. Michael Cullinane, *Ilustrado Politics: Filipino Elite Responses to American Rule, 1898–1908* (Manila, 2003), 53.

8. Caroline Sy Hau, ' "Patria é intereses": Reflections on the Origins and Changing Meanings of Ilustrado', *Philippine Studies*, vol. 59 (2011), 3–54.

9. Lisandro E. Claudio, 'Postcolonial Fissures and the Contingent Nation: An Antinationalist Critique of Philippine Historiography', *Philippine Studies*, vol. 61 (2013), 45–75.

10. 'America's Global Image Remains More Positive than China's', PewResearch Global Attitudes Project, 18 July 2013.

11. ' "West PH Sea" Now Official: So What?', 12 September 2012, <http://www.rappler.com/nation/12277-west-ph-sea-now-official-so-what>.

12. Personal Interview. Manila 24 February 2012.

13. See <http://www.forbes.com/philippines-billionaires/list/>.

14. Caroline S. Hau, 'Conditions of Visibility: Resignifying the "Chinese"/"Filipino" in *Mano Po* and *Crying Ladies*', *Philippine Studies*, vol. 53 (2005), 491–531.

15. Caroline S. Hau, 'Blood, Land, and Conversion: "Chinese" Mestizoness and the Politics of Belonging in Jose Angliongto's *The Sultanate*', *Philippine Studies*, vol. 57 (2009), 3–48.
16. Ibid.
17. Malaysia occupied Swallow Reef in 1983; Mariveles Bank and Ardasier Reef in 1986; Investigator Shoal and Erica Reef in 1999. It has not occupied Louisa Reef which is also claimed by Brunei.
18. 'China–Malaysia Trade to Touch US$100b', *The Star*, 16 March 2012.
19. Cheng-Chwee Kuik, 'Making Sense of Malaysia's China Policy: Asymmetry, Proximity, and Elite's Domestic Authority', *Chinese Journal of International Politics*, vol. 6 (2013), 429–67.
20. See <http://www.china.org.cn/china/2012-05/12/content_25367605.htm>.
21. <http://www.fmprc.gov.cn/eng/wjb/zzjg/yzs/gjlb/2762/2764/t929748.shtml>.
22. Bill Bishop, 'Today's China Readings May 10, 2012', *The Sinocism China Newsletter* (website), available at <http://sinocism.com/?p=4684.
23. See <http://news.sohu.com/20120426/n341700751.shtml> (in Chinese).
24. David Lague, 'Special Report: China's Military Hawks Take the Offensive', 17 January 2013, <http://www.reuters.com/article/2013/01/17/us-china-hawks-idUSBRE90G00C20130117>.
25. Long Tao, 'The Present is a Golden Opportunity to Use Force in the South Sea', *Global Times* (Chinese edition), 27 September 2011. Note that the phrase was changed to, 'Everything will be burned to the ground should a military conflict break out. Who'll suffer most when Western oil giants withdraw?' when the republished article was republished in the English edition on 29 September 2011 as 'Time to teach those around South China Sea a lesson', http://www.globaltimes.cn/content/677717.shtml.
26. Zhang Jianfeng, 'Luo Yuan the "Hawk" ', *Southern Weekend*, 9 April 2012. Translation at <http://southseaconversations.wordpress.com/2012/05/03/luo-yuan-a-profile/>.
27. Mark Stokes and Russell Hsiao, 'The People's Liberation Army General Political Department: Political Warfare with Chinese Characteristics', *Project 2049 Institute Occasional Paper*, 14 October 2013. Available at <http://project2049.net/publications.html>.
28. See<http://southseaconversations.wordpress.com/2013/06/07/the-enigma-of-cefcs-chairman-ye/>.
29. Andrew Chubb, 'Propaganda, Not Policy: Explaining the PLA's "Hawkish Faction" (Part One)', *China Brief* (Jamestown Foundation), vol. 13, issue 15, 26 July 2013.
30. <http://www.news.xinhuanet.com/ziliao/2005-03/16/content_2705546.htm>. Translation in Zheng Wang, 'National Humiliation, History Education, and the Politics of Historical Memory: Patriotic Education Campaign in China', *International Studies Quarterly*, vol. 52 (2008), 783–806.
31. See <http://english.cntv.cn/program/cultureexpress/20110304/106181.shtml>.
32. Leni Stenseth, *Nationalism and Foreign Policy: The Case of China's Nansha Rhetoric*, thesis, Department of Political Science, University of Oslo (1998), 92.
33. David Bandurski, 'How Should We Read China's "Discourse of Greatness"?', 23 February 2010. Available at <http://cmp.hku.hk/2010/02/23/4565/>.
34. Yuan Weishi, 'Nationalism in a Transforming China', *Global Asia*, vol. 2, no. 1 (2007), 21–7.

Chapter 7: Ants and Elephants: Diplomacy

1. US Embassy, Beijing, Cable 09BEIJING3276, 'MFA Press Briefing', 8 December 2009. Available at <http://wikileaks.org/cable/2009/12/09BEIJING3276.html>.
2. US Embassy, Beijing, Cable 09BEIJING3338, 'MFA Press Briefing', 15 December 2009. Available at <http://wikileaks.org/cable/2009/12/09BEIJING3338.html>.
3. US Embassy, Phnom Penh, cable 09PHNOMPENH925_a, 'Update On Uighur Asylum-Seekers in Cambodia', 16 December 2009. Available at <https://search.wikileaks.org/plusd/cables/09PHNOMPENH925_a.html >.

4. US Embassy, Phnom Penh, Cable 09PHNOMPENH954, 'Corrected Copy – Deportation Scenario For 20 Uighur Asylum-Seekers', 21 December 2009. Available at <http://wikileaks.org/cable/2009/12/09PHNOMPENH954.html>.

5. 'Two More Uyghurs Get Life Sentences', *Radio Free Asia*, 27 January 2012. Available at <http://www.rfa.org/english/news/uyghur/life-01272012201754.html>.

6. US Embassy, Beijing, Cable 09BEIJING3507, 'PRC: Vice President Xi Jinping Strengthens Relations with Cambodia during December 20–22 Visit', 31 December 2009. Available at <http://wikileaks.org/cable/2009/12/09BEIJING3507.html>.

7. 'Selected Comments during the Visit to New Bridge Prek Kadam', Cambodian Prime Minister's Office, 14 September 2009. Available at <http://cnv.org.kh/en/?p=1438>.

8. It should be said that, at the same time, the United States was dealing with its own Uyghur human rights problem 22 Uyghur men captured in Afghanistan or Pakistan had been wrongly accused of terrorism and incarcerated at Guantanamo Bay before being 'released' into compulsory exile.

9. 'U.S. Suspends Some Aid to Cambodia over Uighur Case', Reuters, 1 April 2010.

10. See <http://www.army.mil/article/42598/soldiers-jump-into-history-with-cambodians-during-angkor-sentinel-2010/>.

11. Carlyle A. Thayer, 'The Tug of War Over Cambodia', *USNI News*, 19 February 2013.

12. Craig Whitlock, 'U.S. expands counterterrorism assistance in Cambodia in spite of human rights concerns', *Washington Post*, 15 November 2012. Available at <http://articles.washingtonpost.com/2012-11-15/world/35503439_1_human-rights-asia-advocacy-director-cambodia>.

13. Saing Soenthrith and Paul Vrieze, 'Hun Sen's Second Son in Meteoric Rise Through RCAF Ranks', *Cambodia Daily*, 30 January 2012.

14. Vong Sokheng, 'China Steps up Military Aid', *Phnom Penh Post*, 24 January 2013.

15. US Embassy, Beijing, Cable 09BEIJING3507, 'PRC: Vice President Xi Jinping Strengthens Relations with Cambodia during December 20–22 Visit', 31 December 2009. Available at <http://wikileaks.org/cable/2009/12/09BEIJING3507.html>.

16. Deborah Brautigam, 'Chinese Aid in Cambodia: How Much?', *China in Africa: The Real Story*, 17 May 2010. Available at <http://www.chinaafricarealstory.com/2010/05/chinese-aid-in-cambodia-how-much.html>.

17. 'Cambodia: An Ant Dodging Elephants', *Eugene Register-Guard*, 22 October 1964.

18. Donald K. Emmerson, ' "Southeast Asia": What's in a Name?', *Journal of Southeast Asian Studies*, vol. 15 (1984), 1–21.

19. Nicholas Tarling, 'From SEAFET and ASA: Precursors of ASEAN', *International Journal of Asia Pacific Studies*, vol. 3, no. 1 (2007), 1–14.

20. Robert Gates, 'Challenges to Stability in the Asia-Pacific', Shangri-La Dialogue 2008, 31 May 2008. Available at <https://www.iiss.org/en/events/shangri%20la%20dialogue/archive/shangri-la-dialogue-2008-2906/first-plenary-session-1921/dr-robert-m-gates-bce8>.

21. Kurt M. Campbell, 'The United States, China and Australia', Address to United States Studies Centre's Alliance 21 project, Emerging Asia, Customs House, Sydney, 14 March 2013.

22. Personal interview by telephone. 6 November 2013.

23. Hillary Rodham Clinton, Remarks at Press Availability, Hanoi, 23 July 2010. Available at <http://m.state.gov/md145095.htm>.

24. Ian Storey, 'China's Missteps in Southeast Asia: Less Charm, More Offensive', *China Brief* (Jamestown Foundation), vol. 10, issue 25 (17 December 2010). Available at <http://www.jamestown.org/uploads/media/cb_010_07d25e.pdf>.

25. 'China Pledges US$ 70m Aid to Cambodia', 1 April 2012. Available at <https://sg.news.yahoo.com/china-pledges-us-70m-aid-cambodia-075004737.html>.

26. 'Hu Wants Cambodia Help on China Sea Dispute, Pledges Aid', Reuters, 31 March 2012. Available at <http://www.reuters.com/article/2012/03/31/us-cambodia-china-idUSBRE82U04Y20120331>.

27. 'China Offers $20 Million in Military Aid Ahead of Asean Meeting', *Voice of America, Khmer Service*, 29 May 2012. Available at <http://www.voacambodia.com/

content/china-offers-20-million-in-military-aid-ahead-of-asean-meeting-155432515/1356122.html>.

28. 'Cambodia Takes $430m China Loan', *Phnom Penh Post*, 14 June 2012. Available at <http://www.phnompenhpost.com/business/cambodia-takes-430m-china-loan>.

29. Carlyle Thayer, 'Securing Maritime Security in the South China Sea: Norms, Legal Regimes and Realpolitik', paper presented to the International Studies Association Annual Convention, San Francisco, 6 April 2013.

30. Carlyle A. Thayer, 'ASEAN'S Code of Conduct in the South China Sea: A Litmus Test for Community-Building?', *The Asia-Pacific Journal: Japan Focus*, vol. 10, issue 34, no. 4 (20 August 2012).

31. 'Cambodian Prime Minister Hun Sen Meets Yang Jiechi', *Xinhua*, 10 July 2012.

32. Ernest Z. Bower, 'Southeast Asia from the Corner of 18th and K Streets: China Reveals Its Hand on ASEAN in Phnom Penh', *CSIS Newsletter*, vol. 3, no. 14 (19 July 2012). Available at <http://csis.org/publication/southeast-asia-corner-18th-and-k-streets-china-reveals-its-hand-asean-phnom-penh>.

33. 'Setting the Record Straight' (letter from Koy Kuong, Cambodian government spokesperson), *Phnom Penh Post*, 25 July 2012.

34. 'US, China Square off over the South China Sea', *Associated Press*, 12 July 2012.

35. 'Cambodia Rejects ASEAN Ministers' Plea to Issue Joint Communiqué', *Japan Economic Newswire*, 13 July 2012.

36. Jane Perlez, 'Asian Leaders at Regional Meeting Fail to Resolve Disputes Over South China Sea', *New York Times*, 12 July 2012.

37. 'South China Sea: ASEAN Talks Fail; No Joint Statement', *Zeenews*, 13 July 2012.

38. Personal interview by telephone. 6 November 2013.

39. Personal interview. Yangon 20 November 2013.

40. Personal interview by telephone. 4 August 2013.

41. Kurt M. Campbell, 'The United States, China and Australia', Address to United States Studies Centre's Alliance 21 project, Emerging Asia, Customs House, Sydney, 14 March 2013.

42. Kim Beazley, 'A Shift in Thinking Is Needed to Clear Indo-Pacific Hurdles', Special Issue: In the Zone: Crisis, Opportunity and the New World Order, *The Australian*, 7–8 November 2009.

43. Kurt Campbell and Brian Andrews, 'Explaining the US "Pivot" to Asia', Programme paper, Chatham House, August 2013, available at <http://www.chathamhouse.org/publications/papers/view/194019>.

44. Vinay Kumar, 'India, Australia Raise the Pitch on Maritime Cooperation', *The Times of India*, 5 June 2013.

45. Sandeep Dikshit, 'India Offers Vietnam Credit for Military Ware', *The Hindu*, 28 July 2013.

46. Barton Gellman and Greg Miller, 'U.S. Spy Network's Successes, Failures and Objectives Detailed in "Black Budget" Summary', *Washington Post*, 29 August 2013.

47. Bill Carey, 'Congress Passes 2014 Defense Authorization Bill', *Aviation International News*, 3 January 2014.

48. See <http://www.treasurydirect.gov/NP/debt/current> (accessed 23 May 2014).

49. Christian Le Mière, 'Rebalancing the Burden in East Asia', *Survival: Global Politics and Strategy*, vol. 55, no. 2 (April–May 2013), 31–41.

50. Personal interview by telephone. 4 August 2013.

Chapter 8: Shaping the Battlefield: Military Matters

1. Quoted in J.M. Van Dyke, 'Military Ships and Planes Operating in the Exclusive Economic Zone of Another Country', *Marine Policy*, vol. 28 (2004), 29–39, esp. 36.

2. Dennis Mandsager, 'The U.S. Freedom of Navigation Program: Policy, Procedure, and Future', *International Law Studies*, vol. 72, 1998, 113–27.

3. 'Short Term Energy Outlook', US Energy Information Administration, 8 October 2013. Available at <http://www.eia.gov/forecasts/steo/outlook.cfm>.
4. See <http://eng.mod.gov.cn/Database/WhitePapers/2013-04/16/content_4442755.htm>.
5. US Department of Defense. Joint Operational Access Concept. 17 January 2012. Available at http://www.defense.gov/pubs/pdfs/joac_jan%202012_signed.pdf.
6. Jason E. Bruzdzinski, 'Demystifying *Shashoujian*: China's "Assassin's Mace" Concept', in Andrew Scobell and Larry Wortzel, *Civil-Military Change in China: Elites, Institutions, and Ideas After the 16th Party Congress* (report issued by the Strategic Studies Institute, US Army War College, 2004), 309–64. Available at <http://www.mitre.org/publications/technical-papers/demystifying-shashoujian-chinas-assassins-mace-concept>.
7. Nan Li, 'The Evolution of China's Naval Strategy and Capabilities: From "Near Coast" and "Near Seas" to "Far Seas" ', in *The Chinese Navy: Expanding Capabilities, Evolving Roles* (Washington, 2011), 109–40.
8. Wendell Minnick, 'PACAF Concludes 2nd Pacific Vision Exercise', *Defense News*, 17 November 2008.
9. Greg Jaffe, 'U.S. Model for a Future War Fans Tensions with China and Inside Pentagon', *Washington Post*, 1 August 2012.
10. Personal interview by telephone. 29 October 2013.
11. Information from the Stockholm International Peace Research Institute (SIPRI) Military Expenditure Database, released 15 April 2013. Available at <http://www.sipri.org/research/armaments/milex/milex_database>.
12. 'Annual Report to Congress: Military and Security Developments Involving the People's Republic of China 2014', Office of the Secretary of Defense, May 2014.
13. US Naval Vessel Register. Available at <http://www.nvr.navy.mil/nvrships/FLEET.HTM> (accessed 6 January 2014).
14. Personal interview. Beijing 8 November 2013.
15. Wendell Minnick, 'Chinese Media Takes Aim at J-15 Fighter', *Defense News*, 28 September 2013.
16. Ministry of National Defense of China, 'Military Forces in Urgent Need of Standardization', *PLA Daily*, 10 December 2013. Available at <http://news.mod.gov.cn/headlines/2013-12/10/content_4478350.htm>, translation available at <http://chinascope.org/main/content/view/5995/105/>.
17. Roy Kamphausen, Andrew Scobell and Travis Tanner (eds), *The 'People' in the PLA: Recruitment, Training, and Education in China's Military* (report issued by the Strategic Studies Institute, US Army War College, 2008). Available at <http://www.strategicstudies-institute.army.mil/pdffiles/pub858.pdf>.
18. 'PLA Chief of General Staff Stresses on Cultivating [sic] High-quality Military Personnel', *People's Daily Online*, 31 May 2013. Available at <http://english.peopledaily.com.cn/90786/8265768.html>.
19. Personal interview by telephone. 31 October 2013.
20. Barry D. Watts, 'Precision Strike: An Evolution', *The National Interest*, 2 November 2013.
21. David A. Fulghum, 'USAF: Slash and Burn Defense Cuts Will Cost Missions, Capabilities', *Aerospace Daily & Defense Report*, 30 September 2011, 6.
22. Jeff Stein, 'CIA Helped Saudis Secret Chinese Missile Deal', *Newsweek*, 29 January 2014. Available at http://www.newsweek.com/exclusive-cia-helped-saudis-secret-chinese-missile-deal-227283.
23. Jeff Himmelman, 'A Game of Shark and Minnow', *New York Times*, 27 October 2013.
24. US Department of Defense, 'Media Availability with Secretary Panetta in Cam Ranh Bay, Vietnam', *News Transcript*, 3 June 2012. Available at <http://www.defense.gov/transcripts/transcript.aspx?transcriptid=5051>.
25. 'SECNAV Visits Logistics Group Western Pacific and Navy Region Center Singapore', *Naval News Service*, 8 August 2012; Ian Storey, personal communication, February 2014.
26. International Institute for Strategic Studies, 'Military Balance 2013 Press Statement', 14 March 2013. Available at <http://www.iiss.org/en/about%20us/press%20room/

press%20releases/press%20releases/archive/2013-61eb/march-c5a4/military-balance-2013-press-statement-61a2>.

27. Michael Richardson, 'Indonesia to Acquire One-Third of Navy of Former East Germany', *The New York Times*, 5 February 1993.

28. Benjamin Schreer, 'Moving beyond Ambitions? Indonesia's Military Modernisation', Australian Strategic Policy Institute, November 2013. Available at <https://www.aspi.org.au/publications/moving-beyond-ambitions-indonesias-military-modernisation/Strategy_Moving_beyond_ambitions.pdf>.

29. Office of the Spokesperson, US Department of State, 'DoD-funded Integrated Maritime Surveillance System', *Fact Sheet*, 18 November 2011. Available at <http://www.state.gov/r/pa/prs/ps/2011/11/177382.htm>.

30. Rodney Tasker, 'Ways and Means: Manila plans an expensive military upgrade', *Far Eastern Economic Review*, 11 May 1995, 28.

31. Personal interview. Beijing 8 November 2013.

32. Stein Tønnesson, 'The South China Sea in the Age of European Decline', *Modern Asian Studies*, vol. 40 (2006), 1–57.

Chapter 9: Cooperation and its Opposites: Resolving the Disputes

1. Food and Agriculture Organization of the United Nations, 'Philippines, Fishery Country Profile', November 2005. Available at <ftp://ftp.fao.org/FI/DOCUMENT/fcp/en/FI_CP_PH.pdf>.

2. Statement of the Southeast Asian Fisheries Development Center to the Ninth Regular Session of the Scientific Committee of the Western and Central Pacific Fisheries Commission, 6–14 August 2013, Pohnpei, Micronesia.

3. Ibid.

4. Food and Agriculture Organization of the United Nations, 'Philippines, Fishery Country Profile', November 2005. Available at <ftp://ftp.fao.org/FI/DOCUMENT/fcp/en/FI_CP_PH.pdf>.

5. Ministry of Agriculture Bureau of Fisheries, *China Fishery Statistics Yearbook 2011* (Beijing, 2011), quoted in Zhang Hongzhou, 'China's Evolving Fishing Industry: Implications for Regional and Global Maritime Security', *RSIS Working Papers*, no. 246 (Singapore, August 2012). Available at <http://www.rsis.edu.sg/publications/WorkingPapers/WP246.pdf>.

6. Zhang Hongzhou, 'China's Evolving Fishing Industry: Implications for Regional and Global Maritime Security', *RSIS Working Papers*, no. 246 (Singapore, August 2012). Available at <http://www.rsis.edu.sg/publications/WorkingPapers/WP246.pdf>.

7. 'China Starts Annual South China Sea Fishing Ban', *Xinhua*, 16 May 2013. Available at <http://english.people.com.cn/90882/8246589.html>.

8. Kor Kian Beng, 'Fishing for Trouble in South China Sea', *Straits Times*, 31 August 2012.

9. Ibid.

10. John McManus, 'The Spratly Islands: A Marine Park?', *Ambio*, vol. 23 (1994), 181–6.

11. Daniel Coulter, 'South China Sea Fisheries: Countdown to Calamity', *Contemporary Southeast Asia*, vol. 17 (1996), 371–88.

12. United Nations Environment Programme, 'Terminal Evaluation', Reversing Environmental Degradation Trends in the South China Sea and Gulf of Thailand, 22 May 2009. Available at <http://www.unep.org/eou/Portals/52/Reports/South%20China%20Sea%20Report.pdf>.

13. Rommel C. Banlaoi, *Philippines–China Security Relations: Current Issues and Emerging Concerns* (Manila, 2012).

14. The regulations (in Chinese) are available at <http://www.sbsm.gov.cn/article/zxbs/xzxk/fwzn/200709/20070900001890.shtml>.

15. Zhiguo Gao and Bing Bing Jia, 'The Nine-Dash Line in the South China Sea: History, Status, and Implications', *The American Journal of International Law*, vol. 107 (2013), 98–124.

16. International Crisis Group, 'Stirring up the South China Sea (I)', *Asia Report*, No. 223, 23 April 2012, 14.

17. 'China's CNOOC Starts Deepwater Drilling', *UPI*, 10 May 2012

18. Nayan Chanda and Tai Ming Cheung, 'Reef Knots: China Seeks ASEAN Support for Spratly Plan', *Far Eastern Economic Review*, August 1990, 11.

19. State Council Information Office, 'White Paper on China's Peaceful Development', 6 September 2011. Available at <http://www.china.org.cn/government/whitepaper/node_7126562.htm>.

20. 'Commentary: Turn South China Sea Dispute into China–Vietnam Cooperation Bonanza', *Xinhua*, 13 October 2013.

21. Carl Thayer, 'China–ASEAN Joint Development Overshadowed by South China Sea', *The Diplomat*, 25 October 2013.

22. 'News Analysis: "Breakthrough" Helps China, Vietnam Build Trust, Boost Cooperation', *Xinhua*, 15 October 2013.

23. Clive Schofield (ed.), *Maritime Energy Resources in Asia: Legal Regimes and Cooperation*, National Bureau of Asian Research Special Report, no. 37, February 2012.

24. Hasjim Djalal, *Preventive Diplomacy in Southeast Asia: Lessons Learned* (Jakarta, 2002), 57.

25. Hasjim Djalal and Ian Townsend-Gault, 'Managing Potential Conflicts in the South China Sea: Informal Diplomacy for Conflict Prevention', in Chester A. Crocker, Fen Osler Hampson and Pamela Aall (eds), *Herding Cats: Multiparty Mediation in a Complex World* (Washington, 1999), 107–33.

26. Hasjim Djalal, *Preventive Diplomacy in Southeast Asia: Lessons Learned* (Jakarta, 2002).

27. Ibid., 78.

28. 'Premier Li Keqiang's Keynote Speech at 10th China–ASEAN Expo', *Xinhua*, 4 September 2013. Available at <http://www.globaltimes.cn/content/808525.shtml>.

29. Kristine Kwok, 'China's "Maritime Silk Road" Linking Southeast Asia Faces a Rocky Birth', *South China Morning Post*, 18 October 2013.

30. Virginia A. Greiman, 'Resolving the Turbulence in the South China Sea: A Pragmatic Paradigm for Joint Development', Proceedings of the International Management Development Association Twenty Second Annual World Business Congress, 25–29 June 2013, National Taipei University, Taipei, Taiwan.

31. Joint Submission dated 6 May 2009 by Malaysia and the Socialist Republic of Viet Nam to the Commission on the Limits of the Continental Shelf, through the UN Secretary-General, in accordance with Article 76, paragraph 8, of UNCLOS. Available at <http://www.un.org/Depts/los/clcs_new/submissions_files/submission_mysvnm_33_2009.htm>.

32. Marion Ramos, 'Sulu Sultan Dies; Sabah Claim Lives on', *Philippines Inquirer*, 21 October 2013. Available at <http://newsinfo.inquirer.net/510943/sulu-sultan-dies-sabah-claim-lives-on>.

Acknowledgements and Further Reading

THIS BOOK HAS attempted to describe events in several countries, across thousands of square miles of territory and through 4,500 years of history. In many places I have only been able to give the briefest sketch of events and I am profoundly grateful to all the academics, researchers and analysts who know these subjects vastly better and who have, knowingly and unknowingly, assisted my work. Many of the experts I have consulted are named in the text; however, I need to acknowledge their work properly and offer some guidance to readers who would like to take a deeper interest in the history and present of the South China Sea.

Those interested in the prehistory of the South China Sea should consult the works of: Atholl Anderson; Peter Bellwood (notably the 2004 book he edited with Ian Glover, *Southeast Asia: From Prehistory to History*, RoutledgeCurzon); and Wilhelm Solheim (particularly *Archaeology and Culture in Southeast Asia: Unraveling the Nusantao*, University of the Philippines Press, 2006). For later periods of history Kenneth Hall (particularly *A History of Early Southeast Asia: Maritime Trade and Societal Development, 100–1500*, Rowman & Littlefield, 2011) and the many papers by Derek Hong, Pierre-Yves Manguin, Roderich Ptak, Angela Schottenhammer, Li Tana, Nicholas Tarling and Geoff Wade will be invaluable. The best overview of South China Sea history remains Wang Gungwu's *The Nanhai Trade: The Early History of Chinese Trade in the*

South China Sea, originally published in 1958 but republished several times since; many of his more recent works on the region are equally enlightening. The books of Anthony Reid (notably the two volumes of *Southeast Asia in the Age of Commerce 1450–1680*, Yale University Press, 1988 and 1995, and *Imperial Alchemy: Nationalism and Political Identity in Southeast Asia*, Cambridge University Press, 2009) were tremendous guides and companions.

The history of Hugo Grotius and the Dutch East India Company has been rewritten by Julia van Ittersum (see her *Profit and Principle: Hugo Grotius, Natural Rights Theories and the Rise of Dutch Power in the East Indies, 1595-1615*, Brill Academic Publishers, 2006) and Peter Borschberg (*Hugo Grotius, the Portuguese, and Free Trade in the East Indies*, NUS Press, 2011). Robert Batchelor and Timothy Brook have thoroughly explored the history and context of the Selden map: Batchelor in *London, the Selden Map and the Making of a Global City, 1549–1689* (University of Chicago Press, 2014) and Brook in *Mr Selden's Map of China: The Spice Trade, a Lost Chart and the South China Sea* (Profile Books, 2014). On twentieth-century South China Sea history I have found the works of François-Xavier Bonnet, Ulises Granados, Zou Keyuan and Stein Tønnesson invaluable.

On contemporary events, the writings of Aileen Baviera, David Brown, John W. Garver, Christian Le Mière, Li Mingjiang, Clive Schofield, Ian Storey, Carl Thayer and Mark Valencia have been essential. On legal matters I have relied heavily on the work of Robert Beckman and Greg Austin. Chapter 6 owes great debts to the ideas of Benedict Anderson (*Imagined Communities: Reflections on the Origin and Spread of Nationalism*, Verso, 1991), William Callahan (particularly *China: The Pessoptimist Nation*, Oxford University Press, 2012), Andrew Chubb, Caroline Hau, Kuik Cheng-Chwee, Tuong Vu and Brantly Womack (*China and Vietnam: The Politics of Asymmetry*, Cambridge University Press, 2006). Exchanges with Patricio Abinales, Ari Dy and Benedict Kerkvliet helped me get my thoughts on Filipino nationalism in order.

On the practical side of my research I would very much like to thank the many people who have facilitated my travel and research and developed my thinking though their valuable insights. In China, Dr Wu Shicun, Dr Hong Nong, Dr Kang Lin and other members of staff at the National Institute of South China Sea Studies were wonderfully hospitable and open. In Beijing, Yanmen Xie and Daniel Pinkston of the International Crisis Group, Andrew Chubb and academics at Peking and Tsinghua universities who do not wish to be named were generous with their time and expertise.

In the Philippines I was well looked after by Consuelo Garcia and Colin Steley. Alma Anonas-Carpio greatly assisted with fixing and translating. Victor Paz, Lace Thornberg and the staff of the Archaeology Department of the University of the Philippines opened the doors of prehistory to me. I am very grateful for the help and insights of Rommel Banlaoi, Renato Cruz de Castro and the wonderful Myrna Velasco of the *Manila Bulletin*.

Many people at the National University of Singapore provided insight and expertise, including Professor Wang Gungwu at the East Asia Institute, Hooman Peimani at the Energy Studies Institute and staff at the Institute of Southeast Asian Studies, notably Ian Storey, Rodolfo Severino and John Miksic. Elsewhere in Singapore I had enjoyable and valuable discussions with Yen Ling Song of Platts Energy, Pamelia Lee, Tsutomu Hidaka of NYK, Bryan Ma at IDC, Tony Regan at Tri-Zen and Mark Harris and other members and staff of SEAPEX. The International Institute for Strategic Studies allowed me to attend its Shangri-La Dialogue meeting in Singapore and Admiral Kazumine Akimoto welcomed me to an expert conference organised there by the Ocean Policy Research Foundation of Japan.

The Vietnamese Ministry of Public Security denied me a visa (they haven't forgiven me for my previous book on Vietnam) but members of the Vietnam Studies Group gave me valuable assistance. I particularly thank Balazs Szalontai, Shawn McHale, Alex Vuving and Brett Reilly. Nga Pham, Ngoc Nguyen and other members of the BBC's Vietnamese language service were also very helpful.

In Thailand, Ake Tangsupvattana and Captain Wachiraporn Wongnakornsawang of Chulalongkorn University gave generously of their time and thoughts. Lieutenant Evan Almaas and other members of the public affairs team of the United States Marine Corps helpfully facilitated my attendance at the Cobra Gold exercises.

Others who made vital contributions include Ramir Cloma, nephew of Admiral Tomas Cloma; the family of Gerald Kosh; Vlado Vivoda of Griffith University in Australia; Wendell Minnick of *Defense News*;

Shane Worrell of the *Phnom Penh Post*; Huy Duong; Kerry Brown; and Nora Luttmer. In the UK, Zhang Xiaoyang helped with translations from Chinese as did Pinnhueih Lee in Taiwan, who unlocked the newspaper archives of the Republic of China for me. Thank you all.

I enjoyed wonderful email exchanges with the former director of the Hong Kong Maritime Museum, Stephen Davies, and with François-Xavier Bonnet of IRASEC (the Research Institute on Contemporary Southeast Asia), retired US diplomat David Brown and Carl Thayer of the Australian Defence Force Academy. They and Ian Storey and Stein Tønnesson reviewed my manuscript and greatly enriched it with their comments. My sincere thanks to them. My lovely, patient editor at Yale University Press, Heather McCallum, kept me focused and, I hope, readable; grateful thanks to her.

My wife, Pamela Cox, and our children, Tess and Patrick, tolerated long absences and large piles of paper around the house with good grace and unreasonable levels of understanding. They have my deepest love.

Index